Digital Audio and Acoustics for the Creative Arts

Digital Audio and Acoustics for the Creative Arts

Mark Ballora

New York   Oxford
OXFORD UNIVERSITY PRESS

Oxford University Press is a department of the University of Oxford. It furthers the University's objective of excellence in research, scholarship, and education by publishing worldwide. Oxford is a registered trade mark of Oxford University Press in the UK and certain other countries.

Published in the United States of America by Oxford University Press
198 Madison Avenue, New York, NY 10016, United States of America.

For titles covered by Section 112 of the US Higher Education Opportunity Act, please visit www.oup.com/us/he for the latest information about pricing and alternate formats.

Library of Congress Cataloging-in-Publication Data

Names: Ballora, Mark.
Title: Digital audio and acoustics for the creative arts / Mark Ballora.
Description: New York, NY : Oxford University Press, [2016]
Identifiers: LCCN 2016035031 (print) | LCCN 2016035159 (ebook) | ISBN 9780190236663 | ISBN 9780190651626
Subjects: LCSH: Music--Acoustics and physics. | Sound--Recording and reproducing--Digital techniques.
Classification: LCC ML3805 .B266 2016 (print) | LCC ML3805 (ebook) | DDC 780.285--dc23
LC record available at https://lccn.loc.gov/2016035031

9 8 7 6 5 4 3 2 1

Printed by LSC Communications, Inc., United States of America

Table of Contents

Acknowledgments

I am only able to write this book because of a series of mentors, notably Kenneth J. Peacock, Robert Rowe, and Bruce Pennycook, who have led me along and patiently tolerated my persistent questions and all-too-frequent impenetrability.

My students at McGill University and Penn State University brought me to clarity on many of these concepts through their questions and efforts. They have kept me honest, and are ultimately responsible for any value readers may find in this work.

My editor, Richard Carlin, shepherded this edition into being, remaining steadfast and offering many suggestions and insights. His assistant, Erin Janosik, kept our letters "t" and "i" crossed and dotted, which was no small task. The production team, led by Roxanne Klaas, went above and beyond with the finishing touches.

I am particularly indebted to a number of colleagues and friends. This new version would not be what it is were it not for their contributions:

Curtis Craig is a madcap and occasionally ingenious sound designer who is continually pushing the envelope of theater technologies.

Don Neumuller is probably the handiest person I've ever met. Broadcast technician, recording studio nuts and bolts man, teacher—if something electronic is broken, chances are he can fix it, whatever it is, and he'll be happy to share exactly how he did it.

Bob Klotz is one of the most knowledgeable and insightful recording engineers an artist could work with.

Chris Wahlmark, Penn State's self-made video-streaming guru, has educated me into the nature of what makes a good video broadcast.

Dennis Miller raised the level of my writing on many of these topics; my students and readers of this book are the beneficiaries of his tutelage.

Elizabeth Cohen acted as a chiropractor, applying gentle pressure on some trouble spots to restore proper flow and strength between concepts.

Philippe DePalle is a wizard of spectral manipulation. When I was a graduate student, I would never talk to him without having a notepad handy.

Mickey Hart's ever-expanding curiosity into the interconnectedness of sound and rhythm to other phenomena has led me into many wonderful and unexpected areas; it has been my privilege to be able to contribute to his body of work.

My wife Agatha and our son Ian are my foundation, and always keep my priorities straight. This book would not be possible without them. Someday, somehow, I intend to make it up to them.

This text also benefited from the helpful suggestions made by the reviewers:

Dr. Michael Albaugh, Director of Education at Jazz at Lincoln Center
Will Kuhn, Lebanon High School
John Latartara, University of Mississippi
Dr. Adam Vidiksis, Temple University
Maurice Wright, Temple University
. . . And one anonymous reviewer.

Introduction

This book is a new incarnation of the text *Essentials of Music Technology*, published by Pearson Prentice-Hall in 2003. At that time, computers were still new and unfamiliar to many music instructors, and digital multimedia was an emerging feature on consumer-grade computers. The original text was written from the perspective of someone who had come of age in the 1980s when MIDI-based home studios were coming into being.

Many things have changed since then. People of my age bracket are members of the last generation who had to make the "digital transition" from analog electronic musical instruments to digitally based instruments. As with any paradigm shift, there are positive and negative consequences, as new skills are created while other valuable skills are deemphasized—sometimes temporarily, and sometimes permanently. Personal computers are the norm; many software programs blur distinctions between MIDI and digital audio; colleagues of mine who once became nervous at the mention of email now expect students to submit auditions online via YouTube and actively promote investment into livestreaming technology for concerts. Multimedia production tools that used to require thousands of dollars of peripheral hardware now come fully equipped as software, bundled onto the most low-budget personal computers available.

While many things have changed, the foundational concepts behind audio creation and recording remain the same. The basic components of a music studio are shown in Figure I-1a. A MIDI keyboard controls audio that is generated by a computer. An audio interface allows a computer to send and receive audio. Audio is sent from microphone signals or from the computer to a mixer. The combined signals are sent to loudspeakers. Many small home studios contain these components, which model the capacities of larger, professional studios: a recording studio may have more space to record, and a large mixing board to accommodate dozens of audio channels; a mastering studio might have many sets of loudspeakers to simulate the sound of different playback environments. But the functionality is built on this same basic configuration. Sometimes many of these components are combined (Figure I-1b). Some keyboard workstations are miniature stand-alone production consoles (Figure I-1c).

This is the norm for today's students, who are "digital natives," never having known a time when computer technology was unavailable. They have a different set of prior knowledge and assumptions than did the students from even a decade ago.

This new version of my text clarifies some concepts from the original, removes some obsolete sections, reprioritizes topics, covers some new areas, and is (hopefully) spiced up with historical trivia sprinkled throughout. But the goals are the same: to provide an overview of essential topics, and to find a balance between material that is easy for new readers to grasp while providing explanations that are thorough enough to explain the material without "dumbing it down." Different sections will be relevant for different types of projects or different levels of learning. The text is broken into short

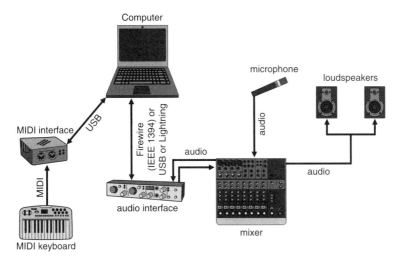

Figure I-1a Components of a music studio/workstation

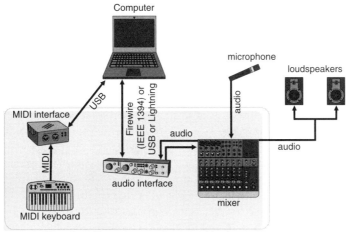

Sometimes these components are combined

Figure I-1b

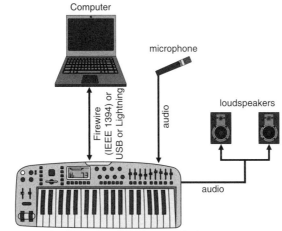

Audio interface / MIDI interface / MIDI keyboard / mixer

Figure I-1c

sections that allow an instructor to assign reading selectively in order to focus on areas that are important for a given group of students.

"Things should be made as simple as possible, but no simpler."—Albert Einstein
(1879–1955)

An effective grasp of basic principles is essential for mastery of anything. When I was an undergraduate, one of my theater professors made a comment that has stuck with me. "Why is it," he exclaimed, "that we bring in the big-name actors for the advanced courses? Anyone can teach a scene studies class! Where we need the masters is the beginning courses, teaching fundamentals." I have since seen firsthand that effective instruction in fundamentals is not always easy to come by, and that without good fundamentals, advanced study is more difficult than it should be. I have been surprised when engineering students who take my introductory course in digital audio tell me that they never understood the Fourier transform until they took my class. This always takes me aback, because it is studied so much more thoroughly in their engineering courses, while I merely give them the view from 10,000 feet. But apparently this is what is missing from their more rigorous courses, where they are thrown into the mathematics but not oriented as to the overarching concepts.

Almost every topic in this book is treated at a more advanced level in other texts. My aim for this text is that it will give students a solid enough grounding in fundamentals that they find themselves equipped to go on to more advanced work.

Hopefully, readers also will come away with the firm impression that digital technology is a set of tools, but nothing more. Every age has its technological innovations; ours has been the transition to digital. A guest lecturer some years ago presented us with pieces written by computers programmed with compositional rule systems. He enjoyed trying to trick musicians, asking them to tell the difference between pieces written by humans and by computer. Afterwards, at dinner with a number of music faculty members, he seemed to find us overly blasé about the idea that computers might someday replace composers. He kept asking us, "Doesn't this *scare* you?" But what seemed most apparent to us was that none of the pieces presented to stump us had been masterworks, but fairly commonplace. My response was that it did not scare me that a computer could write rudimentary music as well as a human could. It would scare me if a computer could write a true musical masterpiece, or even tell me a joke. But we're a long way from that happening.

I recently heard a concert that featured a choir of seventy flutes and a digital percussionist. The group seemed quite excited at the "bazillions" of sounds the digital percussion instrument could make. But, to my ears, the blend was not natural or effective. Besides the fact that the array of percussion sounds far exceeded what would have been possible in a physical setup, the sounds themselves seemed artificial, even downright cheesy, especially when paired with the rich sonority of a live flute ensemble. Their infatuation with this new piece of technology seemed to have fooled their ears.

Listening to this group brought to my mind a quotation from electronic music pioneer Brian Eno:

[The] assumption is that the best synthesizer is the one that gives you the largest number of possibilities. . . . Now, the effect of this . . . is that . . . players move very quickly from sound to sound, so that for any new situation there would be a novel sound for it, because

there's such a wide palette to choose from. . . . Frequently in the studios, you see synthesizer players fiddling for six hours getting this sound and then that sound and so on, in a kind of almost random search. What's clear . . . is that what they're in search of is not a new sound but a new idea. The synthesizer gives them the illusion that they'll find it some- where in there. Really, it would make more sense to sit down and say, "Hey, look, what am I doing? Why don't I just think for a minute, and then go and do it?" (quoted in Armbruster, 1984)

Technology enables us in many wonderful ways, but it will never be a substitute for a good idea. The bottom line will always lie with our ears. My hope is that this book will help people appreciate what technology can do for their music-making and how it can enhance (but never replace) their creativity.

Chapter 1

Basic Acoustics

Acoustic: of or pertaining to sound, the sense of hearing, or the science of sound.

Musical instruments operate by leveraging the properties of acoustics, creating sound in controlled ways. Digital music systems, the main subject matter of this book, create models of these acoustic mechanisms. The first step toward understanding musical instruments and digital music systems is to appreciate the behavior of waves (most particularly *sound waves*) and the properties of resonance.

The Nature of Sound Events

When we toss a pebble into water, we see a splash, followed by ripples ringing out from the splash point. We hear sound when there is a "splash" in the air, and the ripples reach our eardrums. Sound consists of vibrations of air molecules, which may be visualized as tiny Superballs hovering in space, randomly bouncing off each other in all directions. When a sound event occurs, such as when people clap their hands, molecules are pushed together. After the molecules collide, they bounce away from each other, colliding with other molecules. This second collision causes them to ricochet back toward their initial location, where they again collide and ricochet, bouncing back and forth until the energy of their motion dissipates.

When a pebble is thrown into the water, the resulting waves cause the surface to alternately rise and dip. A sound event causes the density of air molecules, also termed *air pressure*, to alternate between bunching together and spreading out. When air molecules are undisturbed, the air is said to be at a normal state of density (or at normal pressure level). When they are pushed together, the pressure level is greater than normal, in a *compressed* state. When they are spread apart from each other, the pressure level is lower than normal, and the molecules are said to be in a *rarefied* state. These three states are illustrated in Figure 1-1.

The air pressure changes that humans perceive as sound are the same phenomena that are discussed in weather reports: high air pressure typically implies a sunny day, whereas low air pressure implies rain and wind. But air pressure changes that determine the weather are at a much greater magnitude and change far more slowly than pressure changes that result in sound. Thus, the pressure changes associated with weather are normally termed *atmospheric pressure*, while pressure changes associated with acoustics or music are normally termed *sound pressure* (Sundberg, 1991).

When a pebble falls into water, the energy generated by this event expands in flat rings (*wavefronts*), moving outward from the point the pebble struck. When energy is

Figure 1-1 Normal, compressed, and rarefied air pressure levels

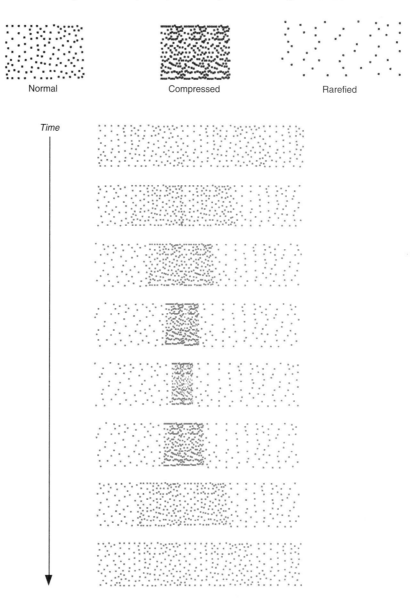

introduced into the air, such as by a pair of hands clapping or by the vibrating tines of a tuning fork, the energy from the event expands outward in spheres. Figure 1-2 shows a two-dimensional slice of this expanding sphere. In the case of the pebble, energy is transported through the medium of water. In the case of the sound, energy is transported through the medium of air. When a medium is disturbed by energy moving through it, it vibrates in response. The vibrations carry the energy as *waves*.

Although sound wavefronts expand in a spherical fashion, as the distance from the sound source increases the surface of the expanding sphere becomes, for many intents and purposes, flat—somewhat like our daily experience of the earth's surface. This flattened property is sometimes called a *plane wave*.

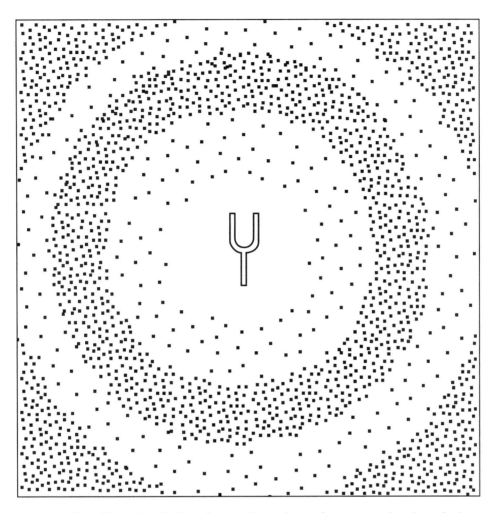

Figure 1-2 Two-dimensional slice of expanding sphere of compressed and rarefied atmospheric pressure resulting from a vibrating tuning fork

It is worth noting that the expanding pressure wave does not consist of individual molecules moving away from the sound source and surfing along with the pressure front. Rather, what spreads is the energy of the wave. The individual molecules simply vibrate about their original position. This is a general characteristic of many waves: they consist of energy moving from one place to another through a medium, while the medium itself is not transported.

Water waves are an example of *transverse waves*, which means that they vibrate back and forth along an axis perpendicular to the wave's propagation. Sound waves are an example of *longitudinal waves*, which are waves that vibrate back and forth along the same axis as the wave's propagation (Figure 1-3).

Sound waves are often illustrated on a graph that plots sound pressure as a function of time. This is what is shown on an *oscilloscope*, which is a testing device that displays electrical wave form signals. An example is shown in Figure 1-4. The horizontal line represents an undisturbed level of molecular density. It is sometimes called the

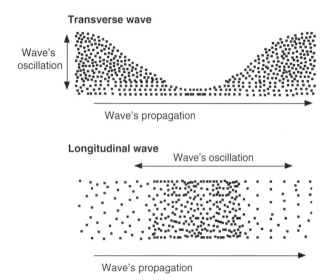

Transverse wave

Wave's oscillation

Wave's propagation

Longitudinal wave

Wave's oscillation

Wave's propagation

Figure 1-3 Transverse and longitudinal waves

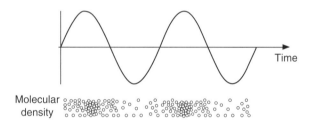

Time

Molecular density

Figure 1-4 Time domain plot

zero line, as it represents no change in pressure from the undisturbed pressure level. Points above the zero line represent pressure levels higher than equilibrium (compressions in air molecules); points below the zero line represent pressure levels lower than equilibrium (rarefactions in air molecules). Since this type of graph illustrates changes over time, it is also called a *time domain plot*.

Wave Propagation

Wave behavior is fundamental to the workings of the universe, the means by which energy is transferred. This section will discuss characteristics of waves and how they propagate.

Simple Harmonic Motion

Sound waves are one example of a *vibrating system*. Everyday life provides many other examples of vibrating systems: tides, springs, pendulums, and so on. Vibrating systems share a number of common properties. Their motion is repetitive, which means that the vibrating body returns to a particular position at regular, predictable time intervals. These intervals are called the *period* of the vibration.

The vibrating motion is created by a competition of forces. A mass-spring system is a good example. Imagine a Slinky toy, hanging from the ceiling, with a weight attached to the bottom of it. At equilibrium position, the weight hangs, motionless. When you pull the weight downward and let it go, the Slinky bounces up and down for a time, above and below the equilibrium point, before finally coming to rest again.

The forces in competition are gravity, which pulls the weight downwards toward the earth, and the spring force, which is the tendency of a spring to return to its equilibrium position. When the spring is held in place while it is either stretched or compressed, it has *potential energy*—it "wants" to move, but is restrained by being held in place. When the spring is released, the potential energy is transformed into *kinetic energy*, the energy of motion.

When the hanging spring is at equilibrium, the downward pull of gravity is balanced by the upward pull of the spring force, and so it remains at rest. When the spring is stretched or compressed, the competition begins. If the spring is stretched downward, the spring force pulling it upward is greater than the gravitational force pulling it downward, and the weight is pulled upward. However, the spring does not simply return to the equilibrium position and then stop. Isaac Newton's (1643–1727) first law of motion tells us that objects remain at rest or in motion until an external force acts upon them. Because there is nothing to stop the spring once it returns to the equilibrium point, its upward momentum pulls it past the rest point, compressing the spring. At a certain level above the equilibrium point, the force of gravity pulling the spring downward becomes stronger than the spring force pulling it upward, and the direction of motion changes. The change in direction occurs repeatedly, moving up and down a little less each time, gradually approaching the initial state of equilibrium.

The mass-spring begins at rest. As the spring is stretched or compressed, tension is created, and a *restoring force* acts to return the weight to its equilibrium position. The farther the mass is pulled from the equilibrium position, the stronger the restoring force in the opposite direction. Thus, the restoring force may be described as being *proportional* to the displacement of the weight. This relationship between force (F), tension (K), and displacement (y) is known as **Hooke's law** and may be written as the following equation:

$$F = -Ky \qquad\qquad (1\text{-}1)$$

The negative value shows that the restoring force is always pulling the object in the opposite direction of its present motion.

Suppose the mass-spring system were attached to a clothesline, and was moved at a constant rate, horizontally, as the mass bounced. The shape of the mass would trace a *sine wave*, which represents a constant change of velocity. If the speed were constant, the shape traced would be a regular zig-zagging series of triangles. If the slope of a sine wave is examined closely, it can be seen that the speed is greatest as the weight passes the equilibrium point. As it reaches the high or low point of each period, the slope flattens, as the speed slows. At the extreme high and low point, the slope is flat for an instant, indicating that motion slows to a stop, before resuming again in the opposite direction. Many vibrating systems exhibit this pattern of velocity change, following the shape of a sine curve like the one shown in Figure 1-4. Vibrating systems that move in this way are said to exhibit **simple harmonic motion**.

Appendix 1 describes sine waves geometrically. Remarkably, this behavior, which describes so many phenomena in the natural world, can be created with nothing more than a compass, straightedge, and pencil.

Characteristics of Waves

Waves in nature may be described by the same features as those characterizing sine waves:

1. *Wavelength*: the distance between corresponding points (for example, the extreme high or low point) from cycle to cycle as the wave repeats itself; the wavelength is often notated with the Greek letter lambda (λ).
2. *Frequency*: how often the wave repeats itself. Frequency is the inverse of wavelength; a higher frequency implies a shorter wavelength, and a lower frequency implies a longer wavelength.
3. *Amplitude*: how high and low the wave's oscillations are, or the amount of deviation from the equilibrium point. This characteristic is completely independent of frequency. Two waves may vibrate at the same frequency but have different amplitudes.
4. *Waveshape:* the waveshape in Figure 1-4 is that of a sine wave, but most actual sound waves exhibit far more complex pressure changes.
5. *Polarity*: a wave's up or down orientation. If a wave is flipped upside down, we say its polarity has been reversed or inverted.

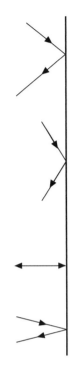

Figure 1-5 Angle of incidence equals angle of reflection

In Chapter 2, these characteristics will be related to the audible characteristics of sound waves.

Diffraction and Reflection

Waves cannot travel undisturbed forever. Sooner or later, they are bound to come into contact with obstacles. Water waves in a swimming pool eventually come into contact with the pool walls, swimmers, floating rafts, and other objects. Air pressure wave-fronts similarly come into contact with walls, furniture, and so on. The behavior of a wave when it comes into contact with an obstacle depends on the wavelength and the dimensions of the object. If the height and width of a surface are significantly smaller than the wavelength, the wave *diffracts* (bends) around the object and continues to propagate. If the dimensions of a surface are significantly larger than the wavelength, the wave is *reflected* away from the object. In the same way that a billiard ball reflects away from the edge of the table, a wave's reflection angle is the same as the angle of incidence (Figure 1-5).

Any change in the medium can function as an obstacle. If you hold one end of a rope and give your wrist a flick, a pulse travels down the rope to its opposite end, then travels back. But the reflection's polarity differs depending on whether the other end of the rope is fixed or free. If the other end is fixed, as would be the case if it were secured to a wall, the reflection is "flipped": if the incident pulse is upward in orientation, the reflection is downward in orientation. This is because the fixed end creates an *opposing force* to the direction of the vibration, which pulls the rope to its opposite polarity. However, if the other end of the rope is free, as would be the case if you were standing on a ladder and holding the rope down toward the floor, the wave's polarity does not change on reflection: if the incident pulse is upward in orientation, so is its reflection. These two conditions are illustrated in Figure 1-6.

Musical applications of vibrations on a rope can be seen in string instruments such as the guitar or members of the violin family. But the same principles also apply to wind instruments. Imagine holding a tube to your mouth and producing an impulsive sound by smacking your lips or clicking your tongue. The impulse creates a high-pressure region that travels down the tube and is reflected back when it reaches the opposite end. If the tube's opposite end is closed, the pulse reflects back at the same polarity, just as does a wave from a free end of a string. If the tube's opposite end is open, a high-pressure front reaching it will immediately dissipate as it reaches the open end and encounters the lower external air pressure. The dissipation of the high pressure impulse produces a rarefied area at the end of the tube, and this low pressure area moves back away from the open end—that is, the reflection is at the opposite polarity, just as in the case of a string with a fixed end. Reflections within a tube are illustrated in Figure 1-7.

Superposition

If you and a friend each hold opposite ends of a rope and each give your ends a sharp flick, you each produce a pulse. Your two pulses travel away from each of you and meet somewhere in the middle. For a moment, their displacement patterns are combined, after which the two waves pass each other and continue, completely unchanged by their encounter with each other. This is called the *principle of superposition*—waves may meet, be combined, and then separate again with their original characteristics intact. Superposition is illustrated in Figure 1-8.

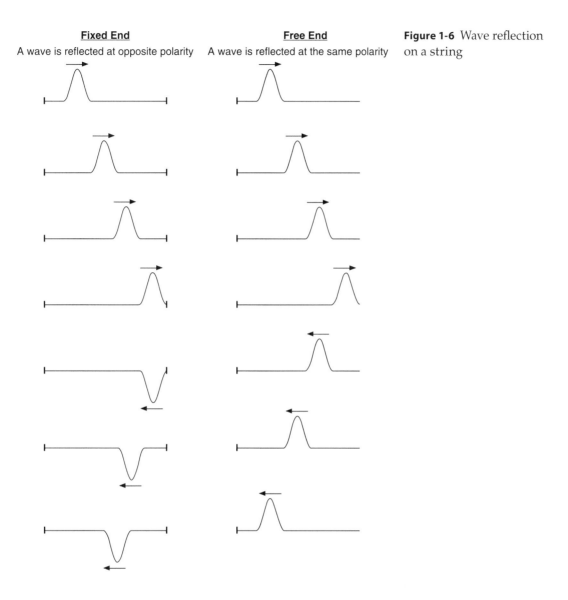

Figure 1-6 Wave reflection on a string

When two waves of similar polarity combine, they exhibit *constructive interference*, which means that a wave of greater amplitude is momentarily constructed. When two waves of opposite polarity combine, they exhibit *destructive interference*, which means that their opposite amplitudes cancel each other out momentarily.

Standing Waves, Resonant Frequencies, and Harmonics

If you secure one end of your rope to a wall, and shake the other end at a regular frequency, a wave pattern appears in the rope. You can observe the combination of reflection and superposition as waves travel down the rope, are reflected back, and, on the way back, interfere with waves traveling in the opposite direction.

There are certain frequencies at which you can shake the rope that will produce wavelengths that are at integer subdivisions of the rope (one-half of the rope's length,

Figure 1-7 Wave reflection within a tube

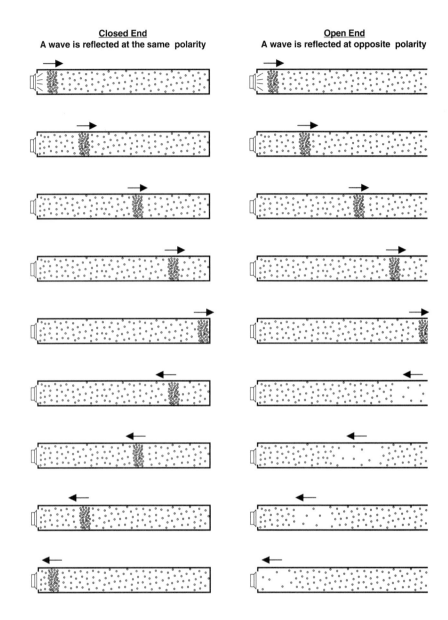

one-third of its length, one-fourth the length, etc.). The superpositions of the waves, moving in opposite directions at opposite polarities, create a series of constructive and destructive interferences. A combination wave is produced that does not appear to propagate at all, but rather oscillates in one place. Such a combination wave is called a *standing wave* (Figure 1-9). There are a series of equally spaced points that remain motionless at all times, called *nodes;* halfway between each node are points of maximum deviation up and down, called *antinodes*.

In general, for a string bound at both ends with a length *L*, standing waves may be produced that have wavelengths at:

$$\lambda = \left(\frac{2}{n}\right)L \qquad n = 1, 2, 3, \ldots \qquad (1\text{-}2)\ (\text{Figure }1\text{-}10)$$

Superposition of two waves at the same polarity

Superposition of two waves at opposite polarity

Figure 1-8 Wave superposition

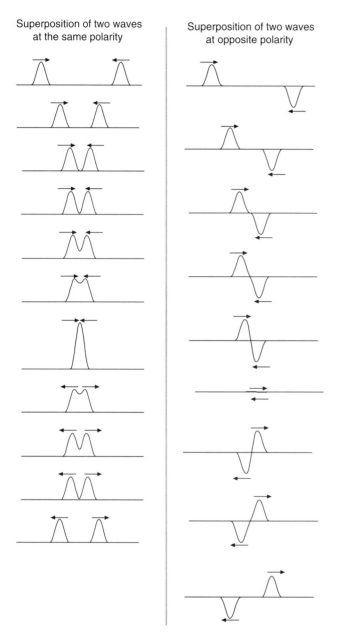

The set of frequencies that produce standing waves in a string are called the string's *characteristic frequencies* or *resonant frequencies*. Each successive standing wave is an integer multiple of the top frequency in the figure. This top frequency, the lowest frequency the string can support, is called the *fundamental frequency* of the string. If the fundamental in the figure has a period of one cycle per second, then, moving down the figure, the frequencies below it have periods of two cycles per second, three cycles per second, four cycles per second, and so on. The set of frequencies that are based on integer multiples of the fundamental is called the *harmonic series*, and each of the standing waves may be called a harmonic of the fundamental.

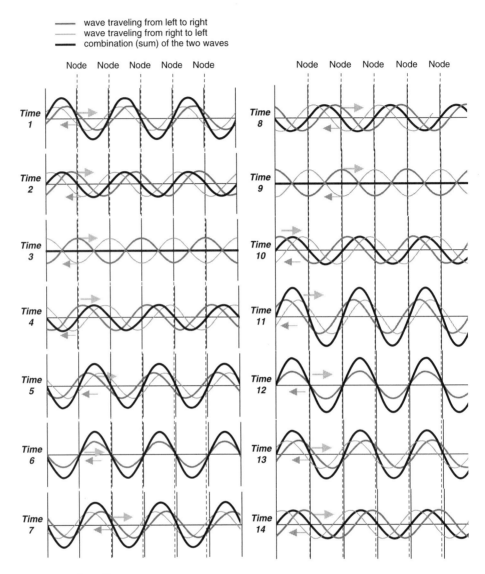

Figure 1-9 Standing waves

Standing waves and harmonics may also be produced by a column of air in a tube. The nature of the wave depends on whether the ends of the tube are open or closed. Consider first a tube with a length of L that is closed at both ends. As longitudinal sound waves propagate back and forth within it, the ends of the tube cause reflections at the same polarity, as described above. A standing wave may be created if pressure changes are generated at a period that produces pressure antinodes at the tube ends, as shown in Figure 1-11. The longest wavelength that meets this condition is twice the tube's length. Additional resonant frequencies may also be created at integer multiples of this frequency, also according to Equation 1-2.

The same set of standing wave frequencies may be created within a tube that is open at both ends, with the difference that the positions of the pressure nodes and antinodes are swapped from the positions they take in a tube that is closed at both ends.

Wavelength
(Times string length)

Frequency
(Times fundamental)

Figure 1-10 Characteristic frequencies of a string bound at both ends

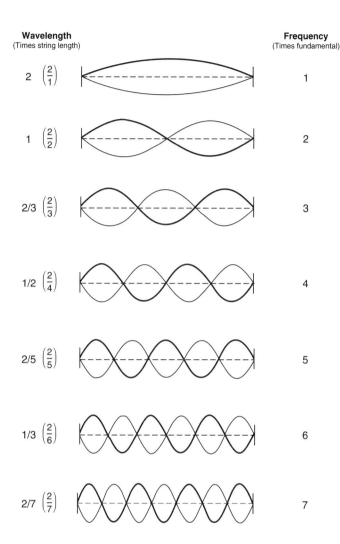

Wavelength	Frequency
2 $\left(\frac{2}{1}\right)$	1
1 $\left(\frac{2}{2}\right)$	2
2/3 $\left(\frac{2}{3}\right)$	3
1/2 $\left(\frac{2}{4}\right)$	4
2/5 $\left(\frac{2}{5}\right)$	5
1/3 $\left(\frac{2}{6}\right)$	6
2/7 $\left(\frac{2}{7}\right)$	7

Because open ends cause reflections at the opposite polarity, a standing wave may be created if pressure changes are generated at a rate that produces pressure nodes at the open ends of the tube (Figure 1-12). As is the case with the tube closed at both ends, the longest wavelength that meets this condition is twice the tube's length, and additional standing waves may also exist at integer multiples of this frequency.

To summarize: the length of a tube that is either open on both ends or closed on both ends is one-half the lowest wavelength (that of the fundamental frequency) that the tube may support. Such tubes are sometimes called *half-wave resonators* (Sundberg, 1991). A flute is a half-wave resonator, as it is effectively a tube that is open at both ends (the embouchure hole may be considered an open end). Figures 1-11 and 1-12 show that, like strings, half-wave resonators can support standing wave frequencies at all harmonics of the fundamental.

A tube that is closed on one end and open on the other can support a fundamental frequency with a wavelength that is four times the length of the tube (Figure 1-13). The reasons for this are a combination of the two end types of half wave resonators: it is impossible for pressure antinodes to exist at an open end, and it is impossible for

Figure 1-11 First five characteristic frequencies of a tube closed at both ends

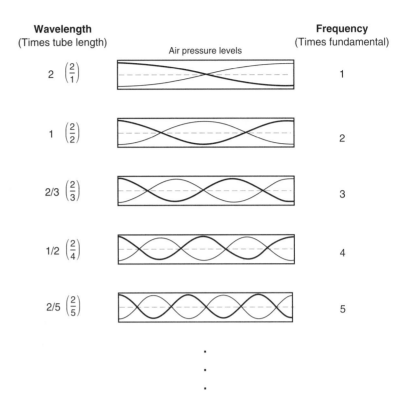

Wavelength
(Times tube length)

Air pressure levels

Frequency
(Times fundamental)

Figure 1-12 First five characteristic frequencies of a tube open at both ends

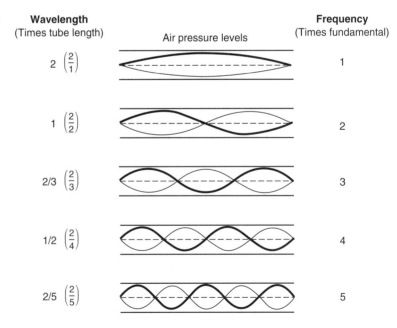

Wavelength
(Times tube length)

Air pressure levels

Frequency
(Times fundamental)

pressure nodes to exist at a closed end. For a tube that has one end open and the other end closed, the fundamental has a pressure antinode at the closed end and a pressure node at the open end. All possible standing waves within such a tube have wavelengths that satisfy this same condition, that is

$$\lambda = \left(\frac{4}{2n-1}\right)L \qquad n = 1, 2, 3, \ldots \qquad (1\text{-}3)$$

Since the length of a tube is one-fourth the wavelength of the fundamental, such tubes are sometimes called *quarter-wave resonators*. Because quarter-wave resonators can support standing waves that consist of a pressure node on one end of the tube and a pressure antinode at the closed end, they cannot support even harmonics of the fundamental frequency. They can support resonant frequencies at odd harmonics only. Reed instruments such as the clarinet or oboe are examples of quarter-wave resonators (the bell functions as an open end, and the reed closes the other end at the mouthpiece).

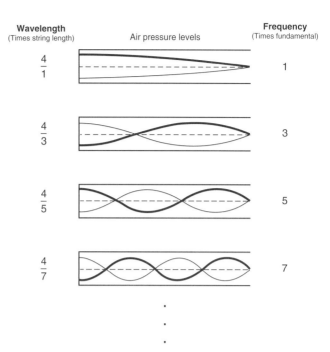

Figure 1-13 First four characteristic frequencies of a tube closed at one end

Standing waves can also occur in enclosed spaces. Showers can be perfect places to demonstrate this phenomenon because they are typically small, and have parallel walls with highly reflective surfaces. If you stand in the shower and sing a low tone and gradually slide the pitch upwards, you'll find that some pitches "ring" out, while others fade. Another experiment is to play a 1 kHz sine wave through a loudspeaker on a floor, facing a wall. Move the speaker to a position about six inches from the wall, and you can hear the level suddenly drop as a node is created between the wavefronts emitted from the speaker and their reflections from the wall. Standing waves in enclosed spaces will be discussed further in Chapter 7.

Standing waves are at the heart of our universe. At an atomic level, the electron used to be considered a tiny particle, orbiting the nucleus. Quantum physicists now prefer to describe electron shells as standing waves, because electrons can never be precisely located, and they can behave like both particles and waves. Thus, the structure of matter as we know it is dependent on standing wave patterns.

The examples thus far have examined one frequency at a time within a medium. However, due to the properties of wave superposition, multiple standing waves may be active simultaneously within a tube or on a string. Simultaneous sets of nodes and antinodes may coexist within a vibrating medium. This capability is an important aspect of the vibrations produced by musical instruments.

Sympathetic Resonance

In a nutshell, resonance describes a mechanical system in which a small amount of input can yield a great deal of output. Helmholtz (1885) explains resonance by using an analogy to cathedral bells. Somehow, these huge metal structures are brought into motion by comparatively small human beings. How can bell-ringers of normal strength bring such huge objects into motion?

The answer lies in their timing. They pull on the bell rope regularly in such a way that they reinforce the motion of the bell. Each time the bell swings away from the rope, they give it another tug, thus reinforcing the motion away. If they were to tug when the bell swings toward the rope, the tug would be contrary to the motion of the bell, and would inhibit motion. As it is, their repeated, timed pulls reinforce the bell's motion, so that each pull amplifies it by a small amount. After a short period of time, the bells take on a sizable swing and ring at great volumes.

Another example can be found on any playground where children play on swing sets. To start the swing, they kick outwards to reinforce motion forward, then pull their feet back to reinforce motion backwards. With each well-timed kick and pull, the swing goes out a bit farther.

When vibrating bodies are reinforced at their characteristic frequencies, just a very little bit of force can produce a disproportionately large degree of output. *Resonance* is this property of high efficiency from even a small input at just the right frequency. Through *sympathetic vibration*, resonance can be passed from one object to another via air molecules. These objects are called *resonators*.

When a tuning fork is struck, its volume is low, and it needs to be held close to the ear in order to be heard. But when it is placed into a wooden box, vibrations are passed from the fork to the wood via *mechanical coupling*, whereby motion is passed from one object to another via physical contact between them. If the wood can vibrate at the fork's frequency, it displaces a good deal more air than does the fork alone. The result is much higher amplitude. We see this in everyday life when a guitar is played. The wooden box amplifies the string's motion (and, as we shall soon see, adds many characteristics of its own into the sound).

If a second tuning fork, tuned to the same frequency, is placed in a similar wooden box in proximity to the first fork/box, the air pressure changes produced by the struck fork come into contact with the second fork. Since they bounce off of the fork at its characteristic frequency, it falls into vibration. This can be confirmed by damping the fork after striking it. The tone continues, as it is being sounded by the second fork.

This is the same principle as the bell rope tugs. Air molecules bounce off the tuning forks all the time. Typically, they do so in a random pattern, so there is little, if any, response from the fork. But if the molecules bounce off the fork at its characteristic frequency, they function as our kicks do on a playground swing, or as the tugs on the rope of a cathedral bell: the fork tines soon vibrate with enough amplitude that the fork's tone becomes audible.

Vibrating bodies can typically respond to a variety of frequencies, and can produce quite complex vibratory patterns. *Chladni patterns* illustrate the variety of motion types, and are named after the physicist and musician Ernst Florens Friedrich Chladni (1756–1827), who first described them. Fine sand is placed onto a metal plate that is near a loudspeaker, which plays a sine wave tone. If the frequency is gradually made higher, it will pass through a series of the plate's characteristic frequencies. At these frequencies, the plate vibrates in sympathy and nodal and antinodal regions that form in the plate's surface. Sand collects in the nodes, and bounces away from the antinodes. A variety of beautiful patterns result, embodying the different modes of vibration as visual designs. The patterns may also be produced if the plate is excited by a violin bow rubbed along its edge. Different patterns emerge if the edges are dampened at various

Figure 1-14 Chladni patterns, shown in John Tyndall's *Sound* (1867)

points, or if clamps are placed on different areas on the plate. Figure 1-14 shows a series of these patterns published in Tyndall (1867).

Phase and Waveshape

Phase describes the position of a wave cycle at a certain time. When multiple waves are traveling within a medium, their interaction creates a shape that is a composite of the respective waves. Depending on the initial phases of the waves, the composite shapes can look quite different from any of the individual waves.

If two waveforms at the same frequency do not have simultaneous zero-crossings, they are said to be *out of phase*. Figure 1-15 shows an example of two sine waves at the

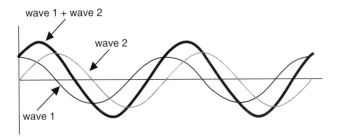

Figure 1-15 Addition of two waves at the same frequency but at different initial phases

same frequency but at different phases. The dark line shows the superposition of these two waves (their sum). The superposition wave is at the same frequency as the other two but out of phase with them. If a wave is shifted in phase by one-half wavelength with respect to another wave at the same frequency, the two will be at opposite polarity. If the waves in Figure 1-15 were one-half wavelength out of phase, their combined positive and negative polarities would cancel each other out entirely.

For reasons that will be covered in Chapter 3, it is often convenient to refer to sine or cosine waves as examples of *sinusoidal waves*, which refers to the waveshape without regard to its initial phase.

Speed and Velocity

The *speed of sound* refers to the speed at which sound wavefronts travel. In air, it is approximately 1125 feet per second (344 meters per second), with slight variations due to altitude, humidity, and temperature. *Air particle velocity* refers to the speed at which individual molecules move back and forth.

Wavefronts travel at the same rate, regardless of frequency or amplitude. In contrast, air particle velocity increases when there is an increase in pressure level and/or frequency. At higher air pressure levels, molecules move farther from equilibrium as they vibrate. We previously noted that frequency and pressure levels are completely independent. This implies that if pressure levels are increased while frequency stays the same, then individual molecules move farther back and forth each cycle than they do when pressure levels are lower, which means that they must move faster to maintain the same frequency.

At the maximum moments of compression during air pressure cycles (the high points on the wave), there is little room for air particles to interact, and thus the particle velocity is at a minimum. Similarly, at moments of rarefaction (the low points on the wave), the increased empty space between the molecules also prevents their interaction. Thus, particle displacement is at a minimum when pressure levels are at maximum and minimum. When pressure levels are at zero (that is, zero change from normal, undisturbed pressure levels), molecules have the greatest opportunity to interact, so the particle displacement is greatest when the air pressure level is at its equilibrium level.

The combination of speed and direction is *velocity*. The relationship between air pressure and air particle velocity is plotted in Figure 1-16. One period of a harmonic cycle of pressure is described by a *cosine curve*; the corresponding variations in velocity are described by an *inverted sine wave*. The velocity curve matches the pressure curve, but with a lag of 90° ($\pi/2$ radians, one-quarter wavelength). The air particle velocity represents the slope of the pressure curve. (Students of calculus may recall that the derivative of a cosine curve is a negative sine curve. This is a real-world example of that principle.)

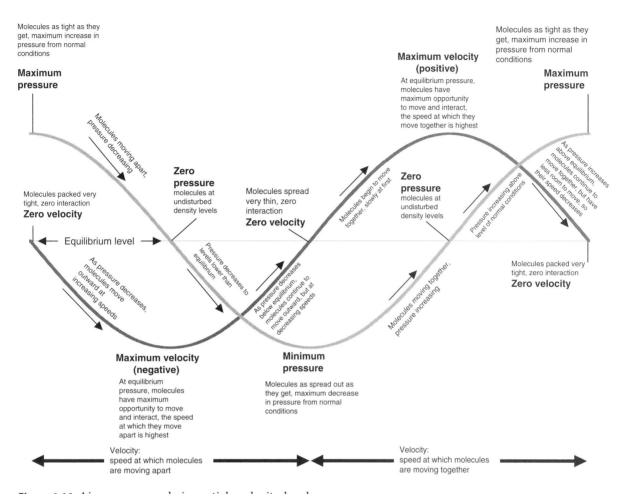

Figure 1-16 Air pressure and air particle velocity levels

Frequencies of Strings and Echoes

String Frequencies

In general, the characteristic frequency of any vibrating object depends on its length and the speed at which vibrations travel within it:

$$f_{vibrations} = \frac{v_{m/s}}{2 \times L_m} \qquad (1\text{-}4)$$

It can be helpful to consider the fraction's measurement units separately, m/s in the numerator and m in the denominator, to see how the units of the final result of "per second" is produced:

$$\text{units of vibration} = \frac{m/s}{m} = \frac{m}{s} \times \frac{1}{m} = \frac{1}{s} \qquad (\text{i.e., "per second"})$$

The vibrations of a string also depend on its length and the speed of vibrations travelling along it. With a string, the velocity is the square root of its **tension** *(T)*, measured in **newtons** (a measurement unit that will be described in Chapter 2), over its mass per unit length (or **linear mass density**, *μ*). Thus, adapting Equation 1-4 for a string produces Equation 1-5:

$$f = \frac{\sqrt{\frac{T}{\mu}}}{2L} \tag{1-5}$$

If these measurement units, newtons and linear mass density, are considered separately, they can be shown to derive the measurement units for velocity, meters per second:

$$\text{newtons } (N) = \frac{m \times kg}{s^2}$$

$$\text{Linear mass density } (LD) = \frac{kg}{m} = \alpha$$

$$v = \sqrt{\frac{N}{\mu}} = \sqrt{\frac{m \times kg}{s^2} \times \frac{m}{kg}} = \sqrt{\frac{m^2}{s^2}} = \frac{m}{s}$$

Echo Rate

When we hear a sound reflection, such as when we stand near a wall and clap our hands, the reflection time, *T*, depends on the velocity, *v* (in meters per second, the speed of sound), and the distance (in meters) to the wall, *d*, as the wavefront travels from our hands to the wall and back:

$$T = \frac{2d_m}{v_{m/s}} \tag{1-6}$$

If we clap our hands while standing between two walls, wavefronts reflect back and forth between them, producing echoes. The echo rate also depends on both the velocity and the distance between the walls:

$$f = \frac{1}{T} = \frac{v_{m/s}}{2d_m} \tag{1-7}$$

Suggested Exercises

- Many objects in everyday life have resonant frequencies that can be brought into vibration, either sympathetically, or by a small, constant stimulation. What examples can you find?
- Using the procedures outlined in Appendix 2, use a spreadsheet to create sine wave plots. Be sure that you can easily modify the frequency, amplitude, and phase of the plots.

Key Terms

acoustics
air particle velocity
air pressure
amplitude
antinodes
atmospheric pressure
characteristic frequency
Chladni patterns
compressed state
constructive interference
cosine curve
destructive interference
diffraction
frequency
fundamental frequency
half-wave resonator
harmonic series
Hooke's law
inverted sine wave
kinetic energy
linear mass density
mechanical coupling
newtons
nodes
opposing force
oscilloscope
out of phase
period
phase

plane wave
polarity
potential energy
principle of superposition
quarter-wave resonator
rarefied state
reflection
resonance
resonant frequency
resonator
restoring force
simple harmonic motion
sine wave
sinusoidal wave
sound pressure
sound waves
speed of sound
standing wave
sympathetic vibration
tension
time domain plot
transverse wave
velocity
vibrating system
wavefront
wavelength
waveshape
zero line

Chapter 2

Music and Acoustics

Chapter 1 discussed waves, sound, and resonance in general terms. Here, the focus will shift to waves that produce musical sound. In a very broad sense, a musical sound may be described in terms of its pitch, its volume, and its timbre. This chapter will examine each of these properties in detail.

Properties of Musical Sound

A musical event can be described by four properties. Each can be explored with descriptive or objective terms.

DESCRIPTIVE	OBJECTIVE
Pitch	Frequency
Volume	Amplitude/power/intensity
Timbre	Overtone content/frequency response/spectrum
Duration in beats	Duration in time

This chapter will examine each of these properties in detail.

What Is the Difference Between Music and Noise?

Every generation seems to have a subjective answer to the question, What is the difference between music and noise? But musical tastes aside, there is a well-defined difference between the two terms. Musical sounds typically have a pitch; pitched wave forms are *periodic*, which means that the sound wave generated by a musical instrument repeats regularly. (This will soon be qualified—musical sounds are more accurately described as *quasi-periodic*—but for the time being, it will do to consider pitched sounds as being periodic.) Noise is *aperiodic*, which means that there is no repeating pattern to the waveform and no perceptible pitch to the sound. Both types of sound are illustrated in Figure 2-1.

The periodic wave is a sine wave (see Chapter 1). The noise wave shows a type of noise called *white noise*, meaning that all values are completely random. As opposed to the predictable nature of a periodic wave, there is no correlation from one point to another in a white noise wave.

Although sine waves are helpful as demonstrations due to their simple behavior, sine wave sounds are virtually nonexistent in nature. Soft whistling comes close, as do the sounds from tuning forks or high notes played on the recorder. But natural phenomena almost always consist of more complex vibrations.

Frequency/Pitch

Frequency and Wavelength

Frequency describes how often a periodic wave repeats itself. It is measured in *cycles per second* or *hertz (Hz)*, named after the physicist Heinrich Hertz (1857–1894). *Pitch* is correlated with frequency: higher frequencies produce higher perceived pitches, while lower frequencies produce lower perceived pitches.

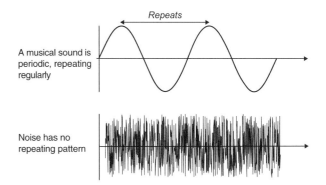

Figure 2-1 Periodic and aperiodic waves

As described in Chapter 1, the *wavelength* (λ) is the distance between corresponding points on a wave's pattern, and *period* is the amount of time that elapses during each wavelength. Period is the inverse of frequency. The speed of sound was defined as approximately 1125 feet per second (344 meters per second). The wavelength can be calculated by dividing the speed of sound, *c*, by frequency, *f*:

$$\lambda = \frac{c}{f} \qquad (2\text{-}1)$$

Figure 2-2 shows the relationship between frequency and wavelength. The speed of sound is here approximated at 1000 ft/second. A wave is shown that has a frequency of 2 Hz, and its wavelength is marked from crest to crest, outlining a single cycle. The arithmetic shows that the period of the wave is the inverse of its frequency, 0.5 seconds per cycle, which means that the wavelength is 500 feet/cycle, according to Equation 2-1.

As another example, the pitch middle A is represented on most tuning devices as 440 Hz ($\lambda \approx 2.3$ ft). (As we will soon see, the precise frequency of the note A may vary in practice.) In broad strokes, longer wavelengths correspond to lower frequencies and pitches, and shorter wavelengths correspond to higher frequencies and pitches. This relationship is seen often in everyday life: longer piano strings are used for the bass notes; longer organ pipes produce lower notes than short pipes; larger bells produce lower pitches than small bells.

The maximum frequency range audible to humans is from 20 Hz ($\lambda \approx 50$ ft) to 20,000 Hz, or 20 kHz ($\lambda \approx 0.05$ ft). (As this is an average range, it varies; some sources give an audible range of 16 Hz–16 kHz, but "twenty to twenty" is an accepted general range.) This upper limit lowers with age; 16–17 kHz is closer to the upper limit norm for most adults who have healthy hearing.

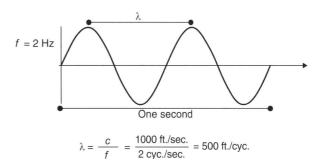

Figure 2-2 Wavelength

As an aside, sound wavelengths are significantly larger than light wavelengths, which explains why we can hear what is happening around a corner, but we cannot see what is happening. Recall the discussion in Chapter 1 on reflection and diffraction of waves. The long wavelengths of sounds, particularly those in lower ranges, can easily diffract around corners and reach our eardrums. Light wavelengths, in contrast, are far too small to diffract around any visible surface; they reflect back without reaching our eyes.

Doppler Shift

It is a common experience that the sound of a moving object, such as a car or train, suddenly drops in pitch when it passes a listener. This has to do with a change in effective wavelength when the object is moving toward and away from the listener. A sound source produces wavefronts at regular intervals. But when it is moving towards a stationary listener, its forward motion lessens the distance between wavefronts, with the result that they arrive more frequently than they would if both the object and the listener were stationary (Figure 2-3). This causes the pitch to be raised. When the object passes the listener and moves away, the distance between successive wavefronts reaching the listener is lengthened, which causes the pitch to fall. This phenomenon is called *Doppler shift* or *effect*, named after the physicist Christian Doppler (1803–1853).

As another aside, it is interesting to compare the Doppler effect with respect to light waves. The phenomenon is the same, although light waves are electromagnetic energy, a different phenomenon from acoustic energy, which can only travel through a medium. Doppler shift is used by astronomers to measure the distances to celestial objects that are moving with respect to the earth. Objects that are moving away from the earth have their light shifted to lower, redder frequencies, a phenomenon they call "redshift," while objects moving toward the earth are "blueshifted," as their light waves are shifted to the higher, bluer-colored frequencies.

Some composers of computer music have made apparent position of sounds a feature of musical works, often incorporating Doppler shift to enhance the effect of sounds moving around the listener. John Chowning's (1934–) *Turenas* (1972) is a particularly effective example.

Frequency Is Fixed and Precise; Pitch Is Flexible and by Convention

Frequency is a quantitative measurement, with no ambiguity. In contrast, the assignment of a note name to a frequency is a matter of common agreement, which can vary. While 440 Hz is the frequency for the pitch middle A that is recognized by the International Organization for Standardization (ISO 16:1975), there are a variety of contexts in which musicians use another frequency as a tuning reference. Many orchestras tune to a frequency of 444 to give added "bite" to the sound. Ensembles that play period instruments often tune to earlier conventions, such as A 415 for some Baroque music, for reasons having

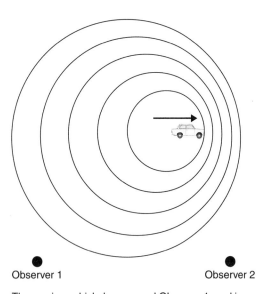

Observer 1   Observer 2

The moving vehicle has passed Observer 1, and is approaching Observer 2. Since it is moving away from Observer 1, its wavefronts are stretched farther apart than they would be if it were stationary, with the result that its pitch falls. Since it is moving toward Observer 2, its wavefronts are pushed closer together than they would be if it were stationary, with the result that its pitch rises. When the vehicle passes Observer 2, she will hear the pitch drop.

Figure 2-3 Doppler effect

to do with the history of the music and the construction of the instruments. When recital performers place piano tuning requests, it's common to ask for a specific piano tuning, such as A 442, to match the tendencies of certain instruments. The appendix in Helmholtz includes a table titled "Historical Pitches from Lowest to Highest," in which European church bells that sound the pitch A are listed according to frequency, date, and country. The frequencies of A range from 370 Hz to 567.3 Hz. This variance is due to the lack of tuning standardization in the Middle Ages. Township boundaries were demarcated by the area within which the cathedral bells were audible, and people rarely traveled beyond their local township. Tuning was a local reference based on the region's cathedral bells or organs.

Human Pitch Perception Is Logarithmic

A critical point concerning the relationship of perceived pitch to frequency is that equivalent pitch intervals are not perceived over equivalent changes in frequency (such as adding a certain number of Hertz to any given frequency), but rather by equivalent changes applied to an exponent that describes a frequency (see Figure 2-4). The raising of a base number by a given quantity is called a *logarithm*. (Fundamentals of logarithms are covered in Appendix 3.)

The top part of Figure 2-4 demonstrates logarithmic pitch perception by using an *octave*. The octave is a perceptual equivalence of pitch class, which occurs with every doubling of frequency. That is, some number of octaves is traversed when a frequency is multiplied by two to the power of an integer. Another example is shown in the bottom part of Figure 2-4, which illustrates the construction of the chromatic scale used in Western music, *twelve-tone equal temperament*. An equally tempered scale refers to an octave being divided into logarithmically (and perceptually) equal increments.

An octave in twelve-tone equal temperament may be constructed by the following steps:

- Choose a starting frequency.
- Multiply it by $2^{n/12}$ for n = 0 to 11.
- Higher octaves may be created by doubling each frequency.
- Lower octaves may be created by halving each frequency.

Frequencies of successive octaves of concert A

55	110	220	440	880	1760	3520
55×2^0	55×2^1	55×2^2	55×2^3	55×2^4	55×2^5	55×2^6

Twelve-tone equal temperament

A	A#	B	C	C#	D	D#	E	F	F#	G	G#
$220{\times}2^{\frac{0}{12}}$	$220{\times}2^{\frac{1}{12}}$	$220{\times}2^{\frac{2}{12}}$	$220{\times}2^{\frac{3}{12}}$	$220{\times}2^{\frac{4}{12}}$	$220{\times}2^{\frac{5}{12}}$	$220{\times}2^{\frac{6}{12}}$	$220{\times}2^{\frac{7}{12}}$	$220{\times}2^{\frac{8}{12}}$	$220{\times}2^{\frac{9}{12}}$	$220{\times}2^{\frac{10}{12}}$	$220{\times}2^{\frac{11}{12}}$
220	233	247	261.6	277	293.6	311	329.6	349.2	370	392	415.3

Figure 2-4 Equivalent pitch distances correspond to equivalent changes of frequency as expressed on a logarithmic scale

Loudness

Loudness is correlated with three related but distinct measurements:

- Power
- Intensity
- Pressure

The distinctions among these measurements will follow, and we'll see how they can be related to each other through some arithmetic sleight of hand.

Power

Chapter 1 had an analogy of a sound event being akin to a stone being tossed into a pond. Continuing with this comparison, a sound's *power* level is comparable to the size of the rock. A larger rock makes a bigger splash. Recall that as a sound wave travels, molecules themselves are not traveling with the sound wave. What is traveling is an expanding sphere of kinetic energy that displaces molecules as it passes over them. The amount of energy contained in this wave, its power, correlates to its perceived loudness. The first sleight of hand trick will be to relate power to air particle velocity (see Chapter 1). This will be done through *force* and *work*.

Air molecules, like any object, are set into motion when force is applied to them. The unit of measurement for force is the *newton* (N). A force of 1 newton applied to an object having a mass of 1 kilogram causes the object to increase its speed (accelerate) by 1 meter per second for as long as the force is applied.

When an object has force applied to it and is displaced, *work* is performed. Work is defined as force times the distance the object moves:

$$work = force \times distance \tag{2-2}$$

The amount of work carried out is unrelated to the amount of the time involved. Whether an object is moved quickly or slowly, the amount of work done is the same. For example, imagine you're pushing a book across a tabletop. You might push it slowly, or you might push it quickly. In both cases, you do the same amount of work.

Power adds time to the equation:

$$power = \frac{work}{time} \tag{2-3}$$

When you push a book quickly across a tabletop, you apply more power than when you push it slowly because you complete the movement in less time. The unit of measurement for power is *watt (W)*, named after the engineer James Watt (1736–1819). One watt corresponds to 1 newton of work performed per second.

In subsequent discussions, power will also be related to velocity, which is defined as:

$$velocity = \frac{distance\ in\ a\ given\ direction}{time} \tag{2-4}$$

Assuming for the moment a constant direction, velocity becomes synonymous with speed (distance/time). This allows power to be rewritten in terms of velocity by combining Equations 2-2, 2-3, and 2-4:

$$power = \frac{work}{time} = \frac{force \times distance}{time} = force \times \frac{distance}{time} = force \times velocity \tag{2-5}$$

We'll return to Equation 2-5 later in this chapter, when some further sleight of hand will be performed to relate power to pressure. But first the focus will shift to show how to create a scale of acoustic power levels.

Complications in Measuring Acoustic Power Levels

Creating a useful scale of acoustic power levels is complicated by two factors. One is that molecules are never completely motionless. There is always some degree of activity among neighboring molecules; there is no level of zero motion by which a given sound's power level may be described in absolute terms. The solution to this complication is to measure power levels *comparatively*. The measurement is derived from a ratio that compares the power of a given sound event to a threshold level of audibility.

However, even after determining a threshold, there remains a second complication, which has to do with the wide range of audible power levels. The difference in wattage between the softest perceptible sound and the threshold of pain is on the order of a millionfold. Working with such a large scale of values quickly becomes counterintuitive. The solution for this second complication is to make the power scale not only comparative but also *logarithmic*. Appendix 3 shows how a large scale may be compressed to a smaller scale through the use of logarithms. The scale created with these solutions in mind has measurement units of the *decibel (dB)*.

The Decibel Scale

Any units of measurement are chosen as a matter of convenience, depending on the scale of what is being measured. The distance from Los Angeles to New York could be described accurately in terms of inches or centimeters, but such small units are not terribly convenient to describe distances of this magnitude; miles or kilometers are usually employed because that scale results in more manageable numbers. This is not the case for all distances, however. When the distance between stars is measured, a larger unit of measurement, the light-year, is commonly employed. By the same token, the distance between hair follicles may also be described in miles, but the resulting fractional number would be too small to have any intuitive value. On smaller scales, inches, centimeters, millimeters, or micrometers are more convenient.

Measurement on a logarithmic scale was discussed briefly in the section on pitch, where equivalent perceptual pitch changes were described as corresponding to equivalent changes in an exponent that describes the difference between two frequencies. Thus, a logarithmic perception of pitch is built into the human auditory system. This section will detail further how a logarithmic scale is applied to acoustic power levels.

Definition of the Decibel

To make the wide range of measurable sound power level values more manageable, Bell Labs created a logarithmic unit of measurement called the *bel (B)*, named for scientist/inventor Alexander Graham Bell (1847–1922).

The scale used for measuring sound power is both comparative and logarithmic. In laboratory settings, the lowest audible sine tone at 1 kHz was found to have a power level of 10^{-12} watts, a power threshold notated as W_0. (Sound at this level would cause the eardrum to move a fraction of the diameter of a hydrogen molecule, which shows just how sensitive the human auditory system is.)

To derive a sound's power level, L, in bels, a measured power wattage, W, is divided by the threshold power wattage W_0, and then the logarithm to base 10 of this ratio is taken:

$$L_W(B) = log_{10}\left(\frac{W}{W_0}\right) \tag{2-6}$$

This creates a scale on which silence is measured at a value of 0 and the threshold of pain at 12, which is a rather small range of numbers for such a large range of sensations. Thus, the bel scale provides a bit too much compression to be helpful. So, as a convenience, the result is multiplied by 10 and termed the decibel (dB).

$$L_W(dB) = 10log_{10}\left(\frac{W}{W_0}\right) \tag{2-7}$$

A doubling of power results in an increase of approximately 3 dB, as can be seen when the power level is taken of a sound at twice the level of the threshold:

$$L_W(dB) = 10log_{10}(2) \approx 3.01\ dB$$

This means that a sound at 13 dB has twice the power of a sound at 10 dB. The level is doubled again at 16 dB, and so on. With the decibel, a useful scale of sound power levels came into being, with silence at a value of 0 dB, and the threshold of pain at 120 dB. The decibel scale is used to describe all three properties associated with loudness.

Intensity

Power levels describe the wattage of a sound event, but they are less helpful at describing loudness from the perspective of a listener. A sound wave is a sphere of energy expanding outward from the sound source. The wave's power is akin to the energy contained in the sphere's surface. The power level remains constant, spread evenly over the surface of the sphere. As the sphere expands to greater distances from the sound event, the power at any given square meter on its surface is less than it was at closer proximity to the source. As an analogy, imagine a balloon being inflated: the mass of rubber does not change, but as the balloon grows, the rubber gets thinner and thinner.

Perception of loudness is a function not only of the sound's power level but also the distance of the listener from the sound event. We have all experienced that events sound louder close up than they do at a distance. Power combined with distance is expressed as ***intensity (I)***, which is measured in watts per square meter (W/m^2), and is also measured in decibels:

$$L_I(dB) = 10log_{10}\left(\frac{I}{I_0}\right) \tag{2-8}$$

where $I_0 = 10^{-12}\ W/m^2$

Table 2-1 shows typical intensity levels of everyday events. Intensity is the primary measurement associated with perceived loudness, as it takes into account both the power levels of the sound event and the position of the listener in relation to the event.

Pressure

Power and intensity describe the energy that *causes* a sound event. But in some contexts it is helpful to describe a sound event in terms of disturbances in the air that *result* from

TABLE 2-1 Intensity level of everyday events.

Soft rustling leaves	10 dB
Normal conversation	60 dB
Construction site	110 dB
Threshold of pain	125 dB

the sound event: *pressure* levels. Returning again to the analogy of a rock being tossed into water, power levels are analogous to the size of the rock. As waves travel from the point of impact, they gradually become smaller; their amplitude decreases with distance from the sound source. The total power level instigating the waves doesn't change, but it gets spread equally through ever-increasing circular wavefronts. The amplitude of the ripples corresponds to sound pressure levels. And intensity levels correspond to the degree to which floating lily pads at varying distances from the splash point bob on the water's surface.

The unit of measurement for sound pressure level is newtons per square meter (N/m^2), also called *pascals (Pa)*, named after physicist Blaise Pascal (1623–1662). As shown in Figure 1-4, sound pressure levels are in a constant state of variation. The *peak pressure level* or *peak amplitude level* refers to the highest point on the curved plot: the maximum change in sound pressure level (or, more generally, the maximum displacement from equilibrium position in a vibrating system).

Relationship of Intensity to Pressure

Sound intensity levels and pressure levels are closely related, but not the same. To describe their relationship further, some additional sleight of hand will now be performed.

We have already compared an expanding sphere of sound wavefronts to a balloon being inflated. Intensity levels are similar to the surface area of a sphere:

$$A = 4\pi r^2 \tag{2-9}$$

Because the terms 4 and π are constants (they do not change as the radius changes), we can remove them from the equation and change the equal sign to a proportion:

$$A \propto r^2 \tag{2-10}$$

which reads, "A sphere's surface area is proportional to its radius, squared." Thus, when the radius is doubled, the surface area increases fourfold. When the radius is tripled, the surface area increases ninefold.

As the distance between a listener and a sound source changes, intensity levels drop proportionally by the inverse square of the change in distance:

$$I \propto \frac{1}{d^2} \tag{2-11}$$

Thus, doubling the distance from a sound source causes the intensity to drop by one-quarter. Tripling the distance causes intensity to drop by one-ninth, and so on. This relationship, called the *inverse square law*, applies to many forms of energy.

Pressure levels, on the other hand, drop at a rate that is proportional to one over the change in distance:

$$p \propto \frac{1}{d} \tag{2-12}$$

Thus, a change in distance by a factor of two causes pressure levels to drop by one-half, a change by a factor of three causes pressure levels to drop by one-third, and so on. Thus, we can say that intensity/power levels are proportional to pressure levels squared.

This relationship may be understood further by recalling the relationship defined in Equation 2-5:

$$power = force \times velocity \tag{2-5}$$

Force also appears in the description of pressure levels:

$$pressure = \frac{force}{area} \tag{2-13}$$

Given this common factor between Equations 2-5 and 2-13, Equation 2-5 may be rewritten to reflect the relationship between power and pressure (Sundberg, 1991). Provided the area in question remains constant, Equation 2-13 indicates that an increase in pressure results in an increase in force. Thus, pressure is proportional to force:

$$pressure \propto force \tag{2-14}$$

Equation 2-5 may therefore be rewritten by substituting pressure for force, and by changing the equality to a proportionality:

$$power \propto pressure \times velocity \tag{2-15}$$

As discussed in the Speed and Velocity section of Chapter 1, air particle velocity increases with pressure change. Thus, velocity is proportional to pressure:

$$velocity \propto pressure \tag{2-16}$$

Making this substitution in Equation 2-15 results in:

$$power \propto pressure \times pressure$$

or

$$power \propto pressure^2 \tag{2-17}$$

Equations 2-11, 2-12, and 2-17 all serve to show that power levels are proportional to pressure levels squared. The same holds true for many propagating wave forms, be they mechanical, electrical, or acoustic: the power contained in the wave is proportional to the wave's amplitude squared.

Root Mean Square

Because pressure levels fluctuate, the value used to express them needs to be an averaging of these fluctuations. But a simple averaging of a wave that is regularly positive and negative results in a value of zero. For this reason, acoustic amplitude meters give a reading of **RMS (root-mean-square)** pressure changes. That is, each periodic amplitude reading is squared so that all values are positive. The mean of these values over a period of time is taken. The square root of the mean then gives a useful measurement of average amplitude. (Readers familiar with statistics may find RMS to be similar to the *standard deviation* of a sequence of values, which is derived by a similar process.)

If a sine wave has values within the range of ±1, and these values are squared, the mean of these squared values over one period is 0.5. And the square root of 0.5 is 0.707. Thus, the RMS of a sine wave is its peak amplitude value multiplied by 0.707, a standard acoustic reference. In the Suggested Exercises, readers are encouraged to verify this with the aid of a spreadsheet program.

Pressure and Decibels

Pressure levels are also measured in decibels, but with a modification that relates the pressure level to the equivalent power level. The threshold stimulus from Equation 2-7 translates into a pressure threshold level of 2×10^{-5} Pa, notated p_0. Recalling that power levels are proportional to the pressure levels squared, decibels in watts may be equated to decibels in pascals by using the logarithmic property of exponents (Property 3 shown in Appendix 3):

$$L_W = 10 log_{10}\left(\frac{W}{W_0}\right) = 10 log_{10}\left(\frac{p}{p_0}\right)^2 = 2 \times 10 log_{10}\left(\frac{p}{p_0}\right) = 20 log_{10}(\frac{p}{p_0}) \qquad (2\text{-}18)$$

Thus, Equation 2-18 is used to determine pressure levels, and Equation 2-7 is used to determine power and intensity levels. This change of multiplier, from 10 in Equation 2-7 to 20 in Equation 2-18, means that a doubling of pressure level results in a change of approximately 6 dB in pressure. This can be shown by returning to the example of a pressure level at twice the threshold value:

$$SPL(\text{dB}) = 20\, log_{10}\left(\frac{4 \times 10^{-5}}{2 \times 10^{-5}}\right) = 20\, log_{10}(2) = 6.02 \text{ db}$$

Having two descriptors of decibel levels, one for intensity and the other for pressure, ensures that as the distance from a sound source increases, the change in decibel level remains the same, whether pressure or intensity are being considered. Recall that intensity (in wattage) changes according to the inverse of the relative distance squared, while pressure (in pascals) changes according to the inverse of the distance. The two versions of the decibel equation, Equation 2-7 and Equation 2-18, bridge the difference between the two quantities. When the distance from the sound event doubles, the intensity drops by one-quarter, that is, it drops by 3 dB twice, for a change of −6 dB in intensity. In turn, the pressure level drops by one-half, a change of −6 dB of pressure. Similarly, if the distance changes by a factor of one-half (the listener is half as close to the event as in the previous example), the intensity changes by one over one-half squared, or by a factor of four. This corresponds to a change of 6 dB of intensity. The pressure changes by a factor of one over one-half, or by a factor of two; this also corresponds to a change of 6 dB of pressure (see Figure 2-5).

Understanding "Negative" Decibels

It can sometimes be confusing when levels are described as having a negative decibel value. If silence is a level of 0 dB, how can pressure or intensity be negative? The answer is that wattage and pascals are not negative, but that the negative sign results from the

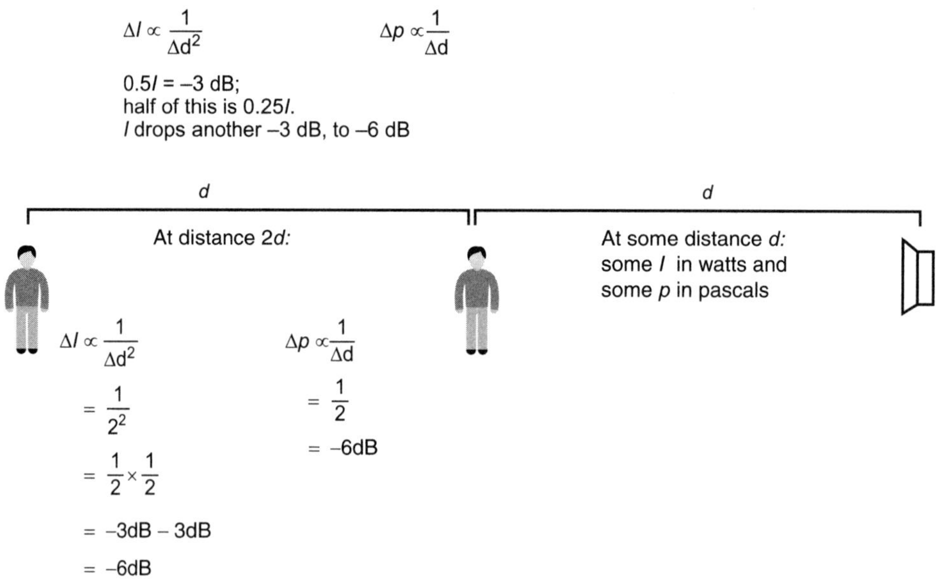

$$\Delta I \propto \frac{1}{\Delta d^2} \qquad\qquad \Delta p \propto \frac{1}{\Delta d}$$

0.5I = –3 dB;
half of this is 0.25I.
I drops another –3 dB, to –6 dB

At distance 2d:

$\Delta I \propto \dfrac{1}{\Delta d^2}$

$= \dfrac{1}{2^2}$

$= \dfrac{1}{2} \times \dfrac{1}{2}$

$= -3dB - 3dB$

$= -6dB$

$\Delta p \propto \dfrac{1}{\Delta d}$

$= \dfrac{1}{2}$

$= -6dB$

At some distance d:
some I in watts and
some p in pascals

Figure 2-5 Doubling distance, decibels of intensity and pressure

conversion to decibels. In these cases, it is helpful to consider decibels as a percentage of intensity change:

$$-3 \times n\text{dB} = \frac{1}{2^n} \text{ of the original intensity level.}$$

For example, if the distance changes by a factor of two, then $n = 2$:

$$-3 \times 2\text{dB} = \frac{1}{2^2} \text{ of the original intensity level.}$$

If the distance changes by a factor of three, then $n = 3$:

$$-3 \times 3\text{dB} = \frac{1}{2^3} \text{ of the original intensity level.}$$

To convert from a decibel level to wattage, the following formula may be used:

$$I_W = 10^{\frac{dB}{10}} \times 10^{-12} \tag{2-19}$$

In audio technology parlance, loudness is frequently equated with the amplitude of the audio signal (which is an analog of acoustic pressure levels) because a volume control adjusts the amplitude (level) of electrical current sent to an amplifier. (Chapter 8 will include an example of when it is important to understand the relationship between audio amplitude levels and intensity levels.)

Timbre

Timbre is the difference in sound quality between different instruments. It is what makes a trumpet sound different from a violin or a flute. While everyone can hear that these instruments sound different, the exact nature of the differences has long eluded precise definition. The American National Standards Institute (ANSI) definition of timbre from 1994 reads:

> *Timbre is that attribute of auditory sensation in terms of which a listener can judge that two sounds similarly presented and having the same loudness and pitch are dissimilar. . . . Timbre depends primarily upon the spectrum of the stimulus, but it also depends upon the waveform, the sound pressure, the frequency location of the spectrum, and the temporal characteristics of the stimulus.*
> *ANSI S1.1-1994 (R1999)*

While this is helpful as a starting point, it is a limited definition in that it really only describes what timbre isn't, rather than what it actually is (although, in fairness, it does hint that a number of characteristics may come into play). As we examine these characteristics, it will become clear that timbre is an ***emergent property***, that is, something that comes into being as a result of a number of factors, a whole that is greater than the sum of its parts.

Modes of Vibration

Sine waves were used as the basis for creating Figures 1-4, 1-15, 2-1, and 2-2, even though—as we have noted—these waveshapes rarely occur in nature. Sine waves are useful as demonstrations because they represent a wave consisting of only one frequency component. For this reason they are often termed ***pure tones***. Pure tones, however, have to be synthesized artificially. Natural sounds are composed of a multitude of frequencies. To understand how a wave can be composed of multiple frequencies, consider the behavior of a wave in a bounded medium, such as a string secured at both ends, as described in Chapter 1.

When a string is plucked, wave motion is initiated. The lowest wavelength is twice the length of the string, as shown in Figure 2-6. The perceived pitch corresponds with the *fundamental frequency*, the speed of sound divided by the wavelength.

The curved shape shown in the figure represents an averaging of the string's maximum deviation. But a more accurate conception of a string's motion is to consider the string as consisting of a number of suspended masses (like popcorn strung together to hang from a Christmas tree, but with masses heavier than popcorn kernels). Imagine a string with only one suspended mass, halfway along its length. When the string is plucked, the mass moves up and down, and the string may be described as having one ***mode of vibration***. Now, imagine a string with two suspended masses. When this string is plucked, there are two possibilities: the two masses may move up and down together, or they may move in opposition to each other. (In fact, the string's total motion is likely to be some combination of these two modes of vibration.) Each time a mass is added to the string, another mode of vibration is introduced.

Now, consider a string consisting of an extremely large number of small masses. When the string is excited, there are many simultaneous and independent vibrations

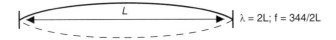

Figure 2-6 Wavelength of a vibrating string

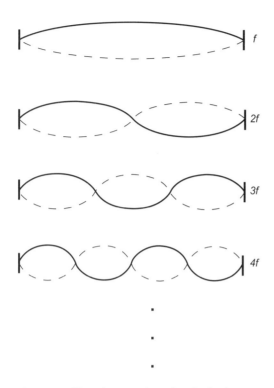

Figure 2-7 Four harmonics of a plucked string

and frequencies occurring along the string. At the moment that the string is plucked, its equilibrium is thrown into chaos, with frequency content that is theoretically infinite. However, the bounded nature of the string eventually limits the range of frequencies it can support. This is a key point: the only stable modes of vibration for a string are its characteristic frequencies, or standing waves. As discussed in Chapter 1, the set of standing waves that a string can support are *harmonics*, integer multiples of the fundamental. Immediately after a string is plucked, its motion is chaotic, but many of the frequencies in that chaos are quickly canceled out as their waves travel along the string. Only the string's resonant frequencies, or harmonics, can continue to propagate, as shown in Figure 2-7 (notice the similarity with Figure 1-10).

Harmonic frequencies create a *linear progression*, as they are successive additions of the fundamental. But earlier in this chapter it was pointed out that, because human pitch perception is logarithmic, linear frequency progressions do not span equal pitch space. Because equivalent pitches are produced by successive exponential intervals, this means that harmonics are not all at the same pitch. Thus, the pitches of a vibrating string compose a *chord*. The set of frequencies produced by an instrument (or any vibrating object) is called its *spectrum*.

The Fourier Analysis

The mathematician Joseph Fourier (1768–1830) is responsible for proving a critical theorem of complex waves that also happens to underlie much of the physics of music:

- All complex periodic waves may be expressed as the sum of a series of sinusoidal waves.
- These sinusoidal waves are all harmonics of the fundamental.
- Each harmonic has its own amplitude and phase.

The decomposition of a complex wave into its harmonic components, its spectrum, is known as a *Fourier analysis* or *transform*. Think of what happens when you direct white light through a prism. You see a rainbow of colors that comes out the prism's opposite side as the white light is broken into its spectral components. In the same way, a Fourier analysis breaks down a complex wave into its component parts. A Fourier analysis is completely reversible. An *inverse Fourier transform* does the same thing in reverse: the spectral components are combined to recreate the original complex wave.

A Fourier analysis can be used to describe any waveform type; Fourier made his discovery when examining heat waves (Fourier, 1822). It was Helmholtz who first described musical timbres in terms of spectral content. Because he knew that musical waves were repetitive, he concluded that they must operate according to the principles of any other repetitive wave, as described by Fourier. Helmholtz invented resonators in the form of enclosed air cavities that he could place into his ear. Based on the differing levels he heard from different resonators, and using only a pencil and paper to plot them, he derived remarkably accurate approximations of musical timbres.

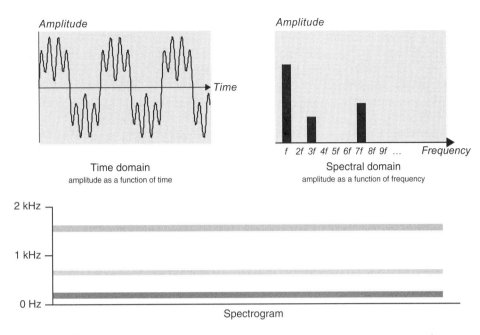

Figure 2-8 Comparison of time domain, spectral domain, and spectrogram plots

Spectral Plots

Given that sounds are typically composed of many frequencies, it is often more useful to represent complex waveforms with a ***spectral plot*** as opposed to a time domain plot. A comparison is shown in Figure 2-8. In the top left portion of the figure, a time domain plot shows changes in air pressure over time. Although it is repetitive, this wave is more complex than the sine waves shown earlier; just by looking at it, it is difficult to describe the wave in terms of its frequency content. The top right portion of the figure shows the spectrum of the waveform. From the spectrum it is easy to see that the complex wave consists of the fundamental, the third harmonic at one-third the amplitude of the fundamental, and the seventh harmonic at one-half the amplitude of the fundamental. The bottom portion of the figure will be discussed in the next section.

Limitations of the Fourier Transform

The Fourier transform is highly theoretical. It is based on a strict, mathematical definition of *periodic waves*: that is, a truly periodic wave has repeated in exactly the same way since the beginning of time, and will continue in exactly the same fashion until the end of time. The very fact that musical instrument (and other) sounds are finite in duration shows that, in fact, no sound that we hear is truly periodic. While we have been describing musical, pitched sounds as periodic, it would be more accurate to describe them as *quasi-periodic*: highly repetitive, but not periodic in the formal sense.

Another reason to describe musical sounds as quasi-periodic is that they change over time. The precise nature of their spectral content varies over the evolution of a tone. Bells and pianos, for example, have extremely complex sets of behavior among their spectral components. A spectrum, representing a forever-unchanging wave pattern, is, by definition, unchanging. Thus, a more useful representation of musical spectra would take changes in time into account.

The time domain and spectral domain plots are both two-dimensional, showing one property as a function of another. The two may be combined in a *spectrogram plot* (also called a *sonogram*), where both frequency and amplitude are shown as a function of time. A spectrogram plot is shown in the bottom portion of Figure 2-8. In a spectrogram, time is represented by the horizontal axis. Frequency is illustrated as a function of time (the vertical axis), with higher frequencies appearing at higher vertical positions. Intensity levels are represented by color intensity or darkness level. In this plot, three predominant horizontal bands represent the three harmonics of the complex wave. The bottom band, representing the fundamental, is darkest, as this is the spectral component with the highest amplitude. The next band, representing the third harmonic, is lighter as it has one-third the darkness of the fundamental. The highest band, representing the seventh harmonic, is one-half the darkness of the fundamental.

The Harmonic Series and Intonation

As described above, harmonics are a linear progression of frequencies, and therefore musical harmonics form a series of pitches—a chord. Harmonics are numbered beginning with the fundamental, which is considered the first harmonic. Taking 220 Hz as a fundamental frequency, the pitches of the lowest six harmonics, which are usually the spectral components with the greatest intensity, are shown in Table 2-2.

People can learn *analytic listening*, which involves learning to "hear out" the individual harmonics of a sound like a plucked string. But the natural auditory response is for harmonically related tones to fuse and create a single pitch, based on the lowest of the frequencies, with a timbre that results from the spectrum. More energy in the higher harmonics will create a sound that is "brighter" than a sound with less energy in higher spectral regions.

Pitches Are Just Ratios

The musical intervals of the harmonic series, shown in the bottom row of Table 2-2, are obtained by *normalizing* each frequency so that it lies between the fundamental, *f* (220 Hz), and an octave higher, 2*f* (440 Hz in the table). Pitch class identity is maintained when a frequency is transposed by octaves, either by raising it an octave with a multiplication of 2 or by lowering it an octave with a multiplication of 1/2. (This property of pitch perception will be discussed further in Chapter 3.)

The pitch intervals of the harmonic series may be identified by halving each frequency as many times as is necessary for the frequency to fall between the fundamental and the next octave, in this case between 220 and 440 Hz. Treating the third and sixth harmonics in this fashion, they are transposed to a frequency of 330 Hz, a ratio of 3/2 to the fundamental, which corresponds to a *perfect fifth*. Treating the fifth harmonic in this fashion transposes it to a frequency of 275 Hz, a ratio of 5/4 to the fundamental, which corresponds to a major third.

These ratios are examples of *just intonation*, a tuning system that relies on simple integer ratios to derive each interval of a musical scale. The term *intonation* refers to

TABLE 2-2 The six lowest harmonics.

220	440	660	880	1100	1320
Fundamental	Octave	Perfect fifth	Octave	Major third	Perfect fifth

pitches based on simple integer ratios. *Temperament*, such as the system shown in Figure 2-4, refers to a scale in which the ratios of each pitch to the fundamental are irrational numbers. The musical intervals found in the harmonic series are approximated in twelve-tone equal temperament. The difference between an interval in just intonation and in twelve-tone equal temperament is audible. Just intervals are noticeably more consonant than equal-tempered intervals. The major third, in particular, is nearly a quarter-tone sharper in twelve-tone equal temperament than its just ratio. However, just intervals do not represent equal subdivisions of the octave, and thus it becomes difficult to modulate or change keys in just intonation. Equal temperament represents a compromise in consonance that allows composers to modulate freely from one key to another, a hallmark of Western common practice music.

The subject of tuning ratios and *microtonality* (use of pitches that fall "between the cracks" of the equally tempered pitches that are found on a piano) is a fascinating one, and is guaranteed to broaden one's perspective on the pitch vocabulary of music. Readers interested in delving further into this area may wish to consult Wilkinson (1988) and Loy (2006) for more detail.

Harmonics in Performance

String players produce harmonics by dampening strings with light finger pressure. For example, the first harmonic may be obtained by dampening the string at its halfway point. Dampening a string is not the same as pressing the finger fully onto the string, which effectively shortens it and causes it to vibrate at a frequency that is an octave higher. By dampening the string with more gentle pressure from the finger, a node is created. The string as a whole continues to vibrate, but the fundamental vibration is suppressed due to the dampening, and therefore only frequencies higher than the fundamental, the second harmonic and higher, can sound. Dampening the string at one-third its length dampens all frequencies below the third harmonic, and so on. This technique produces a higher pitch, but with a different timbral quality than is obtained by shortening the string with full pressure. The sound of harmonics is thinner and hazier sounding than the more full-bodied sound produced by shortening the string by depressing it fully.

Brass players obtain different pitches by producing harmonics from their instruments. They buzz their lips into the mouthpiece to bring the tube that is the body of the instrument into resonance. Through embouchure and breath control, players learn to buzz their lips at different frequencies to produce successive harmonics of the tube length. By depressing the instrument's valves, extra lengths of tube are opened, thus lengthening the tube. The fundamental pitch is lowered and a set of harmonics based on this lower fundamental becomes possible.

A Partial by Any Other Name . . .

One of the themes of this section on timbre is that a vibrating body is active at a number of frequencies. The frequencies, considered in total, are termed its *partials*. The first partial is the fundamental. The relative levels of the partials that compose an instrument's tone play a large part in creating an instrument's timbre.

Harmonics refer to that set of partials that are integer multiples of the fundamental frequency. Partials are not necessarily harmonic. Bell sounds, for example, typically contain a number of inharmonic partials that are determined by the size and composition of the bell.

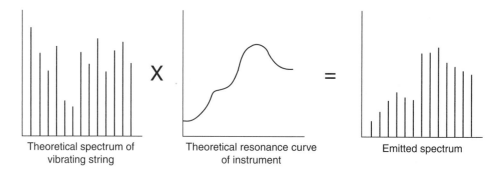

Figure 2-9 Resonance curve
Source: Adapted from Roederer (1995)

Another term, *overtones*, refers only to partials higher than the fundamental. This changes the numbering sequence, in that the first overtone refers to the second partial, the second overtone refers to the third partial, and so on.

Formants

As discussed in Chapter 1, the standing wave patterns on the vibrating part of the instrument—whether it is a string, an air column, a skin, or something else—are eventually passed on to the body of the instrument via mechanical coupling. The term was introduced in the context of a tuning fork that is placed onto a sound box, which amplifies the fork's vibrations.

An instrument's body not only amplifies the vibrations produced by the string or air column, but also produces its own spectrum. Depending on the size, shape, and construction of the instrument's body, certain frequencies will be favored. Regardless of the fundamental frequency (i.e., pitch) being played, certain partials will always have a prominent amount of spectral energy. Thus, an instrument's body is said to produce *formants*, which are consistent spectral peaks, regardless of the pitch being played. The difference in sound between one violin and another is due to the formants of their two bodies.

Thus, the spectrum of the vibrating part of the instrument is combined with the resonance curve of the instrument's body (its formants). The combination of the two creates the spectrum of the sound that is emitted by the instrument (Figure 2-9).

Timbre: To Be Continued . . .

This concludes a basic discussion of acoustic factors that contribute to timbre. A fuller understanding requires a discussion of perceptual issues as well as acoustic factors. Perceptual issues will be taken up in Chapter 3.

Making Waves: Building Blocks of Sound Synthesis

Classic sound synthesis relies on building blocks that are typically expressed in terms of wave type and spectrum. The topic of synthesis will be taken up in more detail in Chapter 10, but this introductory point on waveshapes applies to the topics covered in the present chapter on musical properties, as well as in many that follow.

Synthesizers produce sound waves with *oscillators*, which produce a repeating wave form of some kind. In addition to oscillators that produce noise and sine waves,

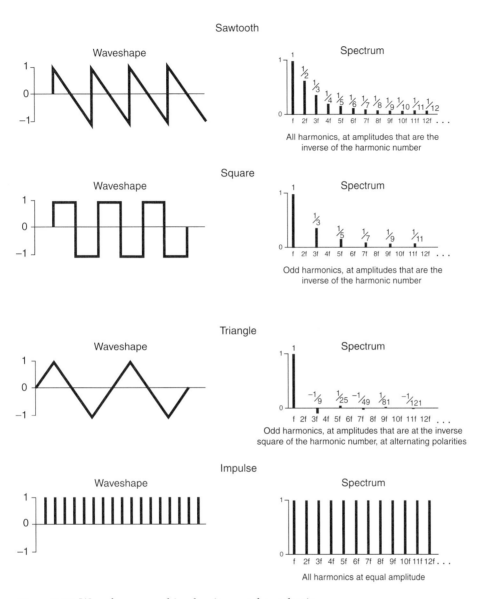

Figure 2-10 Waveforms used in classic sound synthesis

four other basic oscillators produce *sawtooth*, *square*, *triangle*, and *impulse train waves*. These waveshapes and their spectra are shown in Figure 2-10.

These are "legacy" waveshapes that were developed for early electronic equipment. The earliest demonstrations of electrical current were done with spark gap oscillators, which produced electrical current that flowed in simple harmonic motion: quick movement from one direction to another and then back again. This alternating current produced a corresponding magnetic field, which induced a corresponding electrical signal in a nearby conductor. (Chapter 4 will provide an introduction to basic electronic principles.) The transmitted signal could be amplified and sent to a loudspeaker as a radio broadcast. Next, the cathode-ray oscilloscope was invented in 1897, which enabled electrical signals to be viewed in real time. The oscilloscope display was created with a horizontal-sweep oscillator, which produced a sawtooth signal. This acted as a guide for the scanner to sweep linearly from left to right, over and over again, thousands of times per second, plotting a glowing dot as it went. Oscilloscopes and other testing devices became the key components of an electrician's toolkit. The sawtooth oscillator later became the basis for television displays. Square and triangle wave oscillators were created for testing purposes. When they were fed into an electrical system, the output was viewed with an oscilloscope. If the output did not match the input, it was an indication of a problem somewhere in the system.

With the invention of the modular analog synthesizer in the 1960s, these waveforms were produced by making sound from changes in electrical voltage. A sine wave oscillator produced a sine tone via a voltage that alternated according to a sine-shaped pattern. A sawtooth oscillator's change in voltage over time was linear in one direction, immediately returned to its original position, and then returned to a linear rate of change. A square wave oscillator's current moved at a constant speed in one direction, then reversed. A triangle wave oscillator's voltage alternated between high and low levels, similar to a sine wave except that the voltage change over time was linear rather than sinusoidal. The impulse train oscillator produced periodic, instantaneous amplitude bursts with zero amplitude between them.

The waveshapes in Figure 2-10 are idealized in a number of ways. For one thing, all harmonics are in phase. Their waveforms would look very different if the harmonics

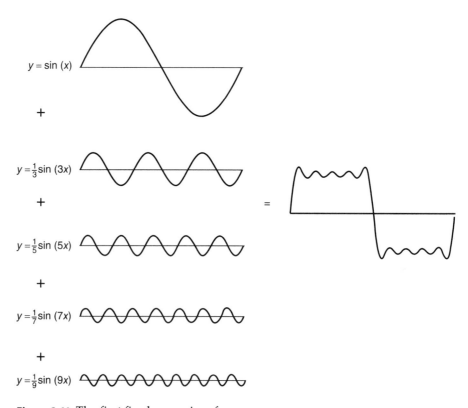

Figure 2-11 The first five harmonics of a square wave

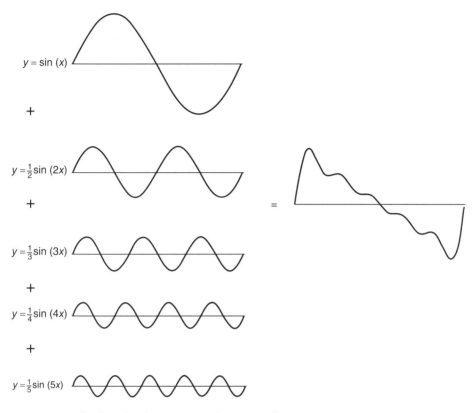

$y = \sin(x)$

$+$

$y = \frac{1}{2}\sin(2x)$

$+$

$=$

$y = \frac{1}{3}\sin(3x)$

$+$

$y = \frac{1}{4}\sin(4x)$

$+$

$y = \frac{1}{5}\sin(5x)$

Figure 2-12 The first five harmonics of a sawtooth wave

were not in phase, although they would not sound any different (a topic that will be discussed in Chapter 3). Also, large changes in voltage cannot occur instantaneously. Thus, the vertical lines in reality have a finite slope.

These idealized shapes illustrate a series of harmonics that extends to infinity. The waves look somewhat different when there is a practical limit to their frequency range. Figures 2-11 and 2-12 show square and sawtooth waves that consist of five component partials. Both shapes show pronounced ripples. As more harmonics are added, the ripples lessen and the overall shape approaches the angularity shown in Figure 2-10. In practical terms, there is always some degree of ripple in any synthesized waveform. (Sound synthesis techniques will be discussed further in Chapter 10.)

Suggested Exercises

- Using a spreadsheet and the steps shown in Appendix 2, create one period of a sine wave. Square all values, then take their mean. Take the square root of the mean to confirm that the RMS value is 0.707.
- Using a spreadsheet and the steps shown in Appendix 2, plot some of the wave forms shown in Figure 2-10. Observe how adding more partials to each creates a more jagged appearance to the wave's shape.

- Go to a website that has instrumental samples (audio files) available. Two excellent sites are the University of Iowa Electronic Music Studios (http://theremin.music.uiowa.edu/MIS.html) and the Philharmonia Samples page (http://www.philharmonia.co.uk/explore/make_music). Download some files and open them in an audio analysis program such as Sonic Visualiser (http://www.sonicvisualiser.org). View the samples as spectrograms, and observe what information can be gleaned from this rendering. Among the characteristics you might observe, consider:
  o identifying the transient and steady-state portions
  o identifying the fundamental
  o whether the file is harmonic or inharmonic
  o does the file have much noise?

Key Terms

analytic listening
aperiodic
bel (B)
chord
cycles per second or hertz (Hz)
decibel (dB)
Doppler shift or effect
emergent property
force
formant
Fourier analysis or transform
impulse train
intensity (I)
intonation
inverse Fourier transform
inverse square law
just intonation
linear progression
logarithm
microtonality
mode of vibration
normalize
octave
oscillator

overtone
partial
pascals (Pa)
peak pressure level or peak
    amplitude level
perfect fifth
periodic
power
pressure
pure tone
quasi-periodic
RMS (root-mean-square)
sawtooth wave
spectral plot
spectrogram plot or sonogram
spectrum
square wave
temperament
timbre
triangle wave
twelve-tone equal temperament
watts (W)
white noise
work

Chapter 3

Perceptual Issues in Acoustics

Chapters 1 and 2 covered issues of acoustics, describing phenomena that are objective and measurable. Actual human perception of acoustic events, however, is less straightforward, and is often difficult to measure precisely. Our auditory perceptions are not based on objective acoustical analyses, but rather on a variety of filters, interpretations, and best guesses that the brain assembles. These interpretations are presumably evolutionary adaptations that came into being to improve our species' chances for survival.

In this chapter, we will take up some issues that connect acoustics and perception, an area known as *psychoacoustics*. Subsequent chapters will show how an understanding of psychoacoustics allows artists to make effective audio production choices. To create art that is meant for the ear, it is important to understand how the ear interprets the information it receives.

What Is the Difference Between Consonance and Dissonance?

Musicians and composers are educated about consonant and dissonant intervals: when pitches played in combination sound pleasing or agreeable, they are said to be *consonant*; when they clash or sound disagreeable, they are said to be *dissonant*. However, listeners do not always agree on whether a particular note combination is consonant or dissonant. As this chapter will discuss, there are some perceptual issues that walk a fine line between measurable and interpretive. But there is one absolute in human musical perception, which is the *octave*, a duplication of pitch class that occurs whenever a frequency is doubled, halved, or transposed by some other integer power of two (as shown in Figure 2-4). Thus, the octave is the perfect consonance, because wave cycles between two sounds separated by some number of octaves always coincide. When people sing pitches an octave apart, it can be difficult to tell that there are two singers, because the tendency is for the pitches to fuse into one due to their cyclic coincidences.

Pitch perception is sometimes described as having two dimensions. The *tone height* describes the pitch of a note within the range of pitches from the lowest to the highest. The *chroma* describes a pitch within the span of an octave. As tone height rises, the chroma repeats itself through successive octaves. Lerdahl (2004) describes the theorist M. W. Drobisch's suggestion, made in 1855, that the relationship between the two can be illustrated with a helix, a shape like a stretched slinky. The loops of the slinky represent successive octaves. If a chroma represents a certain angle along the loop, then the chroma is repeated from cycle to cycle as the slinky continues to pass through this angle as the tone height rises.

The Mystery of the Octave, and the Evolutionary Basis of Music

Octave equivalence, or *octave generalization,* is exclusively a phenomenon of hearing; there is no similar phenomenon in vision, whereby one color seems to be an "octave duplicate" of another. Our perception of the octave is so strong that familiar songs can be played with notes that are transposed by various octaves, and the melody still sounds recognizable and familiar. Octave equivalence is the fundamental miracle of human hearing; without it, we might have music, but it would be quite different.

Our perception of the octave duplication raises fascinating questions. One active research area at this writing is the field of evolutionary psychology (Scaletti, 2016). Some writers, such as cognitive scientist Steven Pinker (1997), suggest that music is a *spandrel,* an evolutionary byproduct without any inherent utility, or, as he puts it, "auditory cheesecake." Others, such as archaeologist Steven Mithen (2007), consider music to be a linguistic necessity that helped to ensure our survival, and remains with us an essential component of our humanity. Lakoff and Johnson (2003) describe language as enabling *distributed cognition*, a mutual sharing of ideas whereby cumulative experiences create emergent phenomena: while any individual, under the right circumstances, may intuit the creation of a sling or bow and arrow, it is unlikely that any one person would develop higher mathematics or literature, which have their basis in combined, societal experiences. Anthropologist and evolutionary psychologist Robin Dunbar views music as something akin to the kind of grooming practiced by various primate species as they clean each other's fur (Dunbar, 1998). He describes "auditory grooming"—language, laughter, music, and other sound-based communications—as an aid in group cohesion, and in maintaining social networks.

I have personally had experiences common to many music teachers who are faced with a classroom full of noisy children—when I resort to singing instructions, the children immediately quiet down and listen. There seems to be an innate responsiveness to musical delivery that commands people's attention. Perhaps octave pitch duplication aided in early singing. Perhaps it aided the blending of men's and women's voices, and aided in mating, just as songs are a part of other species' mating rituals.

Speculation aside, it can be safely asserted that music is a human universal; while different people may like different types of music, it is difficult to find someone who does not respond strongly to music of some kind. (There are extremely rare cases of people who are identified as having congenital amusia, a complete lack of musical comprehension, but occurrences of it are anomalous [Mithen, 2007].) While music perception has long been thought to be related to a number of brain areas that are also responsible for perception of speech and other sounds, researchers, with the aid of emerging technologies such as functional magnetic resonance imaging (fMRI) brain scans, are beginning to find evidence of a dedicated "music center" (Norman-Haignere et al., 2015). The responsiveness to music seems unique to the human species; furthermore, while other species, notably birds and whales, practice singing, instances of any sort of octave generalization are rare among other species (Rothenberg, 2008, p. 95), although Levitin (2007, p. 31) lists cats and monkeys as two species that show evidence of perceiving octave equivalence. Why some species hear octaves and how this pitch-class duplication might have served the human species as a survival mechanism remains an open-ended and compelling question.

Perspectives on Consonance and Dissonance

Beyond the octave, the nature of consonance and dissonance, which was once considered to be a purely factual matter, is now a bone of perceptual contention. Students of counterpoint are familiar with the classification of different intervals as being either consonant or dissonant, and the rules that govern when each can be used. As common-practice music became increasingly complex, the composer Arnold Schoenberg (1874–1951) described in 1926 the "emancipation of dissonance" (Schoenberg, 1975) as the basis for his experiments into free atonality. Schoenberg suggested that the quality of consonance or dissonance was contextual, dependent on the tonal world established by the composer, which could vary from piece to piece.

Some suggest a more objective approach, based on harmonic content. When pure tones at different frequencies are sounded simultaneously, the perceptual effect differs depending on the frequency difference between them. When the frequencies are close together, usually within 10 Hz of each other, only one pitch is perceived. The perceived frequency is the average of the two tones, and there is a modulation, or *first-order beating*, in volume at a rate that corresponds to the frequency difference. For example, when a frequency of 440 Hz is combined with a frequency of 444 Hz, the perceived frequency is 442 Hz, and there is a perceptible volume oscillation at 4 Hz. This amplitude modulation is the result of repeated constructive and destructive interference between the two waves.

If the frequency difference between two tones is increased, the volume modulation becomes more rapid. Eventually, it becomes impossible to perceive them as volume cycles; instead, it takes on a perceptual "roughness." This range of frequency proximity, characterized by modulations and roughness, is known as the *critical band*. As frequency differences move outside the critical band, the two tones become autonomous and are perceived as two separate pitches.

Before the invention of electronic tuning devices, piano tuners performed their work by listening for beats between simultaneous pitches. They obtained the desired pitch relationships by counting the beats per second when two notes were played in combination, and made the necessary adjustments until all intervals were correct.

This beating and roughness explains why composers generally do not write thick chords in the bass ranges. Recall that in Chapter 2, pitch perception was described as logarithmic. This means that at lower pitches, the frequency proximity of pitches is much closer, and the resultant beating and roughness often produces a "muddy" sound. When the same pitches are combined in higher ranges, however, there is greater frequency separation and thus they sound clearer when combined.

A physical definition of consonance and dissonance, based on the perceptual effects of frequency proximity, is illustrated in Figure 3-1. When two pitches are separated by an octave, all harmonics coincide. When two pitches are separated by a perfect fifth, many of their harmonics coincide. Based on this figure, it is easy to see why these intervals are considered consonant: there is a smooth aural blend between the two tones due to their overlap in harmonic content. When two pitches are separated by a major second, few (if any) harmonics coincide. Instead, harmonics from the two pitches frequently fall within each other's critical band, the result being a beating or roughness among the partials that is perceived as dissonance.

Sound Spectra in Time

Humans rely primarily on their eyes and ears for sensory information. Other species have far greater reliance on smell and taste. This is particularly true for species who are

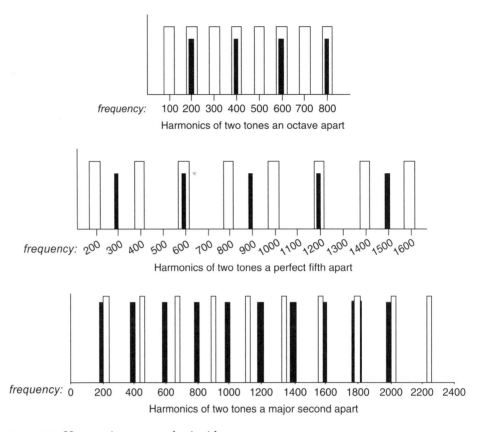

Figure 3-1 Harmonic spectra of coincident notes

lower to the ground; we upright humans get information about our world through seeing and hearing. Biologist E. O. Wilson (1998) points out that this audio/visual preference is species-wide, and not part of any local culture. Evidence can be seen in linguistics: in various languages used worldwide, 75 percent of words describing sensory impressions describe vision and hearing.

While the auditory and visual senses are complementary in many ways, they also supplement each other, with each having its particular strength. The eyes are most effective for providing static information about characteristics such as size, shape, texture, color, and so on. The ears are particularly effective at providing dynamic information about changing events. While we rely primarily on information from the eyes, there is a great deal of information that our ears bring to us that we commonly overlook. Writers such as Barry Blesser (2006) point out that, when blindfolded, we can learn to "see" with our ears more quickly than we might imagine, as we become attuned to nuances in echo, reverberation, and directional hearing. Human perception of sound and music events is largely determined by the behavior of frequencies and their amplitudes over time.

Figure 2-8 represented unchanging complex waves with a set of harmonics at a constant level. But in real life, sounds are rarely, if ever, so consistent. The energy in different spectral regions often changes over the duration of a sound event. These spectral changes often correspond to changes in overall volume.

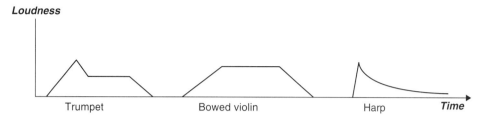

Figure 3-2 Amplitude envelopes

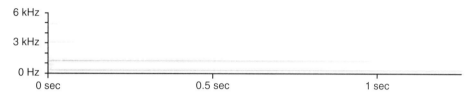

The instrument's sound is characterized by the fundamental at 293 Hz and the fourth harmonic at 1172 Hz. The attack also contains noise below 2 kHz, and partials near the tenth harmonic at 2390 Hz and the 17th harmonic at 4981 Hz. Once the steady-state portion sets in, the fourth harmonic fades first, followed by the fundamental.

Figure 3-3 Spectrogram of a vibraphone at middle D (293 Hz)

The nature of a sound's amplitude changes over time is called the *amplitude envelope*. An approximation of the amplitude envelopes of three different instruments is shown in Figure 3-2. The sound of most instruments begins with an initial *transient*, or *attack*, portion. The transient is characterized by many high partials, mixed with noise. For example, the scraping of a bow on a violin or the puff of breath from a flute both have high degrees of noise content. After a moment, the instruments begin to vibrate and a pitch becomes audible. An instrument's distinctive sound is determined primarily by this transient portion. In the 1950s, when the first synthesizers were being developed by RCA, their inventors made claims that these instruments would remove the "impurities" of sounds created by acoustic instruments: the clicking, blowing, and scraping that form the initial vibrations in an instrument. It did not take long before people realized how canned and artificial sounds became without these "undesirable" transients. Far from being undesirable impurities, the transients make a timbre sound natural and interesting. Later, it became a common exercise in electronic music classes for students to record the sound of a piano note, then employ a razor blade and remove the attack portion of the sound from the tape. The lesson was that without the attack, it was very difficult to identify the sound as originating from a piano.

Following the transient, instruments usually produce a *steady-state*, or *sustained*, *sound*. In contrast to the attack, the steady state is characterized by quasi-periodicity. As per the Fourier theorem, a periodic waveform is composed of a harmonic spectrum. Figure 3-3 shows the spectrogram of the note middle D (293 Hz) played on a vibraphone. It is easy to recognize the additional partials and noise that characterize the attack—the immediate result of the mallet striking the metal bar—and the small number of partials that constitute the sound's steady-state portion.

It is difficult to come up with a simple definition of an instrument's spectrum. With the introduction of computer music systems, early work in timbre study found that the overtone content produced by an instrument varies depending on a number of factors, including its volume level and the register in which the notes were played, as well as modifications a player might make with changes in embouchure, breath pressure, or other playing techniques (Risset and Mathews, 1969). Subtle variations in spectra from note to note over the course of a piece are part of what make the performance interesting and compelling to the listener.

Localization of Natural Events

In addition to its sensitivity to dynamic frequency changes, the human auditory system is also equipped to make estimations of a sound source's location. Human localization is most acute for sounds arriving from the front. It is less accurate for sounds arriving at the rear. The least accuracy is for sounds arriving from the side, where a "cone of confusion" exists (Blauert, 1997). This term refers to listeners being able to make a close estimation of angle, but often confusing front from rear, or high elevation from low elevation.

Not all sound types are equally easy to localize. *Localization blur* quantifies the margin of error in localizing various sound types. High sinusoidal tones are difficult to localize, while the sounds of people speaking, particularly voices known to the listener, are easier to locate. When asked to identify locations of vocal sound sources, listeners in test environments are able to estimate the source angle with a greater average degree of accuracy than when they are asked to identify high sinusoidal tones. As there is a greater variance in identification, the sinusoidal tones are said to have a higher level of localization blur.

The auditory system makes localization estimates with three factors: *interaural time delay (ITD), spectral shadows*, and *pinnae filtering*.

Interaural Time Delay (ITD)

Interaural time delay refers to the difference in time between a wavefront arriving at the near and far ear. When a sound occurs directly from the front, there is an equal distance from the sound source to both ears. When a sound occurs to one side, the wavefront must travel a greater distance to reach the farther ear. The delay between the near and the far ear, short as it may be, is the cue used by the auditory system to make an estimation of location for sounds below 1500 Hz or so. When wavelengths are larger than the dimensions of a surface they come into contact with, the wave diffracts around the object (see Chapter 1). Thus, interaural time delay is the primary means of localizing frequencies below 1500 Hz, as these longer wavelengths diffract around the head to reach the farther ear a moment later.

Spectral Shadowing, or Interaural Level Delay (ILD)

Spectral shadows, or *interaural level delay (ILD)*, describe the difference in spectra received by the two ears. As discussed in Chapter 1, when wavelengths are smaller than the dimensions of a surface they come into contact with, the wave is reflected away from the object. In the case of sound wavefronts, frequencies above 1500 Hz or so have wavelengths that are shorter than the width of the human head (7" or 17 cm). Thus, these wavefronts reflect back away from the head. The result is a *spectral shadow* at the farther ear, where there is less high-frequency content. This shadowing effect is the predominant localization cue for frequencies above 1500 Hz.

Spectral differences of stimulus test tones can cause sounds to appear from the front or the rear. The reason is that sounds arriving from the rear tend to reach the auditory system with attenuated high-frequency content, as these shorter wavelengths are reflected away from the backs of the pinnae (the outer ears). Playing a stimulus signal and gradually attenuating its high-frequency content can give the illusion of a sound moving from front to rear.

Pinnae Filtering

Finally, the auditory system makes a judgment of elevation from changes in a sound's frequency content that result from reflections within the pinnae. As wavefronts bounce around the various nooks and crannies of the outer ears, they enter the ear canal as a series of reflections at varying delay times. The superposition of these reflections causes pinnae filtering, a shaping of the overall spectrum that enters the ear. (In Chapter 6, we will discuss how filtering results from combining an audio signal with a delayed version of itself.) The degree of spectral shaping is determined by the angle and elevation level of the sound.

Everyone's pinnae are different. A given individual's elevation sensitivity is learned through one's own particular pinnae shapes (Bregman, 1990). This has been verified in experiments in which listeners had their pinnae covered with clay, with a flexible tube inserted through the clay to the auditory canal. With the pinnae thus disabled, listeners were able to hear listening stimuli, but had difficulty identifying their elevation. When molds of the listeners' pinnae were attached to the end of the tube, sensitivity to elevation was restored. But when molds of someone else's pinnae were used instead, listeners, once again, had difficulty identifying elevation.

Mismatches Between Measurement and Perception

Given the various properties and emergent factors of sound, we can think of sound events as being multidimensional "objects," with dimensional axes that include pitch, noise content, volume, spectrum, pan position, attack time, and distance. It is the combination of these dimensions that characterizes what is heard. Yet many times auditory events are perceptually more than the sum of their parts. The perceptual impression of a given dimension may vary according to the context in which it is heard.

Phase

Some books on the psychology of music equate timbre with waveshape. This may be true most of the time, but it is ultimately a misleading description. While it is true that sounds having different timbres have different waveshapes, different waveshapes do not necessarily create different timbres. Figure 2-10 illustrated examples of waveshapes created by standard synthesizer oscillators. If the initial phases of the partials were changed, the waveshapes would also change. However, when the relative phases of a steady-state sound are altered, there is no perceptible change in the sound, although the shape of the wave may change noticeably. Thus, adding spectral components to a sound changes the shape of the wave, but a change in waveshape does not necessarily produce a change in spectral content.

This phenomenon, while it may be counterintuitive, makes sense when viewed from an evolutionary perspective. Consider two musicians playing a duet on the same instrument. If one of them should take a step backwards or forwards, the phase relationship of the sounds emanating from these instruments changes, which changes the shape of the composite wave produced by both instruments. If this change in relative phases and composite waveshape were to result in a significant change in the character of the sound, a concert would be a very inconsistent auditory event unless the musicians were careful to remain completely motionless during the performance. Generalizing this phenomenon, life would be extremely confusing if combinations of sounds in the environment changed along with slight changes of distance among sound sources.

However, the fact that phase differences in steady-state sounds are inaudible does not mean that phase is perceptually inconsequential. As was discussed earlier, musically interesting sounds are not steady-state, but in a constant state of evolution. In particular, the behavior of spectral components during the attack segment of a sound is likely to be far more complex than in the steady-state segment. So, for one thing, changing the phase of attack components can change the character of the attack. For another thing, solo performance sounds different from group performance because no two players can ever initiate sound at precisely the same moment; thus the attack from the two instruments is blurred. Because an instrument's characteristics are defined primarily by its attack, the phase of attack components is critical to the character of the sound.

Transients are also an essential component of everyday sounds, particularly speech. The various echoes and reflections that enter the auditory canal alter the character of transients in important perceptual ways, as was discussed in the section on localization. In subsequent chapters, we will soon see that that the treatment of a signal's phases is critical in the evaluation of audio filters.

Timbre

Timbre is often associated primarily with spectral content, as was noted in the ANSI definition in Chapter 2. But this definition is quite open-ended. Defining timbre as "not volume and not pitch" leaves open a great many other characteristics, all of which may fall under the general umbrella of "timbre." One factor is a sound's envelope. Chowning (1977) observed that the verisimilitude of a synthesized imitation of an instrument depends more on characterizing its envelope shape than on matching its spectral content. With an accurate facsimile of the instrument's envelope, a simple approximation of the instrument's partials will be enough for listeners to recognize the imitation of an instrument.

We have noted that the attack portion is critical to the definition of a sound. While sounds that have high-frequency spectral components are described as "brighter" than those with less high-frequency energy, sounds with a faster attack are also often described as "brighter" than sound with slower attacks. Thus, a fast attack can be perceptually confused with the presence of high partials.

Considerable research has gone into the creation of *timbre space*, a multidimensional plot in which timbres are placed according to overtone content, envelope, and attack time (Wessel, 1979). Despite these efforts, a precise definition of timbre remains elusive, and there is no definitive scale of measurement for timbral characteristics. As was stated in Chapter 2, timbre is an example of an emergent property, meaning that is not a single parameter in and of itself, but arises as a consequence of a number of other parameters working in combination, creating an overall effect that is greater than the sum of its parts. These parameters include spectrum, spectral evolution, transient, and formants, among others.

Loudness

The perception of *loudness* is also an emergent property that eludes precise definition. While intensity is the measurement most closely correlated to loudness, the perception of volume is based on a number of factors, not all of them entirely measurable.

One of these factors is that perceived loudness is frequency dependent. In 1933, it was reported that certain frequencies, at certain intensity levels, sound less "loud" than other frequencies at the same intensity levels (Fletcher and Munson, 1933). They produced a set of equal loudness curves that were used as a standard reference until a revised set of equal loudness contours was created in 1956 (Robinson and Dadson, 1956) (Figure 3-4). It is clear from the figure that the auditory system is more responsive to changes in power with frequencies near 1 kHz. Like many other perceptual mechanisms in this chapter, sensitivity in this frequency region is likely another nod to evolutionary adaptation, as this spectral range corresponds to the range of human speech. Speech is a particular characteristic of our species, and our ears are specially wired to understand it. At higher and lower frequencies, a far greater change in power is required to create a perceptually equivalent change in loudness. This is why some headphones feature a bass boost switch. It is meant to give added volume to low frequencies so that when music is played at low volumes the bass ranges are not lost to our ears.

Another curiosity is that within close frequency ranges, perceived loudness is proportional to the cube root of intensity. For example, two violins playing the same pitch generate twice the intensity of one violin, but do not sound twice as loud. To achieve twice the volume, eight violins are required (since $2^3 = 8$). This phenomenon is known as the *cube root intensity law*. However, if two instruments are playing two different pitches, the perceived loudness matches the doubling of intensity.

Adding to the perceptual mix is the fact that perceived loudness is also bandwidth-dependent. Increasing the *bandwidth* (frequency content) of a synthesized

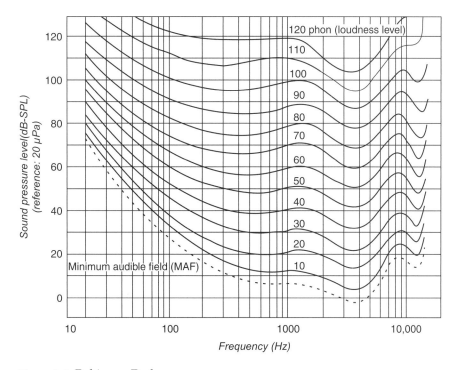

Figure 3-4 Robinson-Dadson curves
Source: From Ken Pohlmann, Principles of Digital Audio, *3rd ed. (1995). Copyright McGraw-Hill Education.*

sound often results in listeners describing the sound as "louder," even if the intensity is kept constant.

Psychologists have developed a variety of scales in attempts to classify perceived loudness. The *phon* is a subjective measurement that uses a pure tone at 1000 Hz as a reference. At 1 kHz, the phon level matches the dB level. Sounds that are perceived as matching this loudness are considered to be at the same phon level.

However, the phon measurement reflects only the perception of extended steady-state tones. Equal loudness measurements need to be modified to account for transients, which occur in natural sounds. To account for transients—which typically contain a greater degree of higher frequencies than the steady-state portion of a sound—a bias is given to the measurements to give greater weight to the higher frequencies in the final loudness determination.

To address this problem, the *sone* was a measurement proposed by S. S. Stevens in 1957. A 1000 Hz pure tone at 40 dB is assigned a level of one sone. Stevens found that a tone at 50 dB was generally perceived as being twice as loud, and assigned an increase of 10 dB to be an increase of one sone. Stevens's finding was used to determine the cube root intensity law. But it is less useful to describe stimuli other than sine tones.

Further studies have attempted to quantify loudness perception by breaking complex sounds into frequency bands (usually with bandwidths of one-third octave), assigning the loudness of each band according to the cube root intensity law, and then summing the loudness of each power band to determine the total loudness of the sound. However, the bandwidth of a sound also adds to the perceived volume level. Noises at a fixed intensity but variable bandwidth increase in perceived loudness once the bandwidth exceeds 175 Hz or so.

A definitive loudness scale remains elusive. Numerous tests have produced varied results, depending on factors such as the range of stimuli, first stimulus presented, instructions given to the subject, and other variables. It cannot be said with any certainty that any perceptual scale measures loudness more effectively than does a measurement of intensity.

It has also been argued that the perception of loudness in everyday life is due to a number of higher-level processes that estimate the distance, context, and import of a sound event (Handel, 1989). Our ears are effective at source identification. We typically know immediately whether a sound originates from an animal, an automobile, thunder, or something else. It has been found that, based on sound alone, listeners can make accurate estimations of the characteristics of rolling balls, including their size, the material that they are made of, speed, and so on (Hermes, 2000). But we have difficulty describing exactly what allows us to make these identifications. In everyday listening, our auditory system synthesizes a variety of acoustic characteristics to make an estimation of the nature of a sound source, one feature of which is perceived loudness.

Masking

Because loudness is context-dependent, when the context becomes complex—as when two or more sound events occur simultaneously—our perception of sound changes. *Masking* refers to a phenomenon by which certain sounds may cause other sounds to disappear (to be "masked") perceptually. Anyone who has tried to have a conversation while walking along a city street is likely to have experienced this phenomenon. The sound of a companion's voice can often be masked by the frequent intrusion of loud passing vehicles and other sounds. More precise analyses of masking show it to be related to the physiology of frequency perception.

The eardrum and middle ear convert incoming sound waves into mechanical energy. This mechanical energy is then transduced into electrical impulses in the cochlea, located in the inner ear. Within the cochlea, roughly 30,000 hair cells are arranged in rows along the basilar membrane. These hair cells fire electrical impulses that are interpreted by the brain as auditory signals. Not all cells fire simultaneously, however. Different regions of the hair cells fire when vibrations at different frequencies are received. A given frequency causes a particular region of cells to fire. The width of the region that is activated by a given frequency is called a *critical band*. A given frequency creates maximum excitation in a small set of hair cells, plus lesser amounts of excitation in neighboring cells. The term "critical band" can also refer to the frequency range to which all of these cells respond. The relationship of critical bands to frequency is not linear, but logarithmic. Bandwidth increases for higher frequencies. For example, a frequency of 350 Hz may stimulate the region of cells that responds to frequencies from 300 to 400 Hz. But a frequency of 4000 Hz may excite a region of cells that responds to frequencies within the range of 3700 to 4400 Hz. Human hearing is typically subdivided into twenty-four critical bandwidths, spanning the frequency range from 20 Hz to 15.5 kHz, according to the *Bark scale*, which was proposed in 1961 by acoustician Karl Eberhard Zwicker (1924–1990). He named it after the physicist Heinrich Barkhausen (1881–1956), who was one of the first to explore subjective loudness measurements.

Frequency domain masking occurs when two tones, one louder and one fainter, are heard simultaneously. If they are within a certain frequency range of each other, the fainter tone needs to be played at a higher volume to be audible. Put another way, the presence of the louder tone (masker) raises the *audibility threshold* of the softer tone (Figure 3-5).

Sound perception is integrated over time intervals of about 200 ms. *Temporal masking* has to do with tones played one after the other, usually within this timespan. A louder sound can raise the audibility threshold of another sound that is played within 100–200 ms later, a phenomenon called *forward masking*. There is also a phenomenon called *backward masking*, by which a louder sound can mask a softer sound that occurs before it. While this is counterintuitive, it appears that within the time window of 200 ms, one sound can mask another, regardless of which one occurs first.

As will be explored in succeeding chapters, masking is relevant to a variety of topics, from concert hall acoustics to audio compression formats.

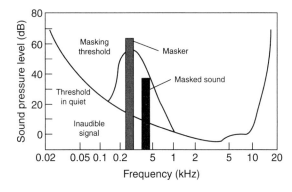

Figure 3-5 Perceptual masking
Source: From Ken Pohlmann, Principles of Digital Audio, *3rd ed. (1995). Copyright McGraw-Hill Education.*

Hearing Things That Aren't There

Many of the phenomena that we've discussed have physical explanations: the beating between two tones that are near in frequency to each other is due to interference patterns between their waveforms; masking is (at least partially) due to an "overload" of a hair cell region. Other phenomena are more peculiar, without any clear explanation, in that they involve our actually perceiving something that is not occurring acoustically. Many of these are part of ongoing research in audition.

SECOND-ORDER BEATS

First-order beating has a clear acoustic explanation: If two sine waves at slightly differing frequencies are plotted and added together, the result has regular amplitude modulations due to constructive and destructive interference that regularly occurs between the two waves. (In the Suggested Exercises section of this chapter, readers are encouraged to verify this by using a spreadsheet to plot the sum of two sine waves at similar frequencies.)

Less straightforward is a phenomenon that occurs for tones that are below 1500 Hz. If two tones are played that span an interval very close to an octave, for example 219 Hz and 440 Hz, a beating pattern occurs that does not have a clear acoustic explanation. These *second-order beats* are the result of neural processing—they happen as some sort of interpretive mechanism, rather than reflecting some acoustic phenomenon.

BINAURAL BEATS

Another interesting interpretive effect occurs when two slightly differing frequencies are sounded separately into our two ears. For example, if the tones 440 Hz and 444 Hz are presented, respectively, over left and right headphone channels, listeners report hearing a single tone that appears to move in circles within their heads, at the frequency that is the difference between the two (in this case, four circles per second).

THE MISSING FUNDAMENTAL

When two tones are played together that could be harmonically related, people often report hearing a third tone that would be the common fundamental for both of them. For example, if tones at 440 and 660 Hz are played together, people would often report hearing a tone of 220 Hz, a *missing fundamental* to both of the tones that are playing. Somehow, a signal reaches the brain that reports the presence of energy in a frequency region where there is, in fact, no energy present.

A related phenomenon is *fundamental tracking*. If groups of harmonically related tones are played in succession, a lower tone can often be perceived that would be the common fundamental to each of these tone groups. For example, if presented with these sequences of tone combinations:

- 440 and 660 Hz
- 660 and 880 Hz
- 880 and 1100 Hz
- 1100 and 1320 Hz
- 660, 880, and 1100 Hz
- 880, 1100, and 1320 Hz

it is common for listeners to report hearing the constant presence of a tone at 220 Hz throughout.

DIFFERENCE TONES

When two tones are played loudly together, a third tone can often be heard at the difference between the two. For example, combining pitches at 2200 Hz and 2300 Hz can produce an audible third pitch at 100 Hz. These *difference tones* are sometimes called *Tartini tones,* named after the composer, violinist, and theorist Giuseppe Tartini (1692–1770), who noted this phenomenon in 1754.

The Physical Basis of Pitch Perception

Examples like these—where listeners hear things that are not actually present—throw a wrench into the works whenever a theory of pitch perception is presented. A common theory of pitch perception is *place theory*, which is named after the motion of the cochlea within the inner ear in response to auditory stimulus. Particular frequencies displace particular *places* along the basilar membrane, and this displacement stimulates regions of hair cells that fire in response. Thus, the motion of the basilar membrane can appear to be the determining factor of pitch perception—until, that is, one tries to account for the missing fundamental, whereby people hear information that is not present in the acoustic signal, and therefore not the result of basilar membrane displacement.

An alternative to place theory is *periodicity theory*, which suggests that the basilar membrane displacement is not what gives the auditory system its cue for pitch perception, but that the perception of pitch is due to the repetitive pattern of pitched waveshapes. Tones that are harmonically related may be summed, and a pattern can be easily discerned that corresponds to their common fundamental, even though this fundamental is not present. Periodicity theory handily accounts for the missing fundamental. On the other hand, it would seem that the relative phases of the tones would be important if waveshape is responsible for pitch perception. But, as we've noted, changing the relative phases of a steady-state sound can drastically change the shape of the wave with no perceptual difference. So the periodicity theory also seems to fall short of a complete explanation.

Loy (2006) postulates that because pitch perception is a critical survival skill, it may be too important to be based on only one mechanism for perception. Rather, it seems likely that it is the result of analyzing multiple redundant cues and coming to a best estimate based on the information that is available. This suggestion concurs well with the ideas that will be discussed in the next section.

Auditory Scene Analysis

Auditory scene analysis is the study of organizational principles found in hearing. Related to these principles is the idea of *perceptual completion*, whereby we are able to infer the presence of an entire object based on incomplete information.

We can see these organizational principles at work in visual perception. *Gestalt principles* are an essential factor in visual organization. These principles include proximity, similarity, good continuation, habit/familiarity, belongingness, common fate, and closure. They are likely a survival mechanism that came about as an evolutionary adaptation: a species that can recognize a predator when much of it is obscured by forest or landscape has a better chance of survival than a species that has to see the entire figure before the fight-or-flight response takes effect. Thus, visual perception involves inference and analysis of probabilities. The brain makes its best judgment with whatever information it's given.

Figure 3-6 The Scale Illusion (discovered by Diana Deutsch): listeners report tones grouped by frequency proximity, rather than the actual ear of presentation.
Source: Figure from Diana Deutsch, "Grouping Mechanisms in Music," in The Psychology of Music, *2nd ed., edited by Diana Deutsch, © 1999 by Academic Press, reproduced by permission of the publisher.*

Many of these inference and perceptual completion mechanisms apply to audition, and analysis of the complex wave of sounds that reaches the eardrums. This single wave is parsed into **auditory streams**, which are the identification of discrete entities in the listening environment. A simple example of an auditory stream is the sound of footsteps. The series of steps are distinct from each other, but they are automatically grouped by the auditory system into a single identity due to their similarity of timbre, proximity of sound source, and other rule-based perceptual mechanisms that the auditory system employs innately. The writings of psychologists Albert S. Bregman (1990) and Diana Deutsch (2012) in this area include many compelling examples of auditory illusions, and illuminate a remarkable set of analytical capacities that are part of the human creature.

One of them is "The Scale Illusion," described in Deutsch (2012). As shown in Figure 3-6, a different sequence of tones is presented to each ear via headphones; listeners consistently report a different grouping of the tones than what is actually presented: tones are grouped by frequency proximity and described as arriving at the same ear when in fact they arrive at different ears. Another is described in Levitin (2007): psychologist Richard Warren presented listeners with the recorded sentence, "The bill was passed by both houses of the legislature," but with a piece of the sentence removed and replaced by noise. Listeners reported hearing the sentence intact in addition to a burst of noise, although reports of exactly where they heard the noise burst varied. This suggests that the speech and noise were processed as separate streams or sonic entities, with the result, once again, that listeners heard something that wasn't actually there. This is a distortion, but one that makes good sense as an evolutionary survival adaptation.

Turn It Down!

One final note on the nature of listening: *the ears are fragile.* They cannot be closed, as can the eyes, when exposed to stimuli that are at damaging intensity levels. While there is an acoustic reflex that lowers responsiveness at high volume levels by about 20 dB, it is slow, not taking full effect until after the potential damage is done. Once the damage is done, it may be irreparable. There may be hearing loss at some frequencies, or *tinnitus*, a constant ringing. Prolonged exposure to loud sounds may not only damage the auditory system; it can also lead to insomnia, tension, headaches, heart disease, and even sexual impotence (Loy, 2006).

Bottom line: if you find your ears ringing after listening to loud music, it's not cool, kids. It's a warning sign from your body: turn it down before you hurt yourself!

Suggested Exercises

- Using the steps shown in Appendix 2, plot two sine waves that differ slightly in frequency. Add the corresponding points of each wave, and create a plot that is the sum of the two waves to show the amplitude modulation effects described in the sections on consonance and dissonance and beating.
- Go to a website that has instrumental samples available, such as the two suggested in the Exercises in Chapter 2. Download some instrumental samples (audio files) and open them in an audio editor such as Audacity (http://sourceforge.net/projects/audacity). Remove the transient portion of a note and create a smooth fade into the steady-state portion. Try playing the edited sound for some people and see if they are able to identify what the instrument is.

Key Terms

amplitude envelope	localization blur
audibility threshold	loudness
auditory scene analysis	masking
auditory stream	missing fundamental
backward masking	octave
bandwidth	octave generalization
Bark scale	perceptual completion
beating (first order)	periodicity theory
chroma	phon
consonance	pinnae filtering
critical band	place theory
cube root intensity law	psychoacoustics
difference tones or Tartini tones	second-order beats
dissonance	sone
distributed cognition	spectral shadow
forward masking	steady-state or sustained sound
frequency domain masking	temporal masking
fundamental tracking	timbre space
Gestalt principles	tinnitus
interaural level delay (ILD)	tone height
interaural time delay (ITD)	transient or attack

Chapter 4

Fundamentals of Electricity

Electroacoustic music involves transducing acoustic musical signals into electrical current. Electricity is used by the various components in a music studio to exchange these signals. In the 1960s, when commercial synthesizers first became available, customers were expected to have some basic knowledge of electronics. For example, users had to solder various modules of a synthesizer system together. While it is no longer necessary to have these skills to use equipment out of the box, electrical terminology is still used in describing electronic music components, so it behooves a digital musician to have more than just a cursory definition of these terms. Some knowledge of electrical principles also comes in very handy when it comes to creating custom configurations. There are a variety of DIY kits available that allow easy creation of instruments that can send MIDI and other types of messages (described in Chapter 10), which allows the creation of custom-built instruments, such as specialized percussion pads, baton-type controllers, or sound-making sculptural pieces.

For these reasons, this chapter will provide some basics of how electrical energy flows from one device to another. The history of how this invisible power was harnessed so that it could provide light and do work is a testament to human deduction and ingenuity. This power is now the technological basis for our civilization.

Static Electricity

Electricity = Electrons

In the 1700s, electricity was not yet well understood, and served primarily as a parlor trick. Using a glass rod, a silk scarf, a wool scarf, and a pith ball suspended from a stick, experimenters thrilled audiences by causing these objects to be attracted to or repulsed from each other once the rod and the ball were rubbed with the scarves. An experimenter/showman might perform with the following steps:

- First: rub the glass rod with silk, touch it briefly to the pith ball, then rub it again with the silk. Then hold the rod near the ball, and . . . presto! Watch the ball magically float away from it!
- Next: rub the rod with wool, hold it near the ball, and . . . presto! The ball magically floats toward it!

How could simply rubbing the rod with these objects in this order cause objects to float in space toward and away from each other?

The American inventor (and later statesman) Benjamin Franklin (1706–1790) concluded that the effects were due to two opposite types of charge, which he termed *positive* and *negative*. We now know that electrical charge is due to an imbalance of **protons** and **electrons**. When an uncharged object gains extra electrons, it acquires a **negative charge**. When an uncharged object loses electrons, it acquires a **positive charge**. A charged atom is called an **ion**. When an atom has more electrons than protons, it is a negatively charged ion. When it is missing electrons, it is a positively charged ion.

Certain types of objects are particularly susceptible to being charged. Rubbing an object with silk removes electrons, giving it a positive charge. Rubbing an object with wool causes it to gain electrons, giving it a negative charge.

In the first parlor trick, rubbing the glass with silk removed some of its electrons, giving the glass a positive charge. When the glass was touched to the ball, electrons on the ball became attracted to the positive charge of the glass, and flowed from the ball to the glass, neutralizing the ball's charge. But when those electrons left the pith ball, they left behind "holes," another term for a positive charge. Rubbing the glass again with the silk removed electrons, once again giving it a positive charge. Because both the glass and the pith ball were positively charged, they repelled each other: the ball moved away from the glass when they were held near each other (Figure 4-1).

When the glass rod was rubbed with the wool, and the wool shed electrons onto the glass, the glass acquired a negative charge. The ball, still having its positive charge, was then attracted to the oppositely charged glass (Figure 4-2). Touching a finger to both objects removed the charges, thus neutralizing both objects.

Objects can also be attracted or repulsed from each other if only one of them is charged. Rubbing the uncharged glass with the silk removed electrons from it, once again giving it a positive charge. Now, when the glass was held near the uncharged ball, the ball's electrons redistributed themselves, rushing to the side of the ball near the glass. This gave the ball's near side a negative charge, which caused it to be attracted to the glass rod and float toward it (Figure 4-3).

A similar thing happened when the wool rubbed the uncharged glass, giving it a negative charge. When the negatively charged glass was held near the uncharged ball, electrons on the near side of the ball were repulsed and moved to its far side, giving the ball's near side a positive charge. This caused the glass and the ball, once again, to be attracted to each other (Figure 4-4).

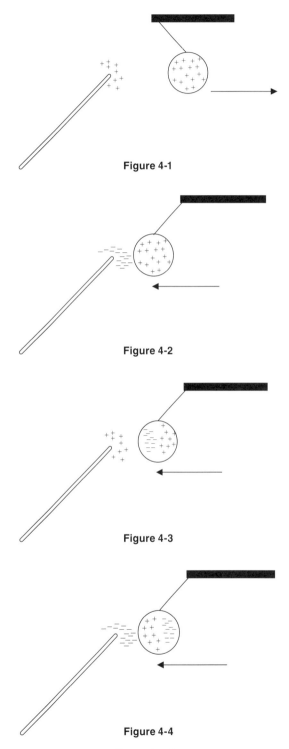

Figure 4-1

Figure 4-2

Figure 4-3

Figure 4-4

Figures 4-1 to 4-4 Opposite charges attract, similar charges repel.

These parlor tricks are examples of *static electricity*, which involves interactions between charged objects. However, the electrons were not static during those extremely brief moments when the objects were brought into contact, which transferred charges between objects. An electrical *current* is produced when electrons move from one place to another in order to make the charges neutral. In fact, when there is a large mismatch in charge between objects, the attraction may be great enough that the electrons "jump" to the positively charged object, emitting a dramatic spark that neutralizes the objects. In this case, the static charge is said to be *discharged*.

From Parlor Tricks to Lightning Storms

Before 1746, it was also known that charged objects could attract or repel each other in a vacuum. Experimenters also knew that some materials are *insulators* and others are *conductors*. Wrapping a charged object in rubber stops the charge from leaving the object, making rubber an effective insulator. On the other hand, connecting a copper wire between two oppositely charged objects causes the charge to travel along the wire from the negative object to the positive object. Copper is thus an effective conductor, as are gold and silver.

These metals work as conductors because of their atomic structure: unlike the lighter elements, they have multiple rings of electrons. The outer rings, being farther away from the nucleus than the inner rings, are not as tightly bound to it. As a result, these outer electrons, called valence electrons, are regularly swapped among atoms, even under normal, uncharged conditions. When extra electrons are introduced, they are simply passed from one atom to another, as in a game of hot potato (or "hot electron"). Thus, electrons move easily through metals.

Experimenters who took their pursuits beyond simple parlor tricks used large *friction machines* (Figure 4-5) to charge objects, such as glass or sulfur, by turning a crank to spin the objects against each other. In 1746, scientists in Leyden, the Netherlands, found a way to store the charge by using a jar lined with foil and charging the foil. The charge could be contained in the jar until they chose to discharge it. The *Leyden jar* (Figure 4-6) demonstrated the capacity to store an electrical charge, and was the first example of what is now termed a *capacitor*, which was the forerunner of the battery.

Benjamin Franklin was daring, and could be naïvely reckless, when it came to lightning. In those days, lightning was not well understood. When it would strike a building and set it ablaze, the event was considered the will of God. Therefore fire companies made a point of only extinguishing fires in neighboring buildings, leaving the one that had been struck to burn itself out in accordance with divine will. Apparently dissatisfied with this protocol, Franklin invented the lightning rod, preventing many such fires altogether by attracting lightning and absorbing it before it had a chance to reach the house. He then earned scientific immortality by proving that lightning was, in fact, electricity. On May 10, 1752, he flew a kite in a thunderstorm that

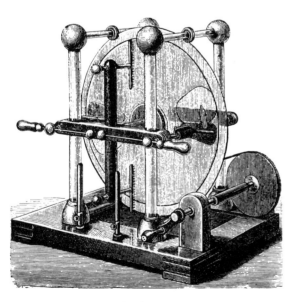

Figure 4-5 Friction wheel
Source: © iStock.com/Nikola Nastasic

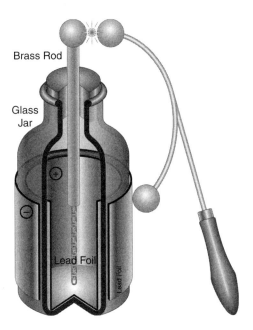

Figure 4-6 Leyden jar
Source: © iStock.com/Fouad A. Saad

had a metal key tied to the twine. When lightning struck near the kite, he noticed that the kite string's fibers stood up. When he touched the key it caused a spark (and gave him a strong shock), showing that electrical current had traveled down the twine to the key. He then found he could fill a Leyden jar with the charge from a lightning bolt. While we are indebted to Franklin for this discovery, we are also fortunate that he survived to carry out further work. The next year, Georg Wilhelm Richmann (1711–1753), a physicist in St. Petersburg, brought about his own demise by attempting to perform the same experiment. Trying to touch lightning with bare hands was relegated to the "Don't try this at home!" file.

While Franklin's work laid the groundwork that eventually revolutionized civilization, his lack of formal education kept him from joining the higher echelons of science. Without skills in higher mathematics, it was left to others to more systematically explore and exploit the power that electricity offered.

Current, Voltage, Resistance, and Power

As we have discussed, when two oppositely charged objects are connected by a conductor, a current of electrons flows from the negatively charged object to the positively charged object. This is known as the *electromotive force (EMF)*, which is measured in *volts*, and describes the potential for current to flow. Physically speaking, it is the difference in the number of electrons between one place and another. The greater the difference, the stronger the impetus for electrical current, and the greater the voltage.

Many descriptions of electricity (Upton, 1957) compare current to flowing water. A greater difference in charge creates greater attraction, thus higher voltage. Imagine water flowing down a hill: the steeper the hill, the greater the force behind the current.

Similarly, the greater the difference between opposite electrical charges, the greater the voltage.

If two channels of water are flowing down the same hill but one of them is wider, then the wider channel delivers more water in a given period of time—the current increases. Electrical current, measured in *amperes*, describes the number of electrons that pass a point over a given period of time, while voltage measures the force driving the electrons. A 100-watt light bulb draws about an ampere, while devices such as microphones draw current in levels of milli- and microamps (milli- indicates one thousandth, micro- indicates one millionth; these and other prefixes that refer to numbers at various powers of ten are shown in Figure A4-1 in Appendix 4).

Electrical *power* is the product of current and voltage, and is measured in *watts*:

$$power = current \times voltage \qquad (4\text{-}1)$$

But not all current flows with equal ease. Consider again water flowing through a channel. If a channel narrows, the force behind the flowing water increases because the water becomes concentrated into the narrower passage. *Resistance*, measured in *ohms*, inhibits current flow. With greater resistance, less current can flow per unit of time, but the impetus to flow increases.

The relationship between the three is described by *Ohm's Law*:

$$voltage_E = current_I \times resistance_R \qquad (4\text{-}2)$$

Thus, increasing either current or resistance increases the voltage.

Substituting Equation 4-2 into Equation 4-1 produces:

$$power = current \times (current \times resistance) = resistance \times current^2 \qquad (4\text{-}3)$$

Assuming resistance remains constant, this implies that

$$power \propto current^2 \qquad (4\text{-}4)$$

(Note the similarity between Equations 4-4 and 2-17.)

The Battery

One of the primary tools for working with electricity is a *battery*, which is a vessel containing a chemical solution that tends to break down into positively and negatively charged ions. Two electrodes (conductor plates, or *terminals*) of different materials are dipped into the solution and become charged: one plate has electrons taken from it by the positive ions in the solution; the other acquires electrons from the negative ions in the solution. When there is nothing connecting the two terminals, the difference in charge between them can be measured in volts, which represents the attractive force in the form of potential energy. When the two terminals are connected by a conductor (typically a wire), that potential energy is transformed into kinetic energy as the extra electrons in the negative terminal flow to the positive terminal in a direct path in an attempt to neutralize it. (Potential and kinetic energy were introduced in Chapter 1.)

This type of flow is called *direct current (DC)*. It is analogous to connecting a pipe between two containers of water, where one container holds more water than the other. Water flows from one container through the pipe to the other container until the amount of water in each is equal.

A switch along the wire can enable or disable the connection between the terminals. When the current is able to flow from one terminal to the other, the system is termed a *closed circuit*. When the connection between the two terminals is broken, the system is termed an *open circuit*.

An incandescent light bulb is essentially a glass tube placed at one point along a closed circuit. As the bulb contains no air, it is an example of a *vacuum tube*. The circuit's connection continues through the tube, but the wire within the tube is narrower than the wires leading to and away from it. This makes it more difficult for electrons to flow through it, as it has greater resistance. The resistance causes the wire to heat up. But since there is no air in the tube, the wire cannot burn, and it glows from the heat instead.

Magnetism

As intriguing as charged objects can be, the real "wow factor" of electronics lies in *magnetism*, a property by which some objects are attracted to or repelled from each other, and by which a force field causes particles to align themselves around two poles. Our fascination with this phenomenon dates back to ancient Greek writers living near the city of Magnesia, who described the properties of a *lodestone*. When placed on a piece of wood floating in water, the lodestone appears to move the wood, aligning in a north to south direction. A lodestone has two distinct magnetic *poles*. One end always faces the north, the other always faces the south.

When two lodestones are in each other's proximity, the unlike poles attract each other, while the like poles repel each other. When a lodestone is broken in two, each piece has the two poles. Lines of magnetic force may be shown by sprinkling tiny strands of iron around a lodestone. The magnetic force causes the strands to move and settle into positions shown in Figure 4-7. The lodestone is the predecessor to the compass, which behaves as it does because the earth itself is a giant magnet. In response to the earth's magnetic field, the compass orients itself along a north-south axis.

The level of attraction between a magnet and an object depends on their relative distance from each other, and can be described with the inverse square law (described in Chapter 2), although the attraction can be reduced by applying heat to the magnet.

Magnetism and Electrical Current

The "wow factor" mentioned above lies in an intrinsic relationship between magnetism and changes in electrical current. For some time, many scientists knew that there was some connection, and labored to unlock what it was. The discovery came in 1819, when Hans Christian Ørsted (1777–1851) accidentally discovered that switching a battery on and off caused a compass needle to be briefly deflected. At the moment an electrical current is

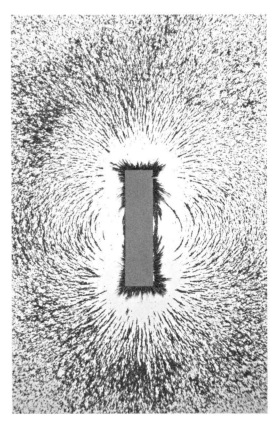

Figure 4-7 Magnetic field pattern
Source: © iStock.com/Awe Inspiring Images

created, a brief burst of magnetism is also created. Conversely, a magnetic field can create a jolt of current at the moment that a conductor is moved through it. The magnetic field is perpendicular to current direction. The degree of magnetism increases substantially when the wire is coiled, a configuration known as an *electromagnet*.

Magnetic Induction

Changing an electrical current produces a magnetic field, and a magnetic field can produce an electrical current; the two are inseparable. Michael Faraday (1791–1867) demonstrated this in 1831 with two coils of wire. The primary coil was connected to a battery, while the secondary coil was connected to a voltage meter.

When the circuit was closed and current flowed from the battery into the primary coil, there was a brief burst of current in the meter connected to the secondary coil. The secondary burst of current went in the opposite direction of the primary current. When the primary current was stopped, the secondary coil showed a brief burst of current, this time in the same direction as the primary current. Curious about whether it was indeed magnetism that was causing the secondary current, Faraday repeated the experiment with only the secondary coil and a magnet. Moving the magnet in and out of the coil produced the same burst of current.

This *induction* occurs when there is a change in electrical current, and it disappears when the current is steady. Once again, water-based analogies can be helpful: consider the change in a waterwheel's motion in response to flowing water. When the water is still, there is no motion in the wheel. When the water first starts to flow, the wheel remains still initially. Recall Newton's first law of motion, discussed in Chapter 1: an object at rest stays at rest until it is forced to move. At first, the wheel resists moving in response to the water: it pushes back in the opposite direction. But after enough water force builds up, the wheel begins to turn at a constant rate. Again according to Newton's first law, once the wheel is in motion, its tendency is to remain in motion. Thus, when the water stops, the momentum of the wheel continues in the same direction of the current for a moment before it comes to a stop.

Faraday expanded on this design with the *induction coil*, which was connected to a power source that was constantly being turned on and off. Since the current was constantly changing, a secondary current was constantly induced, first in one direction and then in another. In contrast to the unidirectional direct current that was described earlier, current that regularly changes direction in this way is known as *alternating current (AC)*.

Electromagnetic Resonance

Faraday provided rigorous descriptions of how voltage and the coil were related. The relationship can be summarized with two fundamental principles:

1. The number of wraps in the coil determines the voltage level of the current that gets generated within it.
2. Two coils maintain a constant power relationship (current times voltage, Equation 4-1). If the secondary coil is twice the length of the primary coil, its induced current has twice the voltage and half the current of the primary coil.

Faraday's descriptions of *mutual induction* in the electromagnetic domain are similar to the properties of sympathetic resonance that were described in Chapter 2. Mutual induction occurs when voltage changes in one coil induce voltage in another due to the electromagnetic field that the primary voltage changes produce. A *transformer* is created when two coils are placed in each other's proximity for the purpose of inducing current, usually "stepping" the voltage up or down in the process.

Mutual induction is the key to modern-day power transmission. DC voltage is difficult to transmit because it weakens as it travels from its source. AC does not have this problem. High-voltage AC can be transmitted over long distances, stepped up along the way by transformers.

Impedance

We've discussed resistance and its relationship to DC voltage (Equation 4-2). In an AC system, *impedance (Z)* is the equivalent of resistance in a DC system, and is also measured in ohms. But impedance and resistance are not exactly the same thing. Impedance is not consistent, but exhibits *reactance*, which means that its effects vary with AC frequency. There are two kinds of reactance: *inductance* (the ability to exhibit induction) and *capacitance* (the capacity to store an electrical charge). Impedance refers to limitations on current flow that are due to the combination of inductance and capacitance, each of which will be discussed below.

COILS AND AC: INDUCTANCE

Inductance is the result of electrical current encountering magnetism. As described above, mutual induction occurs within a coil when a current is sent through it. The result is self-inductance, as the magnetic field produced by the current running through the coil extends outward from the current, affecting current flow in prior turns.

Inductive reactance is limited at DC and low frequencies, but has a greater effect at higher frequencies. Recalling the analogy of waterwheel motion, there is a brief moment of resistance before current may pass through the coil. In the case of direct current, electrons flow through the coil smoothly once the initial resistance is overcome. But in the case of alternating current, in which electrons periodically change directions within the wire, each surge of current into the coil is met with resistance. For high-frequency alternating current, in which the electrons change direction frequently, little (if any) current emerges from the end of the coil. The higher the frequency of the alternating current, the less current may flow through the coil. Should there be a voltage spike in the current, the coil's inductance smooths the spike (Figure 4-8).

Thus, the coil, with its inductive reactance, acts as a *lowpass filter*, allowing lower AC frequencies to pass through with less hindrance than higher frequencies. Lowpass filters may be described by their *cutoff frequency*, which is the AC rate above which frequencies begin to be significantly attenuated. Frequencies below the cutoff frequency

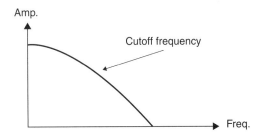

Figure 4-8 Lowpass filtering due to a coil; lower AC frequencies pass through while higher frequencies are attenuated

pass through the filter relatively undisturbed, while frequencies above the cutoff frequency are at reduced amplitude levels. (Digital audio filters will be described more fully in Chapters 5 and 6. The coil- and capacitor-based filters described here can be found in many loudspeaker crossover systems, which will be discussed in Chapter 7.)

CAPACITOR PLATES AND AC: CAPACITANCE

The Leyden jars of Franklin's time were the first human-made capacitors. When Franklin showed that lightning was a form of electricity, he had no way of knowing that it was in fact due to the capacitance of clouds. Clouds absorb electrons, accumulating a negative charge. Down below, the earth is the ultimate sponge for electrons, always having room to store more of them. As the number of electrons within a cloud builds up, an attraction grows between the clouds and the earth. They are separated by air, which is an effective insulator. The attraction between them builds until the charge overcomes the air's resistance and a spark shoots down to the earth. The spark heats the air, which weakens the air's resistance, which allows more electrons to travel along the spark's path. The burst of current also creates a magnetic field, which produces self-inductance (current in the opposite direction). So a current also travels back up from the earth to the cloud. This induced current also induces yet another current flowing back down to the earth, which in turn produces another current going back up to the cloud, and so on. Lightning is this two-way current, at a frequency of about a million hertz, between the earth and the cloud. When heated by the current, the air becomes white hot and expands. This expansion causes the cracking sound of thunder.

Modern-day capacitors consist of a pair of metal plates that have opposite charges. The plates may be charged by attaching them to the terminals of a battery. Attracted to the positively charged plate, electrons crowd into the negatively charged plate, increasing its negative charge. The larger the plate, the more capacity the plate has to hold extra electrons. But capacity is determined by proximity as well as by size. If the plates are moved closer together, the attraction increases, and more electrons are able to flow into the negatively charged plate. When the plates are moved apart, the capacitance drops, which causes electrons to flow out of the negatively charged plate. If the difference in charge between two plates builds up to a sufficient level, electrons can actually jump the gap, creating a spark—a miniature version of lightning.

When capacitor plates are placed along a wire conductor, they form a roadblock to current flow. Imagine current flowing into a negatively charged plate on the left, with a positively charged plate on the right. Direct current is stopped short at the negative plate. But there is far less impedance for alternating current. As the current changes direction, the capacitance of the plates constantly changes. Electrons rush towards the positive plate, only to be stopped short at the negative plate, which increases the plate's negative charge. Across the divide, electrons on the rightmost, positively charged plate move away from the leftmost, negative plate, repulsed by the sudden increase of the electrons there. As the current reverses direction, electrons leave the negatively charged plate. This allows electrons to return to the opposite, positive plate.

The effect of capacitance on AC is the opposite of the coil's inductive reactance: direct current and lower AC frequencies are inhibited by a capacitor, while higher frequency voltage may be transferred across the divide with much less hindrance. Thus, a capacitor acts as a *highpass filter* (Figure 4-9). Like lowpass filters, highpass filters may be described by their cutoff frequency, which is the AC rate below which frequencies begin to be significantly attenuated. Frequencies above the cutoff frequency pass through the filter relatively undisturbed, while frequencies below the cutoff frequency are at reduced amplitude levels.

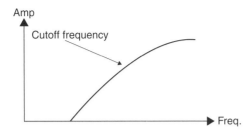

Figure 4-9 Highpass filtering due to a capacitor; higher AC frequencies pass through while lower frequencies are attenuated

Impedance, Voltage, and Current

Water-based analogies have also been used to describe impedance (Keltz, 2015), comparing it to a nozzle control on a hose. (Even though water flowing through a hose is more similar to direct current than to alternating current, these water comparisons offer great intuitive appeal.) The hose itself is low impedance—it allows all current to flow through it freely. The nozzle controls impedance and, by extension, voltage. Table 4-1 shows how impedance, pressure, and flow all change as the nozzle control is adjusted. When the nozzle is closed, water presses against it; there is no current flow (kinetic energy), but a high degree of pressure (potential energy, voltage). As the nozzle is opened, current increases as the voltage decreases. At low impedance, the nozzle is fully open; water flows freely, but not with the force it had when the nozzle was squeezing it into a jet. Greater impedance results in greater water force (voltage).

Controlling Current: From Vacuum Tubes to Microprocessors

Using electricity involves controlling the flow of current, directing and adjusting it so that it can perform the work that powers our devices. Advances in electric technology are based on using current with ever-greater efficiency. The first steps were built on the functionality of the light bulb, which was described earlier.

Vacuum Tubes

As we've noted, a light bulb is a filament within a vacuum that heats up and glows when current passes through it. More complex electronic devices were created using more advanced versions of the light bulb, called *diodes* and *triodes*. These were the basis of

TABLE 4-1 The nozzle on a hose illustrates the relationships between impedance, voltage, and current.

NOZZLE POSITION	IMPEDANCE	PRESSURE/VOLTAGE	FLOW/CURRENT
Closed	High	High (maximum)	0
Slightly open	Not as high	High (but not maximum)	Small
Open	Reduced	Reduced	Increases
Fully open	Low	Very low	High

vacuum tube technology, acting in a manner akin to a valve on a hose, which controls the level of water that it produces. (In fact, English and Commonwealth countries refer to vacuum tubes as *valves*.) Vacuum tubes controlled the direction and amplitude of electrical current.

Early audio amplifiers were all vacuum tube–based. In some cases, the vacuum tubes colored the sound in characteristic ways. Tube-based electric guitar amplifiers often create a desirable saturation when they are overdriven—that is, when the signal input exceeds the amplifier's ability to reproduce it accurately. In some cases, the input wave is "squashed," which adds harmonic distortion to the wave. This distortion adds higher harmonics in small amounts, and the overall effect is one of "warmth."

Before the 1950s, any kind of device that needed current control relied on vacuum tubes. The first computer system, the ENIAC (Electronic Numerical Integrator and Computer), created in 1944, was powered by 19,000 vacuum tubes. A massive cooling system was required to dissipate the heat these tubes generated, and it required enough electricity to light a small town. Its vacuum tubes were constantly burning out, so the machine was "down" almost as much of the time as it was operational. As electronic machines became more sophisticated, vacuum tubes became less and less practical, and smaller, more reliable systems became necessary. The answer came in the 1950s.

Semiconductors

Earlier, we saw that some materials, such as copper wire, act as electrical conductors, while materials such as rubber act as electrical insulators. Other materials, such as silicon, are something in between: they can allow current to flow under certain conditions, if treated properly. These materials are neither conductors nor insulators, but something in the middle, and are thus described as *semiconductors*. In the 1950s, *solid state* products began to appear, in which current was controlled with small silicon wafers instead of vacuum tubes. This development brought tremendous advantages: the silicon crystal structures were much smaller than tubes, which meant that products could be much smaller, and the wafers did not generate the heat levels or require the frequent replacement that were a fact of life for vacuum tube devices.

The *transistor* (*trans*fer re*sistor*) was first created at Bell Labs in 1947. In 1954, IBM began to create solid state computers. That same year, the transistor radio was introduced, which soon became the fastest-selling retail item of all time. In 1959, *integrated circuits* were introduced, which were systems of connected transistors. With the aid of techniques such as photolithography (which allows the production of materials from a photograph) and computer-aided designs, complex systems of thousands of transistors could be assembled on smaller and smaller surfaces, at lower and lower prices.

The next quantum leap in computational power came with the creation of *microprocessors*. These are groups of microscopic transistors wired together on a single chip or wafer, forming a complete computation engine capable of carrying out mathematical operations. The first was the Intel 4004, introduced in 1971, which contained 2,300 transistors. This chip could add and subtract four bits at a time, making it as powerful as the basement-sized ENIAC computer had been in the 1940s (bits are described in Appendix 4). Since then, developments have increased exponentially. *Moore's Law* is based on a 1965 observation by Gordon Moore (1929-), the cofounder of Intel, that the number of transistors per square inch on integrated circuits was likely to double each year, a prediction that has been borne out. Hearing aids, personal computers, and cell phones are among the everyday devices made possible by semiconductor technology.

Electronics and Music

As was stated in the introduction to this chapter, the term "electroacoustic" refers to transforming energy between the electrical and acoustic domains. Telecommunications (and electronic music) are based on creating an *analog* of acoustic pressure variations in the voltage variations of alternating current. When electrical current can be made to match the fluctuations of an acoustic wave, the sound signal may be transmitted from one place to another or encoded into some form of storage media.

Telephone Communication

Chapter 7 will describe how principles of induction underlie the workings of microphones and loudspeakers. These two inventions can be traced back to the creation of the telephone, which was patented by Alexander Graham Bell in 1876. This device sent voice transmissions by creating an electrical current having voltage variations that mirrored the sound pressure variations produced by speech. The mouthpiece contained a thin diaphragm made of flexible material that acted as an analog to the eardrum, vibrating in tandem with air pressure changes produced by speech. The diaphragm was placed near an electromagnet. Its movements took place within the magnetic field, which caused voltage changes from the magnet's wire coil to be sent along a wire. The process was reversed at the receiving end: an electromagnet received the incoming voltage, which caused a nearby diaphragm within an earpiece to vibrate accordingly. The diaphragm's vibrations caused air pressure changes that reproduced the source sound for the listener.

The Bell Telephone Company, founded in 1877, went on to become a major source of research and development in telephony and acoustics. Among its other distinctions, it was to become the birthplace of computer music.

Vinyl Records

The inventor Thomas Alva Edison (1847–1931) also employed a diaphragm that responded to acoustic pressure changes in his invention of the *phonograph* (named from the Greek words for "sound writer") in 1877. A sheet of foil was wrapped around a cylinder. The diaphragm was at the small end of a megaphone-like horn—into which someone spoke, sang, or played an instrument—which was connected to a stylus. Recording was achieved by turning a handle that caused cylinder to revolve as the horn/diaphragm traveled horizontally across it. Motion from the diaphragm caused the stylus to make an impression in the tin foil. As the stylus moved horizontally across the foil, it left a spiral impression. To play the sound back, the stylus was returned to its original position. Turning the handle caused the stylus to pass through the spiral impression, and the impression was passed to the diaphragm, which reproduced the sound. This invention marked the birth of recorded sound. It made sound into a tangible, transportable object, and the world has never been the same since.

Edison's cylinders were eventually supplanted by vinyl discs and electrical turntables. The discs store an analog of an electrical signal as a groove of varying height (and also width, in the case of stereophonic recordings). A needle runs through the groove as the disc spins. The motion of the needle presses against a quartz crystal. For reasons that will be explained further below, this produces an electrical current that is reproduced as sound. Vinyl was the principal format for commercial recordings for some seventy years—quite a long time in an age of rapid technological advances. As will be discussed in Chapter 5, the vinyl medium, which was thought to be all but defunct a few years back, has re-emerged as a desirable format for the audiophile market.

Tape

Tape-based media consisted of a plastic strip that was coated with microscopic, cigar-shaped magnetic particles. On a blank tape, the polarity of these particles (the direction of electron flow) was randomized. The tape would then be run over a *record head* on a recording machine, where an audio signal in the form of AC current was sent. As the tape passed over the head, the electromagnetic field from the signal saturated the tape, altering the average polarity of the particles to match the frequency and amplitude of the signal (Figure 4-10). To play back the recorded signal, the tape was passed over a *playback head*, which transduced the polarity fluctuations on the tape to electrical current, which was then amplified and sent to a loudspeaker.

High-quality tape recording was expensive. The wider the tape and the faster it was sent over the heads, the larger the area of particles that was affected per second of audio. The larger the area of tape per second, the higher the audio fidelity was. Professional-quality studios would use tape that was between 1/4″ and 2″ wide and that played at fifteen or thirty inches per second. Blank tape came at a high cost, and a good deal of it was required to record an album of music.

While recording to tape has been largely outmoded by less expensive and cleaner-sounding digital processes (which will be described in Chapter 5), a market remains in place for tape-based recording. Just as vinyl remains a high-end niche playback format for audiophiles, recording to tape remains a high-end niche recording format. While the tape medium colors the sound, many prefer the coloration to the sound of digital recordings, finding that it has an added "warmth" and a certain attractive quality that can be difficult to describe in words. In Chapter 10, we will see that there are sound processing software programs that many artists purchase that emulate the "imperfections" of analog tape.

Analog emulations aside, many artists prefer to make their initial recordings onto analog tape, and then transfer these recordings to a digital system as a later step in the production process. To be sure, this is not the most economical way of going about

Blank tape—random polarity

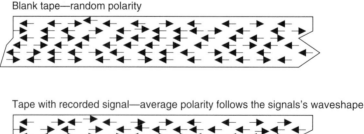

Tape with recorded signal—average polarity follows the signals's waveshape

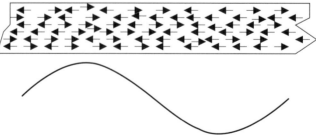

Figure 4-10 Polarity of magnetic particles on recording tape

producing music. But many artists choose this route, finding that the initial analog step adds a quality to the sound that is not present when recordings are made directly to a digital system.

Radio Broadcasting

In classic radio broadcasting, the program material is transduced to voltage variations, which are used to modulate a *carrier* signal of much higher frequency. The electromagnetic field produced by the modulated carrier wave is broadcast into the atmosphere, where antennae tuned to the same carrier frequency can resonate to the signal, transmitting it to a radio receiver in its building. The signal is then demodulated, which means that the carrier signal is removed, leaving only the program material to be sent to a loudspeaker on the receiving end. (Musical applications of the broadcasting process will be discussed in Chapters 8 and 10.)

Early radio receivers were called *crystal sets*, as they operated by means of a receiver in the form of a pointed wire that made contact with a quartz crystal. (This is similar to the mechanism of a vinyl turntable, described above.) Quartz crystals exhibit *piezoelectricity*, which is a current emitted when physical pressure is applied to them. When the wire changed position in response to the current that originated from the broadcast signal, it would press against the crystal, causing it to emit a current that could be treated by a vacuum tube called a *cat's whisker diode*, and sent on to a loudspeaker.

Studio Connections

Grounding

We will now apply our knowledge of electronics to the context of creating a music studio. This involves making a number of electrical connections between devices. The most fundamental connection is to the initial source of power, which is typically a wall outlet. As electrons are passed from place to place, it is not uncommon for some of them to go astray. We will shortly see how stray electrons can be problematic in an audio studio, but the initial point to be made is that an electrical system needs an easy way for stray electrons to be drained so that they do not become an audible problem. When we described how lightning was formed, we mentioned that the earth always has room to absorb more electrons. A vital component of electrical systems is *grounding*, which refers to a connection to Mother Earth where the extra electrons may be drained.

Earlier, there was a description of a light bulb powered by a battery. But when we flip a light switch in everyday life, the current does not come from a battery, but rather from the building's power system. Through a series of transformers, AC power is delivered to buildings from a utility supplier. This power is tapped via wall outlets. These consist of a *hot pin*, through which electrons are supplied, and a *common pin*, which leads electrons back to ground. The common pin is often connected to a ground pin as an additional precaution against stray electrons. When a device is plugged into a wall outlet, its electrical cable contains two wires. The *hot wire* is connected to the outlet's hot pin, and the *neutral wire* is connected to the outlet's common pin. The common wires from all of a building's outlets go to the breaker box, which is, in turn connected to something in the earth, such as a large water pipe.

In a music studio, electrons are circulating in all directions, all the time. The audio cables contain the hot and common wires necessary to get current in and out of each device, so that they may pass the audio signal among themselves. In addition to the audio signal currents, there is also current that originates from a wall outlet to power each device. The wall outlet is also the receptacle where stray electrons may be shed. But electrons do not drain equally from all outlets. The voltage at each may vary depending on minute differences in resistance among the wires, or how far an outlet is from the main breaker. An outlet's current flow can also be hampered due to interference induced by nearby electromagnetic-generating devices. As a result of all these factors, there is no such thing as "perfect grounding," whereby the voltage is equal at all outlets, such that all electrons drain uniformly to ground.

Voltage mismatches among outlets and/or devices are at the heart of *ground loops*, which are like whirlpools in the oscillating current. Imagine an amplifier plugged into outlet A and an effects box plugged into outlet B, with an audio cable connecting them. If outlet B's voltage is slightly lower than outlet A's voltage, some electrons draining from the effects box may become "confused." As the AC current is pushed and pulled back and forth, they may be inclined to drift not toward ground, but toward the other outlet, and into the amplifier. The audio cable then carries some of these electrons back to the effects box, creating a loop. The loop's cycle time is determined by the frequency of the AC signal supplied by the outlets. In the United States, current changes direction 120 times per second, which is rendered as an audible 60 Hz hum.

This system-level resonance, once present, may take some trial and error to remove. One precaution is to use one outlet to power everything: instead of using multiple wall outlets, use just one and plug all devices into a power bar. Another precaution is to run plugs from noise inducers (such as fluorescent lights) to outlets nearer to the main breaker than the audio devices. Sometimes changing the position of something, like unwrapping a cable, can remove a loop.

Audio Levels

Electronic-music devices output one of three voltage levels:

- *Mic level*, from microphones, is the lowest, at 3 mV, and currents of a few micro-amperes, with impedance of 50 to 250 ohms.
- *Line level*, from keyboards and many processing devices, is higher, at 0.5 to 1.5 volts, and currents of a milliampere or so, with impedance at 100 to 600 ohms.
- *Power level* applies to amplifiers and loudspeakers. These range from 10 to 100 volts, with a current of 1 to 10 amperes, and impedance at 4, 8, or 16 ohms.

The focal point of a music studio is the *mixer*, where signals from various devices are combined and their volume levels balanced. Mixers will be discussed further in Chapter 8; for now, it will suffice simply to say that the mixer is the device that everything else is connected to. Depending on the mixer type, it may have the capacity to receive and output signals at any or all of these three power levels.

Audio Cables and Impedance

Line-level signals are usually delivered over *unbalanced cable*. Recalling the hot and common pins in electrical outlets described earlier, in unbalanced cable the hot wire is surrounded by a braided metal sleeve or *shield* (Figure 4-11a), which acts as the signal common wire. Unbalanced cables may have either three-pin *XLR connectors* or 1/4" *tip-sleeve connectors*.

When an XLR connector is used, the wire carrying the audio signal is soldered to pin 2, the "hot" pin (the one that delivers electrons). The cable's ground wire is

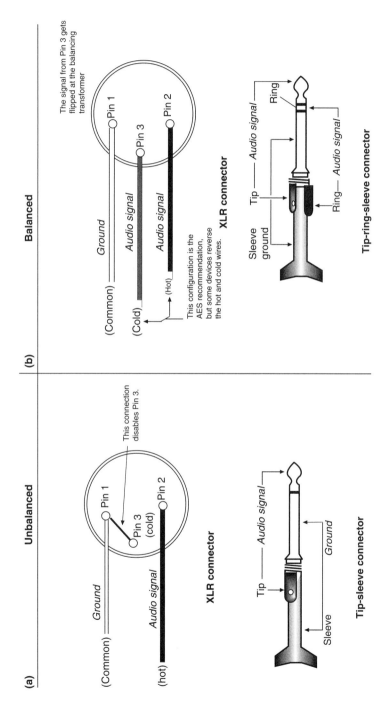

Figure 4-11 Balanced and unbalanced audio cables

connected to pin 1, the "common" pin. The connector's pin 3 is not used, and is connected to pin 1, which effectively disables it.

When a 1/4" tip-sleeve connector is used, the current-carrying cable is connected to the tip, and the ground is connected to the sleeve.

The shield does two things: it absorbs interference from electromagnetic-emitting sources like television broadcasts or cell-phone signals, and it acts as the common wire. This inexpensive, easy delivery works for lengths up to about ten feet. For longer runs, the interference tends to get passed from the shield to the hot wire, and to mingle with the audio.

For short cable runs, using high impedance instruments or microphones can be an advantage, because the mixer does not need to boost the signal and potentially add noise. However, when cable lengths exceed ten to fifteen feet, high impedance signals become susceptible to interference from outside sources. Thus, for longer cable runs, high impedance devices are typically plugged into a *Direct Box (DI)* before the signal is sent any great distance. The DI lowers the impedance of the signal, and sends it over a balanced line.

Balanced cables (Figure 4-11b) deliver duplicate versions of the signal over two wires ("hot" and "cold") at opposite polarities—that is, one copy of the signal is flipped. Balanced cables may use either three-pin XLR connectors or 1/4" *tip-ring-sleeve (TRS) connectors*. When an XLR connector is used, the ground wire is connected to pin 1. The "hot" (positive) wire is connected to pin 2. The "cold" or "neutral" wire (the one that carries the polarity-flipped version of the signal) is connected to pin 3. When a TRS connector is used, the hot cable is connected to the tip, the cold cable is connected to the ring, and the ground is connected to the sleeve.

Devices receiving balanced signals contain a *balancing transformer* that reverses the polarity of one of the wires and then sums their two signals when they are both at the same polarity. This procedure—flipping one copy of the signal, sending it over the cable, and then flipping it back again on the receiving end—removes any interference that may have arrived along the way, because the interference would have been introduced at the same polarity in both cables. When the balancing transformer reverses one cable's polarity, this has the effect of reversing the polarity of the interference, and thus it gets canceled out when the signals are recombined at the same polarity. Balanced cables are more expensive than unbalanced cables because the signal is duplicated, but they deliver a cleaner signal, and are thus most often used in professional environments.

Professional-grade microphone signals are typically low impedance, and delivered over balanced cable.

Keeping a Squeeze on the Current

A source signal needs to have lower impedance than the input of the device receiving the signal. Recalling our hose example (Table 4-1), the water has to be flowing freely for the nozzle to be able to squeeze and focus it with its impedance. If the water isn't flowing, the nozzle has nothing to work with. A receiving device needs to squeeze its signal, not open itself to it: that is, it should introduce greater impedance, rather than lowering the impedance. Adding impedance to the signal raises the voltage level, and allows the source voltage to remain constant at the input. Lowering the impedance drops the voltage. It's like suddenly making the hose wider: the water flows less forcefully through it when it has the added room. If an audio signal is sent at higher impedance than the receiving device, the level is reduced ("loaded down") and the noise level increases. One rule of thumb is to ensure that the input impedance for a device is at least ten times the source signal's impedance.

Suggested Exercises

- Compare a vinyl record album with the same album on CD. Listen to them both and observe any differences in sound quality between the two. The differences between the vinyl and CD formats will be introduced in Chapter 5, but for now let your ears be the sole judge of what the differences are (if any).
- A *multimeter* is a basic testing tool in any electronic toolkit, measuring current, voltage, or resistance. They can be obtained for about $5 at a hobby shop, although more expensive types will offer more features.

    Multimeters consist of two probes that can transmit a current. When the two probes are touched to each other, current will flow from one to the other, and evidence of the current will be shown in the display meter. If the multimeter has a numeric display, it will display a zero, indicating zero resistance. If it doesn't have a numeric display, it will emit a beep to indicate continuity of current.

    A component may be checked by putting its ends between the two probes. To test a battery, for example, place each probe on one of the battery terminals. If the battery is charged, current will flow, and the meter will display the battery's voltage.

    In the same way, an audio cable may be tested. Loop the cable so that each end can be reached by a multimeter probe, and touch the probes to corresponding pins on each end. The beep or zero will indicate whether or not current is flowing properly through the cable. If the cable is damaged, you have the option of replacing it or repairing it. Repairing it will require the use of a soldering iron, and is covered in the next exercise.
- If signal is not flowing properly through a cable, the most likely explanation is that one or more of the audio wires inside it have become detached from the connector. In this case, they need to be reattached with *solder* (pronounced "sodder"), which is a metal conductor that can be melted and applied at the connection point to act as a kind of glue, creating a bond between the wire and a connector pin and restoring current flow. A soldering iron can be obtained for as little as $20. For electrical work, it is important to use an iron that has a fine tip to it, and to get solder that is meant for electronic work, rather than plumbing or other metal work.

    Depending on the connector type, it may be easy or difficult to remove the cable wrapping to expose the connections to the connector. Unmolded cables can have connectors removed to expose the wiring, often by simply unscrewing them. Molded cables are the most difficult to excavate, and it is often easiest just to replace them. When trying to fix them, one usually winds up taking away too much of the rubber and weakening the cable; if repairs are attempted, a better approach is usually to just chop the end off and use a new connector so the cable is not molded.

    Soldering is not a skill that can be learned from a book. It is a manual procedure best learned in person from someone with expertise, or from an online video if no live instructor is available. But the basic procedure is to coat (or "tin") each part that has to be put together, both the wire and the receptacle. Once they are tinned, they may be reheated and the wire may be held to the connector. The solder on both pieces melts, and both mix together, as though they "want" to be together. It takes a bit of practice and patience to get this technique just right. The goal is to avoid saturating the ends in solder.

Once the connection is made, it is important not to move the wire while the solder is drying: resist the temptation to try to speed up the drying process by blowing on the connection. Doing either of these things can lead to a "cold solder joint," which has high resistance. Cold joints tend to look gray, while intact solder joints have a shinier appearance.

When the soldering tip sits unused, it can oxidize, so before switching it off, "tin" the tip with a few drops of solder to coat it until the next work session. Most soldering irons come with a small piece of sponge. The wet sponge allows excess solder to be removed from the iron between applications, keeping the tip clean and precise.

While most cable problems are at the connectors, occasionally there is a break in the middle of the cable, where it may have been stepped on or crushed under wheels or furniture. If the multimeter seems to reflect an intact connection but the signal is still intermittent, the problem may be in the middle of the wire somewhere. A repair may be attempted, preferably with a partner, by one person anchoring a probe at each end, and the other manipulating the length of the wire, slightly bending it gradually along its length, until the meter indicates a break in continuity. The wire may then be cut and repaired at this point.

Key Terms

alternating current (AC)
amperes
analog
balanced cables
balancing transformer
battery
capacitance
capacitor
carrier
cat's whisker diode
closed circuit
common pin
conductor
crystal set
current
cutoff frequency
diode
Direct Box (DI)
direct current (DC)
discharge
electromagnet
electromotive force (EMF)
electron
friction machine

ground loop
grounding
highpass filter
hot pin
hot wire
impedance (Z)
inductance
induction
induction coil
insulator
integrated circuit
ion
Leyden jar
lodestone
lowpass filter
magnetism
microprocessor
mixer
Moore's Law
multimeter
mutual induction
negative charge
neutral wire
ohms

Ohm's Law   solder
open circuit   solid state
phonograph   static electricity
piezoelectricity   tip-ring-sleeve (TRS) connector
playback head   tip-sleeve connector
pole   terminal
positive charge   transformer
proton   transistor
reactance   triode
record head   unbalanced cable
resistance   vacuum tube
semiconductor   volt
shield   XLR connector

Chapter 5

The Basics of Digital Audio

This chapter is a culmination of the introductory chapters that preceded it, and brings us to the main focus of the book, which is digital music systems. Chapter 1 covered waves and resonance, Chapter 2 covered musical acoustics, Chapter 3 covered psychoacoustics, and Chapter 4 covered electroacoustics. The next step is to explore how these concepts translate into a digital system. It is commonly said that ours is the digital age. This is as true for music as it is for everything else. Digital recording and processing is the basis of the vast majority of music that we hear; it is far more common to hear digital audio than it is to attend live concerts or to listen to vinyl records or analog tapes. The first step in understanding the nature of digital music is to understand the digital conversion process. We can then move to basics of digital signal processing in a discussion of filters. The chapter concludes with an overview of the digital recording and playback process.

Historical Context

Digital audio was born in 1938, when British engineer Alec Reeves (1902–1971) patented a system of communication that was an alternative to the analog "voice-shaped current" that was used in telephone communications (described in Chapter 4). With *pulse code modulation (PCM)*, a communication signal's amplitude could be measured, or *sampled*, periodically, and the sample values could be transmitted as a series of binary numbers that represented instantaneous amplitude levels of a sound wave. (The nature of binary numbers is discussed in Appendix 4.) By converting the wave fluctuations to binary ones and zeroes, the contents of the wave could be transmitted electronically by alternating between two voltage levels that corresponded to the binary digits. Transmitting just two discrete values also greatly reduced the noise and errors that would accumulate over standard telephone lines.

While the theory was solid, hardware of the 1930s was not fast enough to perform conversion of an analog waveform to a series of hundreds samples per second. A commercial implementation would have been out of the question. However, there was such a system put in place during World War II by Bell Labs to serve as a secure means of communication between U.S. President Franklin D. Roosevelt and British Prime Minister Winston Churchill.

During the war years, Bell Labs evolved from a communications research firm to a more general think tank. They recruited scientists from many universities to work on radar and emerging technologies. To attract the finest innovators, the company gave them freedom to pursue other interests. Their research facility in Murray Hill, New Jersey, was near a nature preserve. Scientists were encouraged to walk in the woods and let their minds wander. Artists were also recruited, as it was felt that an aesthetic sensibility was necessary to bring meaning to new technologies. A great deal of creative cross-pollination arose from interactions among the researchers. The open-ended nature of Bell Labs continued through the 1960s, as the race to develop space-based technologies provided continuing impetus for innovation.

Max Mathews (1926–2011) joined Bell Labs in 1955 after receiving his doctorate in electrical engineering from MIT, and became the Director of Acoustic and Behavioral Research. He was tasked with creating computer equipment to model telephony, in order to study the audio transmission of telephones and find ways to improve it. Revisiting pulse code modulation technology, Mathews developed some of the earliest equipment to digitize sound (*analog-to-digital converter*, or *ADC*), and to create sound from digital information (*digital-to-analog converter*, or *DAC*).

Having made digital-to-audio conversion possible, Mathews became interested in using the computer to create musical audio. He created a new type of software known as an *acoustic compiler* that could produce musical sounds. He developed a series of these programs over the course of the next decade, named MUSIC I through MUSIC V (collectively these are known as the MUSIC N software series). These extracurricular interests earned him the informal, honorary title of "the father of computer music."

Variations on his music programs were developed at a handful of universities and research centers through the 1970s and 1980s. As computing dropped in price, digital audio software spread to the commercial sector and diversified in focus and emphasis. By the early twenty-first century, audio recording and playback was standard on consumer-grade personal computers, and there is now a vast array of software available for purposes ranging through recording, synthesis, processing, performance, and production.

Digitizing Audio: The Big Picture

The Central Problem

Waves in nature, including sound waves (air pressure changes as a function of time), are *continuous*. The mathematical definition of this term means that between any two points in time, even two points representing a virtually instantaneous interval, an infinite number of amplitude points may be identified (Figure 5-1).

Analog audio (vinyl, tape, voltage-controlled synthesizers, etc.) involves the creation or imitation of a continuous wave. But analog waves are incompatible with computers, which do not have the capacity to represent continuity (or infinity). Computers can only work with *discrete* values. In a nutshell, computers store values in memory locations and perform fast and accurate calculations with them (that is, accurate within certain limits—this is a topic that will be discussed in subsequent sections). While the idea of computers working with audio is commonplace now, using these high-end calculators as music-making machines was quite a conceptual leap in the 1950s. This leap was accomplished by converting continuous values to discrete values.

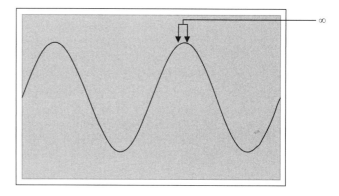

Figure 5-1 Between any two points on a continuous wave, an infinite number of points may be identified

Digital Conversion

Digitizing a continuous wave is a matter of taking instantaneous amplitude measurements (samples) at regular time intervals. In this way, the continuous wave is outlined by a series of discrete measurement values, which may be stored in a digital system (Figure 5-2). Digital audio is analogous to movie film. It is common knowledge that "moving pictures" do not really move; when we go to the movies, what we are seeing is simply a series of still pictures. The appearance of motion is created by sampled images that outline an object's position over time. The images are then projected fast enough that the effect has the appearance of continuous motion. It is the same with digital audio: a sound is sampled often enough, and the samples are played back fast enough, that the effect is apparent auditory continuity.

The workings of the acoustic compilers created by Mathews remain fundamental to the production of digital audio. For computer synthesis, a waveform is calculated in the form of a series of samples that are stored in a *wavetable*. To play back the waveform at different pitches, the table is read different rates by skipping every n samples, in other words, by adjusting the *sampling increment*. Audio is produced by sending the sample values through a digital-to-analog converter (DAC), which converts them to voltage values that are used to drive an amplifier and loudspeakers. Wavetables are used in many commercial instruments, and will be discussed further in Chapter 10.

To record a sound and convert it to a series of samples, voltage levels read from a microphone are fed to an analog-to-digital converter (ADC), which converts the signal to a series of samples and stores them. The samples can later be sent through a DAC for playback.

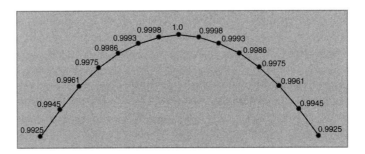

[0.9925, 0.9945, 0.9961, 0.9975, 0.9986, 0.9993, 0.9998, 1.0, 0.9998, 0.9993, 0.9986, 0.9975, 0.9961, 0.9945, 0.9925]

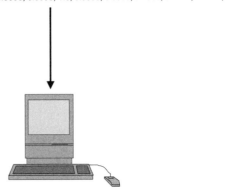

Figure 5-2 A continuous wave may be digitized by sampling its amplitude regularly; once digitized, it may be stored and processed in a computer

Does Digital Sound as Good as Analog?

Audiophiles have argued over whether digital sound is as good as analog recordings since the widespread release of compact discs in the 1980s, and there is no sign of the argument abating. As is the case with many human endeavors, sometimes there is no definitive answer, and the real point of the argument is the pleasure of having a heated discussion (rather like going to a sports bar and arguing whether Lou Gehrig was a better ballplayer than Joe DiMaggio). But when people actually compare audio specifications, the following are some key points.

ARGUMENTS FOR ANALOG

One argument sometimes posed in favor of analog audio is that digital is only an approximation of the audio signal. But the same can be said of analog recordings. Even though their information is continuous and not discrete, that should not be taken to mean that the analog waveform is a perfect mirror of the acoustic signal.

It is also argued that analog has a "richer" or "warmer" sound. Enough listeners have made this claim that it cannot be discounted. The problem is that it is difficult to find concrete definitions of these two words. The differences between analog and digital recordings may be attributable to differences in frequency response and distortion, both of which can affect subjective responses to timbre. *Frequency response* refers to how fully different frequencies are represented in a digital audio system, and will be discussed further in the section on filters in this chapter. *Distortion* refers to a reshaping of an audio wave.

Although the term might imply negative connotations, "distortion" describes any system in which the output is not exactly equivalent to the input. This is not always a bad thing. Many analog components offer a degree of distortion that listeners find pleasing. *Symmetrical distortion* refers to an equivalent alteration of the extreme high and low ends of a wave. Symmetrical distortion may tend to flatten a wave, adding odd harmonics to it as the wave shape approaches a square wave (see Figure 2-10). *Asymmetrical distortion* produces different changes on the high and low portions of a wave and tends to add even harmonics.

Many analog tapes add asymmetrical distortion, and other sources of distortion arise from vintage microphones, amplifiers, or from slight variations in the motor speed (*wow*) of vinyl turntables. Many audio systems manufacturers are actively engaged in identifying the precise differences between high-end digital and analog systems and creating digital simulations of these analog characteristics.

ARGUMENTS FOR DIGITAL

The primary argument in favor of digital recordings is that they contain significantly lower background noise levels than analog recordings. The hiss and crackle that were part and parcel of listening to vinyl records is not a factor with CDs. The absence of noise used to surprise people when they made the transition from record players to CD players.

In addition, the discrete numbers that are the basis of digital recordings are more reliably stored and duplicated than analog recordings. Duplicating a digital signal is just a matter of copying numbers from one place to another, rather than copying an electromagnetic waveform. Copying tapes used to degrade the audio quality, while copying a digital recording is, in theory, an exact duplication. Digital audio is also easier to manipulate: with analog circuits, filtering and other processing operations (which will be discussed presently) are a matter of changing the shape of a continuous wave. In the digital domain, these operations are a matter of storing sample values in memory and subjecting them to numerical operations. Subsequent chapters will discuss types of audio manipulation that can only be accomplished by digitally based techniques.

Finally, the principal digital medium, the optical disc (examples of which include audio CDs, computer CD-ROMs, and DVDs), does not degrade with multiple playings. Vinyl and tape media are based on friction: either a needle running through a groove or tape rubbing against a playback head. Each time they are played, they degrade slightly due to the friction. The laser-based optical system is not based on friction, so the act of playing it does not cause any damage to the disc. However, it should be noted that the material of optical discs has been known to degrade over time, while vinyl can last for centuries.

SO WHERE DOES THAT LEAVE US?

The practical advantages of digital audio have made it the dominant commercial format. Vinyl, however, has undergone a resurgence in sales in the first decade of the twenty-first century. Turntablists use vinyl records for scratching techniques, and many albums are now released on multiple formats, with vinyl as a high-end option for audiophile customers. The tangible effect of having a physical product, as opposed to a virtual one (such as a downloaded digital file) is also a factor for many listeners. In the case of vinyl records, the fact that the discs were somewhat fragile, and had to be handled with care, gave a certain "white glove, fine crystal" flavor to the listening experience that undoubtedly contributed to appreciating the music.

But tangibility is also a factor in the low-tech market. There is a DIY subculture of artists who produce and distribute their music on cassette tape. This is unquestionably a low-fidelity route, but for artists who are starting out and have limited funds, it is an economical way to distribute their work. Even beyond economics, cassettes have a certain grunge appeal, as well as a legacy from the 1970s and 1980s when mix tapes were created on cassettes to be distributed and traded in an underground social market, which was the ancestor of today's social media and digital download culture.

Characteristics of Digital Audio

A more concrete discussion of digital audio's characteristics begins by considering two measurements:

1. *Sampling rate*/sampling frequency
2. *Sample size* (also called *bit depth*, *word size*, and *quantization level*)

Sampling Rate

This number describes how often an audio signal is sampled: the number of samples per second. The more often an audio signal is sampled, the better it is represented in discrete form (Figure 5-3). This raises the question of what is the optimal sampling rate: how often is often enough?

Harry Nyquist (1889–1976) of Bell Labs addressed this question in a paper concerning telegraph signals (Nyquist, 1928). The answer is surprising but true: given that a wave is eventually to be smoothed by a subsequent filtering process, it is sufficient to sample a wave both its peak and its trough (Figure 5-4). This idea is the basis of the *sampling theorem* (also called the *Nyquist theorem*):

> *To represent digitally a signal containing frequency components up to X Hz, it is necessary to use a sampling rate of at least 2X Hz.*

Conversely:

The maximum frequency that can be contained in a signal with a sampling rate of SR Hz is SR/2 Hz.

The frequency $SR/2$ Hz is also termed the **Nyquist frequency**. Therefore, at least in theory, since the highest frequency humans can hear is 20 kHz, a sampling rate of 40 kHz should be sufficient to recreate a signal containing all audible frequencies.

Most commonly, audio signals are **oversampled**, meaning that its frequencies are below the Nyquist frequency, as shown in Figure 5-3. If a signal is sampled at precisely the Nyquist frequency, it is said to be **critically sampled**. The risk of critical sampling is that the peaks and troughs may be missed, with only the zero crossings being recorded (Figure 5-5). The solution to this problem will be covered in the section on filtering.

The most significant problem that digital audio must prevent is **undersampling**, which is when frequencies are present that are greater than the Nyquist frequency. Misrepresented frequencies, such as those shown in Figure 5-6, are termed **aliases**. In general, if a frequency F is sampled at a sampling rate of SR, and SR exceeds the Nyquist frequency, that frequency will alias to a frequency of

$$-(SR - F)$$

where the minus sign indicates that the frequency's polarity is inverted. The range of possible digital audio frequencies is often shown on a polar diagram, as shown in Figure 5-7.

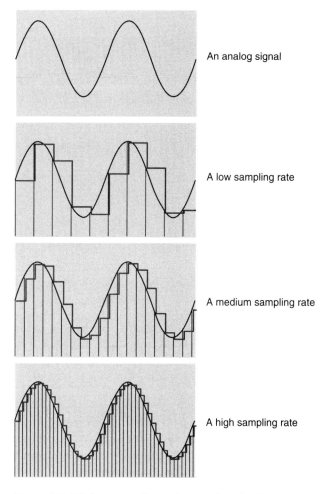

An analog signal

A low sampling rate

A medium sampling rate

A high sampling rate

Figure 5-3 Higher sampling rates produce better representations of continuous waves

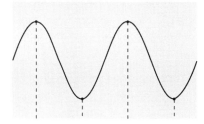

Figure 5-4 To re-create a digitized wave, it is sufficient to sample only its peak and trough

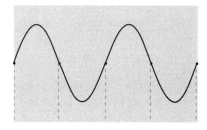

Figure 5-5 Critical sampling runs the risk of only sampling zero crossing points

Figure 5-6 An undersampled frequency is misrepresented (aliased)

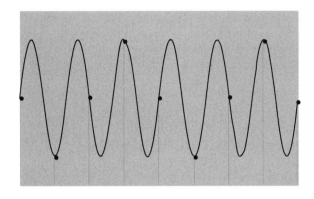

Audio signal of 30 kHz, sampled at 40 kHz

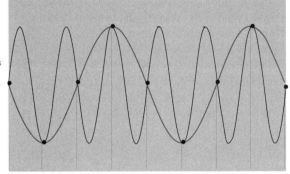

RESULT: The frequency is misrepresented at 10 kHz, at reverse phase

Aliasing has a visual counterpart that is often seen in film Westerns in shots of wagon wheels turning:

- When the wagons move slowly, the wheels advance by less than one-half of a complete revolution per frame; the motion is recorded accurately and the wheels appear to be moving forward.
- As the wheels increase in speed, they may reach a point at which they make exactly one or one-half revolution per frame. The motion of the wheels is thus critically sampled, and the spokes of the wheels appear motionless.
- If the wheels turn between one-half and one full revolution per frame, the spokes appear to move backwards, in the direction opposite to the vehicle's direction.

While wheels apparently moving in reverse may be part of the charm of cinema, the auditory correlate is far less tolerable. In the recording process, filters are used to remove all frequencies above the Nyquist frequency *before* the audio signal is sampled. This step is essential because any recorded aliases cannot be removed later without also removing actual spectral content of the music. But, counterintuitive as it may seem, as long as frequencies above the Nyquist frequency are not present in the sampled signal, the signal may be sampled and later reconverted to audio *with no loss of frequency information.*

The Sampling Rate of CD Audio and Its Origin

The sampling rate for audio CDs is 44.1 kHz. The origin of the CD sampling rate dates back to early video storage formats. When digital audio recording was introduced, audiotape was not capable of storing information at the density of digital signals—encoding thousands of samples per second would have required "hard" saturation in one direction or another, changing regularly, as opposed to the "softer" average saturation needed for analog signals, as described in Chapter 4. Therefore, the first digital recordings were stored on videotape in which sample values, represented as binary numbers with digits of 1 and 0, were stored as video levels of black and white.

The sampling rate was determined by the format of videotape (Figure 5-8). Video pixels are drawn left to right in horizontal lines, starting from the top of the screen and moving down. First the odd-numbered lines are drawn, then the even-numbered lines. This format gives each frame of video two subsets: the odd field and the even field, which lie adjacent to each other along the videotape. A certain number of lines are left blank for information such as synchronization code or closed captioning. The audio sampling rate was chosen to be compatible with the two video broadcast formats:

1. *USA (NTSC):* 525 lines, 30 frames per second, minus 35 blank lines, leaving 490 lines per frame, which equaled 60 fields per second, 245 lines per field.
2. *European (PAL):* 625 lines, 25 frames per second, minus 37 blank lines, leaving 588 lines per frame, which equaled 50 fields per second, 294 lines per field.

With the pseudo video format of black and white pixels, three samples could be stored on each line, allowing:

NTSC: 60 × 245 × 3
= 44,100 samples per second

or

PAL: 50 × 294 × 3
= 44,100 samples per second

Although by the 1980s videotapes were no longer necessary for storing digital audio, 44.1 kHz was chosen as the standard sampling rate for CD audio playback. But it is common to record at higher frequencies, and many inexpensive audio recording devices record at 96 or 192 kHz. The Nyquist frequencies of these sampling rates, 48 and 96 kHz respectively, may seem excessive, given the human upper limit of 20 kHz. But we'll soon see that there are reasons to capture frequencies in a recording that are theoretically higher than the human hearing range. There also are ways of manipulating the audio signal that preserve higher-frequency information in a CD version with a lower sampling rate.

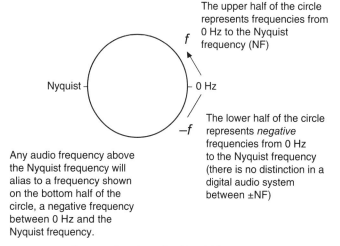

The upper half of the circle represents frequencies from 0 Hz to the Nyquist frequency (NF)

The lower half of the circle represents *negative* frequencies from 0 Hz to the Nyquist frequency (there is no distinction in a digital audio system between ±NF)

Any audio frequency above the Nyquist frequency will alias to a frequency shown on the bottom half of the circle, a negative frequency between 0 Hz and the Nyquist frequency.

Frequencies above the Nyquist frequency
do not exist in a digital audio system

Figure 5-7 The range of frequencies in a digital system illustrated with a polar diagram

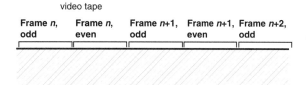

video tape

Frame *n*, odd | Frame *n*, even | Frame *n*+1, odd | Frame *n*+1, even | Frame *n*+2, odd ...

Figure 5-8 The format of videotape

Sample Size

The sampling rate describes how *often* the amplitude of the wave is measured. Sample size describes the *accuracy* of these measurements. (A new term for this characteristic seems to come up every few years. Readers may also encounter the terms *word size*, *quantization level*, or *bit depth*.)

Generally speaking, the effectiveness of any measurement depends on the precision of the ruler that is used. Imagine trying to build a cabinet or a bookshelf from a set of instructions that calls for lengths in sixteenths of an inch. If your ruler only has increments of eighth or quarter inches, you will find yourself having to approximate these cuts, and your carpentry project will likely have a few rough or uneven edges.

In pulse code modulation audio, the precision of sample values is always estimated. It's similar to the *coastline paradox*, a mathematical conundrum explored by Lewis Fry Richardson (1881–1953) and Benoit Mandelbrot (1924–2010). They found that there is no definitive answer to what seems like a straightforward question: what is the length of the British coastline? Why do different authorities and references report different measurements? They found that coastline measurements vary because their accuracy depends on the size of the ruler being used. The smaller the ruler, the more precisely it accounts for tiny curves and inlets. Thus a shorter ruler measures a greater length than a longer ruler does. Because there is no ruler small enough to capture every detail with perfect precision, any measurement will be an estimate of some kind (Mandelbrot, 1967).

In audio, the subtle changes in a signal's amplitude are no less intricate than the details of a coastline. Just as there are practical limits to how often audio signals may be sampled, there are practical limits to the level of precision of the amplitude measurements, due to a finite number of measuring increments.

Sample values are stored as binary numbers, and the number of bits determines how precise they are. With more bits, smaller increments can be stored between the extreme high and low levels. Every instantaneous amplitude level (sample) is stored as the value of the nearest measuring increment (Figure 5-9). (The term "quantization level" is taken from quantum physics, which shows that electrons orbit an atom's nucleus at fixed distances. An electron may orbit at distance *A* or distance *B*, but never anywhere between the two.)

Working with a higher-bit system is like working with a ruler that measures in 1/32-inch increments instead of 1/8-inch increments. But no matter how many bits are used, sample measurements can never be infallibly accurate. There is always some degree of distortion due to differences between actual acoustic levels and the nearest measuring increments. The problem is compounded at low amplitude levels because the highest and lowest sample values don't get used, making the error a greater percentage of the signal. For CD audio, 16 quantization bits (2-byte words, as described in Appendix 4) are used.

Thus, there are practical limitations to the accuracy of digital audio. As far as the sampling rate goes, aliasing is eliminated if a signal contains no frequencies above the Nyquist frequency. As far as the sample size goes, quantization error can never be completely eliminated. Every sample is within a margin of error that is half the quantization level (the voltage change represented by the least significant bit).

SIGNAL-TO-ERROR RATIO

The signal-to-error ratio for a given signal varies depending on the nature of the audio contents. As a base case example, for a full-level sine wave signal represented by *n* bits, the signal-to-error ratio is

$$S/E \text{ (dB)} = 6.02n + 1.76 \tag{5-1}$$

Recall that the acoustic pressure wave is transduced into
an electrical signal, from which these measurements are
taken. Each change of bit represents a change in voltage level.

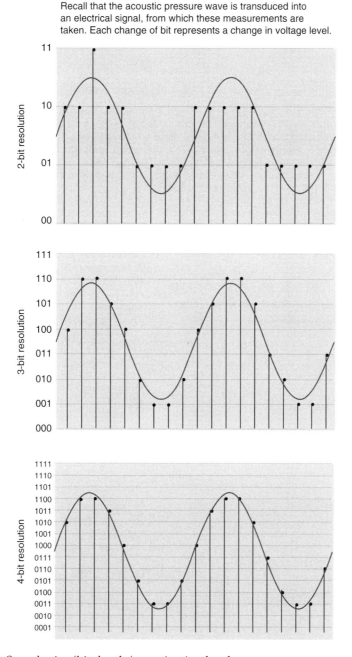

Figure 5-9 Sample size/bit depth/quantization level

The derivation of this value is shown in Figure 5-10. This error ratio may be accept-able for high signal levels. However, low-level signals do not use all available bits, and therefore the signal-to-error ratio is greater. Thus, while quantization error may not be audible at high audio levels, it can become a problem at low levels. Figure 5-11 illustrates a worst-case scenario, where a low-level sine wave is interpreted as a square wave. (The spectrum of a square wave was shown in Figure 2-10.) Unlike the constant hissing

RMS of the Audio Signal

For a signal with quantizing interval Q, with 2^n bits, half the bits will describe the positive and negative regions of the wave. Thus, the peak amplitude will be $Q2^{n-1}$. As discussed in Chapter 2, the RMS of a sine wave signal is its peak amplitude times 0.707. For our digital signal, the RMS is:

$$\frac{Q2^{n-1}}{2^{0.5}}$$

RMS of the Error

Unlike the sine wave signal, which is completely deterministic from sample to sample, the error signal is assumed to be random. The error may be described for any sample as having an instantaneous amplitude of e, and thus its instantaneous power is e^2. The probability of this signal being at a given amplitude for any sample is defined by the probability curve of the error signal. The mean of all possible values (which translates into the amplitude of the error signal) over a continuous area (the probability curve) is mathematically defined as the integral of the product of the signal and its probability curve. In the case of this digital audio signal, the probability curve is uniform over the length of one quantization interval, since there is an equal probability of the analog signal being measured at its actual value $\pm Q/2$. This means that the integration is only an integration of the signal itself, scaled by the probability curve.

What is the mean of all possible values within this area?

The weights of all possible values must equal 1, implying 100 percent of the range of possible values. Since this probability curve is uniform, it may be described as a rectangle, with a length of Q and a height of $1/Q$, giving it an area of 1.

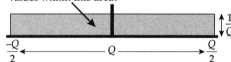

Calculation of the RMS of the Error:

$$E_{rms} = \left[\int_{-\infty}^{\infty} e^2 p(e)\, de\right]^{1/2}$$

$$= \left[\frac{1}{Q}\int_{-Q/2}^{Q/2} e^2\, de\right]^{1/2}$$

(since $p(e)$ is $1/Q$ within the interval $\pm Q/2$)

$$= \left[\frac{1}{Q}\left(\frac{1}{3}e^3\, de\right)\right]^{1/2}$$

$$= \left[\frac{1}{Q}\left(\frac{1}{3}\left(\frac{Q}{2}\right)^3 - \frac{1}{3}\left(\frac{-Q}{2}\right)^3\right)\right]^{1/2}$$

$$= \left[\frac{1}{Q}\left(\frac{1}{3}\left(\frac{Q}{2}\right)^3 - \frac{1}{3}\left(\frac{-Q}{2}\right)^3\right)\right]^{1/2}$$

$$= \left[\frac{1}{Q}\left(\frac{Q^3}{24} + \frac{Q^3}{24}\right)\right]^{1/2} = \left[\frac{1}{Q}\left(\frac{2Q^3}{24}\right)\right]^{1/2}$$

$$= \left[\frac{1}{Q}\left(\frac{Q^3}{12}\right)\right]^{1/2} = \left[\left(\frac{Q^2}{12}\right)\right]^{1/2} = \frac{Q}{\sqrt{12}}$$

Calculation of the Signal-to-Error Ratio:

$$\frac{S}{E} = \left[\frac{S_{rms}}{E_{rms}}\right] = \frac{\left(\frac{Q2^{n-1}}{\sqrt{2}}\right)^2}{\left(\frac{Q}{\sqrt{12}}\right)^2} = \left(\frac{Q2^{n-1}}{\sqrt{2}} \times \frac{2\sqrt{3}}{Q}\right)^2 = \left(\frac{2^n\sqrt{3}}{\sqrt{2}}\right)^2 = \frac{3}{2}(2^{2n})$$

$$\frac{S}{E}(dB) = 10\log_{10}\left[\frac{3}{2}(2^{2n})\right] \text{(power)}$$

$$= 20\log_{10}\left[\sqrt{\frac{3}{2}(2^{2n})}\right] = 20\log_{10}\left[\frac{\sqrt{3}}{\sqrt{2}}(2^n)\right] \text{(amplitude)}$$

$$= 20\log_{10}\left(\frac{3}{2}\right)^{1/2} + 20\log_{10}(2^n)$$

$$= 20\log_{10}\left(\frac{3}{2}\right)^{1/2} + 20n\log_{10}(2)$$

$$= 20\log_{10}(1.2247) + 20n\log_{10}(2)$$

$$= 1.76 + 6.02n$$

Thus, the amount of error is dependent on the voltage range of Q. The smaller the range of one quantization increment, the less the RMS of the error.

Thus, more quantization bits produce a higher ratio, meaning that there is more signal and less quantization noise.

Figure 5-10 Derivation of signal-to-error ratio

noise of analog recordings, quantization error is correlated with the digital signal, varying with the signal level, and is thus a type of distortion that comes and goes as volume levels change, as opposed to a constant noise. This would result in a compromised listening experience. But, paradoxically, noise is the answer to the problem.

DITHER

The problem of quantization distortion is addressed by *dither*, which is low-level noise added to the audio signal before it is sampled (Figure 5-12). Dither adds a level of *random* error to the signal, thus transforming the quantization distortion into added noise. The noise is a constant factor that is not correlated with the signal, as is the case with quantization error distortion. The result is a slightly noisy signal, rather than a signal broken up by distortion.

Although intuitively this may not seem like much of an improvement, dither leverages interpretive faculties of the auditory system, replacing an unacceptable problem with a forgivable problem. Recall from Chapter 2 that loudness is correlated with the average power of sound. And recall from Chapter 3 that noise seems to be processed separately by the auditory system from material such as speech or music. The auditory system integrates information at all times; listeners never hear individual samples, but an averaging based on a

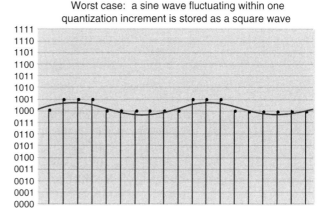

Figure 5-11 Quantization error

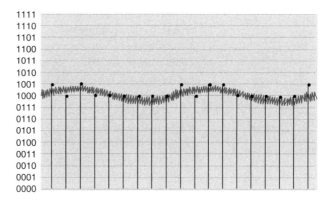

Figure 5-12 Dither

block of samples that spans 100–200 milliseconds. With dither, this averaging allows low-level segments of the musical signal to coexist with the noise, rather than be temporarily eliminated due to distortion.

Because of this averaging, dither allows resolution below the least significant quantization bit. Without dither, digital recordings would be far less satisfactory than analog recordings, and the market for digital audio equipment and recordings would have been dead on arrival. And even though dither does add some degree of noise, there is still significantly less noise in digital recordings than in analog recordings.

Sample Size vs. Sampling Rate

To summarize what we've learned so far:

- The sampling rate determines the signal's frequency content.
- The sample size determines the level of noise in the signal (fewer bits require a higher level of dither to span the margin of error of plus or minus half the voltage change represented by the least significant bit).

The following arithmetic derives the size of audio files, based on the sampling rate, the sample size, and the number of stereo channels:

44,100	× 2	× 2	× 60	≈ 10 MB/min
samples per second	bytes per sample (16 bits)	channels (for stereo audio)	seconds per minute	

There are occasions where the size of audio files is far larger than is practical, particularly in contexts involving transmission. (Data reduction techniques will be discussed in the section on perceptual coding.)

Many programs allow both the sampling rate and the sample size to be either increased or reduced. This may be necessary for a variety of reasons. If memory is tight, it may be necessary to reduce a file's size by eliminating some of its information. Or a given software program may work only with files having a given sampling rate and sample size, requiring that audio files be converted to these specifications before they can be imported into these programs.

If the sampling rate is raised or the word size is increased, no information is added by the conversion. Increasing the bit depth simply adds more bits with a value of zero to each sample value. When the sampling rate is increased, additional samples are added between existing samples. The new samples are given values that either duplicate the preceding sample, or they are assigned values that interpolate between the preceding and succeeding sample (interpolation will be discussed further in Chapter 8).

There are likely to be audible results from decreasing either the sampling rate or the sample size. But, given the choice, it usually is preferable to decrease the sampling rate, which simply lowers the frequency range of the file, since lowering the sampling rate lowers the Nyquist frequency. Reducing the bit depth can have one of two results. A lower bit depth requires a higher level of dither in the file to remove quantization error distortion. If the converter adds the appropriate level of dither, then the level of noise in the signal (its *noise floor*) is increased. If the converter does not add dither, then the conversion adds quantization error distortion to the converted file.

It may not be immediately apparent whether a particular converter adds dither when it reduces a file's bit depth. To test the process with a certain converter, a sine wave file may be used as a test file. If the converted file sounds buzzy, this is likely the sound of quantization error distortion, and it is likely that dither was not added; if it sounds noisy, with a "sh" or hissing sound in the background, it is likely that dither was added.

Filtering

What Is Filtering?

The purpose of any filter—be it a swimming pool's water filter, a coffee filter, or a camera's color filter—is to allow some things to pass through while preventing other things from getting through. In the case of audio, filtering refers to spectral shaping. A filter modifies the spectrum of a signal by emphasizing or deemphasizing certain frequency ranges. Filtering is a critical aspect of audio production, and is operationally simple to perform with digital components. Simple arithmetic can have large-scale effects.

Filter Types

There are four basic filter types, shown in Figure 5-13. The top two were introduced in Chapter 4, when coils and capacitors in AC circuits were discussed. The spectral shaping performed by each filter type is shown by its treatment of a white noise input signal. White noise was introduced in Figure 2-1, as a random waveshape. Digital white noise consists of random values only, with no correlation from one sample to the next. The spectrum of a signal created from pure randomness is flat, which means that the average power of all frequencies is equal. This makes it a useful signal type for demonstrating the effects of filters.

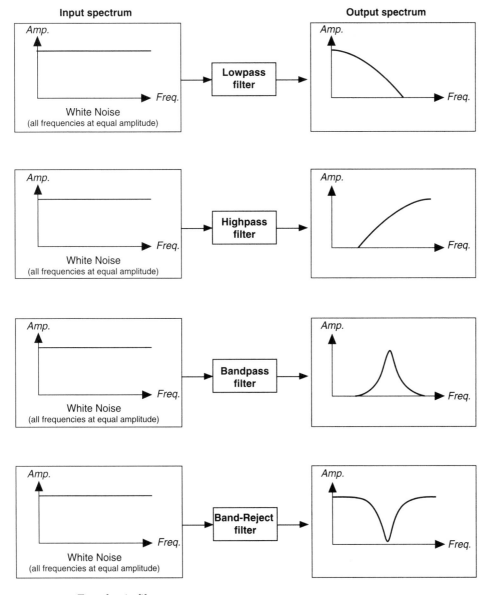

Figure 5-13 Four basic filter types

LOWPASS FILTER

A lowpass filter attenuates higher frequencies (it "lets the lows pass"), and is described by its cutoff frequency. This is the spectral component for which the amplitude on output is 0.707 of its amplitude on input. The value of 0.707 is used because of the relationship between amplitude and power levels. Amplitude is directly related to pressure levels. Recall from Equation 2-17 that power is proportional to pressure squared: $0.707^2 = 0.5$. Therefore, the cutoff frequency represents the half-power level, –3 dB. As we've discussed, lowpass filters are an essential component in the design of digital recorders. The audio signal must be lowpass filtered before it is sampled to eliminate frequencies above the Nyquist frequency.

A lowpass frequency response such as that shown in Figure 5-13 is created by a *feedforward filter,* which creates dips ("zeroes") in the spectrum of its input. Feedforward filters are simple in-out devices: a signal goes in, and comes out with its spectrum adjusted by the filter.

Another lowpass filter type is a *feedback filter* (also called a *resonant* or *recursive filter*). A feedback filter recirculates its output back into its input, so that the filter's output is combined with the incoming signal input. This is similar to what happens with a PA system when a microphone is placed too near a loudspeaker. A loud squeak is heard because the loudspeaker's output is picked up by the microphone and sent back to the loudspeaker in a recirculating fashion. In the same way, a feedback filter adds a spectral "hump" near the cutoff frequency. The filter is said to resonate at this spectral peak, just as natural materials have resonant frequencies (as discussed in Chapter 2). The filter's resonance adds a distinct coloration to the input that is often useful in musical applications.

Figure 5-14 compares the frequency responses of a feedforward and a feedback lowpass filter. Figure 5-15 shows spectrograms of feedforward and feedback lowpass filters. The resonant peak of the feedback filter, the pronounced ringing effect, can be seen in the dark band. A wah-wah pedal, a characteristic effect popularized by Jimi Hendrix and many other rock guitarists, is a resonant lowpass filter, with the cutoff frequency determined by the pedal position.

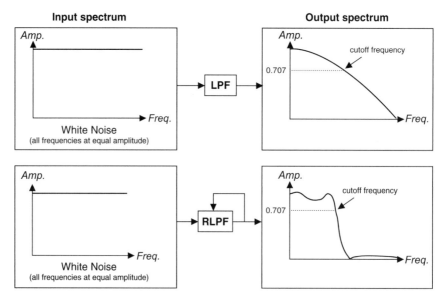

Figure 5-14 Frequency responses of feedforward and feedback lowpass filters

Oscillating cutoff frequencies: 400–4000 Hz

Feedforward

Sawtooth wave at 220 Hz (note the harmonic spectrum indicated by the horizontal lines)

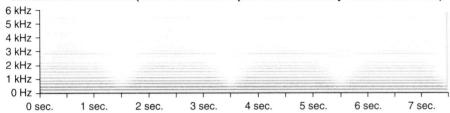

White noise

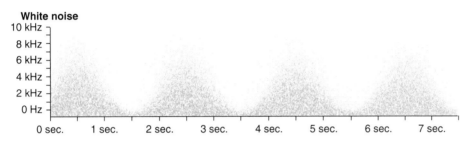

Feedback
Note the spectral resonance at the cutoff frequency

Sawtooth wave at 220 Hz (note the harmonic spectrum indicated by the horizontal lines)

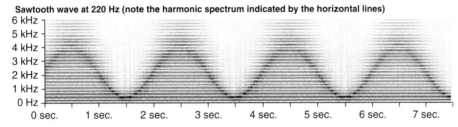

White noise

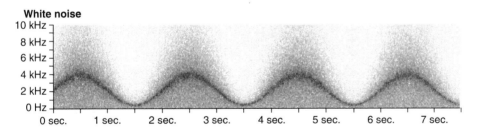

Figure 5-15 Spectrograms of lowpass filtered signals

HIGHPASS FILTER

A highpass filter is the opposite of a lowpass filter. It attenuates or eliminates lower frequencies (it "lets the highs pass"). Highpass filters share much in common with lowpass filters. They are characterized by a cutoff frequency, the spectral region at which the amplitude on output is 0.707 of its amplitude when input. Highpass filters may also be feedforward or feedback. Figure 5-16 compares the frequency responses of a feedforward and a feedback highpass filter, and Figure 5-17 shows spectrograms of both highpass filter types.

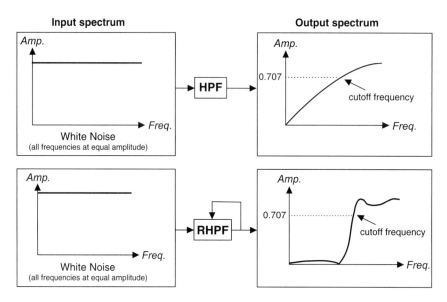

Figure 5-16 Frequency responses of feedforward and feedback highpass filters

BANDPASS FILTER

A *bandpass filter* attenuates or eliminates frequencies above and below a specified band of frequencies, the *passband* (it "lets a band of frequencies pass"). A bandpass filter is characterized by two values: *center frequency* and *bandwidth*, as illustrated in Figure 5-18. The center frequency is at the midpoint of the passband. The bandwidth is the difference between spectral components on either side of the center frequency that are lowered in power by 3 dB. Figure 5-19 shows spectrograms of bandpass filters.

Putting noise through a bandpass filter with a narrow bandwidth produces a windy, pitched sound. Many electroacoustic composers have created pieces from filtered noise, and a project of this sort is included in the Suggested Exercises at the end of this chapter.

BAND-REJECT FILTER

A *band-reject filter* is the opposite of a bandpass filter. It attenuates or eliminates frequencies within a specified band of the spectrum. Like the bandpass filter, a band-reject filter is characterized by center frequency and bandwidth, as shown in Figure 5-20. Band-reject filters are more specialized than the other three types and are not as likely to be used for musical effects. One possible use would be to attenuate a narrow band of noise from a recording. Figure 5-21 shows spectrograms of band-reject filters.

"EVERYTHING IS A FILTER!"

This assertion (Smith, 1985) underlines the central importance of filters in audio systems. Anything that transmits sound filters it in some way. Audio speakers filter their signals, and serious audiophiles look at the frequency response of speakers before buying them. When a person speaks and puts a hand in front of her mouth, the sound of the voice is lowpass filtered, as the higher frequencies reflect off the hand and back toward the mouth. This is also the effect obtained by brass players who use hat mutes. The size and shape of a room filter the sound propagating within it. Thus, filters underlie audio at every stage of recording, processing, transmission, and production.

Oscillating cutoff frequencies: 400–4000 Hz
Feedforward

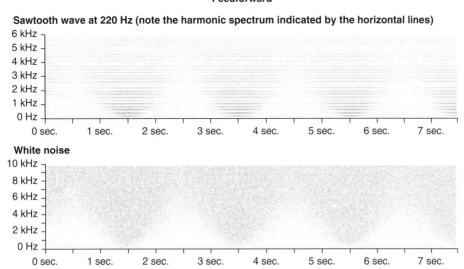

Sawtooth wave at 220 Hz (note the harmonic spectrum indicated by the horizontal lines)

White noise

Feedback
Note the spectral resonance at the cutoff frequency

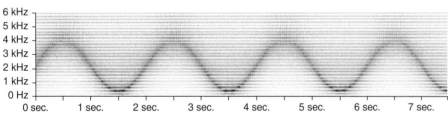

Sawtooth wave at 220 Hz (note the harmonic spectrum indicated by the horizontal lines)

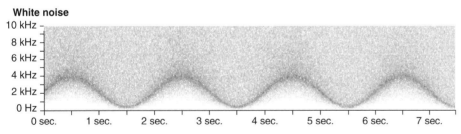

White noise

Figure 5-17 Spectrograms of highpass filtered signals

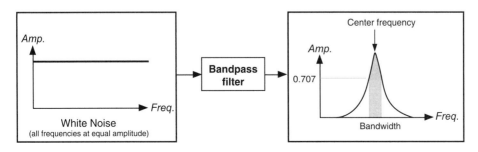

Figure 5-18 Frequency response of a bandpass filter

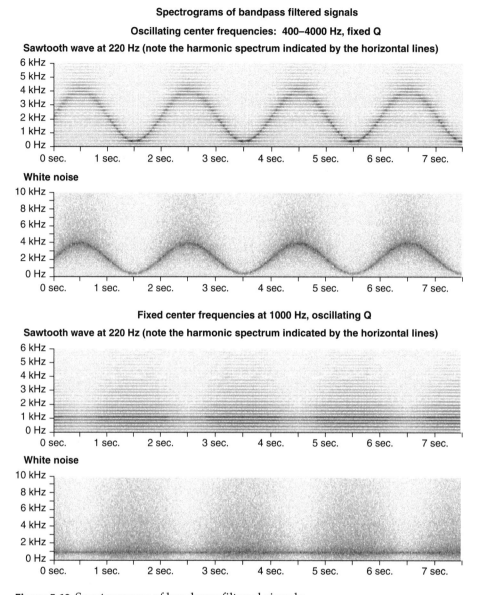

Figure 5-19 Spectrograms of bandpass filtered signals

The Digital Filtering Process

We've now studied the basic filter types and asserted the overall importance of filters in general. The introduction to filters stated that they are quite simple operationally, involving storage and mathematical operations on stored values. We will now go a bit deeper into the nuts and bolts of filtering operations.

By convention, an audio signal is termed x. A digitized audio signal is termed $x[n]$, with n representing a series of discrete sample values (Figure 5-22). The letter n may either be thought of as the specific position (also termed *index* or *address*) of any given

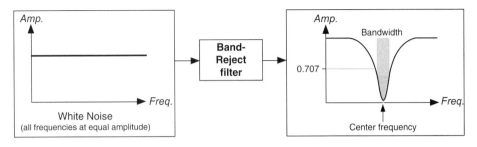

Figure 5-20 Frequency response of a band-reject filter

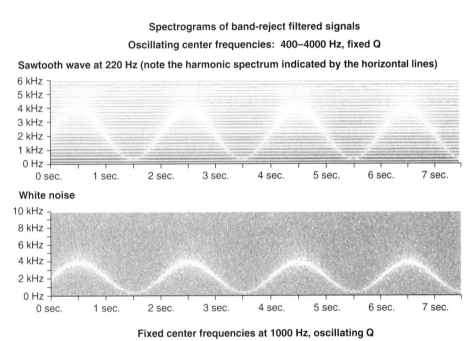

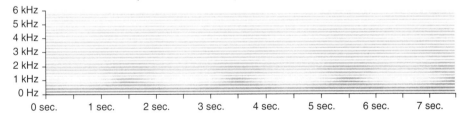

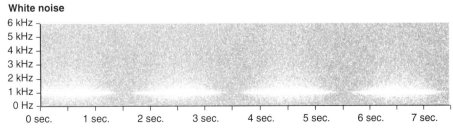

Figure 5-21 Spectrograms of band-reject filtered signals

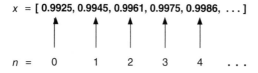

Figure 5-22 A digital signal is termed $x[n]$

Figure 5-23 A filter's output is termed $y[n]$

sample within signal x, or it may be generalized to represent the entire set of discrete values that make up the signal. The output of a filter is termed $y[n]$ (Figure 5-23). The digital filter combines the present sample with multiples of past samples to compute each output sample, as shown in Equation 5-2:

$$y[n] = a \times x[n] + b \times x[n-1] + c \times x[n-2] + d \times x[n-3]\ldots \qquad (5\text{-}2)$$

This general description is called the ***filter difference equation***. The symbol n may be interpreted to mean "now," or "the current sample value." $x[n-1]$ may be interpreted as "the value of the sample just previous to the present sample," $x[n-2]$ as "the value of the sample two samples previous to the present sample," and so on. The values multiplied by the series of samples, $[a, b, c, d, \ldots]$ are the equation's ***coefficients***.

Although the connection is not intuitive from the filter difference equation, the number of coefficients and their values make it possible to calculate a filter's frequency response and thus derive specific spectral shapes such as those shown in Figure 5-13.

There are a number of texts on ***digital signal processing (DSP)*** that provide outstanding descriptions of how the filter difference equation translates into the frequency response, and that were written to bridge the fields of music and electrical engineering (McClellan, Schafer, and Yoder, 1998; Park, 2010; Pirkle, 2012; Steiglitz, 1996). Figure 5-24 shows how the frequency response of a simple averaging lowpass filter may be derived, although coming up with the frequency response of more complicated filters is a bit more involved. The general overview provided here is meant to demonstrate a practical value of digital audio: all that is necessary to alter the spectrum of an audio signal is hardware that is able to delay samples for a specified number of sample periods and to quickly perform basic arithmetic on the samples held in memory.

Feedforward vs. Feedback Filters

A filter difference equation such as Equation 5-2 combines the present input sample with past input samples, which makes it an example of a feedforward filter. As we've discussed, feedforward filters create areas of attenuation (or *zeroes*) in the spectrum of their output. Table 5-1 illustrates the mechanics of taking a simple "dummy" signal of [0.4, 0.5, 0.6, 0.7] and filtering it with a difference equation with the coefficients [0.3, 0.15, 0.3].

A feedback filter performs multiplications on past output samples as well as past input samples. Thus the difference equation of a resonant filter has two sets of coefficients, the feedback coefficients and the feedforward coefficients:

$$\begin{aligned} y[n] = a \times y[n-1] + b \times y[n-2] + c \times y[n-3] \\ + \ldots d \times x[n] + e \times x[n-1] \ldots \end{aligned} \qquad (5\text{-}3)$$

Feedback filters create areas of amplification (***poles*** or ***resonances***) in the spectrum of their output. Table 5-2 performs the same processing on a dummy signal as Table 5-1, with the addition of a feedback coefficient of [0.5]. Feedback filters need to be handled with a bit more care than simple feedforward filters; the coefficients need to be chosen carefully to ensure that the filter's feedback loop does not allow the output to "blow up." However, feedback filters are able to perform fine degrees of spectral shaping with fewer coefficients than would be possible with a feedforward filter.

This filter averages the present and past sample. Intuitively, we can understand this as a kind of smoothing applied to any rough edges in the signal. Analytically, we can see how this works by starting with the filter difference equation:

$$y[n] = 0.5x[n] + 0.5x[n-1]$$

Start by abstracting the sample streams. Rather than dealing with the sample $x[n]$, consider the entirety of the input signal to be $X[n]$. Similarly, consider the entirety of the output to be $[z]$. Consider a delay of one sample to a stream of samples to be z^{-1}. Instead of thinking of one sample delay as $x[n-1]$, consider the entire signal delayed by one sample as being $X[z]z^{-1}$.

Rewriting the difference equation in this form is called the z-transform.

$$Y[z] = 0.5X[z] + 0.5X[z]z^{-1}$$

The z-transform allows the operations of the filter to be considered algebraically. First, it can be factored:

$$Y[z] = X[z] \, (0.5 + 0.5z^{-1})$$

The transfer function, $H[z]$, describes what is done to the input signal by creating a ratio of the output to the input:

$$H[z] = \frac{Y[z]}{X[z]} = 0.5 + 0.5z^{-1} = 0.5 + \frac{0.5}{z}$$

Finding the zeroes of this equation, the values of z that cause the equation to equal zero, indicate zeroes in the filter's frequency response. For this equation, the zero is at

$$z = -1$$

The filter's frequency response is created by considering this zero as a complex number, $-1 + 0j$, and plotting this point on the unit circle (recall Figure 5-7):

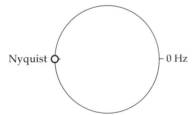

This indicates that the filter has a zero at the Nyquist frequency. The magnitude of other frequencies can be measured as the distance from this zero to each corresponding frequency point on the circumference.

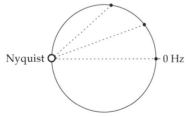

This shows that the maximum magnitude of the frequency response occurs at 0 Hz, with a gradual attenuation that culminates in a zero at the Nyquist frequency.

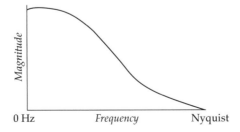

Figure 5-24 Frequency response of a simple averaging lowpass filter

TABLE 5-1 Mechanics of a feedforward filter.

Input signal: $X(n) = [0.4, 0.5, 0.6, 0.7]$
Coefficients: [0.3, 0.15, 0.3]
Filter difference equation: $y[n] = 0.3x[n] + 0.15x[n-1] + 0.3x[n-2]$
$Y(n) = [0.12, 0.21, 0.375, 0.45, 0.285, 0.21]$

NOW	PREVIOUS SAMPLE	TWO SAMPLES PREVIOUS	OUTPUT NOW
n	$n-1$	$n-2$	$y[n]$
0.4	—	—	
×	×	×	
0.3	0.15	0.3	
↓	↓	↓	
0.12 +	— +	— =	0.12
0.5	0.4	—	
×	×	×	
0.3	0.15	0.3	
↓	↓	↓	
0.15 +	0.06 +	— =	0.21
0.6	0.5	0.4	
×	×	×	
0.3	0.15	0.3	
↓	↓	↓	
0.18 +	0.075 +	0.12 =	0.375
0.7	0.6	0.5	
×	×	×	
0.3	0.15	0.3	
↓	↓	↓	
0.21 +	0.09 +	0.15 =	0.45
—	0.7	0.6	
×	×	×	
0.3	0.15	0.3	
↓	↓	↓	
— +	0.105 +	0.18 =	0.285

(continued)

TABLE 5-1 Mechanics of a feedforward filter. (*continued*)

NOW		PREVIOUS SAMPLE		TWO SAMPLES PREVIOUS		OUTPUT NOW
n		$n-1$		$n-2$		$y[n]$
—		—		0.7		
×		×		×		
—		—		0.3		
↓		↓		↓		
0	+	0	+	0.21	=	0.21

TABLE 5-2 Mechanics of a feedback filter.

Input signal: $X[n] = [0.4, 0.5, 0.6, 0.7]$
Feedforward Coefficients: [0.3, 0.15, 0.3]
Feedback Coefficient: [0.5]
Filter difference equation: $y[n] = 0.5y[n-1] + 0.3x[n] + 0.15x[n-1] + 0.3x[n-2]$
$Y[n] = [0.12, 0.27, 0.51, 0.705, 0.6375, 0.52875, 0.264375, 0.1321875, 0.06609375, 0.033046875, 0.016523438 \ldots]$

PREVIOUS OUTPUT		NOW		PREVIOUS SAMPLE		TWO SAMPLES PREVIOUS		OUTPUT NOW
$y[n-1]$		$x[n]$		$x[n-1]$		$x[n-2]$		$y[n]$
—		0.4		—		—		
×		×		×		×		
0.5		0.3		0.15		0.3		
↓		↓		↓		↓		
—	+	0.12	+	—	+	—	=	0.12
0.12		0.5		0.4		—		
×		×		×		×		
0.5		0.3		0.15		0.3		
↓		↓		↓		↓		
0.06	+	0.15	+	0.06	+	—	=	0.27
0.27		0.6		0.5		0.4		
×		×		×		×		
0.5		0.3		0.15		0.3		
↓		↓		↓		↓		
0.135	+	0.18	+	0.075	+	0.12	=	0.51

(*continued*)

TABLE 5-2 Mechanics of a feedback filter. (*continued*)

PREVIOUS OUTPUT $y[n-1]$	NOW $x[n]$	PREVIOUS SAMPLE $x[n-1]$	TWO SAMPLES PREVIOUS $x[n-2]$	OUTPUT NOW $y[n]$
0.51	0.7	0.6	0.5	
×	×	×	×	
0.5	0.3	0.15	0.3	
↓	↓	↓	↓	
0.255 +	0.21 +	0.09 +	0.15 =	0.705
0.705	—	0.7	0.6	
×	×	×	×	
0.5	0.3	0.15	0.3	
↓	↓	↓	↓	
0.3525 +	— +	0.105 +	0.18 =	0.6375
0.6375	—	—	0.7	
×	×	×	×	
0.5	0.3	0.15	0.3	
↓	↓	↓	↓	
0.31875 +	— +	— +	0.21 =	0.52875
0.52875	—	—	—	
×	×	×	×	
0.5	0.3	0.15	0.3	
↓	↓	↓	↓	
0.264375 +	— +	— +	— =	0.264375
0.264375	—	—	—	
×	×	×	×	
0.5	0.3	0.15	0.3	
↓	↓	↓	↓	
0.1321875 +	— +	— +	— =	0.1321875

(*continued*)

TABLE 5-2 Mechanics of a feedback filter. (*continued*)

PREVIOUS OUTPUT		NOW	PREVIOUS SAMPLE	TWO SAMPLES PREVIOUS	OUTPUT NOW
$y[n-1]$		$x[n]$	$x[n-1]$	$x[n-2]$	$y[n]$
0.1321875		—	—	—	
×		×	×	×	
0.5		0.3	0.15	0.3	
↓		↓	↓	↓	
0.06609375	+	— +	— +	— =	0.06609375
0.06609375		—	—	—	
×		×	×	×	
0.5		0.3	0.15	0.3	
↓		↓	↓	↓	
0.033046875	+	— +	— +	— =	0.033046875
0.033046875		—	—	—	
×		×	×	×	
0.5		0.3	0.15	0.3	
↓		↓	↓	↓	
0.016523438	+	— +	— +	— =	0.016523438

Lowpass Filters

A simple feedforward lowpass filter may be created by taking the average of the current and preceding sample. This is the simple averaging lowpass filter used as an example in Figure 5-24:

$$y[n] = 0.5x[n] + 0.5x[n-1] \qquad \text{Coefficients: } [0.5, 0.5] \qquad (5\text{-}4)$$

An intuitive way of understanding the effect of Equation 5-4 is to bear in mind that a waveform with sharp edges contains many high frequencies. Recall as an example that the jagged sawtooth and square wave illustrations shown in Chapter 2 (Figure 2-10) were idealized: an infinite number of harmonics are necessary to produce such sharp waveforms. In a digital system, the harmonics do not extend to infinity, but only to the Nyquist frequency. As more harmonics are added, the wave shape approaches the angular shape of the idealized waveform, but the ripples never disappear entirely.

Thus, the sharper the edges of a waveform, the more high frequencies it contains. Relating this to Equation 5-4, the equation's averaging effect serves to smooth the edges of the output, which lessens the high-frequency content of a complex wave.

Highpass Filters

A simple feedforward highpass filter may be created by taking the average of the *difference* between the current and the preceding sample:

$$y(n) = 0.5x[n] - 0.5x[n-1] \qquad \text{Coefficients: } [0.5, -0.5] \qquad (5\text{-}5)$$

Equation 5-5 has the opposite effect of the lowpass filter. The minus sign in the equation means that the waveform's edges are made sharper, which accentuates high frequency content.

Bandpass and Band-Reject Filters

These two filter types are typically feedback filters, as it is difficult to do their degree of spectral shaping with feedforward filters. Some music synthesis software programs term bandpass filters *resonz*, since they resonate at a center frequency.

Center frequency and bandwidth are often combined to create the descriptor **Q** **(*quality*)**, which is the ratio of the center frequency to the bandwidth (CF/BW). Q is often a more useful description than simple bandwidth. ***Constant Q filters*** maintain a set ratio of CF/BW as the center frequency is changed. Recalling from Chapter 2 that human perception of pitch is logarithmic, a constant Q represents a constant musical interval, with a narrower bandwidth for low center frequencies and a wider bandwidth for high center frequencies.

Other Filter Characteristics

A filter's ***transient response*** describes the filter's initial output when there is a sudden change in the input (such as the attack of a new note). Because the transient is a key portion of a musical timbre, as discussed in Chapter 3, a filter's transient response is critical to the way a filter's effect is perceived. Figure 5-25 illustrates the output of the same filter illustrated in Table 5-1. The input signal is more characteristic of an actual audio example in that it is periodic, consisting of a sinusoidal wave. The output of the filter is calculated in the same way that it was calculated in Tables 5-1 and 5-2. As the figure shows, there is an initial transient of six irregular samples from the filter output before it settles into a periodic pattern.

Other useful observations may also be drawn from this figure. A filter's transient response is followed by its ***steady-state response***. The initial transient output eventually settles to a steady state that corresponds to one of the four basic filter types shown in Figure 5-13. In Figure 5-25, the steady-state output is a periodic signal with the same frequency as the input. However, its peak amplitude is lower than that of the input signal. Therefore, the filter in Figure 5-25 attenuates this frequency. The figure also shows that once the steady-state response is reached, the phase of the output is offset by one-quarter of a cycle from that of the input. The demonstration input signal for this illustration consists of one frequency component; for a more complex input signal, the amount of delay would vary for different frequencies. A filter's ***phase response*** describes how much it delays the spectral components of its input.

Filter design is a weighing of compromises. An ideal "brick wall" filter, such as that shown in Figure 5-26, cannot be implemented. In practice, sharp cutoffs result in resonance as well as phase distortion near the cutoff frequency. Practical filter design

A periodic input signal causes an initial transient response
before the output settles to a periodic pattern

Filter Difference Equation: y[n] = 0.3 x [n] + 0.15 x [n–1] + 0.3 x [n–2]

x [n] = [1, 0.707, 0, –0.707, –1, –0.707, 0, 0.707, 1, 0.707, 0 . . .]

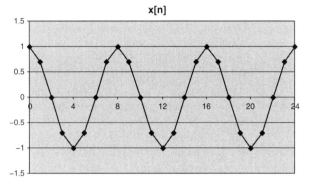

y [n] = [0.09, 0.362, 0.406, 0, –0.406, –0.406, –0.574, –0.406, 0, 0.406, 0.574, 0.406, 0, –0.406, –0.574, –0.406, 0, 0.406, . . .]

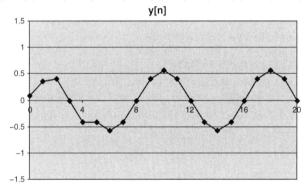

Figure 5-25 Filter transient response

involves consideration of ripple in the passband, *stopband* (the spectral region attenuated by the filter), and the slope of the cutoff (expressed in dB/octave). A more realistic frequency response is shown in Figure 5-27. In general, a sharper cutoff frequency results in a longer impulse response; the filter is said to "ring." This can cause a filter to behave almost as a musical instrument in and of itself. Ringing filters can sound quite lovely; feeding them an impulse signal is the digital equivalent to a mallet strike to a bell or chime. (Impulses will be discussed further in Chapter 6.)

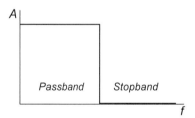

Figure 5-26 An ideal lowpass frequency response

The Digital Recording and Playback Process

Recording

Now that the workings of filters have been discussed, the steps of digital recording can be listed in sequence. (Many of these steps will be covered in more detail in Chapter 6). Figure 5-28 illustrates the process for a two-channel stereo recording. Each step is discussed briefly below.

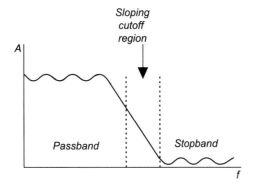

Figure 5-27 A more realistic lowpass frequency response

DITHER
Low-level noise or dither is added to the signal prior to sampling to reduce quantization error distortion.

LOWPASS (ANTIALIASING) FILTER
The lowpass/antialiasing filtering step is essential to remove frequencies above the Nyquist frequency. Given the practical limitations of filters, extra caution is taken. Because an ideal brick wall filter is impossible, the cutoff starts a few thousand hertz below the Nyquist frequency. To ensure that no aliasing occurs, the filter's stopband may begin at a frequency lower than the Nyquist frequency. Thus, the problem of critical sampling, shown in Figure 5-5, is avoided because these filtering steps ensure that are always more than two samples per period of any signal.

SAMPLE AND HOLD
The *sample and hold circuit* measures the analog voltage levels. The measurement values must then be held long enough to be read by the analog-to-digital converter.

ANALOG-TO-DIGITAL CONVERTER (ADC)
The ADC prepares the information for storage. It reads values from the sample and hold circuit, determines the quantization level nearest to the actual value, and outputs it as a binary number for storage. The binary values are transmitted through pulse code modulation (PCM): alternations between two voltage levels to transmit binary ones and zeroes.

MULTIPLEXER
In the *multiplexer*, the parallel data streams from each stereo channel are transformed into a serial bit stream for storage. Samples from the two channels are alternated in the stream, and extra encoding bits are added to each sample that indicate which stereo channel it belongs to.

ERROR CORRECTION
Digital audio would not be economically feasible without effective error correction. Given the density of digital data, optical discs would be prohibitively expensive if they had to be robust enough to ensure flawless storage and reproduction. Therefore, effective error correction is required. This is an entire subfield of digital audio engineering, involving various forms of encryption.

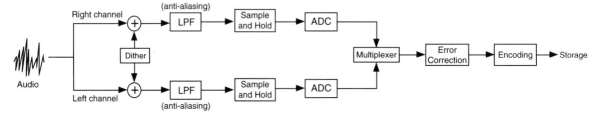

Figure 5-28 Components in the digital recording process
Source: Adapted from Ken Pohlmann, Principles of Digital Audio, *3rd ed. (1995). Copyright McGraw-Hill Education*

A variety of bookkeeping measures are taken at this stage. Samples are stored in groups known as *frames*. Each sample is accompanied by bits that identify its frame number and stereo channel. In addition to this extra information accompanying each sample, the beginning of each frame is marked by a unique series of bits that allow unambiguous identification of a frame's beginning. This *subcode* information allows listeners to fast-forward or reverse a CD and have playback begin at the beginning of the chosen frame.

A variety of measures may also be taken to reduce errors. For example, the sum of all sample values in a frame is stored in a few bytes reserved for bookkeeping. On playback, if the sum of samples in a frame does not match the stored sum value, the mismatch indicates that an error is present. A variety of algorithms may be employed to try to correct it.

Another error-correction approach involves scrambling the order of the samples, a process known as *interleaving*. The samples are reordered on playback. Interleaving ensures that if an area of the storage medium undergoes damage, the samples affected will not be contiguous. Noncontiguous errors may be remedied by correction algorithms, whereas a series of damaged samples may be irreparable.

ENCODING
Before being transferred to the storage medium, the data must be *encoded* to ensure that it can be read accurately on playback. The nature of the encoding will be discussed in Chapter 6 in the section on Storage Media.

Playback
The process of playing digital audio is essentially the reverse of recording it, as shown in Figure 5-29.

BUFFER
The creation of audio from a series of stored sample values is a precisely timed operation. To ensure that samples are processed at a constant rate, they are initially held in a *buffer* from which they may be steadily dispensed. A buffer may be compared to a pail of water held under a spigot (Pohlmann, 1995). Although water may emerge irregularly from a spigot into the bucket, a small hole in the bottom of the bucket ensures that a consistent stream of water flows out.

ERROR CORRECTION
Stored bits are de-interleaved and checked for accuracy in the error correction module. Errors may be eliminated up to a certain point. Depending on the degree of error

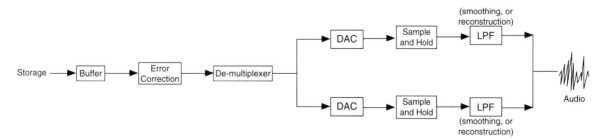

Figure 5-29 Components of the digital playback process
Source: Adapted from Ken Pohlmann, Principles of Digital Audio, *3rd ed. (1995). Copyright McGraw-Hill Education*

present, a number of steps may be taken. Should absolute correction be impossible, a variety of concealment techniques may be employed. In some cases, a sample may be interpolated by assigning it a value based on the mean of samples that precede and follow it. Given the deterministic, periodic nature of musical signals, interpolation is often a workable alternative. If this approach proves impossible, a worst-case scenario is simply to mute the signal momentarily until samples become verifiable again.

DIGITAL-TO-ANALOG CONVERTER (DAC) AND SAMPLE AND HOLD
The digital-to-analog converter reads binary sample values and translates them into voltage values. This is not an instantaneous process, however, and *glitching errors* may result from some bits being translated before others. For example, if one digital word is

     01111111 11111111

and the next is

     10000000 00000000

the most significant bit may register in the DAC before the other bits, thus creating a short voltage spike resulting from the value of

     11111111 11111111

before the intended value is output. To remove these voltage glitches, a sample and hold circuit acts as an intermediary between the DAC and the actual voltage output. The sample and hold circuit reads values from the DAC when the DAC has reached a stable state during each sampling period. This value is held until the DAC reaches a stable state during the next sampling period. Thus, glitches are eliminated, but the result is a staircase waveform, such as those shown in Figure 5-3. As we've discussed, sharp edges in a waveform create high-frequency content that is not part of the musical signal. These edges, therefore, need to be smoothed by a lowpass filter.

OUTPUT LOWPASS FILTER
As a final step before the realization of audio, the staircase wave produced by the sample and hold circuit is smoothed by a lowpass filter. Output lowpass filters often employ a three-step process of oversampling:

1. Samples are inserted between the original samples, and the output sampling rate is correspondingly multiplied. For example, at 4× oversampling, three samples at a value of zero are inserted between each sample, and the sampling rate is multiplied by 4. At 8× oversampling, seven samples at a value of zero are inserted between each sample, and the sampling rate is multiplied by 8. The audio is thus produced at this higher sampling rate.
2. These added samples have their values converted from zero to interpolated values between the original samples so that they fit the curve of the signal. This process smooths the staircase wave from the sample and hold unit.
3. Because the increased sampling rate also increases the Nyquist frequency, the smoothing process may then be polished off by a filter that has a more gradual and smooth cutoff slope, as it extends to regions beyond audible frequencies. The resulting signal is cleaner than conversion at the original sampling rate.

Oversampling is often complemented by *noise shaping*, a process that highpass filters quantization error so that the distortion is pushed to frequencies above the audible range. Noise shaping will be discussed in more detail in Chapter 6.

Suggested Exercises

- Import a music file into a digital audio workstation (DAW) or audio editor. Save a few versions of it at different sampling rates and sample sizes. Listen to them closely and compare the results.
- Do an Internet search for spoken word fragments: speeches from politicians or from movies and TV, for example. Open them in an audio editor and extract short segments, no more than two words in succession. Copy them into a new file to assemble a new sentence that contains words from any number of sources. Using the audio editing functions, try to make the new patchwork file sound as smooth and as natural as possible.
- Prepare a series of examples for a music history or theory class. Copy audio files from CDs that you own to a computer, open them in an audio editor, and create the excerpts to be used as class demonstrations. (To avoid any copyright infringement, take care not to distribute these.) Create a playlist of excerpts that is saved to an iPod or other mobile device. The end result should be an easily navigable set of tracks that may be chosen and played quickly in class, as opposed to repeatedly changing CDs, finding the desired track, and fast-forwarding to the desired point in that track.
- Import a recording into a DAW and lower its volume until it is just above silence. Export the file to a series of audio files, each with a different type of dither added. Import these files back into the DAW and amplify them to a level close to what the original recording was. This step will also amplify the dither, which will be featured prominently in the newly amplified files. How do the different dither types sound?
- Create a short piece consisting of only filtered white noise. How much musicality can be generated by filter sweeps, changes in bandwidth, changes in volume, and so on?

Key Terms

acoustic compiler	critically sampled
alias	digital-to-analog converter (DAC)
analog audio	digital signal processing (DSP)
analog-to-digital converter (ADC)	distortion
asymmetrical distortion	dither
bandpass filter	encoding
band-reject filter	feedback filter (or resonant or
bandwidth	recursive filter)
buffer	feedforward filter
center frequency	filter difference equation
coefficient	frame
constant Q filters	frequency response

glitching error

index or address

interleaving

multiplexer

noise floor

noise shaping

Nyquist frequency

oversampled

passband

phase response

poles or resonances

pulse code modulation (PCM)

quality (Q)

resonz

sample

sample and hold circuit

sample size (or bit depth, word size, or quantization level)

sampling increment

sampling rate

sampling theorem or Nyquist theorem

steady-state response

stopband

subcode

symmetrical distortion

transient response

undersampling

wavetable

wow

Chapter 6

Working with Digital Audio

Chapter 5 provided an overview of the workings of digitizing audio. Having covered this basic groundwork, we can now dig deeper and explore some of the sonic alchemy that digital audio makes possible. It will also be helpful to cover concrete matters, such as how audio may be stored onto physical media and shared via the Internet.

Analysis and Processing

Spectral Representation

Chapter 5 covered basic mechanics of audio filtering. This section will delve further into the processing that can be done with an audio signal once it has been discretized and stored.

0 HZ = DIRECT CURRENT

A spectral component at 0 Hz is often referred to by an electronics term. As described in Chapter 4, direct current (DC) is current that does not alternate in direction, but moves only in one direction. Because the direct current has no alternation, DC has a frequency of 0 Hz, indicating that there is no oscillation present in the current. The terms "DC" and "0 Hz" are often used interchangeably.

There are times when a current or a signal has a constant value added to it. For example, the equation

$$y = 0.5 + \sin(x)$$

describes a sine wave with a value of 0.5 added to all values. This means that the sine wave does not oscillate equally above and below the value of zero, with a range of ± 1, but rather above and below the value of 0.5, so that it spans a range of -0.5 to 1.5 (that is, the range covers the DC value plus and minus the wave's range: 0.5 minus 1 and 0.5 plus one). The presence of this constant value is termed **DC content** or **DC offset**.

SPECTRA OF DIGITAL SIGNALS

The Fourier transform, introduced in Chapter 2, states that any periodic signal may be expressed as the sum of a series of sinusoidal waves. All are harmonics of the signal's fundamental frequency, and each is at a particular amplitude and phase.

For discrete digital signals, the mathematics of the Fourier transform have been adapted to a process known as the **Discrete Fourier Transform (DFT)**. The transform treats the signal of N values as one period of an infinitely repeating waveform. As with the Fourier transform, the entirety of the signal's past and future can be calculated, due to its assumed periodicity.

The DFT transforms N time domain samples into N spectral values. The fundamental frequency is what the signal as a whole represents: 1 cycle per N samples. The successive spectral values represent multiples of this frequency: 2 cycles per N samples, 3 cycles per N samples, and so on. The DFT produces spectral values—amplitude and phase—of 0 Hz and a set of N–1 harmonics of the fundamental.

As stated in Chapter 2, a Fourier transform is completely reversible. A transform may be done to a set of samples to derive spectral information on the values. An inverse transform may be performed that creates exactly the same series of time domain samples.

The DFT produces a spectrum that is symmetrical. Just as two samples are required to identify a single frequency's peak and trough (as was shown in Figure 5-4), a DFT produces two values for each spectral component, one positive and the other negative, with the energy divided between the two. This symmetry is well represented by the polar diagram that was shown in Figure 5-7. Because the information of the positive and negative components is identical, in some illustrations the negative frequencies are discarded and the amplitudes of the positive frequencies are doubled. There are various ways of representing the transform, as shown in Figure 6-1. For some applications, it may be appropriate to illustrate all frequencies resulting from the transform, both positive and negative. Sometimes the complete results are plotted with the 0 Hz component in the middle position of the graph; other times the negative frequencies are shown to the right of the positive frequencies. Figure 6-1 also shows how increasing the value of N increases the spectral resolution of the transform.

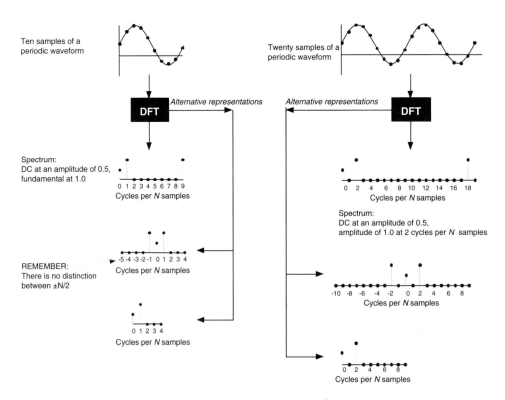

Figure 6-1 Representations of the Discrete Fourier Transform

THE FOURIER TRANSFORM PROCESS

Interested readers may consult the reference list at the end of this book for some accessible explanations of the mathematics involved in the transform. The mathematics are abstract and sublime, and subject to being viewed through a variety of conceptual lenses. The literature on this area is continually being enriched by musicians writing from their own unique perspectives. Five of these perspectives will be discussed below.

Perspective One: Multiplication by Probe Signals

As described in Loy (2007), the transform is achieved by multiplying the source audio signal by a series of probe signals. Because the digital signals consist of a series of discrete values, this step involves multiplying corresponding index values from the signal and the probe:

$$source[n] \times probe[n]$$
$$source[n + 1] \times probe[n + 1]$$
$$source[n + 2] \times probe[n + 2]$$
$$\ldots$$

All these multiplications between the source signal and a probe are then summed into a single value. The idea is expressed more succinctly in summation notation:

$$\sum_{n=1}^{N} source[n] \times probe[n]$$

The process is then repeated for each of the probe signals.

What are these probe signals, and what does multiplying the signal with all of them accomplish? Recall that:

- Multiplying two numbers by the same sign—two positive numbers or two negative numbers—produces a positive value.
- Multiplying a positive number by a negative number produces a negative value.

A sinusoidal wave consists of an equal number of positive and negative values. Thus, multiplying two sinusoidal signals with each other will, in most cases, produce a set of values that are both positive and negative, and that cancel each other out when the products are summed. The one exception to this is when two sinusoidal signals are multiplied that have the same frequency. As shown in Figure 6-2, this creates a set of only positive products, as all the multiplications are either positive-times-positive or negative-times-negative. Thus, when these are summed, the result will not have the cancellations that normally occur when two sinusoidal signals of different frequencies are multiplied and summed.

Returning to the DFT: the audio signal is multiplied by a series of probe signals; and each probe signal is a set of samples that outline a harmonic of the audio signal's fundamental frequency. Therefore, if the signal contains energy at a given harmonic,

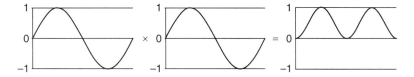

Figure 6-2 Squaring a sine wave

when the audio signal is multiplied by that harmonic's probe frequency and the products are summed, a positive value will result.

Perspective Two: A Harmonic Coordinate System

The harmonics represented by these probe frequencies may be termed a **basis set**, which is a term describing a set of linked (dependent) basis vectors in a system. Any point in the system may be described as a linear combination of these basis vectors; conversely, these basis vectors are able to describe any point in the system. These basis vectors are also described as **orthogonal** axes, which means that they are perpendicular to each other, and that their properties are nonoverlapping. This is an expanded coordinate system of the same sort seen in Cartesian geometry, which describes points in space based on a system of two basis vectors (the x and y axes) or three basis vectors (with the addition of a z axis). All points in two- or three-dimensional space may be described in terms of two or three basis vectors that represent axes in the Cartesian system.

The Fourier transform of a continuous time signal expands this concept. It has a basis set consisting of a large number of vectors that are able to describe many possible frequency components of the analog signal. For a discrete signal of N points, the Fourier transform has a basis set consisting of N vectors, which represent 0 Hz and $N-1$ harmonics of the signal.

Perspective Three: Taking the Inner Product

With this basis set in mind, the audio signal may be considered as a vector existing within the coordinate system defined by the basis set of harmonics. The transform process is the same thing as taking the **inner product**, which is the product of every corresponding index point between two vectors, summed. This process can be shown with a simple example involving two three-point vectors, which describe points on the x, y, and z axes. The inner product of a vector describing a point lying on a Cartesian x axis is taken with a vector describing a point lying on the Cartesian z axis:

Vector A: [1, 2, 0]
Vector B: [0, 0, 1]

The inner product of vectors A and B is:

$$(1 \times 0) + (2 \times 0) + (0 \times 1) = 0$$

The zero result indicates that each vector lies completely along one orthogonal axis, and has no coordinate components from any of the other orthogonal axes.

The DFT involves taking the inner product of the audio signal vector and each of these basis probe vectors. Each probe vector is orthogonal to all other probe vectors. If the result of the inner product between the audio signal and a probe vector is zero, this means that there is no relationship between the audio signal and that given probe frequency, which means that there is no energy from that harmonic present in the audio signal. Inner product values greater than zero indicate a presence of that probe frequency within the audio signal: the greater the inner product value, the greater the energy of that probe frequency harmonic within the audio signal.

Perspective Four: Filter Bank

Yet another way of looking at it is to think of the DFT as the output of a bank of bandpass filters. The center frequency of each filter is a harmonic of the signal's period, and each filter has a fixed bandwidth.

THE FAST FOURIER TRANSFORM (FFT)
The DFT is computationally intensive. A more efficient version, the *Fast Fourier Transform (FFT),* produces identical results, but is fast enough for spectra to be derived and manipulated in *real time*. This means that the results can be displayed as a musical signal is being generated. The FFT algorithm relies on repeatedly breaking the mathematics of the transform into two parts, so a requirement of the FFT algorithm is that the length of the audio signal under analysis must be some power of 2.

TIME DOMAIN LOCALIZATION VS. SPECTRAL RESOLUTION
The theoretically infinite length of the signals, the transform's built-in "assumption" that the signal's cyclic patterns will repeat in exactly the same way forever, makes the Fourier transform an effective process to describe stable (*stationary*) signals. But it has shortcomings in describing irregular (*nonstationary*) signals. The only way it can "explain" any transient behavior in the signal is to create a number of frequency components whose constructive and destructive interference over the total length of the signal combine in such a way to produce the transient. The nonstationary nature of the transient is thus translated as a coincidence brought about by the amplitudes and phases of a number of stationary components, rather than the sudden appearance of new frequencies that quickly dissipate. Thus, it is said that a Fourier transform loses *time localization* of events in a signal, resulting in a tension between time and frequency resolution. A longer signal contains more points, and thus a Fourier transform reveals the presence of more harmonics, with any nonstationary activity "smeared" over the length of the signal. (It's a bit like taking a long-exposure photo of a busy street corner, and then trying to describe what events occurred from the blurry image that results.) The transform of a shorter signal is better able to describe the timing of an event but, due to its fewer data points, is interpreted as containing fewer frequency components. Thus, there is an inverse relationship between time and frequency resolution. This tradeoff is analogous to the *uncertainty principle* in physics, which states that the more accurately a particle's position can be observed, the less accurately its velocity can be estimated, whereas a more accurate measurement of its velocity, by definition, introduces more uncertainty as to its precise position.

Segmenting the Signal: Short Time Fourier Transform and Window Functions
One solution to this tradeoff is to divide a signal into shorter pieces, called *windows,* and to perform a *Short Time Fourier Transform (STFT)* of each window. A suitable window length must be found to provide a workable compromise, because the shorter window divides the spectrum into fewer components. Each window—representing one period of a waveform—has a higher fundamental frequency (due to its shorter wavelength) than the entire signal would have if it were to be transformed. To avoid discontinuities, windows are typically taken of overlapping segments of samples: Samples that end one window are repeated at the beginning of the next window.

Window Length and Spectral Resolution
An important factor of the STFT is the window length. Suppose a given analysis involves a 512-point FFT. Each window of 512 samples is treated as one cycle of an infinitely repeating wave. This cycle is a multiplication of the sampling period. For CD audio, the sampling period is 1/44,100 seconds. Multiplying this value by 512 produces a period of 0.01161 seconds. Chapter 2 described the frequency of a cyclic wave as the

inverse of its period. Thus, the cycle's frequency is the sampling frequency divided by the window length. In the case of a 512-point window applied to CD audio, this is:

$$\frac{44100 \ \frac{samples}{second}}{512 \ \frac{samples}{cycle}} = 86.132 \ \frac{cycles}{second}$$

This value is interpreted as the fundamental frequency of the signal. The transform produces 512 harmonics of this frequency—integer multiples of the fundamental— from 86.132 Hz to 44,100 Hz. (Recall the polar diagram that was shown in Figure 5-7. Because the sampling rate is equivalent to DC in a digital audio system, this is the same as saying that the harmonics will range from 0 Hz to 511 times the fundamental.)

The frequency components resulting directly from the transform are problematic, however, due to the practical reality that most signals contain many frequencies that are not integer multiples of 86.132 Hz. The result of these frequencies is spectral "leakage," which refers to amplitude values assigned to frequency components produced by the transform that are not actually part of the audio signal.

The leakage problem is compounded by discontinuities that appear when windows start or end in the middle of frequency cycles. These discontinuities are also interpreted as additional spectral components that further distort the results of the transform.

Window Functions

The problems of discontinuities are addressed by using blocks of samples that overlap. Rather than appearing one after the other, the ending samples of one block are the same as the beginning samples of the next block, so that the transform works with overlapping the blocks of samples. The difficulties of leakage are addressed by the use of *window functions*. These are symmetrical signals that are multiplied by each window of samples before the window is analyzed (Figure 6-3). The function begins and ends at a value of zero, or close to zero. This fades each block of samples in and out, making it

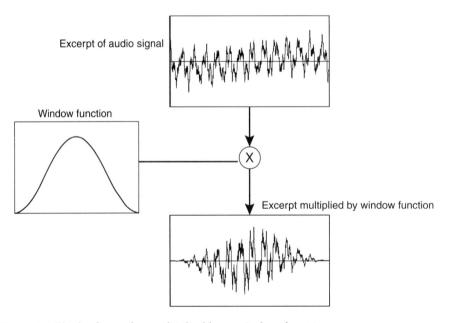

Figure 6-3 Block of samples multiplied by a window function

"appear" more periodic to the transform, resulting in an analysis that is a better approximation of the signal's actual frequency contents.

The window function is a signal as well, however, with its own spectrum. Just as the choice of camera lens can influence what is captured in a photograph, the window function also acts like a tinted lens, imposing its own spectrum on the signal excerpt's spectrum. But the function's "tint" actually acts as a kind of anchor, allowing a stronger estimation of the excerpt's spectrum to be made. Because the transform "knows" the spectrum of the window function, and it can see what comes out when the window function is multiplied by the excerpt, it can take a step backwards and estimate what the excerpt's frequencies must have been to have produced the spectrum that resulted.

There are a variety of window functions that are used in spectral transforms. A straightforward excerpting of a set of samples is called as a *rectangular window*, in that each excerpted sample is multiplied by one and all earlier and later samples are multiplied by zero. Rectangular windows are regarded as highly inaccurate, and are rarely, if ever, used. It is far more common to use a window function such as a *triangular*, *Hamming*, *hanning* or *Welch window* (the window shapes and their formulas are shown in Figure 6-4). The differences among them are subtle, and any of them is a significant improvement over a rectangular window.

Convolution

WHAT IS IT?

At heart, filtering is an example of convolution. *Convolution* is a vector operation that involves sliding one vector over another, multiplying overlapping members, and taking the sum of all multiplications. The vectors are then slid by another increment, and the process repeats.

As a real-world analogy, consider a ritual observed in junior sports leagues. After a game of soccer or tee ball, both teams display sportsmanship by lining up, with team A facing team B. Both lines walk forward, and as players pass each other, each player gives a high five to each member of the opposing team. Now, simply imagine that the players are numbers, that they advance in perfect synchronization, and that each high five is a multiplication. All high fives occur simultaneously. With each step forward, listeners hear the collective sound of all overlapping players high-fiving.

Figure 6-5 illustrates an example with two sequences, $x[n]$ and $y[n]$. The symbol "*" denotes convolution. Notice that it is the same process that was illustrated in Tables 5-1 and 5-2. We may observe two facts:

1. The process is commutative. It does not matter which sequence is reversed; the results will be the same.

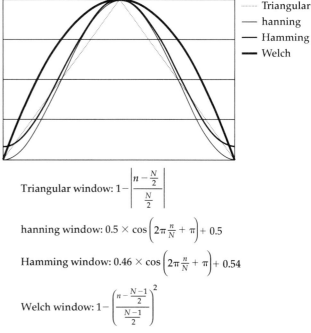

Triangular window: $1 - \left| \dfrac{n - \frac{N}{2}}{\frac{N}{2}} \right|$

hanning window: $0.5 \times \cos\left(2\pi \frac{n}{N} + \pi\right) + 0.5$

Hamming window: $0.46 \times \cos\left(2\pi \frac{n}{N} + \pi\right) + 0.54$

Welch window: $1 - \left(\dfrac{n - \frac{N-1}{2}}{\frac{N-1}{2}} \right)^2$

for a window containing N samples

Figure 6-4 Commonly used window functions

2. The length of the convolved sequence is the sum of the lengths of the two sequences, minus 1.

Figure 6-6 generalizes the process, using index values in place of numbers. If the definition of any two sequences is extended to include an infinite number of zeroes before and after the values listed, a further observation can be made:

At any time n, the output is the product of $x_m \times y_{n-m}$, for values of m that go from zero to n. This may be written in mathematical notation as follows:

$$x[n] * y[n] = \sum_{m=0}^{n} x[m] \times y[m-n] \quad n = 0, 1, 2, \ldots \qquad (6\text{-}1)$$

Note that convolving two sequences is quite a different process from multiplying two sequences. Multiplication simply involves multiplying corresponding members of two sequences to form a third sequence (it is what is done when an inner product is taken, a process described in the last section):

$$x[n] = [\, x_0, x_1, x_2, x_3, \ldots] \quad y[n] = [y_0, y_1, y_2, y_3, \ldots]$$
$$x[n] \times y[n] = [x_0 \times y_0, x_1 \times y_1, x_2 \times y_2, x_3 \times y_3, \ldots]$$

(Imagine the two junior sports league teams standing in two opposite lines, with each member giving one high five only to the facing player.)

$x\,[n] = [1, 2, 3, 4, 5\,]$

$y\,[n] = [\,6, 7, 8, 9\,]$

$x\,[n] * y\,[n] = [\,6, 19, 30, 92, 100, 94, 76, 45\,]$

Time (n)	Output	
0	$(1 \times 6) = \mathbf{6}$	$[\,6, 7, 8, 9\,]$ $[\,5, 4, 3, 2, 1\,]$
1	$(1 \times 7) + (2 \times 6) = \mathbf{19}$	$[\,6, 7, 8, 9\,]$ $[\,5, 4, 3, 2, 1\,]$
2	$(1 \times 8) + (2 \times 7) + (3 \times 6) = \mathbf{30}$	$[\,6, 7, 8, 9\,]$ $[\,5, 4, 3, 2, 1\,]$
3	$(1 \times 9) + (2 \times 8) + (3 \times 7) + (4 \times 6) = \mathbf{92}$	$[\,6, 7, 8, 9\,]$ $[\,5, 4, 3, 2, 1\,]$
4	$(2 \times 9) + (3 \times 8) + (4 \times 7) + (5 \times 6) = \mathbf{100}$	$[\,6, 7, 8, 9\,]$ $[\,5, 4, 3, 2, 1\,]$
5	$(3 \times 9) + (4 \times 8) + (5 \times 7) = \mathbf{94}$	$[\,6, 7, 8, 9\,]$ $[\,5, 4, 3, 2, 1\,]$
6	$(4 \times 9) + (5 \times 8) = \mathbf{76}$	$[\,6, 7, 8, 9\,]$ $[\,5, 4, 3, 2, 1\,]$
7	$(5 \times 9) = \mathbf{45}$	$[\,6, 7, 8, 9\,]$ $[\,5, 4, 3, 2, 1\,]$

Figure 6-5 Convolution of two sequences of numbers

$$x[n] = [\, x_0, x_1, x_2, x_3, x_4 \,]$$

$$y[n] = [\, y_0, y_1, y_2, y_3 \,]$$

Time (n)	Output	
0	$x_0 y_0$	$[\, x_4, x_3, x_2, x_1, x_0 \,]$ $[\, y_0, y_1, y_2, y_3 \,]$
1	$x_1 y_0 + x_0 y_1$	$[\, x_4, x_3, x_2, x_1, x_0 \,]$ $[\, y_0, y_1, y_2, y_3 \,]$
2	$x_2 y_0 + x_1 y_1 + x_0 y_2$	$[\, x_4, x_3, x_2, x_1, x_0 \,]$ $[\, y_0, y_1, y_2, y_3 \,]$
3	$x_3 y_0 + x_2 y_1 + x_1 y_2 + x_0 y_3$	$[\, x_4, x_3, x_2, x_1, x_0 \,]$ $[\, y_0, y_1, y_2, y_3 \,]$
4	$x_4 y_0 + x_3 y_1 + x_2 y_2 + x_1 y_3$	$[\, x_4, x_3, x_2, x_1, x_0 \,]$ $[\, y_0, y_1, y_2, y_3 \,]$
5	$x_4 y_1 + x_3 y_2 + x_2 y_3$	$[\, x_4, x_3, x_2, x_1, x_0 \,]$ $[\, y_0, y_1, y_2, y_3 \,]$
6	$x_4 y_2 + x_3 y_3$	$[\, x_4, x_3, x_2, x_1, x_0 \,]$ $[\, y_0, y_1, y_2, y_3 \,]$
7	$x_4 y_3$	$[\, x_4, x_3, x_2, x_1, x_0 \,]$ $[\, y_0, y_1, y_2, y_3 \,]$

Figure 6-6 Generalized view of the convolution process

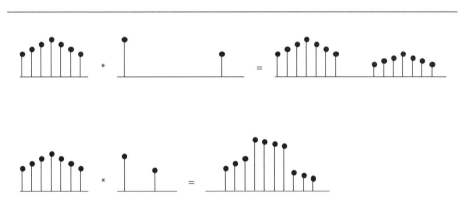

Figure 6-7 Graphic illustration of the convolution process

Figure 6-7 gives a graphic view of convolution, which suggests another interpretation, based on the results of the operation: when sequence A is convolved with sequence B, every member of sequence B produces a scaled duplication of each member of sequence A. When one sequence consists of single impulses spaced widely apart, as in the top part of the figure, the result is discrete copies of the other sequence, scaled accordingly. When the sequences are close together, as in the bottom part of the figure, the discrete copies become superimposed.

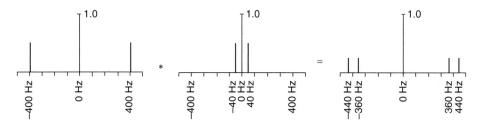

Figure 6-8 Ring modulation: spectral convolution

WHY IS CONVOLUTION IMPORTANT?

Convolution is a critical process in signal processing due to the following tenet:

When two time domain signals are multiplied, their spectra are convolved.

The converse is also true:

When two time domain signals are convolved, their spectra are multiplied.

We can demonstrate these concepts with two examples.

Time Domain Multiplication: Ring Modulation

Ring modulation is a classic analog synthesis effect in which two signals are multiplied. When translated into the domain of digital signals, ring modulation exemplifies spectral convolution. Figure 6-8 illustrates how the multiplication of two sine wave signals results in copies of a signal's spectral components, centered on and scaled by the components of another signal. Thus, a time domain multiplication results in a spectral convolution. Ring modulation will be discussed further in Chapter 8.

Time Domain Convolution: Filtering

In Chapter 5, we studied the filter difference equation (Equations 5-2 and 5-3). Recall that the values of the coefficients and their time delay determine the frequency response of the filter.

Filters are often analyzed in terms of their ***impulse response***. An impulse signal is one that consists of a single impulse with a value of one, followed by a series of values of zero:

```
[1,  0,  0,  0,...]
```

A DFT of an impulse yields a sequence of

```
[1,  1,  1,  1,  1,...]
```

Thus, the impulse response is useful because its spectrum consists of all harmonics at equal amplitude. If a spectrum consisting of all frequencies is sent into a filter, the filter may be described in terms of how it affects each spectral component of the input signal.

Finite Impulse Response (FIR) Filters and Infinite Impulse Response (IIR) Filters

A filter difference equation's set of coefficients may be considered to be a vector of scaled impulse values. An impulse signal sent into a filter results in output of exactly those coefficients (Figure 6-9). Thus, a filter's coefficients are also termed its ***impulse response***. A feedforward filter is also called a ***finite impulse response (FIR) filter***, since the output is an infinite series of zeroes after all coefficients have been multiplied by the impulse. This is not the case with a feedback filter, as was shown in Table 5-2. Because the output

Assume that a filter difference equation is:

$y[n] = 0.5\ x[n] + 0.75\ x[n{-}1] - 0.2\ x[n{-}3]$

Impulse signal = [1, 0, 0, 0 . . .]

Filter coefficients = [0.5, 0.75, 0, −0.2]

Time:　　　n　　$n{-}1$　$n{-}2$　$n{-}3$

Given an input signal of a single impulse,
the output will be the coefficients:

Time (n)	Output	
0	0.5	[. . . 0, 0, 0, 1.0] [0.5, 0.75, 0, −0.2]
1	0.75	[. . . 0, 0, 0.0, 1.00] [0.5, 0.75, 0, −0.2]
2	0	[. . . 0, 0.0, 0.00, 1] [0.5, 0.75, 0, −0.2]
3	−0.2	[. . . 0.0, 0.00, 0, 1.0] [0.5, 0.75, 0, −0.2]
4	0	[. . . 0.00, 0, 0.0, 1.0] [0.5, 0.75, 0, −0.2]
	.	
	.	
	.	

Figure 6-9 Impulse response

is constantly fed back into the filter, it theoretically could continue infinitely. Thus, a feedback filter is also called an *infinite impulse response (IIR) filter*. As was suggested in Chapter 5, care must be taken in the design of IIR filters to ensure that their coefficients produce output values of 1 or less. Otherwise, the feedback would continually output values that "blow up" as the signal recirculates endlessly and snowballs.

Spectral Shaping

The heart of filtering, then, is that an input signal is convolved with a filter's impulse response. The result, as we've discussed, is spectral shaping. That is, the spectrum of the input signal is multiplied by the spectrum of the filter's frequency response. The spectrum of each signal may also be represented as a vector of amplitude values. Corresponding spectral values of the input signal and the filter frequency response are multiplied. Thus, a time domain convolution results in a spectral multiplication.

Oversampling and Noise Shaping

Having covered the concepts of spectra and convolution, we can now examine what happens to a signal that is recorded and played back (Figure 6-10). After a signal has been lowpass filtered to remove frequencies above the Nyquist frequency, then sampled

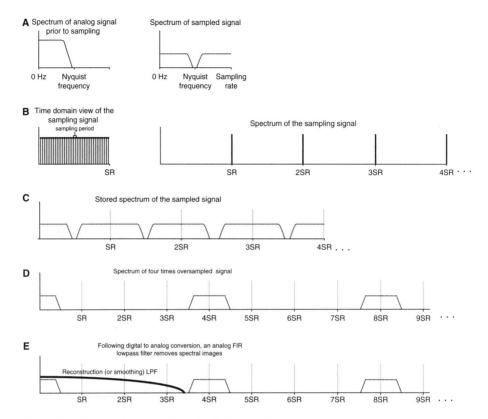

Figure 6-10 Spectral view of the digital recording process

and represented in discrete form, it has a symmetrical spectrum, as was discussed in the sections on the Digital Fourier Transform (6-10a). The sampling process effectively consists multiplication by a *sampling signal*, a series of impulses occurring at each sampling period. Each discrete value of the audio signal—that is, each value held in the sample and hold circuit—is multiplied by an impulse of the sampling signal.

The sampling signal also has a spectrum. It is the spectrum of an impulse train, which was shown in Figure 2-10 to be harmonics of the fundamental, all at equal amplitude. Therefore, the spectrum of the sampling signal consists of harmonics at multiples of the sampling rate (6-10b). Thus, the time domain multiplication of the audio signal times the sampling signal produces a spectral convolution. The result is that the stored signal consists of multiple images of the audio signal's spectrum, centered at harmonics of the sampling signal (6-10c).

At the digital-to-analog conversion stage, the output lowpass filter is tasked with removing these spectral images. With the signal of 6-10c, this would require a cutoff slope sharp enough to leave the frequencies below the Nyquist frequency unaltered. This is a considerable design restraint, as was discussed in Chapter 5 and shown in Figures 5-26 and 5-27. But the task is made feasible through the process of oversampling.

As was discussed in the section on playback in Chapter 5, oversampling is a process that places intermediate samples between the stored samples in the audio signal, with a corresponding increase in the sampling rate. This process gives a smoother rendition of the audio signal, and provides additional benefits as well. Although oversampling does not increase the frequency bandwidth of the original audio, by raising the sampling rate, it raises the Nyquist frequency accordingly and with it the spectral images of the signal (Figure 6-10d). This gives the output lowpass filter more breathing room. Following conversion to analog, a simple analog FIR lowpass filter with a flat passband and long cutoff region is sufficient to remove the spectral images (Figure 6-10e).

Another benefit of oversampling is its treatment of any quantization error noise that was introduced by the digital-to-analog conversion. This error noise is spread evenly throughout the spectrum of the signal. Because oversampling increases the signal's spectral range, the error noise is spread to higher frequencies that are inaudible and possibly removed by the lowpass filter. The redistribution of quantization error is aided by noise shaping, a term that was introduced briefly in Chapter 5. This is a processing technique described by Cutler (1960) that involves feedback, noise, quantization, and probability. Dither is added to the stored samples in the form of a small random value added to each sample. The sample with the added error is then requantized, and the difference between the original stored value and the quantized value is accumulated for each sampling period. Each sample is then combined with the error accumulated with earlier samples in such a way that the error noise undergoes highpass filtering, so that the error noise is redistributed to the high end of the spectrum, often above the audio range. Watkinson (1999) suggests the term "quantizing-error-spectrum-shaping" as an alternative to "noise shaping." It's a more accurate description, although not as catchy a term.

Oversampling, in summary, provides multiple benefits:

- It smooths the audio wave and removes spectral images.
- It also can help to reduce the noise caused by quantization error.

When the term *oversampling* is touted as a feature of a CD player or some other audio component, it typically refers to not only the oversampling plus reconstruction (or smoothing) just discussed, but also some form of noise shaping. Noise shaping also plays a role in reducing accumulated error in DSP operations, a topic that will appear in Chapter 8.

Perceptual Coding

As was discussed in Chapter 5, the sampling process creates a description of an audio waveform as accurately as possible and transmits it as a pulse code modulation (PCM) signal. The CD sampling rate and bit depth produce file sizes on the order of 10 MB/minute. Chapter 3 discussed the differences between what may be accurately measured and what may actually be perceived. The field of ***perceptual coding*** takes these measurable-perceptual disparities a step further. It involves methods designed to reduce audio file sizes by considering two questions:

1. To what degree does the auditory system perceive the complexities of an audio signal?
2. How much can be removed from signals before listeners start to notice?

In Chapter 3, we discussed how the auditory system is selective, providing an interpretation of acoustic information to the brain's processing centers. Perceptual coding data reduction techniques seek to imitate the processes of the auditory system, identifying elements that it would ignore in an acoustic wave, and eliminating these elements from the signal.

Psychoacoustics

Early work in the field of digital synthesis examined recorded instrumental sounds. Moorer and Grey (1977) described timbre studies of the violin, clarinet, oboe, and trumpet. The amplitude and frequency envelopes of trumpet partials are shown in Figure 6-11. This was one of the first thorough examinations into the behavior of individual partials over time. They found that some of the partials had quite complex amplitude fluctuations, which required extensive datasets to represent precisely. They questioned whether listeners actually needed that much information to appreciate the sound quality. They created reductions of the envelope data (also shown in Figure 6-11), and found that line segment approximations of each partial's amplitude envelope could reduce the amount of data significantly, without any great difference in perceived sonic complexity. Their work showed that a good deal of sound's natural complexity is lost on the auditory system; creating highly accurate renditions of these envelope shapes amounted to using unnecessary bandwidth for little perceptual gain.

These line segment approximation envelopes represent an early form of perceptual coding. Although it has become more sophisticated, taking into account psychoacoustics and masking, it is concerned with the same basic question: how can the data of audio signals be reduced without adversely affecting their sound quality?

Masking and Perceptual Coding

Data reduction techniques that utilize perceptual masking perform spectral analyses on blocks of samples. Low-level frequencies that would be masked by louder neighboring frequencies are treated as being less perceptually salient. This material may be eliminated, or it may be resynthesized with fewer bits when the inverse transform is performed. Although this loss of resolution necessarily leads to quantization error in these frequencies, a masking analysis model estimates how much quantization error may be masked within the critical band of louder frequencies. This allows the amount of data to be reduced through allocating bits dynamically, according to the prominence of certain frequencies within a block of samples.

Encoding Techniques

Encoding for compression makes use of the Short Time Fourier Transform. Blocks (or frames) of successive samples are analyzed and compared to a psychoacoustic model, and reductions are made where material is deemed expendable. The effectiveness of

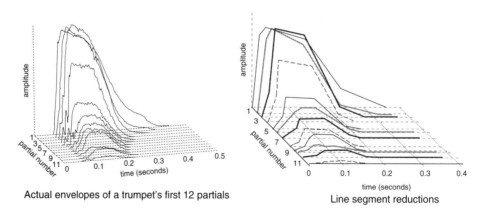

Actual envelopes of a trumpet's first 12 partials   Line segment reductions

Figure 6-11 Envelope segment reductions proposed by James Moorer and John Grey
Source: From "Lexicon of Analyzes Tones. Part 3: The Trumpet," Computer Music Journal *2.2 (Sept. 1978)*

the coding depends in large part on the size of the blocks. Any quantization distortion that results from data reduction extends over the length of a block. In a worst-case scenario, if a block contains silence followed by a transient, the added distortion may act as a pre-echo of the upcoming transient.

In *subband coding*, short blocks of samples are applied to a bank of bandpass filters. The output of each filter is then put through a spectral analysis. Comparison of the activity in each band allows the transform to make a determination of where material may be removed or rendered at lower resolution, based on its predictions of the degree to which the quantization error distortion would be masked by activity in the other bands. Subband coding tends to be strong in time localization at the expense of spectral resolution.

In *transform coding*, longer blocks of successive samples are subjected to an FFT that yields a more detailed spectral view than that of subband coding. As with subband coding, these analyses are used to make the determination of which components are likely inaudible, and which may be requantized at a coarser level. Transform coding tends to be stronger in spectral resolution and weaker in time localization.

Subband coding and transform coding are both *lossy* since, by definition, some material is lost in the compression process. *Lossless encoding* identifies periodicities in the signal, a technique known as *entropy encoding*. Rather than storing every sample of a cyclic waveform, a cycle can be identified, and the number of cycles can be encoded. This results in a smaller file than an uncompressed PCM file, but not as small as that of a lossy compression format.

In 1988, the International Organization for Standardization (ISO) and the International Electrotechnical Commission (IEC) formed the Moving Picture Experts Group (MPEG) to create standards for video and audio *codecs* (en*co*der/*dec*oders), and the distribution of compressed files. The MPEG-1 Layer III standard, more commonly known as MP3, has become the most widely used compression format in the domain of online purchasing, computers, and mobile devices.

MP3 encoding segregates the signal into thirty-two frequency bands, analyzes them according to a psychoacoustic model, removes or requantizes bits according to the model, and then reduces the file size even further through entropy encoding. There is some flexibility in its implementation: users can choose a bit rate (measured in kilobits/second, or kb/s), which defines how much material it must generate per second of content. The bit rate determines the degree of compression, and therefore lossiness, of the file.

File compression is a complex procedure, and there is no such thing as a perfect psychoacoustic model. The masking principles employed are based on statistical averages, which means that actual results may vary depending on the type of music being encoded, the playback equipment, and the listener's preferences.

In 1994, the MPEG-2 standard was introduced in order to address issues of multi-channel audio for applications such as surround cinema sound in movie theatres, HDTV broadcasts, and DVD releases of films that feature multi-channel audio. The audio component on a DVD-video disc is played over six stereo channels (five main channels and one channel for bass material; this format will be discussed further in a later section in this chapter, as well as in Chapter 8). The soundtrack is encoded with the AC-3 compression format (also known as Dolby Digital). AC-3 treats the signal dynamically. Rather than carry out a predefined form of compression on an entire signal, blocks of samples are analyzed and treated based on how active or steady the material is. Prominent spectral components are given longer word lengths, while masked components are given shorter word lengths, within distortion levels considered tolerable by the model.

In addition to AC-3's proprietary psychoacoustic model and encoding method, additional measures are taken to treat the discrete stereo channels. The channels may often be consolidated, given that material may be shared on multiple audio channels, but at different amplitudes to simulate apparent locations between speaker positions (this effect, called *phantom imaging*, will be discussed in Chapter 8). High-frequency material may also be shared on multiple channels, since the auditory system is weak at localizing high-frequency sounds (above 2 kHz or so). Thus, the redundant portions as well as the high-frequency portions of each channel may be combined into a common channel when the audio is encoded. At the decoding stage, this common channel may be sent to the five discrete channels with separate amplitude information for each. This encoding allows the six audio channels to be reduced to a size of less than one-third of what would be required for stereo PCM CD audio.

Perceptual codecs are the "better mousetrap" of audio distribution. There is always room for improvement, and work in this area is ongoing. Other common codecs include MPEG-2 Advanced Audio Coding (AAC) and Windows Media Audio (WMA). Many of these are proprietary, and only work on certain devices. Open source codecs, such as Ogg Vorbis, are popular in the open source and jamband download communities.

Approaches to Improving Audio: Compress Content or Increase Resolution?

The effectiveness of data reduction algorithms is of great interest now that digitally stored music is the norm, and recordings are often downloaded from the Internet rather than purchased as physical media. When purchasing music, customers often have a choice among a number of audio formats, including CD resolution (44.1 kHz sampling rate, 16-bit sample size), high resolution (48 or 96 kHz sampling rate, 24-bit sample size), and compressed formats.

The option of high PCM resolution may seem puzzling, given that the Nyquist frequency of these high sampling rates allows for material in the 30–40 kHz range, which is well above the oft-cited upper limit of hearing at 20 kHz. However, it should be borne in mind that this limit was determined through listening tests in which listeners reported the audibility of sine waves. The fact that sine waves may be inaudible at these frequencies does not necessarily mean that these frequencies have no effect on what we hear in concert halls or in the quality of music recordings. Many audiologists point out that this limit does not reflect actual hearing limitations, but rather limitations in the testing instruments that were used to define the upper limit of 20 kHz (Bryan and Tempest, 1970). One study in music perception involved listeners connected to EEG monitors (Oohashi et al., 1991), and compared their brain responses when listening to recordings with sampling rates of 96 kHz and 44.1 kHz. The listeners were found to have increased alpha brain wave activity during the higher-bandwidth selections.

In my own experience, I once had an opportunity to hear the two resolutions (96 kHz sampling rate/24-bit word size vs. 44.1 kHz sampling rate/16-bit word size) in an A-B comparison of the same performance of jazz music, recorded at both specifications and played over top-quality loudspeakers. There were about twenty of us in the room, and we all found the differences striking. The recordings made at the higher resolution had far greater clarity: higher instruments, such as cymbals, woodsticks, and triangles, were easier to hear, standing out from the other instruments; notes were better differentiated in fast staccato passages; there was a greater sense of localization among the instruments. We soon found ourselves waxing poetical:

- "It's like looking at the stars in the city, and then going to the country and looking at the stars when there are no city lights!"
- "It's like eating really fresh, crisp lettuce, and then eating lettuce that's a day old!"

Based on these examples, it seems that capping human frequency perception at 20 kHz may be an oversimplification. Although humans may have difficulty perceiving sine tones above 20 kHz, this appears to be only one aspect of audio perception. Frequency bandwidth is just one dimension of music. Chapter 3 discusses a number of ways in which musical perception is an emergent phenomenon, dependent on a variety of factors. There are recurring debates on some Internet mailing lists as to the nature of high-definition audio. Many assert that the key to enhanced listening lies in the increased sample size, with the greatly reduced quantization error distortion that results from using 24-bit samples. In Chapter 5, it was discussed how there is no definitive answer as to why some audiophiles prefer the sound of analog formats to digital formats. The same can be said of high-definition digital audio: to date, there is no definitive study showing why it may be superior to CD quality or compressed audio, yet people seem to know the difference when they hear it.

Thus, two approaches to audio production and transmission may be considered:

1. The high-definition audio approach involves more accurately representing the audio signal.
2. The compression approach considers masking and psychoacoustics, making a determination of material that the auditory system would disregard anyway, and removing this material.

The introduction of compressed formats in the 1990s had enormous significance for the audio industry, given their implications for transmission, storage, and commerce. They were developed through rigorous study by bodies such as the Motion Pictures Expert Group and the International Telecommunication Union, Radiocommunication Bureau (ITU-R), and described in numerous journals, conferences, and books. Readers wishing to delve further into the area may wish to begin with two entries in the References section. Brandenburg (1999) is a conference paper that offers a general introduction to the MP3 and AAC formats, while Bosi and Goldberg (2003) is longer and more thorough, providing a foundation for those wishing to create their own codecs.

The formats were introduced following numerous listening tests with strict controls to ensure consistent, reproducible conditions in all testing environments. Given the reduction in word sizes, there is a predictable risk of audible distortion, with greater degrees of distortion resulting from higher degrees of compression. In addition to quantization-related distortion, other potential artifacts include:

- Pre-Echo
  This was mentioned briefly when encoding techniques were introduced, and is related to the tradeoff between time localization and frequency resolution, which was discussed earlier in relation to the Fourier transform process. If a transient should occur within a block under analysis and adjustments are made to the quantization level as a result of it, those adjustments will be spread throughout the block, with the possible result that quantization noise that is intended to be masked by the transient may be audible before the transient takes place.
- "Birdies"
  This describes an artifact that can result from bit allocations changing from block to block for high-frequency content. The result can be a timbral change in the high frequency regions, which has been likened to a chirping sound.
- Speech Reverberation
  This artifact results from the same issues that cause pre-echo. Speech is particularly challenging to encode, given the transient nature of fricatives and plosives (sounds

such as /f/, /p/, /sh/, etc.), and the high frequency resolution required for the more tonal vowels. With large block sizes, the loss of time localization can result in a kind of "metallic reverberation" sound.

- Multi-channel Artifacts
  Sometimes stereophonic imaging can be affected by the encoding process, wherein the image appears to blur or shift over time.

Tutorials containing detailed examples of these artifacts can be heard on Erne (2001).

In formal studies such as these, the priority is on creating conditions that are reproducible and verifiable. They are held under tight, clinical conditions to ensure consistency in results among different test subjects in different places and at different times. The tests carried out by MPEG and ITU-R had strict specifications in terms of playback equipment, room acoustics, and presentation material (typically excerpts lasting a minute or less). There is a certain irony in the fact that these test conditions may not match typical everyday listening environments of a typical consumer living room. While this was considered and debated, it was ultimately determined that there was simply no way to account for the differences among consumer listening environments. The tests could not reveal anything definitive unless they were carried out under well-controlled conditions.

Thus, given the variability of musical material, playback equipment, listening room acoustics, differences between objective acoustic measurements and human perception (discussed in Chapter 3), and listener preference, it can be difficult to make definitive statements that are applicable outside the specific testing context. Further complicating things is the fact that a large key to the success of MP3 and AAC is the open nature of these standards. Anyone willing to pay a licensing fee is free to develop a codec. Thus, not all codecs are equivalent, and different codecs may produce different results with different types of music (Brandenburg, 1999). In short, the terms "MP3 quality" or "AAC quality" are not simple, generally applicable definitions.

The subject of music compression formats remains a matter of concern among producers and artists, who worry that listener appreciation of high-fidelity audio is waning. In American Academy of Arts and Sciences (2009), Jonathan Berger of Stanford University caused some consternation in the audio industry with a claim he made that was based on eight years of informal tests that he had carried out with incoming college students. He found that young listeners actually prefer the "sizzle sound" they are familiar with in compressed music to full-fidelity uncompressed music, which they are less accustomed to hearing.

A more recent study (Wilson and Fazenda, 2013) attempted to evaluate listener perception of MP3 and uncompressed audio of various music genres. It found that most listeners find bitrates below 192 kb/s to be clearly inferior to uncompressed audio, while higher bitrates of 192, 256, or 320 kb/s are often difficult to distinguish from CD audio. Perceived differences seem to depend on the type of music being heard and the listener's level of audio expertise. When differences are audible, listeners describe the compressed files as having high-frequency "metallic sounding" artifacts, reduced "clarity" for material with high-frequency content or for sharp transients such as drum hits or cymbal crashes, as well decreased dynamic range overall.

There are also any number of seasoned musicians and audio professionals who affirm, albeit anecdotally, that absolutely no one listens to compressed files for extended periods of time, the way people used to listen to a 20–30-minute side of a vinyl record (Blackmer, 2015; Giles, 2012; Keen, 2012). They claim that the fidelity of compressed music just does not stand up to extended listening sessions. Indeed, perhaps the greatest concern over most formalized listening tests is that, as a purely practical matter, listeners are typically presented with short segments of material to evaluate. It is difficult to evaluate long-term listening in a manner that is verifiable and reproducible.

The listening environment has as much to do with the listening experience as does the fidelity of the audio. Listeners who use inexpensive headphones in crowded, noisy places may not notice the effects of lossy compression as much as audiophile listeners who listen over high-end playback systems in quiet critical listening rooms. Ultimately, the bottom line is a listener's own ears. Musicians commonly perform their own listening tests to find out what differences they can hear. In the Suggested Exercises section at the end of this chapter, readers are encouraged to do similar tests on their own to see what differences they can hear among file types.

In the long run, the most important lessons that can be imparted to students in the audio field are not nuts-and-bolts techniques of how to use audio software, but rather the essential skills of audio ear training. Learning to appreciate the sound of well-mixed, well-recorded audio is a lifelong pursuit, and is a skill that can always be refined. My own informal observation is that students whose listening experience consists mostly of hearing compressed music over low-quality earbuds in noisy environments are often at a distinct disadvantage in audio production classes. Only through continually sensitizing their ears can students develop the level of critical listening that is essential for effective audio production.

Storage Media

Some students I have spoken to scoff at the idea of purchasing physical CDs. Because they tend to listen to music from computers or portable devices, they see little point in buying a physical disc, and are in the habit of purchasing music online as digital downloads. Still, physical media are not dead just yet, and they still play a role in music distribution. This section will discuss how digital information is stored on various media and how it is retrieved for playback.

Compact Disc

RETRIEVING DATA

The commercial digital music era began in 1982 with the release of the compact disc, or CD. This marked the entry into the marketplace of the *optical disc* medium, a data storage format that had been invented in 1958. Data is retrieved from an optical disc by means of a laser that shines onto the disc's surface. Binary values are stored on the disc in the form of microscopic holes, called *pits*, in its surface; the areas between the holes are called *lands*. The length of the pits and lands is variable, and it is these lengths that are encoded as binary values. The pits and lands are laid out in a spiral starting from the inner edge of the disc, as shown in Figure 6-12. If the pit track on a standard-sized audio compact disc (a diameter of 12 cm, or 4.72″) were laid out in a straight line, it would extend approximately 3.5 miles (5.6 km). (A brief housekeeping note: given the spiral layout of CD data, when cleaning compact discs it is advisable to

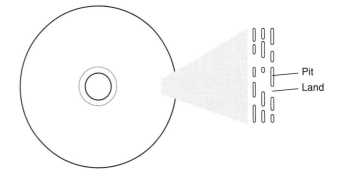

Figure 6-12 Pits and lands on the surface of a CD

use a cloth and wipe the disc in a line along the disk's radius, from the center outward. Wiping in a circular motion runs the risk of damaging consecutive data should any scratches result. A scratch along the disk's radius, over non-consecutive areas of data, may be remediable with error correction.)

A compact disc holds a maximum of 783 MB of data, allowing a playback time of 74 minutes of audio material. Some variation in the format, such as squeezing the pit/land spiral a bit tighter, allows for playback of 80 minutes or more.

The data is retrieved for playback by a fine laser beam, which is focused along the pit/land track, as shown in Figure 6-13b. The beam is reflected to an optical pickup that translates the intensity of the reflected beam to an electrical signal. The coating that covers the surface of the disc causes the laser beam to *refract*, reflecting away from the disc at an angle toward the pickup. When the beam is focused on a flat area within a pit or on a land, the wave is reflected intact. When the beam is focused at an edge between a pit and a land, part of the beam reflects from the land and part of the beam reflects from the pit. The depth of the pit is one quarter of the wavelength of the laser. Thus, the laser beam begins reflecting from the pit one-quarter wavelength later than the beam reflecting from the land; it then takes another quarter wavelength before the reflections from the pit combine with the reflections from the land. The result is that the reflections from the pit are one-half wavelength out of phase with those from the land, and the reflection is largely canceled, sending a lower-intensity reflection to the pickup. The interpretation of a binary digit depends on the intensity of the reflection reaching the pickup. Low-intensity reflections from a pit edge are translated into a digit of 1, and high-intensity reflections from a pit or land are translated into a digit of 0.

The mechanism of laser beam and electrical pickup makes the optical disc a cleaner medium than vinyl and tape. Both of these earlier media types rely on friction to generate the playback signal, which causes the media to degrade with repeated playings. On a vinyl phonograph player, a needle running over the grooves of the disc (described in Chapters 4 and 5) creates friction. Over time, the friction of the needle against the grooves causes them to dull, degrading the signal that may be played back. With a tape player (also described in Chapters 4 and 5), the friction is due to the audiotape passing over the playback head. Every time a tape is played, a small number of particles become dislodged from the tape. (Proper care of tape machines includes regularly cleaning the heads to remove these particles.) Over time, the tape loses fidelity due to the loss of particles. Optical discs, in contrast, do not produce audio by means of friction. While

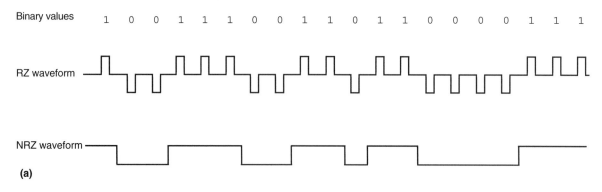

(a)

Figure 6-13 a. Comparison of RZ and NRZ encoding. b. Optical system by which data is read from compact disc via NRZI encoding

The beam reflected from a pit or a land is reflected away from it, and read as a 0.

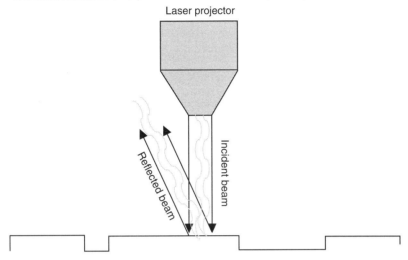

When the beam is focused on a pit edge, the reflection from the pit cancels out the reflection from the land. This is read as a 1.

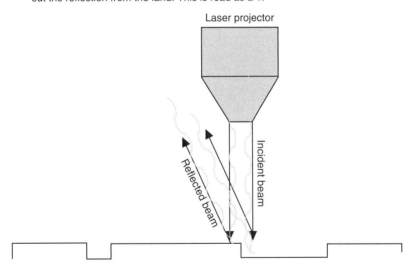

Comparison of a sequence of pits and lands, the waveform derived from the laser, and the resulting binary values.

Binary values
 1 0 0 1 0 0 0 0 1 0 0 0 1 0 0 0 0 0 1 0 0 1 0 0 1

Pits and lands on CD Surface

NRZI waveform

(b)

Figure 6-13 (Continued)

the disc material does degrade over time, playing optical discs does not involve the same level of wear and tear.

THE FORM OF THE DATA

Playback from a CD is a time-critical process. Values must be read at a constant rate, whether they are taken from the inner or the outer regions of the disc. Thus, a CD player's motor spins most quickly, at 500 rpm, when data is read from the extreme inner edge. As the laser moves outward, the spinning speed gradually slows to 200 rpm. As the laser focuses over the length of the pit/land track, its progress must be carefully clocked so that values are retrieved accurately. Timing could be a problem if a long series of the same digit had to be reproduced. The laser tracker would have to be extremely accurate across a long land or pit region to transmit the beginnings and ends of bits accurately. To ease demands on the tracker, the stored data values—audio samples and the associated bookkeeping described in Chapter 5 (multiplexing, error correction and subcode)—are encoded to ensure that transitions between the two binary digits occur regularly. The encoding vocabulary is structured to ensure the tracker's timing accuracy.

Timing accuracy in reading binary numbers is critical in all computing and telemetry, and channel coding methods have evolved along with the hardware technology. Early computers, which saved data to magnetic tape, used *Return to Zero (RZ) encoding* (Figure 6-13a). Each bit was encoded by changes between three voltage levels: high, low, and zero (which fell between high and low). A change from zero to high level indicated a bit of 1, a change from zero to low level indicated a bit of 0. After the voltage change, the voltage was reset to a value of zero until the next bit was recorded. This meant that there were two voltage changes per bit: a positive change followed by a negative change indicated a 1 (first up and then back down to zero again), while a negative change followed by a positive change indicated a 0 (first down then back up to zero again). These transitions meant that this method was *self-clocking*, because every data-reading increment was clearly marked by these two voltage changes. However, all these transitions were inefficient, produced a high signal-to-noise ratio, and the neutral state between bits made it impossible to overwrite data onto the tape.

Non–Return to Zero (NRZ) encoding was more efficient in that there were only two levels used, positive and negative. The voltage did not return to a neutral (zero) state between bits, but stayed where it was, either high or low. It only changed when the bits changed value. A stream of bits with a value of 1 would have a constant positive value, while a stream of bits with a value of 0 would have a constant negative value. The problem with this method was that if a bit were missed due to an error, all subsequent voltage levels would be the opposite value of the data bits.

Non–Return to Zero Inverted (NRZI) encoding does not associate bit values of 1 and 0 with high and low voltage, respectively. Instead, a value of 1 inverts the voltage, while a value of 0 keeps it at its present level. Thus, a series of bits with a value of 1 produces voltage changes that alternate between high and low, while a series of bits with a value of 0 produces a constant voltage at either high or low level, depending on the result of the last transition produced by a bit of 1. Because this encoding, like NRZ encoding, can produce a series of bits that all have the same corresponding voltage value, they are not self-clocking.

NRZI encoding is used on CDs, as shown in Figure 6-13b. Since NRZI is not self-clocking, the bits need to be encoded in such a way that transitions occur with some frequency to avoid clock drift. As described in Chapter 5, the samples are grouped in frames. Each frame contains 16 samples, 8 for each channel. At the encoding stage, the values are split into 8-bit bytes and interleaved for purposes of error correction. To achieve timing accuracy from regular bit transitions, each 8-bit byte is translated into a 14-bit byte that meets the following two conditions:

1. Successive digits of 1 must be separated by at least two digits of 0.
2. There can never be more than 10 consecutive 0 digits.

Each of the 256 possible 8-bit binary numbers is translated into a 14-bit binary number that meets these two criteria. The translation is done with a simple lookup table, wherein each possible 8-bit value has a 14-bit counterpart.

In order to ensure that successive bytes of data do not violate these rules (for example, if a particular byte ends with a 1, and is followed by a byte that begins with a 1), three extra bits are placed between each 14-bit word. These extra bits are calculated on a byte-by-byte basis to ensure that the bit sequence follows the encoding conditions and that the average number of high and low values in the resulting NRZI waveform maintains a balance between the high and low levels.

Thus, every 8 bits of data from the original audio is represented by 17 bits of data encoded on the CD. The increased number of stored bits means that, on playback, bits must be read at a rate much faster than the sampling rate: 17-bit values must be translated back into 8-bit values, checked for error, reassembled, reordered, and still produce audio samples at a rate of 44,100 per second.

CD Recorders

A CD recorder stores data on a disc by melting pit and land patterns into its surface. A write-once (WO) recorder can perform this process only one time. A read-write (RW) recorder has the capability to erase a CD's data by smoothing the surface with heat, after which the disc may have new pit/land patterns imprinted.

DVD

The DVD disc is the same size as the CD, but was created for larger-capacity storage of video and audio material for film and multimedia releases. The abbreviation "DVD" originally stood for "digital video disc," which was modified to "digital versatile disc," and now does not actually stand for anything. The DVD format offered improvements over two earlier video storage formats.

The laser disc succeeded videotape as a medium for storing multimedia. With a twelve-inch diameter, these were the same size as vinyl records. This format was particularly popular for opera releases. But its video content, although at a definition that was superior to that of VHS video tapes, was still in analog form. This made the video incompatible with computer-based storage and editing.

The video compact disc (VCD) allowed films to be stored digitally onto CDs, although at decreased visual resolution. This format was particularly popular in Asian countries.

DVD is intended to store both audio and visual material at high digital resolution. Although identical in dimensions to the compact disc, a more compact pit/land track and a more focused laser provide a storage capacity of 4.7 GB, allowing storage of 120 to 135 minutes of high-quality audio and video. DVD players are backward compatible. Its narrow laser can easily fit into the larger pit-land track of audio CDs, allowing DVD players to play both disc types.

In addition to high-quality video, DVDs are designed to store stereo CD-quality audio in 5.1 channels, via Dolby Digital encoding. This is the stereo format used in cinema and high-definition television (HDTV), and will be described more fully in Chapter 8.

Super Audio CD (SACD)

While the vast majority of commercial digital audio hardware and software was created to use PCM formatted samples, there are, in fact, other ways of digitizing analog information. In the late 1990s, the Philips and Sony corporations, which had created the original PCM format for CD audio, created the SACD format to improve on the 44.1 kHz sampling rate and 16-bit resolution of PCM storage. SACD relies on a format known as Direct Stream Digital® (DSD®). An alternative method of storing values is used, called *delta-sigma encoding* (or *sigma-delta encoding*). The DSD delta-sigma recording utilizes a sampling rate of 64 times the CD sampling rate (2.8224 MHz) and a word size of one bit. The single bit at each sampling interval functions as a sign bit: a digit of 1 means that the audio wave ascends, and a digit of 0 means that the wave descends (Figure 6-14). Each digit is sent to an *integrator* that keeps a running total of the sample level. At each sampling period, the audio level is compared to the level stored in the integrator. If the audio level is above the integrator level, a value of 1 is output. If the audio level is below the integrator level, a value of 0 is output. With sharp increases or decreases, an ascending wave produces a stream of the value 1, and a descending wave produces a stream of the value 0. A wave that remains at a constant level is approximated with each sampling period: the integrator value is alternately above and below the audio level, producing alternating values of 1 and 0. Thus, the density of the pulses represents the shape of the wave. This type of encoding is also known as *pulse density modulation (PDM).*

PDM has inherently less noise than PCM because it does not require as many filtering steps. As discussed in Chapter 5, successful PCM recording relies on ensuring that an audio wave is sampled at its peak and its trough, with an analog lowpass filter ensuring that the sampled signal's bandwidth is within the Nyquist frequency. When the samples are played, another analog lowpass filter is required to smooth the staircase wave that is constructed from the stored samples. Analog processing always adds some degree of noise. But these filtering steps are not necessary with the PDM format, which does not have a Nyquist frequency and the associated concern with aliasing. This

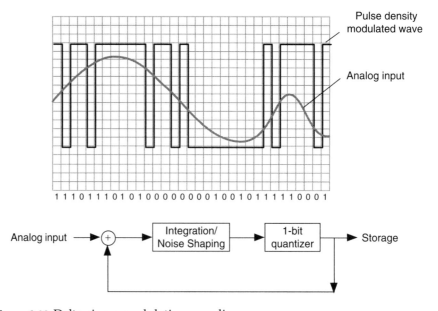

Figure 6-14 Delta-sigma modulation sampling

reconsideration of the sampling process eliminates the need for the analog filtering stages and their added noise levels. The single-bit resolution does have the potential for greater error than PCM recording, but advanced noise shaping processes are employed to push the error noise above the audible frequency ranges. PDM is distinguished by the fact that all processing is all done in the digital domain, so the noise acquired in the analog processing stages of PCM conversions is not a factor.

SACDs offer increased *dynamic range* (the difference between the loudest and softest levels) and frequency response. With the established market base of PCM-based products, SACDs are directed at a niche user base. While not a widespread commercial success, they remain a presence within the audiophile community.

DVD-Audio

This was another niche audiophile format that was in competition with the SACD format beginning in 2000 until 2007, when it became inactive. It was based on a PCM format, but at higher specifications than audio CDs, with a sampling rate of 96 kHz and 24-bit sample size. It was meant to bring DVD audio quality to a level that matched the highest quality vinyl and tape audio.

High Definition Compatible Digital (HDCD)

This PCM format works with audio at CD specifications, but it employs custom dither and noise shaping techniques to deliver 20-bit resolution within the 16 bits of PCM audio. Discs in this format are playable in standard CD players, although an HDCD player is required for full fidelity.

Blu-ray

The Blu-ray format was designed to produce video resolution superior to what was possible on DVD-formatted discs. It has greater storage capacity due to a pit/land track that is denser than a DVD pit/land track. Its name is derived from the fact that a blue laser is used to read the track; this is the higher-frequency end of the color spectrum, which has a shorter wavelength than the red laser used to read DVDs and CDs. Its greater data capacity enables increased pixel resolution of the imagery, and displays the video material at a faster frame rate than that found on DVDs. Depending on the player used, the audio tracks may be decoded into a variety of digital formats, at various sampling rates, word sizes, and numbers of stereo channels.

Hard-Disk Recording: The Convergence of Multimedia

Digital Workstations

As the price of computer memory storage drops and processor speeds rise, computer hard drives have become increasingly common as a storage medium for large video and audio files. Recording is easily done through small recorders that can store high-fidelity PCM audio, which can then be easily transferred to a computer editing system. It is also common to record directly to computer. Because new storage/playback media appear every few years, long-term storage on computer hard drives has a greater chance for longevity than archiving material onto media such as optical discs.

Digital audio editors, such as the one shown in Figure 6-15, typically work with an interface similar to an analog tape deck. More advanced programs are *Digital Audio Workstations (DAWs),* which function as complete studio environments. DAWs will be discussed more fully in Chapter 10.

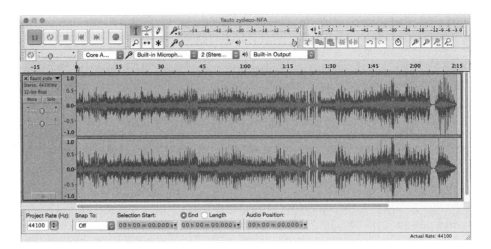

Figure 6-15 Digital audio editing software
*Source: Audacity® software is copyright © 1999–2015 Audacity Team. Website: http://
audacityteam.org. It is free software distributed under the terms of the GNU General
Public License. The name Audacity® is a registered trademark of Dominic Mazzoni*

Hard-disk recording offers the advantages of ***random access***: the ability to jump
instantly to any point in an audio file without having to fast-forward or rewind, as is the
case with tape. Random access allows extreme flexibility in editing. Audio may be cut
and pasted as easily as text is manipulated in a word-processing program. Volume and
stereo pan controls may be automated, typically by drawing an envelope over a graphic
of the track's waveform. Crossfades may be specified between two audio segments on
the same track, allowing separate sound elements to be integrated seamlessly.

The digital editing environment represented a marked departure from the analog
environment of tape, where use of the same audio required physically copying a section
of tape, and arranging separately recorded material required razor-blade editing. Once
the tape had been cut, there was no turning back—it could be reconnected, but it
wouldn't sound quite the same. In a software environment, all edits are ***nondestructive***, as the original audio files are not affected by the operation. A splice or a crossfade
may be undone without affecting the audio data. Different versions of the same operation may be stored in memory before a final selection is made.

The capabilities of digital music programs are made expandable via ***plug-ins***,
which are specialized software modules that may be used in conjunction with a larger
program to perform processing operations. For example, while most audio editors come
bundled with a number of effects, it is often possible to expand one's collection of
processing capabilities with separately purchased plug-ins. Many plug-ins are also
available in the form of apps for mobile devices such as smartphones and tablets.
(Effects will be covered in detail in Chapter 8.)

Transferring Data Between Devices

Digital information may be transferred among storage devices directly, without analog
conversion, through three PCM or transmission protocols: ***S/PDIF, AES/EBU***, and
Lightpipe.

S/PDIF (Sony/Philips Digital InterFace) transmits two channels of digital audio,
and can also transmit extra information to allow copy protection in some devices, enabling producers of material to build in prohibitions against copying. This is the type of

transmission often used on consumer-grade equipment, typically transmitted over RCA cables (such as those used in home stereo systems to connect devices to the amplifier) or over fiber optic cable with TOSLINK connectors.

AES/EBU (Audio Engineering Society and European Broadcasting Union) is another two-channel transmission format. The physical connection is usually via a three-pin balanced connector, the same type used for professional microphones (see Figure 4-11). This is meant to be the "professional grade" format, capable of transmission over long distances (up to 100 meters, or longer if extra processing "boosts" the signal along the way) and lower in *jitter* (signal irregularity) than S/PDIF.

Lightpipe is also transmitted over fiber optic cables and TOSLINK connectors, and is meant for multi-channel transmission. A single cable can send eight channels of 24-bit audio at a sampling rate of 48 kHz. With some extensions, higher resolution may be used, transmitted over fewer channels.

Transferring data among devices is a synchronized procedure. Steps must be taken to ensure that bit start and stop times in the sending device match the bit start and stop times in the receiver. The source device must be placed into a mode that defines it as the clock master, and all receiving devices must be placed into a slave mode, with the clock source determined by the input format, which needs to be set to match the format of the data originating from the source device. A common error is to accidentally keep a receiving device on an internal clock mode (as would be appropriate when recording an analog signal), which can result in distortion due to mismatches between the sender's and receiver's bit start and end times.

Audio File Types

Audio files come in a number of flavors. Some of the more common file types are described below. The differences among them are attributable to differences in storage and processing requirements for different computer platforms. To some extent they are interchangeable, and it is usually an easy matter to convert a file to another format. Most DAWs and audio editors can convert file types via a **Save As . . .** or **Export . . .** command. For example, different formats may store samples within different number ranges, in which case converting to the other format involves multiplications on each sample, a process that takes place "under the hood." There may also be bookkeeping differences among file types. The various formats are differentiated by a header portion of the file that precedes the actual sample values. Some file types are composed of a series of different header subdivisions, known as "chunks." The header(s) give information about the file, such as the sampling rate, sample size, or number of stereo channels. Therefore, converting from one file type to another involves altering the header information as well as converting the sample values.

NeXT/SUN

NeXT/Sun is the earliest audio file format type and was intended for Unix computers, primarily for voice files and telephone transmission. These files can typically be identified by the extension ".au" or ".snd." Four sampling rates are supported: 8, 8.012, 22.05, and 44.1 kHz, although the lower rates are more common. Files of this type are likely to be legacy, and not often used in high-resolution multimedia projects. However, historical sound files may be found that are of interest even if they are of low fidelity, just as aged, grainy photographs may be valuable in certain video projects.

AIFF

AIFF (Audio Interchange File Format) is a format native to Macintosh and SGI platforms, and was created as part of these companies' mission to provide platforms for high-quality multimedia work. These files can be recognized by the extension ".aiff" or ".aif." AIFF stores stereo channels in interleaved format, which means that samples are transmitted serially, with alternating samples belonging to different channels. For example, in a two-channel file, the samples will follow a succession of

[(sample n, left), (sample n, right), (sample $n + 1$, left), (sample $n + 1$, right), . . .]

Each set of successive of samples that is to be played simultaneously on different channels is termed a *sample frame*. The file header contains information about the size of the file, the number of channels, sample rate, sample size, and the number of samples contained in the file. The samples are stored as two-byte integer values, with the most significant byte listed first ("big endian"). AIFF can also support high-resolution files with 24- or 32-bit sample sizes, and sampling rates higher than 44.1 kHz.

The AIFF format was designed to work with uncompressed PCM audio. A modification of the format, AIFF-C (which may have the extension ".aifc"), also supports compressed audio formats. When a compression format type is used, it is identified in one of the header chunks. When Apple created its OSX operating system, it also created a "little-endian" version of the AIFF format, which means that the least significant byte is stored first. Because little endian is not supported in the original AIFF specification, a "dummy" compression format is used to accommodate the little-endian byte order. The difference between the two byte formats is rarely of any consequence to a user; the only time it may come up would be if an older audio program could not read a file in the new format. In this case, a simple conversion would take care of the problem.

AIFF can store loop point markers, which allows them to be used in sampling instruments (samplers will be discussed further in Chapter 10). Information about up to two loop points may be stored in a file. Typically, the loop points represent the steady-state portion of an audio wave, so that the samples between the loop points may be repeated until the note is released.

SDII

SDII (Sound Designer II) files are also native to Macintosh computers, and typically are named with the extension ".sdii." SDII originated from the digital editing program Sound Designer, one of the first audio editors created for the personal computer. Unlike the interleaved format of AIFF, SDII files are "split stereo," which means that stereo channels are stored as separate files that are played simultaneously. Information about the file is also kept separate from the audio samples, rather than in a chunk that must precede them. SDII files are thus less fixed in form than AIFF files and may be more suited to some DAW environments, particularly if the file is meant to be extended through additional recording. Many such programs convert AIFF files to SDII files when they are imported.

WAVE

The RIFF WAVE (Resource Interchange File Format Waveform) was created by Microsoft and is native to Intel platforms (Windows machines). Files are often named with the extension ".wav" and have a structure similar to an AIFF file, with added bookkeeping to aid in buffering samples in advance of playback and minor differences in data storage, such as storing 2-byte sample values with the least significant byte listed first ("little endian"). As is the case with the AIFF format, samples are stored as integers, and like AIFC files, the RIFF WAVE specification also allows for a variety of compression types. WAVE can also support high-resolution files with 24- or 32-bit sample sizes, and high sampling rates. WAVE files may also be embedded with metadata according to the

Audio Definition Model (EBU 3364), which describes spatialization data, such as number of "objects" (instruments or other entities) in an audio file and where they should be placed in a stereo field, and how many channels should be rendered.

CAF

The *Core Audio Format (CAF)*, invented by Apple in 2005, was created to provide greater levels of flexibility than were part of the AIFF specification. While the AIFF and WAVE formats have a file size limit of 4 GB, CAF files have no file size restrictions. They also offer a safer method of recording in that the file header's size field does not need to be updated after a recording is completed. With WAVE or AIFF files, a file can be rendered unusable if there is an error in updating the size field after a recording. With the CAF format, a recording may be appended without the size field being updated. CAF can serve as a generalized wrapper for many types of audio file formats, in a manner that is similar to QuickTime's ability to play multiple media formats. CAF files can also store extra data, such as text annotations, markers, or channel layouts.

Video Streaming and Networked Music

Since 2006 or so, many performance companies have come to rely on Internet broadcasting to reach larger audiences. Internet broadcasting may be done on many scales. At the low end, a smartphone or tablet device might send a low-fidelity, monophonic transmission to a performer's family member in a distant location. At the high end, organizations such as the Metropolitan Opera's *Live in HD* series, London's *National Theatre Live*, or sold-out stadium concerts can send high-definition broadcasts to theaters that are contracted to serve as venues. These facilities need to be equipped with digital projection systems, satellite connections, and surround sound audio, and are meant to be the "next best thing to being there." Some commentators have noted that high-definition opera broadcasts are actually changing the nature of performance, as singers are becoming accustomed to adapting to close-up shots, which affects the way they perform.

Between the low and high ends of the Internet broadcast spectrum, there is no particular standard. Colleges and universities put together systems that fit their needs and their budgets, making performances available to family, prospective students, and alumni who have Internet connections and personal computers. While configurations vary, a basic setup is outlined in Figure 6-16. While video cameras typically come equipped with microphones, when streaming music events it is generally preferable to use professional microphones meant for music recording (microphones will be discussed in Chapter 7). The video camera's microphone is likely to be of lower fidelity than those used in concert recording; furthermore, the camera may be at a distant spot from the stage, and its microphone signal may be weak as a result. While a distant visual view may be tolerable, a "distant" aural perspective is likely to be unsatisfying. Therefore, a set of microphones is combined at a mixer, the output of which is sent to the audio input jack of the camera, overriding the camera's microphone signal. Sending the audio directly to the camera ensures that the audio is synchronized with the video. The audio and video are then digitized in a video capture unit, then sent to the Internet via a computer, and on to a video streaming service.

Streaming refers to a computer receiving a continuous signal and buffering it (see the description of buffering in the Digital Playback section of Chapter 5). The storage buffer allows the material to be rendered as it arrives and then discarded, leaving room

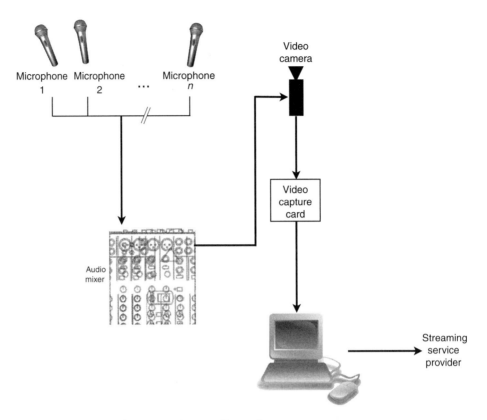

Figure 6-16 Basic video streaming configuration

in the buffer for more incoming material. When streaming is successful, the buffer is able to gather material faster than it needs to render it, so that viewers are treated to continuous playback. When it is unsuccessful, the buffer is unable to store the new information fast enough, and the content is stopped during playback while the buffer is filled. Streaming is increasingly being used for all kinds of multimedia content. Whereas people used to rent films on video or DVD, it is now more common to subscribe to a streaming service of some kind, which makes a variety of film, television, or music selections available for on-demand viewing/listening.

Institutions that are entering the concert streaming arena have to create a hardware/software system that suits their budget. Part of this process involves choosing a streaming service. There are a variety of streaming services available, and they are chosen based on price, broadcast quality and speed, whether or not ads are displayed, and the capability of additional material such as graphics or program information being displayed. Some services, for example, may allow other pre-recorded material, such as historical information or interviews with the artists, to be played during intermission, while others may only be able to transmit a single signal from the video camera, which leaves "dead time" during intermission periods.

Expansions to a basic configuration shown in Figure 6-16 may include multiple cameras, in which case they are connected to a video switcher, which allows the program director to switch camera angles during the broadcast. Another consideration is whether the performance is meant to be archived. Some cameras can store material onto a memory card. Alternatively, the computer may store the file, although often it is best to minimize the number of tasks the computer is performing to ensure that the transmission to the Internet is stable. Producers of higher-fidelity broadcasts may not use a computer at all, opting instead to use a dedicated hardware encoder.

The encoding and uploading processes necessarily introduce some degree of delay, and a tradeoff needs to be made between a broadcast's stability and its delay time. A concert stream may prioritize signal stability, and a delay of 30–45 seconds may be perfectly acceptable. But for a master class that involves interaction, whereby viewers may post questions, a delay of this length would be unworkable; in this case, faster transmission, even at risk of dropouts, would be preferred.

A balance must also be struck between encoding methods for the video and audio material. On the one hand, the ear has a greater degree of time resolution than do the eyes. Loss of an occasional video frame may be tolerable, while loss of an audio frame would be unacceptable. On the other hand, viewers are accustomed to high-quality video broadcasts, and they may find degraded images or single camera broadcasts to be unacceptable, regardless of audio fidelity.

An area related to concert streaming is *networked music* (also called *distributed creativity*) events, which feature musicians in different locations who are playing together by means of high-speed, high-bandwidth Internet connections. This is an area of active research and an emerging performance practice. While transmission latency was once a challenge in realizing such performances, this problem has largely been solved. At this writing, the challenges tend to be about coordinating studios in different places, as well as lack of performance intimacy (it can be somewhat alienating to perform with someone when eye contact is impossible). However, those who regularly perform networked music remark that the experience can be quite sublime: when a performer in Calgary is able to entrain with a performer in Beijing, there is a different type of performer intimacy that arises that serves to emphasize the innovations of our digital age (Cayko, 2015).

There are some who have developed *Digital Presence Workstations*, an analog to the Digital Audio Workstation, which serve as control panels that show an overview of a musical network. Other practitioners focus on the challenges of performances that involve some degree of inherent latency. Some solutions include creating a delay to an incoming signal so that it matches a particular beat resolution—rather than there being a delay of some number of millliseconds, which may vary, the receiving computer can simply add enough delay to ensure that there is an offset of a quarter note, eighth note, or some other subdivision. What this implies is that one piece actually exists in numerous forms: there is the version that is played by a performer, and there is the version that is translated by the network, which may vary from performance to performance.

Networked music brings to mind the challenges faced by cathedral organists, who must adapt to the delay between the time at which they depress a key and the resulting sound, which comes from distant pipes. In a similar sense, networked music is an idiosyncratic practice, with its own unique challenges. Many musicians find it compelling because of the technical, musical, and philosophical questions it raises as to the nature of performance, ensemble playing, and listening awareness.

Suggested Exercises

• Using a spectral analysis application such as SoundHack (soundhack.com), experiment with convolving two files. Remember, convolution is a kind of spectral crossbreeding of two sounds. It's easy to do, and you never really know what will come out until you try it, so enjoy the surprises this brings. A few things can be predicted, however. Curtis Roads outlines some general principles in *Microsound* (2004). If either source has a long, smooth attack, the convolved file will too. If the sounds are pitched and long in duration, the convolved file will have both pitches and both spectra intermingled in a way that is more than just simply mixing the two. Convolving an audio file with a series of impulsive sounds (such as a woodblock) will create echo effects. If one of the sounds is an impulsive sound that has a decaying envelope, such as a plucked string, the result can be a reverberation-like effect. If the envelope is reversed, such as using a plucked string played in reverse, the convolution will sound as though it is played in reverse as well. Combining a long and a short sound can give the impression of fictional instruments, such as a harpsichord playing a gong.

- What can you hear if you save an audio file in a variety of compression formats and rates? What is lost in the lossy formats? What differences can you find if you listen to the same piece of music in different formats? Perform some of your own informal tests with different types of material and different formats and try to describe the differences you hear. Your descriptions will not be definitive or necessarily reproducible, but they will be a critical step in your own ear training. An example of an informal listening report is below.

Informal Listening Report Comparing PCM, AAC, and MP3 Audio Using Apple's iTunes software, I created three compressed versions of two audio files—AAC (300 kb/s), and two different levels of MP3 compression (192 kb/s and 128 kb/s). One file was the Maestoso/Allegro movement of Beethoven's *Piano Sonata No. 32, Opus 111*, played by Einar Henning Smebye (1987, Norwegian Music Productions ARCD 1911). The other was the song "Ripple," recorded by the Grateful Dead (1970, Warner Brothers Records Inc. WS1893, 2001 HDCD reissue on Rhino Entertainment Company R2 74397). I used the Max/MSP programming environment (which will be described further in Chapters 10 and 11) to create an interface that played all four versions of each selection (uncompressed and three compressed) simultaneously, with one version at a time being sent to the audio output while the other three played silently. A set of radio buttons allowed a user to instantly switch between the four formats at will. I listened over a set of Bose QuietComfort2 headphones, a set of custom-built desktop speakers, and also played them for a class of students over a pair of QSC K8 loudspeakers. With both recordings, there were audible differences between PCM and compressed versions, and subtle differences between the compression formats. When switching from the PCM to a compressed version, the "shine" on the reverberation became a bit muffled. (The subject of reverberation and the overall "acoustic signature" will be discussed in Chapter 7.) It was difficult to hear differences between the AAC and 192 kbps MP3 versions. The 128 kbps MP3 versions sounded "fuzzier," less crisp with the transients of plucked strings and piano tones. The fuzziness may be due to larger window sizes used in the spectral transform, which would remove some of the precision of the transients. This was particularly evident in a passage from the Beethoven sonata that consisted of quick, growly runs in the bass, which sounded noticeably less defined in the lower-resolution MP3 version. More noticeable (and surprising) was a change in stereo imaging, particularly on the recording of "Ripple," which features vocals, guitars, mandolin, and soft percussion. With the uncompressed recording, it sounded as though the singer and lead instruments were farther front than the supporting instruments. In the compressed versions, the aural image became flattened, as though everything were the same distance from me as a listener, with more obvious signals from each of the loudspeakers. It was as though the process of compression provided a remix of the song. In the short term, it appeared that the compressed version favored some of the supporting instruments. Over time, however, the compressed files seemed less nuanced. The supporting instruments were still audible in the PCM version, but not as "in your face." The uncompressed version seemed to invite more focused listening. With attention, background instruments gradually emerged and the listening experience became increasingly immersive. But in a less optimal listening environment, such as earbuds on public transportation or as background music in a crowded party or bar, the supporting instruments would likely have been inaudible and the compressed versions would have provided more of the sound world.

Key Terms

basis set
AES/EBU transfer protocol
codecs
convolution
Core Audio Format (CAF)
DC content or DC offset
delta-sigma encoding (or sigma-delta encoding)
Digital Audio Workstations (DAWs)
Digital Presence Workstations
Discrete Fourier Transform (DFT)
dynamic range
entropy encoding
Fast Fourier Transform (FFT)
finite impulse response (FIR) filter
Hamming window
hanning window
impulse response
infinite impulse response (IIR) filter
inner product
integrator
jitter
lands
Lightpipe transfer protocol
lossless encoding
lossy
networked music or distributed creativity
nondestructive editing
Non–Return to Zero (NRZ) encoding
Non–Return to Zero Inverted (NRZI) encoding
nonstationary signal
optical disc
orthogonal
perceptual coding
pits
plug-in
pulse density modulation (PDM)
random access
rectangular window
refraction
Return to Zero (RZ) encoding
ring modulation
sample frame
sampling signal
self-clocking
Short Time Fourier Transform (STFT)
S/PDIF transfer protocol
stationary signal
streaming
subband coding
time localization
transform coding
triangular window
uncertainty principle
Welch window
window
window function

Chapter 7

Acoustic Signatures: Room Acoustics, Microphones, and Loudspeakers

When we hear a recording of an instrument being played, such as a violin, we are hearing more than just the instrument. We are hearing the violin, played within a particular space, recorded by a particular type of microphone, produced in a studio with audio processing equipment, and played over a particular set of loudspeakers. All these factors combine to create the sound that reaches our ears, which is designed to suit a particular musical context. I suggest referring to this combination of factors as the final recording's *acoustic signature* (Levitin [2007, p. 156] similarly refers to recordings' "overall sound," "sonic color," or "timbral quality").

The next two chapters will cover the stages of the music production process:

1. A musical performance in a particular venue is captured with a microphone (or multiple microphones).
2. Microphone signals are directed to a mixer. Each signal goes to a particular channel of the mixer. The various channels are adjusted so that their relative volumes are compatible. Filtering and other effects may be added at this stage. The mixing and processing may be hardware-based, software-based, or a combination of the two.
3. The mixed signal is output to loudspeakers, which allow us to hear it.

The discussion of psychoacoustics in Chapter 3 showed that the auditory system does not provide an objective representation of acoustic events, but rather an interpretation of them. The same may be said of the equipment involved in each of these steps. Microphones, audio processing equipment, and loudspeakers all color the sound in some way. Sometimes the coloration is subtle, other times it is overt. Understanding this coloration, and learning how to use it, is the basis of the art of audio production.

This chapter will cover the beginning and end of the chain: microphones and loudspeakers, which in many ways are mirror images of each other. The steps in between, where the audio is mixed and processed, will be covered in Chapter 8.

Room Acoustics

Direct and Reflected Sound

Chapters 1 and 2 discussed physical principles of acoustics as they relate to music. Now the subject of acoustics will be explored in an architectural context: how performance/recording spaces treat acoustic energy. The performance space is inseparable from the musical material performed within it, as both combine to create the listener's impression. If music is analogous to a painting, the acoustic characteristics of the performance space are analogous to the canvas, lighting, frame, and the way it is hung in a gallery space.

All rooms have a characteristic sound (a filtering effect) that is a combination of *direct sound* and *reflected sound*. Direct sound refers to acoustic energy travelling directly from the sound source (instrument) to the listener. Reflected sound refers to acoustic energy interacting with the boundaries of the performance space and the objects within it.

The balance between the two depends on the listener's position in the room. Direct sound attenuates with distance according to the inverse square law, as shown in Chapter 2 (Equation 2-11). Given the quick drop in the intensity of direct sound with distance, at greater distances there is a much higher proportion of reflected sound. A room's treatment of reflected sound depends on its size, shape, wall and ceiling treatment, and the presence or absence of objects within the room. Acoustic reflections within a performance space filter the sound propagating within it.

The nature of "room filtering" differs somewhat between large and small performance spaces, so the two will be discussed separately.

Large Performance Spaces

Sound propagation in large spaces is often described in three stages:

1. Direct sound
2. *Early reflections*
3. *Diffuse reverberation*

DIRECT SOUND

As described above, direct sound refers to wavefronts that travel directly from the source to the listener. Because direct wavefronts travel in a straight line to reach the listener, they have a shorter travel path than wavefronts that reflect from a surface before reaching to the listener. The first wavefront to reach the ear defines the sound's location to the auditory system, even if it is low in intensity. However faint the the first wavefront may be compared to subsequent reflections arriving from different directions, the wavefront that makes the first impression on the ear provides the localization cue, a phenomenon known as the *precedence effect*.

EARLY REFLECTIONS

Early reflections, or first-order reflections, refer to wavefronts that reach the listener after reflecting once from the floor, ceiling, walls, or furniture. Their role in sound perception depends on the amount of delay between direct sound and early reflections. (Delay times will be discussed further in Chapter 8.) Early reflections arriving within 35 ms of the first wavefront have been found to reinforce the direct sound, adding to its clarity and intelligibility. Longer first-reflection times are due to greater distances from source to listener. Therefore, besides providing a sense of reinforcement and added clarity, first-order reflections are also a cue by which the auditory system makes a judgment of a room's size.

Depending on the dimensions of a concert hall, first-order reflections are most likely to come from the walls, although seats located near the auditorium center may receive first reflections from the ceiling. In especially large halls, suspended reflectors are often installed with the intention of providing early reflections to center seats.

DIFFUSE REVERBERATION

Diffuse reverberation refers to second- (and higher-) order reflections. As first-order reflections continue to bounce around the room, reflecting off of its surfaces, they create a wash of sound that eventually dies down as the sound's energy is absorbed by the walls, ceiling, and objects in the room. The *reverberation time* refers to the length of time it takes for the sound pressure level to drop 60 dB ($1/2^{10}$, or approximately 1/1000, of its initial pressure level)—effectively to silence. The reverberation time is generally proportional to the ratio of a room's volume to the combined area of its surfaces and any objects:

$$reverberation\ time = 0.16 \times \frac{volume\ (m^3)}{area\ (m^2)} \tag{7-1}$$

If the room's measurements are in feet, the equation's constant changes:

$$reverberation\ time = 0.048 \times \frac{volume\ (ft^3)}{area\ (ft^2)} \tag{7-2}$$

A large cathedral may have reverberations on the order of five to ten seconds; a typical living room has a reverberation time of less than a second. But true reverberation time is not encapsulated in a single number, as the rate of absorption varies with frequency. In a large auditorium, higher frequencies can be absorbed by the air itself, so longer reverberation times tend to contain a greater proportion of lower frequencies. Different materials in the room also tend to absorb different frequencies. Equations 7-1 and 7-2 are sometimes useful as a rough estimate, usually describing the reverberation time of a sound at 500–1000 Hz in a bare room with equally absorptive surfaces everywhere. More precise graphs of reverberation show reverberation time as a function of frequency.

REVERBERATION RADIUS

There is a certain distance from the performer at which the direct and reverberant sound are roughly equal in intensity. This *reverberation radius* is the optimal point for microphone placement to ensure that a recording captures both the sound of the performer and the qualities of the room. The reverberation radius depends on the room, but a rough estimate can be made based on the room's volume, V, and reverberation time, R_t:

$$reverberation\ radius = 0.056 \times \sqrt{\frac{V(m^3)}{R_t}} \tag{7-3}$$

or

$$reverberation\ radius = 0.039 \times \sqrt{\frac{V(ft^3)}{R_t}} \tag{7-4}$$

Regardless of whether feet or meters are used, the reverberation radius may be expressed in a simplified form based on just the room surface area, A:

$$reverberation\ radius = 0.14 \times \sqrt{A} \tag{7-5}$$

The derivation is shown in Figure 7-1.

Equations such as 7-3 through 7-5 are helpful as guidelines, but, as always, the bottom line lies in what our ears tell us. Readers who have an opportunity to make a

	Meters	**Feet**
Reverberation Time (C = the speed of sound)	$t_r = \dfrac{55 \times V}{C \times A}$	$t_r = \dfrac{55 \times V}{C \times A}$
	$= \dfrac{55 \times V}{343 \times A}$	$= \dfrac{55 \times V}{1125 \times A}$
	$= \dfrac{0.16\,V}{A}$	$= \dfrac{0.048\,V}{A}$
Reverberation Radius	$R_r = 0.056 \times \sqrt{\dfrac{V}{R_t}}$	$R_r = 0.0309 \times \sqrt{\dfrac{V}{R_t}}$
	$= 0.056 \times \sqrt{\dfrac{V}{\frac{0.16\,V}{A}}}$	$= 0.0309 \times \sqrt{\dfrac{V}{\frac{0.048\,V}{A}}}$
	$= 0.056 \times \sqrt{\dfrac{V}{1} \times \dfrac{A}{0.16\,V}}$	$= 0.0309 \times \sqrt{\dfrac{V}{1} \times \dfrac{A}{0.048\,V}}$
	$= 0.056 \times \sqrt{\dfrac{A}{0.16}}$	$= 0.0309 \times \sqrt{\dfrac{A}{0.048}}$
	$= 0.056 \times \dfrac{\sqrt{A}}{0.4}$	$= 0.0309 \times \dfrac{\sqrt{A}}{0.219}$
	$= 0.14 \times \sqrt{A}$	$= 0.14 \times \sqrt{A}$

Figure 7-1 Reverberation radius derivation

recording are encouraged to experiment with listening to the reverberant properties of a space. When the room is quiet, clap your hands and listen to how long the sound lasts. While the musicians are rehearsing, walk slowly up and down the aisles and listen carefully to how the sound changes. It can be surprising to find that there is a certain point at which it sounds as though you're close to the ensemble, but taking a step or two away from them suddenly changes the sound dramatically.

Given the intensity drop of direct sound due to the inverse square law, once one is outside of the reverberation radius, there is virtually no direct sound to be heard. Past that point, changing the distance from the sound source does little or nothing to change the sound quality. The "reverberant soup" is the same, regardless of distance or direction.

IMPULSE RESPONSE
Because rooms filter sound, it is not surprising that acousticians describe the sound of a room by its *impulse response*, just as electrical engineers use an impulse response to describe filters. Before digital analysis was possible by impulse signals (as described in Chapter 6), impulses were created with a short sound burst (hand clap, flick of a lighter,

click from a toy). The room could then be characterized by the intensity and timing of its reflections. These give a quantitative description of how sound is treated in a particular space.

INTERAURAL CROSS-CORRELATION (IACC)

We have noted the importance of using one's own ears as the ultimate arbiter of reverberation quality. It is important to underline that this means using *two* ears. The importance of listening with two ears can be easily appreciated by going to a concert and turning your head so that only one ear faces the stage, and plugging the far ear. The sound immediately "flattens," becoming less distinct, and it becomes difficult to pick out individual parts in an ensemble. Just as two eyes are necessary to give us visual depth perception, two ears are necessary for aural depth and room perception. *Interaural cross-correlation (IACC)* describes the degree of similarity between the wavefront patterns reaching the two ears. Low IACC (that is, greater difference between the ears) is a desirable characteristic, as it improves localization of sound sources and contributes to an impression commonly described as "spacious."

TYPES OF REFLECTION: SPECULAR AND DIFFUSE

Wave reflection was discussed in Chapter 1. Figure 1-5 illustrated the basic wave principle that the angle of incidence equals the angle of reflection. To be more specific, this principle describes the behavior of wave reflections from surfaces that are smooth and regular. Reflections of this type are called *specular reflections*.

However, real-life acoustic reflections are not always so simple. Acoustic waves, particularly musical ones, contain many frequencies. And reflective acoustic surfaces are often irregular, with the result that the simple relationship exhibited by specular reflections becomes something of an oversimplification. When waves come into contact with an irregular surface, the result is not a single angle of incidence and a single angle of reflection. Rather, reflections are scattered in all directions, with the intensity of the reflections being dependent on the angle of the incident wave. *Lambert's cosine law*, illustrated in Figure 7-2, states that the intensity of the reflections is proportional to the

Intensity of reflection ∝ Intensity of incidence × cosine (angle of incidence to surface normal)

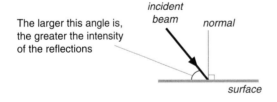

Examples:
Size of the angle represented by the height *h*

Figure 7-2 Lambert's Cosine Law

cosine of the angle of incidence with a line perpendicular to the surface (the perpendicular line is termed a *normal*).

Lambert's cosine law is also important in the study of 3D modeling and shading: reflections of a flashlight on a painted wall, for example, are reflected with greater intensity if the light is pointed directly at the wall (perpendicular to it) than if its light strikes the wall at an angle, and light reflects from a round object differently depending on the angle and intensity of the light beam. Sound wavefronts behave in the same way, and therefore diffuse reflections play a large role in shaping the acoustic signature of a space.

Diffuse reflections differ from specular reflections in two important ways:

1. The intensity of specular reflections is dependent on the observer's position as well as the angle of incidence, while diffuse reflections are independent of the observer's position.
2. Diffuse reflections radiate from a larger area of the reflective surface, rather than from a single point (Figure 7-3).

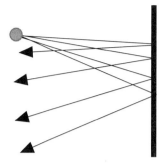

Figure 7-3 Diffuse reflections originate from a larger area of the reflective surface than specular reflections

Because diffuse acoustic reflections are scattered, a listener at any given position receives many reflections of a single sound event. These multiple reflections have a number of consequences. Temporally, there is an overall smoothing of amplitude transients. Spectrally, the reflections filter the sound. Recall from Chapter 5 that filtering is a process of combining an input signal with delayed versions of itself. The multiple reflections have the same effect. Diffuse reflections create a faster buildup toward the reverberation stage of sound propagation and a more uniform reverberant soundfield than is produced by specular reflections. This spreading of the acoustic energy also increases the likelihood of low interaural cross-correlation.

For these reasons, the nature of diffuse reflections plays a significant role in characterizing the most highly rated concert halls. Prior to 1900, theaters were commonly designed with Greek/Roman-styled aesthetic enhancements. Fluted pillars, mouldings, sculptures, and other decorative features served to create diffuse reflections that enhanced the space's acoustics. With the turn of the twentieth century, the International Style of architecture, coupled with economic considerations that encouraged fast construction and increased seating capacities, led to sparser spaces characterized by large, flat surfaces. These spaces do not promote diffuse reflections to the same degree as these earlier, more decorative designs. A room's propensity to produce favorable diffuse reflections is a topic of serious consideration in contemporary acoustics.

SPEECH VS. MUSIC

In a reverberant space, sounds of the past are mixed with sounds of the present, as reverberations from earlier sounds are joined by the sounds being made by the speaker or performer. While reverberation can be flattering to musical sounds, it can obscure speech intelligibility. A venue that is suitable for a lecture presentation may be undesirable for musical performances, and vice versa. For intelligibility, speech presentations require a short reverberation time, typically no longer than one second. Music, however, is better suited for reverberation times lasting two seconds or longer.

Even if space is suitable for music, it may not favor all types of music equally (Sundberg, 1991). For example, early music written for the Church was meant to be performed in cathedrals, which are large, stone spaces with long reverberation times. Its harmonic rhythms tend to be slow, which keeps the reverberations from turning the music into a dissonant mush of harmonies. On the other hand, chamber music was written for smaller spaces with shorter reverberation times. The harmonic rhythms are faster and the rhythmic interplay among parts tends to be more intricate, because the space allows for more complicated activities to be heard. Chamber music played in a cathedral can sound indistinct, while early religious music played in a small venue can sound overly static.

ABSORPTION

Returning to the idea that a room is a filter, and that reverberation is frequency-dependent, the character of a room may be described in terms of which frequencies are allowed to reverberate and which frequencies are more easily absorbed.

The degree to which any given frequency is reflected or absorbed depends on the materials and objects within the performance space. One factor is size: as described in Chapter 1, small obstacles reflect high frequencies, while larger obstacles reflect low frequencies. Another factor is material, or what the surface is made of: different materials tend to absorb different frequencies. A material's tendency to absorb a given frequency is quantified by the material's *absorption coefficient*:

$$absorption\ coefficient = \frac{absorbed\ sound}{incident\ sound} \tag{7-6}$$

A low absorption coefficient describes a majority of sound energy reflecting away from a surface. A perfectly reflective surface would have an absorption coefficient of zero, as it is 0 percent absorptive. A high absorption coefficient means that the majority of sound is absorbed. An open window reflects no incident sound, and would have an absorption coefficient of 1.0, as it is 100 percent absorptive. Figure 7-4 plots absorption coefficients as a function of frequency for a variety of materials.

Different surface types can be categorized according to their absorption characteristics:

- **Highly Reflective Surfaces.** Heavy, stiff materials—such as unpainted concrete and shower tiles—have low absorption coefficients and tend to reflect all frequencies equally.
- **High-Frequency Absorbers (500–1000 Hz).** Soft porous materials—such as curtains, clothing, or carpet—are high-frequency absorbers. The thicker and more porous the materials are, the lower the frequencies they are likely to absorb. Because clothing tends to absorb high frequencies, stone churches and cathedrals tend to be much more reverberant in high frequencies when they are empty. Modern concert halls address this issue by using material on the seats that is designed to match the absorptive characteristics of clothing, so that an empty hall is close to being as absorptive as a full hall.
- **Low-Frequency Absorbers (300–500 Hz).** Materials that can vibrate—such as windows, plaster walls over widely spaced beams, or wooden floors laid on widely spaced beams—act as resonators. They can be brought into vibration by low frequencies, and the energy required to bring these surfaces into a state of vibration results in these frequencies being absorbed by the materials, and attenuated acoustically within the room. Air cavities behind walls can also act as low-frequency resonators and absorb acoustic energy.
- **Midfrequency Absorbers (300–1000 Hz).** A combination of high- and low-frequency absorptive material can be employed to absorb midrange frequencies. An example is a wall covered in a porous material with regularly spaced wood panels placed over it.

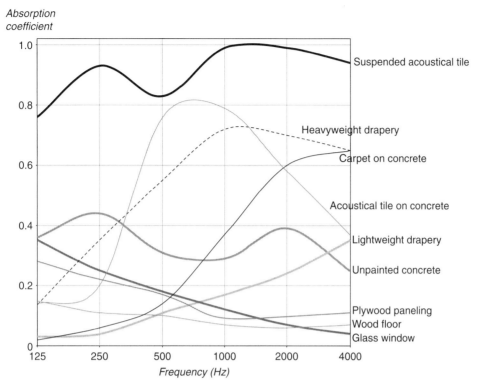

Figure 7-4 Absorption coefficients
Source: Data from Rossing (1990), p. 466

ABSORPTION AND SOUND PROPAGATION

Typically, a combination of low-, mid-, and high-frequency absorbers provides optimal results. A room with only high-frequency absorbers is likely to sound dull, and a room with only low-frequency absorbers is likely to sound thin. Performers should be placed in locations that take advantage of the room's shape and surfaces. A reflective surface near a performer can be advantageous, as the early reflections can enhance the sound. Many venues use acoustic shells behind an ensemble to reflect wavefronts that travel upstage and to focus them toward the audience. Placing an ensemble on a carpet or under a wooden overhang is likely to be counterproductive, as these surfaces will absorb much of the sound. On the other hand, a reflective wall or ceiling can enhance the sound, as long as the reflections are sufficiently diffused so that they fill the space uniformly.

In a documentary on his career (*Laurence Olivier: A Life*, 1982), the famed actor Laurence Olivier apologetically claimed to have "ruined" the acoustics of one of London's National Theatre stages when he was the company's director. In an attempt to bring the onstage action closer to the audiences, he went to considerable expense to extend the stage into the auditorium, without realizing how this would affect the room's sound distribution. Previously, sound from the stage spread over the auditorium floor as well as up to the balcony seats. With the stage extension, sound from the downstage area had no direct path to the balcony, and tended to get swallowed up in the seating area under the balcony, reflect off the balcony back to the stage, or get lost in the ceiling.

A renowned failure in architectural acoustics was Philharmonic Hall in New York City's Lincoln Center for the Performing Arts, which opened in 1962. The hall was heralded as being foolproof, as it was designed by acclaimed acoustician Leo Beranek (1914-). Yet its flaws became immediately apparent when the hall opened:

- *The orchestra members could not hear themselves or each other well.* This was due to an absorptive wall at the back of the stage. This wall also contributed to a lack of reverberation. The sound did not fill the hall well, and some seat locations had echoes.
- *There was an absence of low frequencies, making the cellos and basses practically inaudible.* Although sound clouds had been suspended from the ceiling to reflect sound down to the audience, they were too small to reflect the large wavelengths from these low instruments. The bass sounds were lost in the ceiling, reaching the audience only after multiple reflections; by that time, the sound was disassociated from what the musicians were playing, and came across as rumbly background noise.
- Low-frequency content was also not well served by the stage and seating arrangement. The angle of the stage caused the sound to resonate in the spaces between the rows of seats. The energy of higher frequencies resonating in these areas had the effect of "pushing" longer wavefronts upward, toward the ceiling.

Colleagues of Beranek are quick to point out that these problems were not due to any lack of competence on his part. Rather, his ideas were "nickel and dimed," adjusted by a series of compromises for purposes of visual design or construction efficiency, which were carried out in ignorance of their acoustic ramifications.

Unfortunately, once a hall is constructed, there is little that can be done to improve it, short of gutting the space and starting over. Corrective measures were eventually implemented with a complete redesign in 1976, a few years after the venue had been renamed Avery Fisher Hall for a major benefactor, the founder of Fisher Electronics. The clouds were realigned to reflect all frequencies. Diffusers were put on the side walls to scatter the reflections. The orchestra was put into a solid enclosure that allowed them to hear themselves better. Less-absorptive seats were installed, and an absorptive back wall cut down on echoes. These measures were an improvement, but many musicians, conductors, and audience members still found the hall lacking acoustically. In 2015, as part of a series of renovations to all of the facilities at Lincoln Center, the hall was renamed for producer and philanthropist David Geffen, who was the highest bidder in a fundraising campaign to finance the renovation and purchase naming rights to the refurbished hall.

Contemporary acoustical architects use digital models to trace simulated sound paths and calculate reverberation time and diffusion. Nowadays, when a building is constructed, their views are part of the design consideration, and acousticians are treated as equal partners in the design process. Design teams are more likely to acknowledge that decisions cannot be made for visual appeal only, as there are can be unintended acoustic side effects.

IDEAL CONCERT HALL CHARACTERISTICS

In a 1962 study, Beranek studied the sound properties in fifty-four of the world's most highly regarded concert halls. He played the same "performance" in each, and compared the results. He did this by making a recording in an anechoic chamber, which ensured that there was no reverberation present in the recording. He played this recording over the same high-quality loudspeakers at each hall. With the same source material played in each venue, all variances in reverberation were due to the venues, not the recording. He used a "dummy head" microphone pair, which is a model of a human head with microphones placed into each of the ear canals. The stereo recordings were therefore a close match of what reached listeners' ears in each space. He then played the recordings in an anechoic listening room. By playing them simultaneously through a mechanism that allowed him to choose which location was heard, he could "aurally transport" listeners from one hall to another to compare the differences. He reported that it was quite striking to instantly "travel" from concert halls in Boston, Vienna, and other locations for immediate comparison of the halls' characteristics.

Based on these recordings, he made the following observations about preferred concert halls (Pierce, 1983):

1. Long reverberation times were desired (on the order of two seconds).
2. The more different the sounds were reaching each ear, the better (low IACC is desirable).
3. Narrow halls sounded better than wide halls. (This is presumably because narrow halls ensure that reflections from the walls reach listeners sooner than reflections from the ceiling; because ceiling reflections tend to be uniform, the wall reflections promote the low IACC mentioned above.)

In another article, Barron (2008) cites five subjective dimensions by which concert halls are evaluated:

1. Clarity, the ability to hear musical detail
2. Reverberation
3. Acoustic intimacy, the level to which the audience is personally involved in the sound
4. Envelopment, the degree to which listeners feel surrounded by the sound
5. Loudness

A variety of measures may be taken to focus a space's acoustics to ensure that it treats sound to best advantage. Suspended reflectors can help ensure that sound doesn't get lost near the ceiling, but is directed to where audience members are seated. Many halls and recording studios are enhanced by ribbed wooden reflectors that are meant to reflect different wavelengths at different angles, scientifically designed for optimum diffusion of all frequencies. (When I was much younger, I had an opportunity to tour a studio in construction, where this type of reflector was being installed. Curious, I naïvely asked the designer if he'd explain the principle behind them; his answer was curt and bemused: "No." Architectural acoustics is a specialized and competitive field, and experts tend to be protective of their trade secrets.)

Small Performance Spaces

ROOM MODES

The standing-wave behavior of waves in a tube was covered in Chapter 1. It was easy to see an association between tubes and musical instruments such as the flute, the organ, and the clarinet. However, the example of a tube closed at both ends shown in Figure 1-11 may have seemed more theoretical than practical, having no ready an association with any instrument type. But bearing in mind that a room is a filter, and a factor in the overall sound being produced within it, a comparison may be made between a closed tube and an enclosed room. Small performance spaces have the potential to resonate in the same manner as do closed tubes, in that pressure can maximize at the walls as air molecules are abruptly stopped in their motion and crowd together. Thus, the walls of the room may create pressure antinodes, and standing waves may be produced if steady-state sounds are played that have wavelengths at twice the dimensions of the room or at harmonics of this frequency. This phenomenon, whereby certain frequencies are ampli-fied due to the room's dimensions, is termed *modal enhancement*, and the frequencies that may form standing waves are termed *room modes*. There are three types of room modes: *axial modes, tangential modes,* and *oblique modes,* as shown in Figure 7-5.

Room modes can dramatically affect the frequency response of a small room, par-ticularly at low frequencies. If the room is a perfect cube, the same resonances may be amplified on all three axial modes, creating a cumulative amplification. The same prob-lem can be encountered when a room is based on simple relationships. If a room's length is exactly two times its width, for example, the fundamental of the room's width

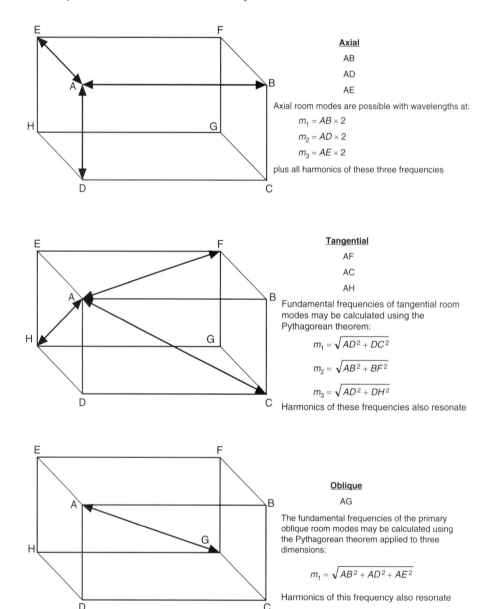

Axial

AB

AD

AE

Axial room modes are possible with wavelengths at:

$$m_1 = AB \times 2$$
$$m_2 = AD \times 2$$
$$m_3 = AE \times 2$$

plus all harmonics of these three frequencies

Tangential

AF

AC

AH

Fundamental frequencies of tangential room modes may be calculated using the Pythagorean theorem:

$$m_1 = \sqrt{AD^2 + DC^2}$$
$$m_2 = \sqrt{AB^2 + BF^2}$$
$$m_3 = \sqrt{AD^2 + DH^2}$$

Harmonics of these frequencies also resonate

Oblique

AG

The fundamental frequencies of the primary oblique room modes may be calculated using the Pythagorean theorem applied to three dimensions:

$$m_1 = \sqrt{AB^2 + AD^2 + AE^2}$$

Harmonics of this frequency also resonate

Figure 7-5 Room modes

corresponds to the second harmonic of the room's length, again creating a cumulative amplification. Ideally, small recording rooms are designed without simple relations and without parallel walls in order to avoid this problem.

An instrument's placement in a small room can also determine the low-end frequency response. A cello positioned in a corner has the potential to create pronounced bass resonances; moving the player away from the wall and into the room can reduce the effect. The same is true for microphone placement. Placing a microphone within a pressure node can exaggerate the presence of a standing wave, while moving the microphone a short distance, so that it is outside of the node, can eliminate the problem.

Due to room modes, sound levels may not be consistent throughout a room for resonant frequencies. By moving short distances, one can walk through nodes and antinodes and notice the changes in sound level. I have had colleagues observe this effect in small lecture spaces, where the character of the presenter's voice changes as he walks back and forth, in and out of nodes and antinodes. For high frequencies, the short wavelengths mean that nodes and antinodes may be quite close together, and a difference in sound quality can be observed by simply tilting one's head to one side or another.

Room modes are typically not a factor in the acoustics of large rooms because the air temperature tends to vary over the room's area. (Recall from Chapter 1 that the speed of sound depends on temperature.) For example, the ceiling tends to be warmer than the floor. The result is that sound waves do not propagate at consistent speeds throughout the space of the auditorium, and pressure waves cannot propagate consistently enough to cause pronounced room resonances.

FLUTTER ECHO

While sustained tones can cause standing waves in small rooms, impulsive sounds can cause *flutter echoes*, which are the result of a transient wave bouncing back and forth between two surfaces. These have the character of a "reverberation tail." Flutter echoes are often noticeable when you first move into a house or apartment and the rooms have no furniture or carpeting. Rooms with parallel walls are particularly prone to flutter echo effects. I know of one recital hall where a stage extension was installed, which seemed like a good idea because it brought performers closer to the audience and allowed more room for large ensembles. Unfortunately, the newly installed downstage area was between flat walls, unlike the older upstage area, which was between diffusers on the stage right and stage left walls. The downstage area was highly prone to flutter echoes; clapping one's hands produced a sound something like a bouncing ping-pong ball.

COMB FILTERING

Along with flutter echo, the combination of acoustic energy with a specular reflection leads to a type of sound coloration known as *comb filtering*. This refers to an uneven frequency response due to regular frequency cancellations that can result when a signal is combined with a delayed version of itself. Two examples of undesirable comb filtering are shown in Figure 7-6. Comb filtering is sometimes used intentionally as an audio effect, and will be discussed in detail in Chapter 8.

ACOUSTIC TREATMENT OF SMALL SPACES

Although it ideally performance rooms are constructed without parallel walls, this is not always an option. Often, recording spaces are repurposed, and those who use them have to make do with what is available in terms of room size and shape. However, a number of steps may be taken to reduce standing wave and flutter echo effects.

Figure 7-6 Accidental comb filtering can result when microphones pick up multiple versions of a signal. The comb filtering results from time misalignment between the signals. Multiple microphones picking up the same signal from different distances (left) or reflections causing a delayed version of a signal to combine with a more direct signal (right) cause cancellations and coloration (filtering) of the signal.

One option is to treat the room with absorptive material in order to reduce resonances. On the other hand, too much absorption can also create a "dead" sound if reflections are eliminated altogether. Rather than attempt to absorb certain frequencies, another approach is to ensure that reflections are diffused. Acoustic companies produce a variety of diffusion products that are meant to enhance or reduce certain frequency ranges. Diffuser kits can be purchased in a variety of sizes to accommodate a range of budgets. Then again, sometimes the answer can be found in lo-fi ingenuity: a bare-bones approach to creating diffuse reflections might be simply to place a bookshelf against a wall or to place some chairs in the middle of the room.

Microphones

Microphones are the ears of a recording. We've discussed some of the nuances that a space adds to a performance's sound. Capturing those nuances in a recording means choosing the right tool for the job. There are a myriad of microphone types used in concert recording, all meant for particular types of contexts.

At the heart of a microphone is a ***diaphragm*** that acts as a ***receptor***, which responds in much the same fashion as our eardrums: it vibrates in response to changes in air pressure, particularly those coming from a particular direction, and the vibrations are converted (***transduced***) to electricity. Microphones may be described by three categories:

- Receptor type
- Transducer type
- Directionality

Receptor Types

The diaphragm of a microphone is a thin, flexible material, such as a sheet of Mylar, that is coated with gold, aluminum, or nickel. A microphone's receptor type depends on how the diaphragm's motion is sensed. Receptors fall into two categories: *pressure* and *pressure gradient* (sometimes simply referred to as *gradient*).

PRESSURE

The diaphragm of a pressure receptor responds to sound pressure changes arriving from only the front side side of the microphone (Figure 7-7). There is nothing in the diaphragm's response that differentiates between wavefronts arriving from different directions.

PRESSURE GRADIENT (VELOCITY)

The diaphragm of a pressure gradient microphone responds to pressure changes arriving from both the front and rear (Figure 7-8). Sound pressure waves arriving from the front diffract around the microphone and, after some delay, strike the diaphragm again from the rear. Similarly, pressure waves arriving from the rear reach the front of the diaphragm after a delay, due to the extra distance . The signal produced is determined by the difference (gradient) of pressure wavefronts arriving from either side of the diaphragm. For long wavelengths, air particle velocity is proportional to the pressure gradient in the vicinity of the diaphragm, so an older term for this receptor type is *velocity* (see Figure 1-16).

Transducer Types

A microphone's transducer determines how the diaphragm's motion is converted into voltage changes. Like receptors, microphone transducers also fall into two categories: *dynamic* and *condenser*.

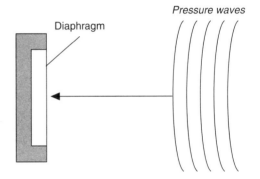

A pressure receptor is sensitive to pressure waves arriving from the front only

Figure 7-7 Pressure receptor

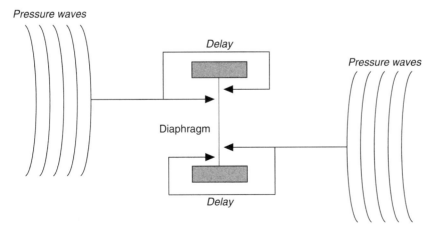

A pressure gradient is sensitive to pressure waves arriving from the front and the rear

Figure 7-8 Pressure gradient receptor

DYNAMIC (ELECTRODYNAMIC, ELECTROMAGNETIC, RIBBON, MOVING COIL)

A dynamic microphone transducer works by magnetic induction. As described in Chapter 4, when a wire (conductor) is made to move within a magnetic field, an electrical current is generated. In a dynamic microphone, coils attached to the diaphragm extend into a magnetic field. As the diaphragm moves back and forth in response to air pressure changes, the corresponding motion of the coils produces an electrical current with voltage levels that are proportional to pressure changes, as shown in Figure 7-9. Dynamic microphones have the advantage of being simple in design. They are inexpensive and sturdy, well suited for live performances of popular music or as a budget microphone for a home recording studio.

A classic dynamic pressure gradient microphone is a design commonly known as the **ribbon microphone**. They played an important role in early broadcasting, and will be discussed further in the section on directionality. The diaphragm wasn't round, as in standard dynamic microphones, but was rather a thin metal ribbon suspended vertically (Figure 7-10). Ribbons were more sensitive than the standard dynamic diaphragm, so these microphones had a superior sound quality. Due to their unique diaphragm shape and sound quality, ribbon microphones are sometimes considered a class unto themselves.

CONDENSER (CAPACITOR)

The second transducer type works by means of an electrical capacitor. As described in Chapter 4, a capacitor consists of two metal plates that are oppositely charged and placed in close proximity to each other. In a condenser microphone, one plate of the capacitor is the microphone diaphragm; the other plate of the capacitor is called the **backplate**. As the proximity between the plates changes due to variations in air pressure, their capacitance changes, which produces a current with voltage changes that correspond to the acoustic pressure changes (Figure 7-11).

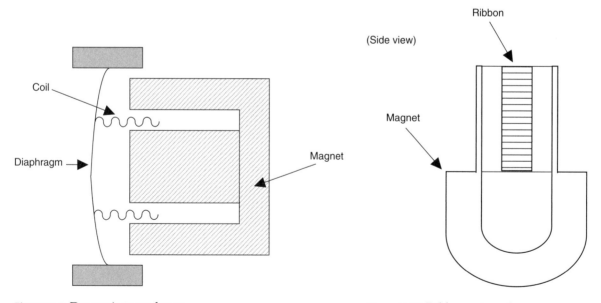

Figure 7-9 Dynamic transducer   **Figure 7-10** Ribbon microphone

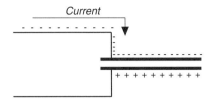

At closer proximity between the plates, there is greater attraction, and greater capacitance (ability to store electrons) in the negative plate, thus producing a current in the negative plate

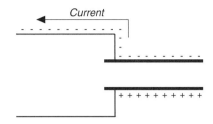

When the plates are moved apart, there is less attraction, and less capacitance (ability to store electrons) in the negative plate, thus producing a current away from the negative plate

Figure 7-11 Capacitor transducer

Condenser microphones are characterized by sharper transients than dynamic microphones, making them well-suited for percussive instruments such as drums and pianos. Their design is more complicated than that of dynamic microphones, making condenser microphones more expensive. To charge the plates, some of these microphones contain a battery. But it is more common for the charge to originate from an external power source, a type of DC signal known as ***phantom power***, which is usually supplied by a mixer or audio interface (phantom power will be discussed further in Chapter 8's section on mixing).

Directionality

The directionality of a microphone describes the magnitude of its response to pressure changes arriving from different angles. It is often expressed as a polar equation with magnitude as a function of a given angle, where 0° represents the position directly in front of the microphone.

OMNIDIRECTIONAL

Omnidirectional microphones respond with equal magnitude to pressure changes from all angles. These microphones may be described as a polar equation:

$$\rho = 1 \qquad (7\text{-}7)$$

which indicates that the microphone is 100 percent responsive, regardless of the sound source's angle in relation to the microphone (that is, at a value of 1 for all 360°). A polar directional plot is shown in Figure 7-12.

By definition, pressure microphones are omnidirectional, because only one side of the diaphragm responds to air pressure changes (as shown in Figure 7-7). But it is more accurate to describe pressure microphones as being omnidirectional *within certain limits*. Lower frequencies diffract around the body of the microphone and are able to reach the diaphragm without attenuation. Higher frequencies, with their smaller wavelengths, tend to reflect away from the

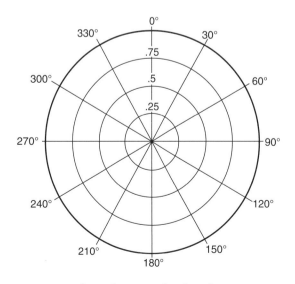

Figure 7-12 Omnidirectional polar plot

microphone, causing a roll-off of higher frequencies (typically starting at 8 kHz) not originating from a frontward direction. Thus, smaller-sized pressure microphones allow better omnidirectionality of high frequencies.

BIDIRECTIONAL (FIGURE 8)

Bidirectional microphones have a figure-8 magnitude response. The response is maximum for pressure changes from both front and back and zero for changes from the side. The polar equation for a bidirectional pattern is

$$\rho = cos\theta \qquad (7\text{-}8)$$

where θ represents the polar angle of the sound's position relative to the front of the microphone, from 0° to 360°. A bidirectional polar plot is shown in Figure 7-13.

Pressure gradient microphones are, by definition, bidirectional because both sides of the diaphragm respond to air pressure changes (as shown in Figure 7-8). Although the magnitude of the response is equal from the front and rear lobes of the diaphragm, the polarity of the response is opposite with each lobe. By convention, the front lobe is termed "positive" polarity and the rear lobe is termed "negative" polarity.

Ribbon microphones were mentioned above as an early example of dynamic microphone. Most were bidirectional, since the hanging ribbon responded to sound pressure changes arriving from the front or rear directions, whereas sounds from the left or right produced equal pressure on both sides of the ribbon and caused little or no displacement. Bidirectional ribbon microphones date back to the early days of broadcasting. They were ideal for interview situations when two people sat facing each other, to the front and rear of the ribbon. Ribbon microphones are a vintage design, having been largely superceded by more recent designs that feature changeable directional patterns.

FIRST-ORDER DIRECTIONAL MICROPHONES

Microphones are made directional through combinations of pressure and pressure gradient characteristics. The most common directional microphones in professional music recording may be classified as *first-order cardioid*. "Cardioid" refers to a heart-shaped directional pattern that describes their responsiveness to sounds arriving from all directions (360°); there are a number of variations on the cardioid pattern, described by polar functions. "First order" refers to a polar function equation that includes a cosine term to the first power. All of the patterns favor pressure changes arriving from the front, with variation in their responsiveness to pressure changes arriving from the sides and rear.

Figure 7-14 shows the layout of a dynamic cardioid microphone. Cardioids can be recognized easily from the openings in the sides of their capsules, which allow pressure changes arriving from the side and the rear to reach the back side of the diaphragm. The back of the diaphragm also responds to pressure changes arriving from the front: after reaching the front of the diaphragm, wavefronts diffract to the side of the capsule, reaching the back side of the diaphragm after a delay.

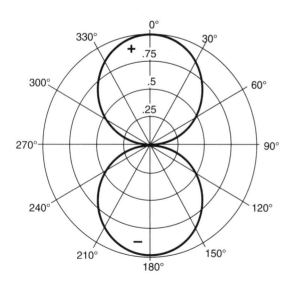

Figure 7-13 Bidirectional polar plot

In the same way, pressure changes arriving from the rear first reach the back side of the diaphragm, and also reach the front side of the diaphragm after a delay. This acoustic (distance-based) delay is compensated by a delay that is built into the microphone circuitry. The combination of the acoustic delay and the electrical delay creates the cardioid directionality pattern.

To understand the role of the electrical delay, recall that the microphone's output level is proportional to the gradient (degree of difference) between the two sides of the diaphragm. Therefore, in an ideal scenario, wavefronts would reach both sides of the diaphragm at the same time. This would cause the same material to affect both sides of the diaphragm simultaneously, and at opposite polarity, which would produce a high gradient between the front and back of the diaphragm.

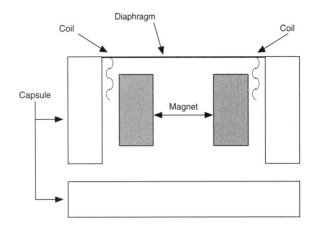

Figure 7-14 Layout of a cardioid microphone

But the front-arriving pressure changes cannot reach both sides of the diaphragm simultaneously due to the acoustic delay, which means that the pressure changes that reach the back side of the diaphragm are a phase-shifted version of the patterns affecting the front side. The result is destructive interference and attenuation of the signal. To remedy this attenuation, the electrical delay is placed upon the signal picked up from the diaphragm's front side. The electrical delay time matches the acoustic delay time. Thus, the combination of the electrical delay and acoustical delay simulates the ideal scenario of simultaneous activity on either side of the diaphragm, which produces a maximum gradient level for front-arriving pressure patterns.

When wavefronts arrive from the side, there is no acoustical delay, as they reach both the front and back of the diaphragm at the same time. In this case, the electrical delay imposed on the signal from the front of the diaphragm causes phase offsets and destructive interference between the activity reaching the diaphragm's front and back, with the result that there is attenuation of side-arriving wavefronts.

When wavefronts arrive from the rear, they first reach the back of the diaphragm, then diffract to the front, which they reach after the acoustic delay time. They then have the electrical delay imposed on them, which increases the phase difference between the front and back diaphragm signals. The result is near complete cancellation of the rear-arriving wavefronts. This produces the cardioid pattern, which is highly responsive to front-arriving pressure patterns, attenuated for side-arriving patterns, and low for rear-arriving patterns.

By adjusting the design of the capsule to lengthen or shorten the acoustic delay, and changing the electrical delay time, variations on the cardioid pattern can be created. First-order directional microphones have a generalized polar equation of

$$\rho = A + B\ cos\theta \qquad (7\text{-}9)$$

where $A + B = 1$. The A term describes the omnidirectional characteristic, and the B term describes the bidirectional characteristic. As was the case with the equation for bidirectional patterns, the angle, θ, applies to a complete circle, 0° to 360°. The most common first-order combinations are shown in Figure 7-15.

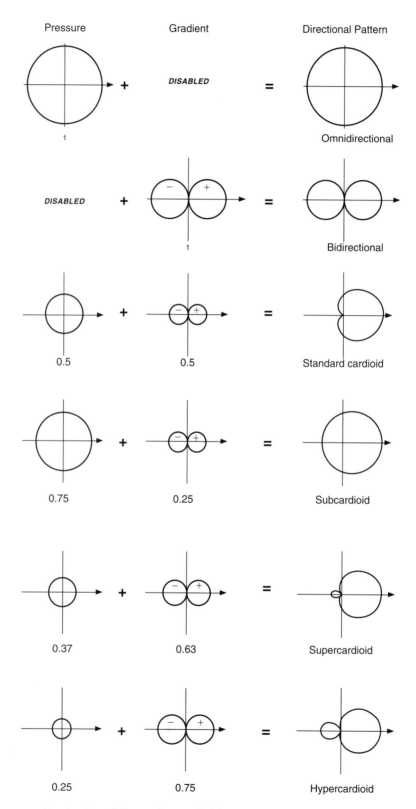

Figure 7-15 Derivation of first-order cardioid patterns
Source: Adapted from Eargle, The Microphone Book, *p. 83, Fig 5-2, Focal Press 2001*

STANDARD CARDIOID

A *standard cardioid microphone* has the most common directional pattern. It is the result of an equivalent combination of omni- and bidirectional characteristics:

$$\rho = 0.5 + 0.5\cos\theta \qquad (7\text{-}9)$$

A directional plot is shown in Figure 7-16.

SUBCARDIOID

Also referred to as the *forward-oriented omni*, a *subcardioid microphone* is often used in classical music recording. It is usually described by the polar equation

$$\rho = 0.75 + 0.25\cos\theta \qquad (7\text{-}10)$$

A directional plot is shown in Figure 7-17.

SUPERCARDIOID

The *supercardioid pattern* has a somewhat tighter front response than the standard and subcardioid patterns and is described by the equation

$$\rho = 0.37 + 0.63\cos\theta \qquad (7\text{-}9)$$

A directional plot is shown in Figure 7-18.

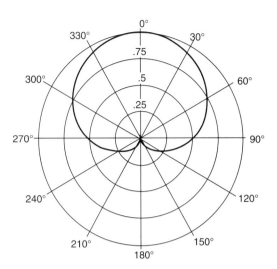

Figure 7-16 Standard cardioid directional polar plot

HYPERCARDIOID

The *hypercardioid pattern* has the tightest forward-magnitude response. It is described by the equation

$$\rho = 0.25 + 0.75\cos\theta \qquad (7\text{-}10)$$

and is illustrated in Figure 7-19.

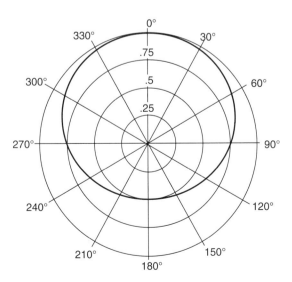

Figure 7-17 Subcardioid directional plot

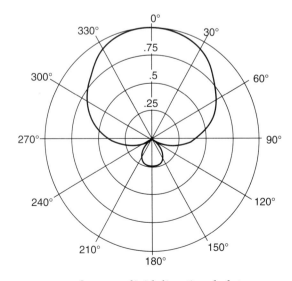

Figure 7-18 Supercardioid directional plot

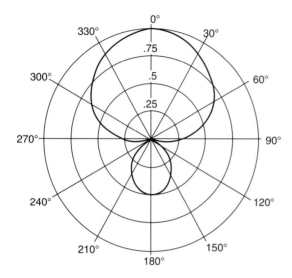

Figure 7-19 Hypercardioid directional plot

Variable Pattern Microphones

Variable pattern microphones allow the directional response pattern to be selected from a variety of patterns. Earlier, the cardioid directional pattern was described as resulting from a combination of acoustic delay, due to additional wavefront travel times from one side of the diaphragm to the other, and delays built into the circuitry to compensate for the acoustic delay. Some variable pattern microphones allow the acoustic delay time to be changed by lengthening the capsule, while others allow the electrical delay time to be changed. The *Braunmühl-Weber dual-diaphragm variable pattern microphone* design consists of two diaphragms that are placed on opposite sides of a single backplate. By means of various combinations of the cardioid patterns from each diaphragm, virtually all first-order patterns can be produced (Figure 7-20).

Directionality and Frequency Response

The acoustic delay of a pressure gradient microphone does not affect all wavelengths equally. Some frequencies experience more cancellation than others. Specifications for cardioid microphones typically include a polar plot with superimposed patterns that illustrate the response of the microphone to different frequencies (Figure 7-21). As described earlier, higher outputs are the result of greater pressure gradients. The amount of gradient depends on two factors: phase drop-off and intensity drop-off.

PHASE DROP-OFF

Phase drop-off is due to the time difference between a wavefront reaching one side of the diaphragm and diffracting to the other side. These differences are much more significant with high frequencies than with low frequencies (Figure 7-22). High frequencies, with their short wavelengths, may be at very different levels in their cycle on either side of the diaphragm. This creates a large difference in pressure levels, which means the microphone has high output. But low-frequency pressure waves, with long wavelengths, create nearly equal pressure levels at both sides of the diaphragm. With minimal pressure differences, the output signal is not as strong.

Thus, a cardioid or figure 8 has a natural tendency to roll off low frequencies and emphasize the highs. Manufacturers compensate for this with an output transformer that has a frequency response curve that is the inverse mirror of the microphone's curve. The sum of the two produces a flatter response.

INTENSITY DROP-OFF

Intensity drop-off results from the longer distance to the far side of the diaphragm, and is significant at close range. Due to the inverse square law, a change by about an inch has a significant effect close to the sound source, but little to no effect at a greater distance, where a change of an inch represents a much smaller percentage of the difference.

At close ranges, the added distance from the front to the rear of the diaphragm adds a significant percentage to the travel path; thus there is a stronger gradient

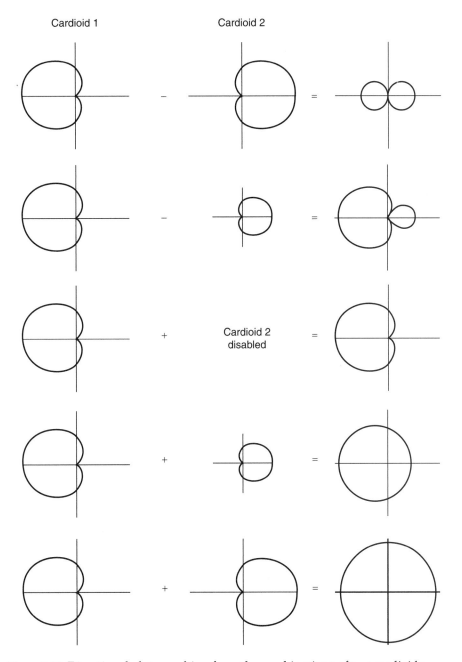

Figure 7-20 Directional plots resulting from the combinations of two cardioids
Source: Adapted from Eargle, The Microphone Book, *p. 102, Fig 5-21, Focal Press 2001*

because the intensity drops significantly by the time the wavefront reaches the far side. This intensity difference affects all frequencies. Even the bass frequencies get an extra "gradient boost" at close range. When combined with the corrective curve of the output transformer, the result is a bass boost at close range. This is known as the

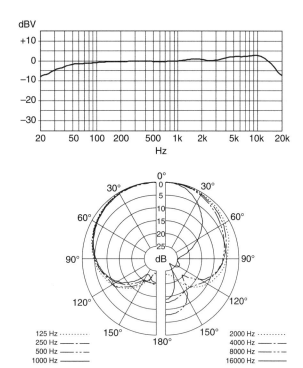

Figure 7-21 Cardioid polar plot with frequency response
Source: Polar diagram of the MK 4 studio microphone (Sennheiser), frequency response curve of the MK 4 studio microphone (Sennheiser)

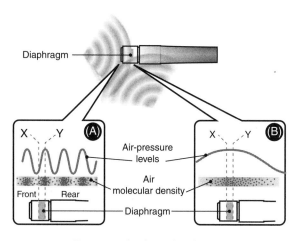

Figure 7-22 Because the far side of a microphone diaphragm represents a longer travel distance for the wave front, the front and rear respond to the same signal, but with a difference in phase. A high-frequency signal (lower left) produces a big difference in pressure levels, while a low-frequency signal (lower right) produces minimal difference in pressure levels at the two sides of the diaphragm.
Source: Chuck Dahmer. Originally published in Ballora, "Square One: Vive la Différence," Electronic Musician 22.3 (2006). Courtesy of NewBay Media

proximity effect, or "bass tip-up." This effect has been a fact part of microphone technology since the early days of high-fidelity audio. It was considered a feature of the ribbon microphones used by crooners and announcers in the 1930s and 1940s. They learned to make subtle adjustments in their distance from the microphone to give their voices a husky, warm timbre, a sound quality that characterizes the ribbon microphones of that era.

Direct vs. Diffuse Sound Responses

Each directional pattern type treats the balance of direct and diffuse sound differently. The directional pattern and the direct-diffuse balance are critical factors to engineers when they make artful microphone choices.

Random energy efficiency (REE)—sometimes termed *random efficiency (RE)*—compares the microphone's responsiveness to sounds arriving off-axis, which are typically diffuse reverberation, to sounds arriving from the front. For example, a hypercardioid has an REE of 0.25, which means that its signal consists of one-quarter off-axis reverberations, and three-quarters on-axis direct sound. The REE of the various directional patterns is summarized in Figure 7-23.

A related measurement is the *distance factor* (or *reach*) of a microphone. This is a comparison of the relative distance a microphone may be placed from a sound source, compared to an omnidirectional microphone, to produce the same direct-to-reverberant

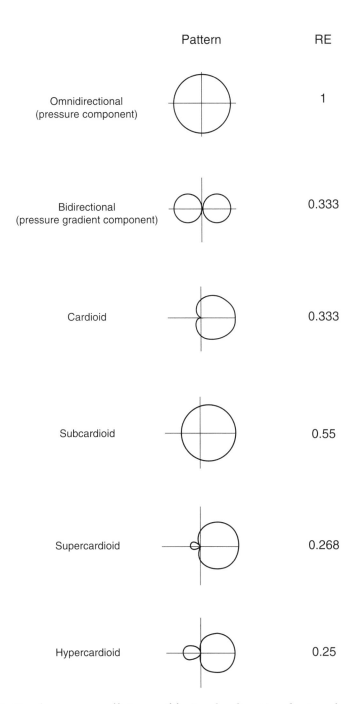

Figure 7-23 Random energy efficiency of first-order directional microphones

response. For example, a hypercardioid, with its reach value of 2, may be placed twice as far from a sound source as an omnidirectional microphone to obtain a signal with the same direct-to-reverberant ratio. The distance factor of the various directional patterns is summarized in Figure 7-24.

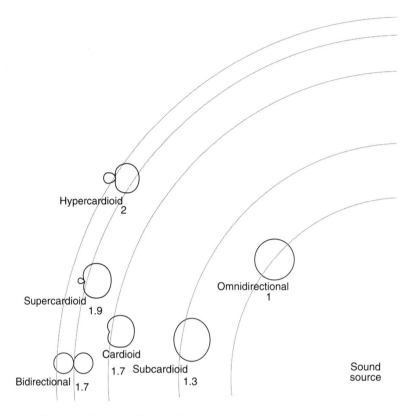

Figure 7-24 Distance factor of first-order directional microphones

Microphone Configurations

When recordings are described, two factors may be considered: *localization* and *spaciousness*. Localization refers to an aural stage picture in which the apparent positions of different players can be easily discerned. Spaciousness refers to an impression of sound being spread over the listening space, with a sense of diffuse reverberation. This section will discuss how these two qualities play into the process of recording. In Chapter 8, they will be discussed in the context of postproduction.

Recording high-quality concert music rarely involves using just a single microphone. At the very least, two microphones are needed to make a two-channel stereo recording; just as music heard through only one ear is a limited listening experience, a monophonic recording of concert music is likely to lack dimensionality. Concert recordings typically use a number of microphones in tandem.

Optimal microphone configurations vary according to context. The size of the room, type of ensemble, and style of music are all factors that determine the precise type and positions of microphones. Recording is a refined art, akin to a musician's ability to interpret a written score. The configurations introduced here are meant to provide starting points for some common recording contexts. A seasoned recording engineer will likely add a number of personal touches, developed through experience and experimentation.

Recording Popular vs. Recording Classical

The simplest multi-microphone configuration is that of a separate, directional microphone for each instrument in an ensemble. The signals are then combined at a mixing board, where adjustments of relative volumes, stereo positioning, and appropriate filtering and effects are applied. Separate instruments on separate audio tracks, often recorded at different times, is the methodology of popular music production, the goal of which is to create a simulated stage picture in postproduction.

In contrast, the goal in concert music recording is to capture the authentic sound of a performing ensemble, with a lifelike sense of volume balance and stage position, set within the reverberation signature of a particular venue. Concert microphone configurations determine the stereophonic imaging and the balance between direct and diffuse sound present in the recording.

Different instruments call for different recording approaches. Direct sound without diffuse sound exists only in the immediate vicinity of the instrument. It can be a surprising experience to move through the area in close proximity to a musician who is playing, because instruments do not produce the same timbral quality in all directions and at all heights. Listening carefully to the tone quality at the front, rear, and sides, as well as comparing the sound near the floor with the sound heard at normal standing height, can reveal wide variations in sound quality. A close microphone, then, can bring about very different results depending on its height and position relative to the player. Dickreiter (1988) and Eargle (2001) provide excellent recommendations on microphone placement for specific instrument types.

As was discussed earlier, the default microphone position is near the reverberation radius, which is the point at which the intensities of direct and reverberant sound are equal. Beyond this placement, however, a number of other configurations may be explored to shape the character of the recording. The two broad approaches to stereophonic recording are based on *time-of-arrival* and *intensity*.

Time-of-Arrival Configurations

A time-of-arrival setup consists of spaced microphones, typically in an arc in front of a large ensemble. Normally, these are omnidirectional microphones placed at a distance of 20 cm to 150 cm (roughly 8″ to 60″) apart. For highly reverberant rooms or rooms with pronounced audience noise, cardioid microphones may be preferred.

With this approach, different instruments are at different distances from the various microphones, meaning that a given instrument's wavefronts will arrive at slightly different times at each microphone. These differences produce apparent sound locations between the speaker locations (due to an illusion called *phantom imaging*, which will be discussed further in Chapter 8). Time-of-arrival recordings provide a good sense of space and are suitable for ensembles in large rooms. The tradeoff is that stereo imaging tends to be less precise than with intensity recording. In some cases instruments may appear to shift position when they play different pitches, due to varying degrees of phase cancellation for different frequencies at the separate microphones.

Also, although it is seldom a problem with contemporary audio playback equipment, in the early days of stereophonic recording it was often necessary to produce monophonic versions for playback over radio or phonographs that were not stereo. Combining the signals from both channels of a two-channel time-of-arrival recording would sometimes cause phase cancellation problems in the mono version.

Two coincident bidirectional microphones,
oriented at 90° to each other

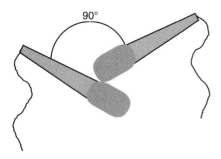

Combined directional characteristics

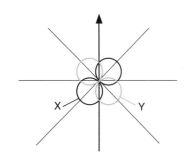

Figure 7-25 XY configuration

Intensity Configurations

Also known as ***coincident microphone recording***, intensity recording consists of placing two directional microphones at the same location, oriented in different directions relative to each other. Because there is no time difference between the signals arriving at the two microphones, the resulting stereo imaging is due to pressure (or intensity) differences between them. Coincident microphones tend to produce more precise spatial imaging than spaced microphones, the tradeoff being a decreased sense of room spaciousness. Coincident microphone techniques may be divided into two main categories, XY and MS.

XY MICROPHONE CONFIGURATION

With an ***XY configuration***, two microphones with identical directional patterns are placed at the same spot, one directly on top of the other, at an angle. A common configuration consists of two bidirectional microphones placed at 90°, as shown in Figure 7-25. This is also called a ***Blumlein configuration***, after its creator, Alan Blumlein (1903–1942). It has the advantage of providing precise stereo imaging from sound sources in front of the microphones plus reverberation that reaches the microphones from the rear.

Cardioid microphones may also be used in XY configurations. Depending on the microphones used, the separation angle may range from 90° to 130°. The signals from the two XY microphones provide left and right stereo signals. The angle of the microphones, plus the panning separation of the two signals adjusted on the mixer, provide the overall width of the apparent stage picture.

MS MICROPHONE CONFIGURATION

An ***MS configuration*** (the M standing for *mono, main,* or *middle*; the S standing for *side* or *stereo*) consists of two coincident microphones, typically with differing directional characteristics. The M component is usually a cardioid microphone pointed toward the sound source. The S component is a bidirectional microphone that is oriented perpendicular to the M microphone (Figure 7-26). A sound arriving from front center hits the null spot of the figure 8, and its signal is sent equally to both sides of the diaphragm. Unlike the signals from XY configurations, the signals from MS microphones do not create two corresponding stereo channels. Rather, the stereo channels are created from combinations of the two microphones created in the mixer. The M signal is directed to one channel and panned center. The S signal is duplicated, and the polarity is reversed on one copy. The two copies are sent to two separate mixer channels, which are panned left and right. The stereo signal is derived by creating the left channel from the sum of the mid and side signals, and the right channel from the difference between mid and side channels. In other words, the left channel is created from the mid signal plus the portion of the signal that reaches the left side of the figure 8, and the right channel is created from the mid signal plus the portion of the signal that reaches the right side of the figure 8.

MS can be done on a hardware mixer. But it is often easier to use a digital audio workstation with three tracks set up. The M signal goes to one track and panned center.

The S signal goes to another track, and is panned hard left or right. A copy of the S signal is placed on the third track, its polarity is inverted, and this channel is panned opposite to the other S track. Ideally, the two side tracks are sent to a subgroup, or their volume faders are linked so that one fader changes their levels in tandem.

The stereo imaging is more flexible with MS configurations than with XY configurations. If the side channels are brought to a zero volume level so that only the mid channel is heard, the result is a monophonic recording. But if the side channels are faded in, the apparent width of a stereo soundfield increases along with their volume levels. With XY configurations, the angle of the microphones is what determines the stereo imaging. With MS, the imaging is determined by level differences rather than through physical microphone placement, so the stereophonic effect can be changed after the recording is made. Another advantage of MS is that the main microphone facing the center of the soundfield gives the aural image a firm foundation (sometimes described as "greater brilliance").

Near-Coincident Configurations

Near-coincident (or *quasi-coincident*) *microphone configurations* attempt to combine the best parts of spaced and coincident microphone placements. Pairs of directional microphones are placed close together with a separation distance up to 30 cm (12″). These configurations feature much of the localizability of coincident configurations while maintaining some of the sense of spaciousness of time-of-arrival configurations.

ORTF

The *ORTF microphone configuration*—named for the French broadcasting group Office de Radio Télévision Française, where it was created—consists of two cardioid microphones separated by 17 cm (6.7″), which is the approximate width of the human head. The microphones are each angled 55° away from center. While the directionality is meant to simulate the sensation that would reach a listener's ears, the open space between the microphones allows each microphone to pick up the full range of frequencies without the spectral shadowing that the head produces.

SPHERICAL STEREO MICROPHONES

Spherical stereo microphones are spherical enclosures that are roughly the size of the human head. They contain two omnidirectional microphones placed on opposite sides to correspond to the position of the ears. Spherical microphones create interaural delay

A cardioid plus a bidirectional

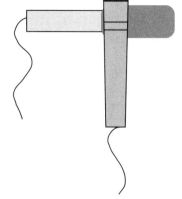

Combined directional characteristics

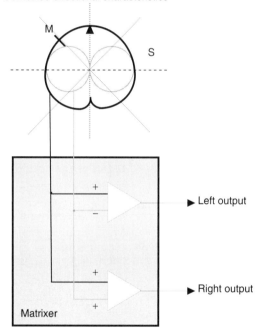

Figure 7-26 MS configuration

and spectral shadowing in much the same manner as the auditory system. They are easy to set up and provide good stereo imaging and ambient sound.

Support (Accent) Microphones

When an orchestra or other large ensemble is recorded, the principal microphones, or *main mics*, are typically placed above the center of the ensemble to provide a good overview of the sound. Depending on the material being recorded, it may also be advantageous to add additional *support* or *accent microphones*, which are placed close to certain instruments in order to give additional highlighting to a soloist's part, an important secondary musical line, or a soft instrument that may not be well represented in the main mic signal. The support microphone signals can be controlled at the mixing board, where their volume and pan positions may be fine-tuned.

The potential drawback of a support microphone signal is that there is a shorter distance between a support mic and an instrument than there is between the ensemble and the main microphones. This means that the support signal is "closer" to the ears than the other signals are. The precedence effect was defined earlier: the first wavefront reaching the auditory system provides the localization cue, no matter how low in intensity it may be. As discussed in Chapter 3, the ear is quite sensitive to slight differences in time. With a support microphone positioned closer to an instrument than to the main microphones, the support signal is picked up earlier than the main signal, causing the instrument to stand out from the rest of the ensemble. Although this added prominence may be helpful in some circumstances, over-reliance on support microphones can distort the sound's balance. The support signals do not share the direct-to-diffuse balance of the main microphones and run the risk of weakening the sensation of spaciousness, "flattening" the sound. These undesirable effects can be lessened somewhat by sending the support signal through a delay of a few milliseconds, so that it is more in sync with the rest of the ensemble.

Multi-Microphone Configuration for Recording Large Ensembles

When recording a full orchestra, a single set of main microphones will likely not provide adequate coverage of the entire ensemble. Because no microphone responds as broadly as our ears do, simply using two microphones will not capture all of the nuances of a concert hall. The art of the recording engineer is to synthesize the sound of the hall into a stereo playback format. A number of microphones may be employed to ensure that sound is captured from a number of perspectives.

The heights of these microphones depend on the venue and is something that engineers learn with experience. Eargle (2001) suggests using two main microphones in an ORTF pattern, typically 1–2 meters from the edge of the stage. In addition, two flanking omnidirectional microphones to either side of the ORTF pair can ensure that the full range of strings is picked up. Their supplemental signal should be 6–8 dB lower than the main microphones' signal.

To ensure coverage of the winds and other upstage instruments, a supplemental ORTF pair can be placed above the center of the orchestra, about halfway back, also at a signal level 6–8 dB lower than that of the main microphones. As the instrument's signals will travel different distances to reach the two ORTF pairs, a slight delay may be put on the supplementary pair to compensate for the time difference.

If there are soloists or featured parts in a particular piece, accent microphones may be placed near those instruments to give them added presence. These accent microphones should also be at a lower level and at a delay from the main microphones to ensure their signals blend well into the overall sound. An additional pair of microphones may also be placed in the back of the venue to capture the sound of the room.

However, there is no hard and fast rule about the number and placement of microphones. This configuration is just one suggestion, albeit one from a seasoned master in the field, which illustrates the kinds of considerations involved in choosing and placing microphones to record large ensembles.

Surround Recording Configurations

The goal of surround recording is to offer enhanced "presence" or "immediacy" to music recordings, giving listeners a stronger sensation of being present in the concert environment than is possible with two channels. The five-channel format has become the norm for cinema stereo soundtracks. This layout consists of three front channels (left, center, right) and two surround channels (left-surround, right-surround). (Multichannel formats will be discussed more fully in Chapter 8.) While there have been limited releases of five-channel music recordings, as of this writing they have not gained significant footing in the commercial market. However, given the prevalence of the format for film and video presentations, it is valuable to consider how music may be recorded effectively in five channels.

In general, the methodology is to use the front microphones as main microphones, with an added center channel providing increased localizability. The surround microphones are used for reverberant sound. Three microphone configurations, shown in Figure 7-27, are described here.

INA 5

The most straightforward configuration is the *Ideale Nierenanordnung ("INA 5; ideal cardioid")*, created by Ulf Herrmann and Volker Henkels of H & H Tontechnik in Dusseldorf. Five cardioid microphones are oriented in five directions to supply the five channels.

THE FUKADA TREE

The *Fukada Tree configuration* was developed by Akira Fukada of NHK (Nippon Hoso Kyokai, or Japanese Broadcasting Corporation). It builds on the INA 5 configuration by employing seven microphones. Five cardioid microphones pick up the five channels. In addition, two omnidirectional microphones are placed "wide," outside the front left and right microphones, and their signals are equally shared between the left front/left-surround and right front/right-surround channels. The added right-of-right and left-of-left omnidirectional signals are meant to supply an expanded spatial impression.

OCT SURROUND

The *OCT surround configuration* is an expansion of the *OCT (Optimum Cardioid Triangle)*, a two-channel stereo configuration developed by Günther Thiele of the Philipps University of Marburg. The OCT consists of a front-facing cardioid microphone combined with two hypercardioids that face 90° to the left and right. In OCT surround, this basic triangle is supplemented by four bidirectional microphones placed some distance behind the front triangle (the exact distance depends on the size of the performance space). These rear microphones provide the material for the surround channels. The main triangle provides directional material, while the rear microphones complement the triangle with diffuse, nondirectional material.

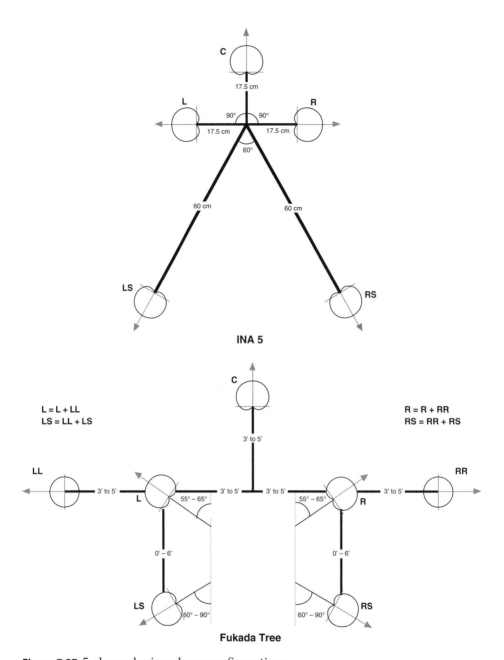

Figure 7-27 5-channel microphone configurations

EXPANSIONS OF THE SPHERICAL STEREO MICROPHONE

Spherical microphones were mentioned above as a type of quasi-coincident configuration, consisting of two omnidirectional microphones positioned like ears within a head. Some offer an expanded configuration that adds two bidirectional microphones to the two standard omnidirectional microphones. The bidirectional microphones are attached beneath the sphere and face forward. Five channels may then be derived from these four microphones. A center channel may be created by summing the signals from

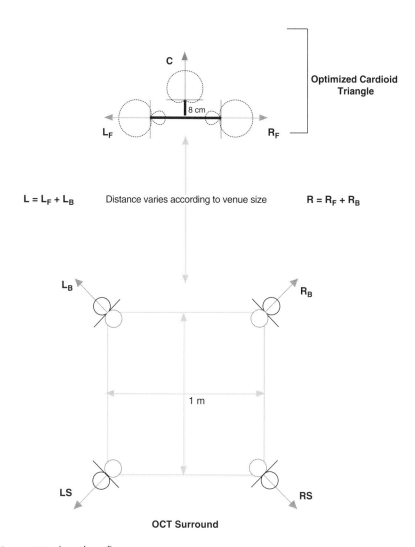

$$L = L_F + L_B \qquad \text{Distance varies according to venue size} \qquad R = R_F + R_B$$

Figure 7-27 (*continued*)

the two omnidirectional microphones. The four corners may be created by treating the omni-/bidirectional pair on each side as an MS configuration, with the front corners derived from the sum of the pair and the rear corners derived from the differences. This addition of the bidirectional pair is meant to give the impression of front and back sound sources.

SOUNDFIELD MICROPHONE

The *Soundfield microphone* consists of four directional microphones arranged in a three-dimensional "X" shape, or tetrahedron (Figure 7-28). It is used in conjunction with a signal processor, which may be either a dedicated piece of hardware or a software program. The processor encodes the signal in a way that allows the recording to be configurable for different playback speaker settings. It is often used with Ambisonics surround sound systems, which will be described in Chapter 8.

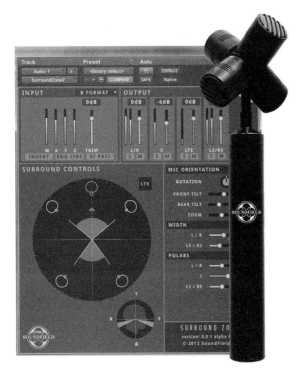

Figure 7-28 Soundfield microphone with SurroundZone2 software
Source: Courtesy of TSL Professional Products Ltd

Loudspeaker Technology

In many ways, loudspeakers and microphones are mirror images of each other. In a microphone, acoustic pressure changes set a diaphragm into motion, and the pressure variations are transduced to voltage variations. In a loudspeaker, voltage variations are transduced into motion, which produce corresponding acoustic pressure changes. A loudspeaker mechanism consists of wire springs, called *voice coils*, that lie within a magnetic field and that are connected to a paper cone. Alternating current that is sent through the coils causes them to move in response (as described in Chapter 4). The movement of the coils is transferred to the cone, which moves in and out in a way that mirrors the audio signal, pushing and pulling the air molecules to create corresponding acoustic energy.

Loudspeakers are like finely tuned motors. And just like automobiles, different models have different characters, appeal to different sorts of listeners, and carry broad cultural associations. They do not simply reproduce audio objectively. The cone has its resonant frequency, and the wooden enclosure also acts as a resonator. To some degree, all speakers filter audio signals.

Loudspeakers may be either active or passive. *Passive loudspeakers* are powered by an external amplifier, to which they are connected with speaker cable. Speaker cable comes in different grades and quality levels. In general, longer cable runs should use thicker cable, which has less resistance than thinner cable, to avoid signal degradation. Beyond this basic premise, speaker cable types are also the subject of some controversy. While some prefer to use expensive speaker cable, others claim that the results are just as good when they use inexpensive electrical wire, available from any home improvement store. Like speaker cable, the electrical wire consists of two cables, which can connect to an amplifier and loudspeakers in the same way that speaker cable may be connected.

Active loudspeakers include a built-in amplifier. They are connected by audio cables to an instrument or a mixer. Many are quite robust, meant for live performances and tours with nightly set up and tear-down. While the amplifier-speaker combination used to imply a low-quality loudspeaker, active speakers are becoming the norm due to their convenience and increasingly high-quality sound.

Since cones have their own resonances, a given cone can be expected to favor certain frequency ranges more than others. Loudspeakers often exist in systems, wherein each component produces a different set of frequencies. *Crossover networks*, consisting of lowpass, highpass, and bandpass filters, split the audio spectrum into regions, and send the discrete regions to a cone-coil system that is designed to respond well to its frequencies.

The larger the cone, the larger the wavelengths it can reproduce. Part of what differentiates the components of a speaker system are the different sizes of cones. Large-coned units are called *woofers*, and produce the low end of the spectrum. In many cases, woofers also rely on psychoacoustics to supplement their frequency range. Many cannot fully reproduce lower frequencies, but produce harmonics of them. From these harmonics, the auditory system interpolates lower bass content via the phenomenon of the missing fundamental (described in Chapter 3).

Tweeters, in contrast, are designed to deliver the higher end of the spectrum. Some types consist of horn/driver systems that act as a kind of megaphone: air is first compressed within its narrower throat end, and then radiated outward through the wider flared end. Other types of tweeters are a dome shape, made of synthetic material that is specially designed to produce short wavelengths at high energy levels. In addition to effectively delivering higher frequencies, tweeters tend to deliver highly directional signals, as their shorter wavelengths have less of a tendency to diffract around to the sides and back of the cabinet than do the longer wavelengths produced by woofers.

Speakers come in two main enclosure types. An *air suspension speaker* is an air-tight, closed box. A *bass-reflex* (or vented box) *enclosure* is not airtight, but has a port-hole in the speaker cabinet that allows it to act as a tuned resonator. This allows better production of longer-wavelength (lower-frequency) content.

Some loudspeakers are *integrated units*, in which both the woofer and tweeter are contained within the same enclosure along with the crossover network. Such a system is called a *two-way system*. A *three-way system* also contains a mid-range speaker. Integrated systems are common for personal computer speakers, studio monitor speakers, or amplification in small venues.

Monitor speakers come with a higher price tag than standard loudspeakers. They are meant for critical listening facilities, such as music studios (rather than for a restaurant, a living room, or an elevator). The higher price is due to their design specifications, which optimize them to deliver all frequencies as equally as possible.

Large venues tend to use *cluster systems*. These are stacks of speakers that are calculated to produce different frequencies in different directional patterns. As these systems are the most versatile, they are also the most expensive, with the greatest capacity to move the large volumes of air needed to fill a large theater, arena, or stadium.

Loudspeakers are the wildcard of an audio system, as they all add their own particular color to the sound they deliver. The way a particular speaker sounds in a particular room also depends on the dimensions and arrangement of that room. Audio can sound quite different when played over a different type of loudspeaker, and the same loudspeaker can sound different when it is moved to a different room. Matching the acoustic character of loudspeakers with the acoustic character of the rooms in which they are placed is part of the artistic side of acoustics, and is often based largely on personal taste. The subjective nature of loudspeakers was wryly described by Beranek (1996):

> It has been remarked that if one selects his own components, builds his own enclosure, and is convinced he has made a wise choice of design, then his own loudspeaker sounds better to him than does anyone else's loudspeaker. In this case, the frequency response of the loudspeaker seems to play only a minor part in forming a person's opinion.

While much loudspeaker development focuses on improving frequency responses, another active area of development is in highly directional speakers that make sound audible in a desired area and virtually inaudible outside of it. They are somewhat akin to the listening booths that are featured at many science museums, which are parabolic shells placed on opposite sides of a room. Energy generated from a focal point of a parabola is reflected as a tight beam, and energy encountering a parabolic shell is focused to a single point. In science museum exhibits, two people sit in the focal points of two parabolas, and are thus able to hear each other across a crowded room. The same type of thing can happen with an integrated array of closely placed speakers. With different speakers having different delay times, the sound they produce can be focused in a manner similar to the single-point reflections produced by a parabolic surface. These speakers are meant for environments such as museum exhibits, retail spaces, or alarms in control rooms.

Other compelling work is in the design of adaptable sound systems. As described in Ross (2015) and Meyer Sound Laboratories (2015), these systems create configurable auditory spaces, which make it possible for theaters, restaurants, or other venues to transform their acoustic ambience into different-sounding spaces by calculated adjustments in echo and reverberation. This addresses the problem described earlier in this chapter of certain spaces being suitable for either music or spoken presentations, but not necessarily both. A restaurant or banquet hall may benefit from low reverberation during crowded mealtimes, by containing conversations into certain areas to reduce overall noise. The same venue may feature a musical performance at another time, when more reverberation would be beneficial, or a spoken presentation at a different time, when it would be beneficial to spread the sound evenly and intelligibly throughout the space. A restaurant may want to change its acoustic character to suit different times of day and different levels of activity. These configurable audio systems operate via microphones placed in special wall paneling. The microphones constantly sample the reverberation of the space, and present a modified reverberation character via unobtrusive loudspeakers. The desired reverberation character can be controlled with a tablet device, allowing a maître d' to quickly change the space to sounding more lively, more subdued, or more reverberant.

Suggested Exercises

- Record a recital. Record each piece at a different input level. When you can, change locations and record from a new spot in the auditorium, at a variety of levels. Edit the recordings to create an audio CD, with one track per piece or movement of a piece. To ensure a seamless listening experience, insert a very short fade-in before each track starts, and a short fade-out after it ends. Compare the results. How well does the recording match what your ears heard at the event? Which location and level sounds best in terms of:
  o How well loud and soft passages are reflected
  o Representing the reverberation in the venue
  o Clarity of the sound—can musical nuances be heard well?
  o Balance between instruments
  o Stereo imaging
- Make some recordings of a musician using some of the different microphone configurations described in this chapter. Compare the results.
- Create a makeshift comb filter by recording some material, putting two copies of it onto two tracks of a DAW, and then delaying one of them by some small amount. How does the sound change as you increase the delay between them?

- Working with a partner, experiment with the directionality of different types of microphones. Put a microphone in the middle of the room, and listen to its input over headphones. While one person listens, have the other person walk in a circle around the microphone. How does the sound change when you switch from a directional to an omnidirectional microphone?

- Work with a partner in a reverberant space, such as a gymnasium or theater. Have one person act as "performer," staying in one place and reading a short passage and playing a short passage on an instrument. Run a tape measure from the performer to the back of the room. Place a microphone one foot away from the performer and start recording. Have the performer "slate" the recording by saying "one foot," then reading the passage of text and playing the passage on the instrument. Stop recording. Move the microphone to two feet away, and repeat. Continue for about twenty-five feet. When the recording is complete, listen to the results. At what distance would you estimate the reverberation radius to be? How does increasing distance affect the intelligibility of the spoken passage and the quality of the music? At what point does additional distance no longer change the sound quality?

- Having studied the reverberant qualities of this space, how closely can you simulate them with the settings of a reverb plug-in? (For reference, recall that one foot of distance equals approximately a one-millisecond delay.)

- Work with some of the multi-microphone configurations described in this chapter. Gradually change the mix in postproduction and listen to how the quality of spaciousness changes. Start with an MS configuration, and gradually widen the stereo field by bringing up the side mics. If possible, try doing a configuration of about eight microphones at various distances from the performer, such as the orchestral configuration described by Eargle. In the studio, raise and lower the volume levels of the different microphones and see how the sense of the recording space changes.

- Look at waveforms from current popular song releases and recordings made in the 1960s or 1970s. How are they different? What differences can you observe about the sound quality of recordings being made today? If possible, compare waveforms of an original release to the same song on a remastered re-release—what is different about the new version?

- Record a mini solo album consisting of at least five stereo tracks. You should not make a recording of yourself performing, but focus instead on the recording quality you can get of someone else performing. If this is your first recording, it's probably best to record a soloist, as recording larger ensembles creates more complex challenges. Configure the microphones to capture a stereo recording with a good balance of direct and reflected sounds. The project should consist of at least three sessions:

  o Session one—testing and preparation. This session is not to record a piece of music, but to carry out tests. Try different positions for the microphones. Play a single held note and a brief melodic pattern from the instrument. Record this material from a number of different microphone positions, with different microphones.

  o Session two—first recording. Based on what you learned in the first session, try recording some music. Then study it later. Compare your recording to a professionally recorded CD of the same instrument. Is the sound brighter? More compressed? More "upfront" or "closer" sounding? It is likely that you'll be able to find ways you could improve the quality of the sound you recorded.

  o Session three—building on the second session, work toward getting the best sound you can that captures the performance and the venue.

Key Terms

absorption coefficient

acoustic signature

active loudspeaker

air suspension speaker

axial mode

backplate

bass-reflex enclosure

bidirectional microphone

Braunmühl-Weber dual-diaphragm
variable pattern microphone

cardioid microphone

cluster system

comb filtering

condenser

crossover network

diaphragm

diffuse reverberation

direct sound

distance factor or reach

dynamic transducer

early reflection

first-order cardioid microphone

flutter echo

Fukada Tree configuration

hypercardioid pattern

Ideale Nierenanordnung ("INA 5; ideal
cardioid") microphone
configuration

impulse response

integrated unit

intensity recording or coincident
microphone recording

interaural cross-correlation (IACC)

Lambert's cosine law

localization

main mic

modal enhancement

monitor speaker

MS microphone configuration

near-coincident microphone
configuration

oblique mode

OCT (Optimum Cardioid Triangle)
surround configuration

omnidirectional microphone

ORTF microphone configuration

passive loudspeaker

phantom power

precedence effect

pressure

pressure gradient or gradient

proximity effect

quasi-coincident microphone
configuration

random energy efficiency (REE)
or random efficiency (RE)

receptor

reflected sound

reverberation radius

reverberation time

ribbon microphone

room mode

Soundfield microphone

spaciousness

specular reflection

spherical stereo microphone

standard cardioid microphone

subcardioid microphone or
forward-oriented omni
microphone

supercardioid pattern

support or accent microphone

tangential mode

three-way system

time-of-arrival recording

transducer

tweeter

two-way system

variable pattern microphone

voice coil

woofer

XY microphone configuration or
Blumlein configuration

Chapter 8

Treating and Mixing Audio

As outlined at the beginning Chapter 7, a series of steps is involved in producing a music recording. As we discussed, both recording and playing back audio are not straightforward, linear procedures. A good deal of artistry is required to capture sonic nuance and to effectively play it back. No microphone can capture the range of sensations that our ears can, and it is equally rare to find speakers that deliver exactly what they receive. The audio production process is one of artistry and synthesis, using a variety of production tools to enhance what is recorded so that, when played back, it gives the impression of being natural (Begauld, 1996). Much of this synthesis occurs between the steps of recording and playing back. The job of a music producer is to shape the sound in a way that is appropriate for the music being delivered. This chapter will cover some of the steps involved in treating and mixing musical material.

Effects: An Introduction

All music that is recorded or amplified relies on effects to enhance its sound. At a rock concert some years ago, I remarked to the person sitting next to me, whom I had just met, that I was eager to hear what sort of effects and processing would be applied during the extended percussion section that would be featured in the second set. He looked at me dubiously, and respectfully contended that he preferred to believe that everything we heard was originating from the hands of the musicians onstage, and not through electronics that were superimposed onto what they were doing. I didn't have the heart to tell him that when concerts take place in a venue like a large basketball arena, *nothing* that the audience hears comes from the stage. Vocals, guitars, drums, and keyboards were all coming to our ears through the extensive speaker cluster system that was hanging prominently in front of the stage. These are more than just auditory magnifying glasses: music delivered to a concert hall through a PA system needs to be filtered to compensate for the room's frequency response. And once you go down that rabbit hole, everything is fair game. Reverberation may be added, or any number of other effects.

The same is true in studio recording. Most recordings are made in small, dry-sounding rooms. In postproduction, the recording is given character through the use of reverberation, equalization, and other types of effects. The same is true for concert recording, although the extent of processing may be different. Effects are essential just to make electronic audio signals resemble natural sound. That said, many artists take things a step further and use effects as instruments, remolding the sound as

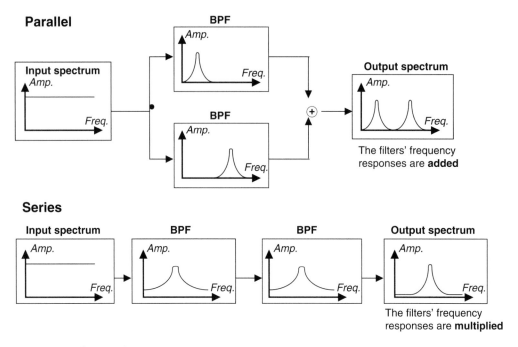

Figure 8-1 Filter combinations

though it were made of modeling clay. This section will cover some of ways that they are able to do this.

Combining Effects

Many effects are the result of filter combinations. Fundamentals of filtering were covered in Chapter 5. This section will go further, starting with two basic ways of combining filters (Figure 8-1):

1. *Parallel:* An input signal is split and each copy of the signal is sent through one or more filters; then the signals are recombined. The frequency responses of the filters are *added* at the output. (Note that a rough bandpass filter could be constructed by using a highpass filter and a lowpass filter in parallel.)
2. *Series* (or *cascade*): An input signal is sent through a succession of filters. The frequency responses of the filters are *multiplied* at the output.

A Few Words on Word Length

Error and Word Length

Many digital audio processors boast high-bit internal processing, such as 32 or 64 bits. Because CD audio is 16 bits (or 24 bits for high-resolution formats), this may lead to some confusion. The key word to bear in mind is *internal.* While the final output will be at 16 or 24 bits, the processor may use more bits to calculate that output. Using more bits helps to reduce errors that can accumulate due to approximation.

Recall that filtering is achieved by arithmetic operations on audio samples. These operations frequently add bits, as shown in the following equations involving binary numbers:

$$100_2 \times 100_2 = 10000_2$$

$$100_2 + 111_2 = 1011_2$$

The same thing happens in base 10. For example, 1.5 times 1.5 equals 2.25; the multiplication adds a decimal place. In a digital system, there are only a limited number of decimal places, so some compromise has to be made. If the result of that multiplication had to fit into only one decimal place, it would have to be rounded—should it be rounded to 2.2 or 2.3? (This issue comes up every month when your bank calculates the interest that should be added to your account. Sometimes, this will come to a fraction of a penny. Guess who gets that extra fraction of a cent. . . .)

Think of the problem tackled by a mosaic artist who wants to create a curved shape, but must do so with pieces of square tile. The smaller the tiles, the more the shape can resemble a curve. But there is a practical limit to how small tiles can be, and the reality is that the mosaic can ever contain a true curve. In the same way, digital audio systems can hold only a finite number of possible values. As described in Chapter 5, a digital recording system measures an infinite number of possible instantaneous amplitude levels, but has to modify (quantize) them, storing them as values of the nearest available measuring increment.

Therein lies the quandary of digital audio. If the result of a calculation requires more than the available number of bits, the only way to proceed is to *truncate* (chop off) the least significant bits before moving on to the next calculation. If multiple operations are involved, then each calculation potentially introduces more error.

Errors are a fact of life in digital audio systems. Some operations average groups of samples, others simply multiply all samples by some value. Even something as simple as adjusting a volume fader is an operation that does arithmetic on samples, and that arithmetic can lead to approximation error. Whatever the operation is, multiplication can lead to longer word sizes.

Converting to Shorter Word Sizes

The precision of sample values is a slippery matter (recall the discussion of quantization error in Chapter 5). For this reason, most processors work with extra-long word sizes to give DSP operations some breathing room. But at some point the word sizes need to be reduced to 16 bits if the project is being prepared for CD. When this point arrives, there are techniques for doing this that minimize error, as was discussed in Chapter 6 in the section on noise shaping.

The crudest solution is truncation—simply lopping off the least significant bits. This can result in lost luster at lower volume lower levels, making aspects like reverb and stereo separation less distinct. You might not miss these lower levels if your destination depth is 24-bit, but truncating from 32 bits down to 16-bit sample sizes will definitely take a bite out of things.

The more refined approach is to use a process called *redithering*. This is related to the dither that is applied during recording (discussed in Chapter 5), when low-level noise is added to the input to refine the dynamic range to allow resolution finer than what is theoretically allowed by the word lengths. A random value is added to the lower bits. If 32-bit samples are being converted to 24-bit samples, a random 8-bit number gets added to each sample, causing elements of the least significant bits to be carried over to the upper 24 bits. Without dither, both the signal-to-noise ratio and the maximum dynamic range of 24-bit audio is 144 dB, and 96 dB for 16-bit audio. With redithering, the effective dynamic range increases by about 20 dB, since at low levels the music can be heard alongside the noise. While adding noise is an imperfect solution, the tradeoff can be minimized through noise shaping, which was discussed in Chapter 6. This is a type of redithering that highpass filters the quantization error distortion, pushing it to the high end of the spectrum, often out of the audio range altogether.

The ideal working process is to stay in a high bit-depth environment as long as possible during all preliminary processing and storage. If, for example, you do your processing in a 48-bit environment, but back up your work to 16-bit files between sessions, you compound the downsizing problems every time you store your work. Noise shaping is helpful, but it's not something to be done over and over. It's more like a final sanding and polishing. Combining files that have had noise shaping applied to them earlier, you might get some unpleasant surprises due to difference frequencies (also called combination tones, which were discussed in Chapter 3).

Suppose you want to crossfade between two files that have been noise shaped. Individually, each may sound fine. But what might not be apparent is that one may have had its quantization error pushed up to, as an example, 18 kHz, while the other file had its distortion pushed to 18.1 kHz. The difference is inaudible until the two files are crossfaded, and the multiplications involved create a kind of sonic grit due to a difference frequency centered at 100 Hz. Like everything else, noise shaping is not a cure-all. It's a tool that should be used only once, at the final step of production.

Latency

Another issue in production is that of processing speed. In computer music systems (as in *all* music systems), timing is everything. As will be described in Chapter 10, software synthesis now allows for the possibility of real-time processing of performers in concert situations. The acoustic performance of a musician may be digitized, processed, and output in fractions of a second. The size of this fraction is critical, however, given that the auditory system can sense inter-onset difference times on the order of milliseconds. At the CD audio rate, the sampling period is 1/44,100 seconds, or 0.0226757 ms. This, theoretically, is the shortest possible amount of time in which a digital audio system can recognize and output audio at this sampling rate. However, it is usually more efficient computationally to fill a buffer of samples and process them all at once, rather than one at a time. Samples may be, for example, processed in blocks of 64, which means that anything done in response to incoming audio requires at least 64/44,100 sec (1.45125 ms) for the new samples to be generated.

Computer operating systems or sound cards may have built-in audio block sizes, typically at 1024, 2048, or 4096 samples. The more samples are held in buffers, the more efficient the computations are and the less suitable the processor is for real-time performance. If live audio is combined with processed audio, large buffers may produce undesirable echoes or comb filtering.

The latency time of a system may be tested by creating an impulse signal on one channel and recording the impulse on the other channel. Then both channels may be viewed and compared in an audio editing program. Viewing them together will show the time difference between them, which represents the system's latency.

Delay-Based Effects

As noted in Chapter 5, the digital filtering process combines a signal with delayed versions of itself. The audible results depend on how much time is involved. Time delays fall into three categories:

1. Delay > 50 ms: audible echoes
2. Delay < 10 ms: coloration, filtering
3. 10 ms < delay < 50 ms: enhancement, increase in volume

Simple Delay

In this most basic delay-based effect type, the signal is combined with a delayed version of itself, resulting in an echo (Figure 8-2), a sonic "two for the price of one." This is called a *simple delay*. Users can typically set the delay time and the volume (gain) of the delayed signal.

Multitap Delay

When a series of simple delays is combined, the configuration is called a *multitap delay*. This term is based on an analogy to plumbing. Picture water flowing through a pipe. If water is drawn from different points along the pipe by inserting taps along its length, it is a multitap plumbing system. With audio multitap delays, the output is combined with a succession of delays. Users may set the time (analogous to the tap location along the pipe) and gain (analogous to the tap width) of each delay (Figure 8-3).

Feedback Delay

As with a feedback filter, a *feedback delay* recirculates the delayed output back into the filter's input. This produces a decaying series of echoes, such as might be heard when yodeling into a canyon. Users may typically set the delay time and the echo decay time (Figure 8-4).

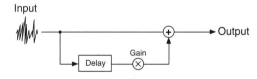

Figure 8-2 Simple delay

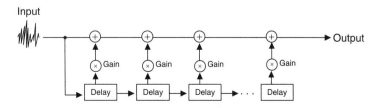

Figure 8-3 Multitap delay

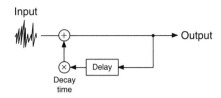

Figure 8-4 Feedback delay

Building Blocks of Delay-Based Effects: Comb and All-Pass Filters

Comb Filters

Undesirable comb filtering was mentioned in Chapter 7, in the context of small-room resonances. While accidental comb filtering can lead to undesirable results, intentional comb filtering is the basis of a variety of effects.

In a basic comb filter, the current sample is combined with a delayed sample, as in this filter difference equation:

$$y[n] = x[n] + a = x[n - D] \tag{8-1}$$

where D is some number of samples. This is similar to the simple lowpass filter discussed in Chapter 5 (Equation 5-4), which had a delay of one sample. Equation 8-1 generalizes Equation 5-4 to describe a delay of an arbitrary number of samples.

The delay time imposed by the filter is D/SR seconds (the number of delayed samples over the sampling rate). The result of this delay has a pronounced effect on the harmonics of the frequency having a period of twice the delay time. As shown in Figure 8-5, the even harmonics of this frequency are reinforced, and the odd harmonics of this frequency are canceled. Frequencies between harmonics are attenuated. The result is a frequency response consisting of a series of regularly spaced spectral peaks and nulls, resembling a comb.

Comb filters may be feedforward or feedback, and may be either *positive sum* (meaning the delayed sample is added to the current sample) or *negative sum* (meaning the delayed sample is subtracted from the current sample).

FEEDFORWARD COMB FILTER (INVERTED COMB FILTER)

The positive-sum comb filter (Figure 8-6) has the difference equation:

$$y[n] = x[n] + x[n - D] \tag{8-2}$$

This filter type produces peaks at:

$$\frac{nSR}{D} \text{ Hz (from 0 Hz to the Nyquist frequency)}$$

and nulls at

$$\frac{(2n - 1)SR}{2D} \text{ Hz (from 0 Hz to the Nyquist frequency).}$$

In other words, spectral peaks are produced at harmonics of SR/D Hz, with nulls occurring halfway between the peaks.

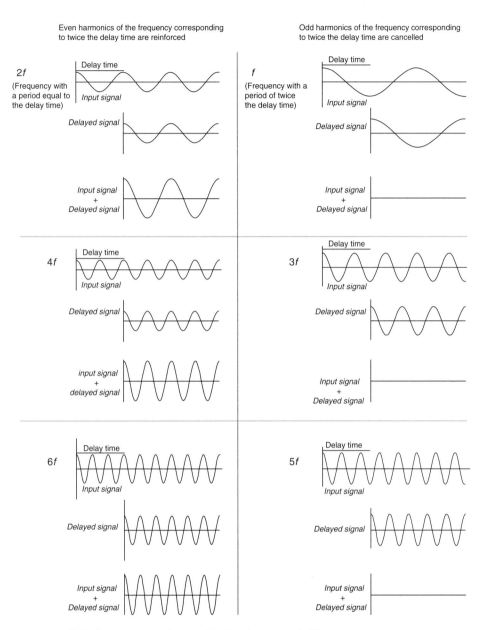

Figure 8-5 Reinforcement and cancellation from comb filtering

A positive-sum comb filter resonates in a similar manner to a half-wave resonator, a tube that is open at both ends (see Chapter 1). Consider a frequency having a wavelength that is twice the tube's length. As shown in Figure 1-12, a tube's resonances are harmonics of this frequency. Recalling the relationship between frequency and wavelength (Equation 2-1), the relationship between Figures 1-12 and 8-5 can be shown by the following:

$$\frac{nSR}{D} = f = \frac{nc}{\lambda}$$

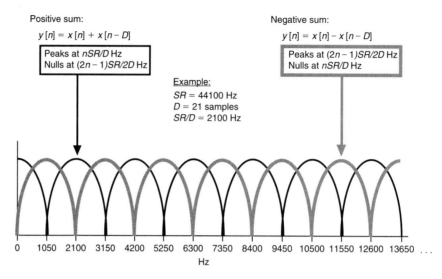

Positive sum:

$$y[n] = x[n] + x[n - D]$$

Peaks at nSR/D Hz
Nulls at $(2n - 1)SR/2D$ Hz

Negative sum:

$$y[n] = x[n] - x[n - D]$$

Peaks at $(2n - 1)SR/2D$ Hz
Nulls at nSR/D Hz

Example:
SR = 44100 Hz
D = 21 samples
SR/D = 2100 Hz

0   1050   2100   3150   4200   5250   6300   7350   8400   9450   10500 11550 12600 13650 ...
Hz

Figure 8-6 Feedforward comb filter frequency response

where the left ratio describes resonant harmonics of a feedforward comb filter based on the delay time, and the right ratio describes resonant harmonics of a tube based on the tube's length. This shows that the delay time of a comb filter is analogous to the length of a tube.

The longer the delay, the greater the number of peaks and nulls. Recalling the spectral symmetry described in Chapter 6, it can be seen that the simple lowpass filter with a delay of one sample, described in Equation 5-4, produces a minimal type of comb filtering: the peaks are at 0 Hz and the sampling rate, and the first (and only) null is at the Nyquist frequency. When the comb filter's delay time is increased, the longer delay simply "squeezes" this frequency response, producing more peaks and nulls within the same frequency range.

As shown in Figure 8-6, the negative-sum comb filter has a change of sign in the difference equation:

$$y[n] = x[n] - x[n - D] \qquad (8\text{-}3)$$

With a negative-sum filter, the position of the peaks and nulls is reversed from the frequency response of the positive sum comb filter: the nulls appear at harmonics of SR/D, and the peaks are halfway between the nulls. The simple highpass filter with a one-sample delay described in Chapter 5 (Equation 5-5) also represents this form. The nulls are at 0 Hz and the sampling rate, and the peak is at the Nyquist frequency.

A negative-sum comb filter is analogous to a quarter-wave resonator, a tube that is closed at one end (Figure 1-13). Consider the frequency having a period of twice the delay time, as in Figure 8-5. The odd harmonics of this frequency are reinforced, while its even harmonics are canceled. In the example above of the positive-sum comb filter, the odd harmonics were canceled. Their presence in the output of the negative-sum comb filter means that the fundamental resonance of the negative-sum comb filter is an octave lower than the fundamental resonance of the positive-sum comb filter, and this frequency is one-half the sampling rate over the delay time. With the negative-sum

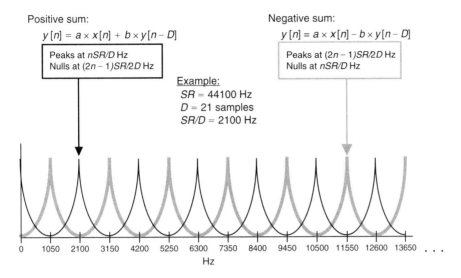

Positive sum:
$$y[n] = a \times x[n] + b \times y[n - D]$$

Peaks at nSR/D Hz
Nulls at $(2n - 1)SR/2D$ Hz

Negative sum:
$$y[n] = a \times x[n] - b \times y[n - D]$$

Peaks at $(2n - 1)SR/2D$ Hz
Nulls at nSR/D Hz

Example:
SR = 44100 Hz
D = 21 samples
SR/D = 2100 Hz

0   1050   2100   3150   4200   5250   6300   7350   8400   9450   10500   11550   12600   13650   . . .
Hz

Figure 8-7 Feedback comb filter frequency response

comb filter, only odd harmonics are produced, and the delay time is analogous to twice the length of a tube.

FEEDBACK COMB FILTER

Feedback comb filters (Figure 8-7) combine the present sample with a delayed output sample. The difference equation's positive- and negative-sum versions are

$$y[n] = \left(a \times x[n]\right) + \left(b \times y[n - D]\right); \quad 0 < a, b < 1 \tag{8-4}$$

(positive sum)

and

$$y[n] = \left(a \times x[n]\right) - \left(b \times y[n - D]\right); \quad 0 < a, b < 1 \tag{8-5}$$

(negative sum)

Feedback comb filters produce peaks and nulls at the same positions as those produced by feedforward comb filters, but the shape of the spectrum is inverted, which means that most of the material between the peaks is eliminated. The result is a pronounced ringing at SR/D Hz (or an octave lower in the case of the negative-sum filter). The amplitude of the ringing depends on the coefficient b. A feedback comb filter may be made to ring at a given frequency by setting the delay time to the inverse of the ringing frequency.

Given:

f – ringing frequency (cycles per second, or Hz)

D – number of samples delayed (samples per cycle of delay)

SR – sampling rate (samples per second)

t – delay time (seconds)

$$(1) \ f = \frac{SR}{D} \frac{samples \ per \ second}{samples \ delayed}$$

which may be rewritten as:

$$(2) \ D = \frac{SR}{f} \frac{samples \ per \ second}{cycles \ per \ second}$$

Since

$$(3) \ t = \frac{D}{SR} \ seconds$$

(2) and (3) may be combined:

$$t = \frac{D}{SR} = \frac{\frac{SR}{f}}{SR} = \frac{SR}{f} \times \frac{1}{SR} = \frac{1}{f} \ sec$$

All-Pass Filters

The "first cousin" of the comb filter is the ***all-pass filter***. Its difference equation combines elements of feedforward and feedback comb filters:

$$y[n] = \left(-a \times x[n]\right) + \left(x[n - D]\right) + \left(a \times y[n - D]\right) \tag{8-6}$$

The name "all-pass" may initially cause some confusion: during its steady state, this filter type passes the average amplitudes of all frequencies equally. This might lead to a misunderstanding that an all-pass filter has no audible effect. However, as was discussed in Chapters 2 and 3, there is much more to a sound than the steady state. For one thing, this filter type has a complex phase response, which gives it a transient response that alters the phases of the sound's attack spectrum. Because the attack is the definitive portion of an audio signal, an all-pass filter audibly colors an input signal that is not steady state.

Furthermore, a sharp transient or decay sent through an all-pass filter is output as a metallic ringing. The filter's impulse response consists of a series of regularly spaced, attenuated impulses. This output effectively smears the finite impulse signal. The succession of attenuated impulses creates a ringing sound at the frequency 1/(*delay time*) Hz, where the delay time is *D/SR* seconds. Thus, the ringing frequency is entirely dependent on the delay time, and is unrelated to the spectrum of the input signal. While this ringing may be created with short delay times, at higher delay times (exceeding the window length over which the human auditory system integrates information, as discussed in Chapter 3), the impulse response of an all-pass filter may consist of discrete sound events, a kind of colored echo.

All-pass filters are particularly effective in cascade configurations. Each filter's impulse response is a series of impulses in response to a single input, and each of these output pulses produces a series of pulses to the next filter in the series. Therefore, the cumulative effect is the multiplication of all pulses output from each of these filters. Even a single all-pass filter has a dense impulse response due to the combination of the feedforward and the feedback components. The cascade configuration thickens this dense output even further. If multiple all-pass filters were configured in parallel, the uneven phase response could potentially cause unexpected amplitude changes in a changing signal. But the blurring effect of a cascade configuration smooths out any unevenness in the filter's output, and produces a diffuse ringing that can be effective in simulating reverberation, a topic that will be covered in the next section.

Delay-Based Effects

Comb and all-pass filters may be combined in different combinations to provide a number of special effects. Many of these have been popular since the 1960s, when artists began to view the recording studio environment as an instrument in and of itself.

Flanging

A *flanger* consists of a feedback comb filter that has a short delay time that oscillates—typically in the range of 1 to 10 ms. The delay time oscillations result in a dynamic comb filter with sliding teeth, continuously expanding and compressing like an accordion. This gives the sound a quality of motion with a varying "whooshing" sound.

Chorusing

A *chorus* is similar to a flanger in that it also combines input with an oscillating delay, but there are two differences. In a chorusing unit, the comb filter is typically feedforward rather than feedback, and the delay time is longer, typically on the order of 20–30 ms. Its output is not as colored as that of a flanger; rather, it sounds something like human singers, who can never initiate notes with exact simultaneity, and thus have a "group" sound due to the blurring of note transients. This chorused sound is often enhanced with a multitap delay, with each delay having a slightly different frequency and gain.

Phase Shifting

A *phase shifter* is another effect that uses modulating delay times. But unlike flanging and chorusing, which are based on comb filtering, phase shifters use a series (cascade) of all-pass filters with oscillating delay times. The shifting, denser delays produce a muted shimmering quality that is gentler than flanging, and less distinct than chorusing, sometimes described as an "underwater-like" sound.

Reverberation

A *reverberator* (or *reverb unit*) simulates the natural propagation of sound in an enclosed space. As discussed in Chapter 7, reverberation is an inherent component of natural sounds. A recording made in a dry recording room, with no reverberation, sounds harsh and unnatural, even when played by an accomplished virtuoso. Therefore, reverberation is considered an essential ingredient in recorded and amplified audio. In the days of analog recordings, there were three classic methods of simulating reverberation, and none offered a great deal of control over the reverb parameters. However, each had its own distinctive—albeit artificial—color, and they became part of the aural vocabulary for recorded music. Today, many digital reverberators have a greater range of controllable parameters, but often include presets that emulate these vintage configurations.

REVERB CHAMBER (ECHO CHAMBER)

A *reverb* or *echo chamber* is the earliest form of artificial reverberation, dating back to the 1930s at Abbey Road Studios in London. Audio was played into a highly reflective room, where it was picked up with at least one microphone; the signal from this room was then mixed with the original signal (Figure 8-8).

SPRING REVERB

In a *spring reverb*, electrical fluctuations were transduced into mechanical fluctuations, which were reflected back and forth along a spring. The mechanical fluctuations from the spring were then transduced back into electrical fluctuations and mixed with the original signal (Figure 8-9). This is a far more compact and inexpensive design than an echo chamber, which requires a dedicated room. Created in 1939, spring reverbs appeared frequently in live performances, often installed into guitar amplifiers or organs.

PLATE REVERB

Plate reverb was invented in the late 1950s. It consists of a transducer that converts the audio signal into mechanical vibrations that are spread over a metal plate. Transducers on the plate convert the vibrations into a signal that is mixed with the original (Figure 8-10). The plates were typically large, weighing on the order of 600 pounds. They were popular in recording studios, either as an alternative to an echo chamber, or as a substitute for one if a studio did not have a dedicated room available.

DIGITAL REVERBERATION

The first computerized reverberation models were introduced in the early 1960s by Manfred Schroeder (1926–2009) of Bell Labs. He created two algorithms that formed the basis of *digital reverberation*, shown in Figure 8-11. In one, a series of five all-pass filters creates a ringing sound that is meant to simulate diffuse reflections within

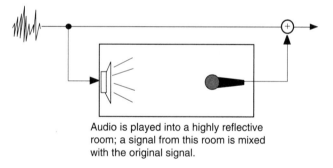

Audio is played into a highly reflective
room; a signal from this room is mixed
with the original signal.

Figure 8-8 Reverb chamber

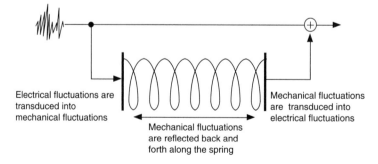

Electrical fluctuations are
transduced into
mechanical fluctuations

Mechanical fluctuations
are reflected back and
forth along the spring

Mechanical fluctuations
are transduced into
electrical fluctuations

Figure 8-9 Spring reverb

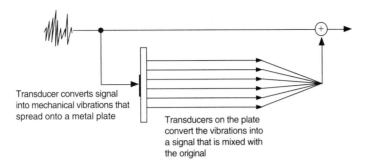

Figure 8-10 Plate reverb

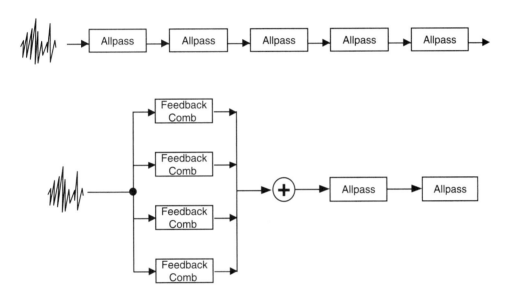

Figure 8-11 Schroeder reverberation algorithms

a room. The filters' gain controls (volume) are used to adjust the echo density. His second algorithm consists of four parallel comb filters, the output of which are summed and sent into a series of two all-pass filters. Both of these designs were particularly effective when filters' delay times were prime to each other, so mathematical relationships among them were minimized, and their delay signals never coincided. This produced a more random-sounding wash than would have been produced by delay times that were simple multiples of each other.

Although Schroeder's reverb algorithms were seminal, they also had their own distinctive coloration. While their sound was attractive in many ways, they tended to simulate the behavior of specular reflections, and had a sound often described as "metallic." However, they represented a baseline that could be explored and expanded. Some elaborated on Schroeder's use of all-pass filters to create a greater sense of diffusion in the reverb tail. Others created designs meant to simulate diffuse reflections for a more natural sound.

As is the case with loudspeakers (see Chapter 7), reverberation is largely a matter of personal taste. Many reverberators have signature qualities that are preferred by some users, and eschewed by others. Often, users do not seek a simulation of real-world reverberation, but a modification of it. For example, many performers prefer a quick buildup of high-density reflections that quickly decay; this was a sound that many described as the "Phil Collins drum sound" in the 1980s, as it was a timbral/stylistic choice he used on many recordings.

Given the variety of moods and sonic spaces that musical artists strive to create, it seems likely that there will never be any one definitive reverb that suits everyone. Rather, the variety of nuances available with different reverbs is another tool in a music studio's palette of choices (Datorro, 1997).

CONVOLUTION REVERB
An alternative to delay-based reverbs are *convolution reverbs* (convolution was discussed in Chapter 6). These allow an impulse response recorded at an actual site to function as the reverb's impulse response, thus "placing" the audio in the space where the impulse response was recorded by convolving the audio signal with the impulse response. They are computationally more complex than delay-based filtering algorithms, but processing speeds of consumer-level computers now make them feasible, and they come as plug-ins for many DAW programs. The tradeoff is that they are not as customizable as manufactured reverbs, which allow specification of room size, reverb time, brightness, and other parameters. But convolution reverbs often have a much more natural sound. The Internet has various sites where impulse responses of castles, caves, factories, and other interesting settings can be downloaded and loaded into convolution reverberators. It can be quite interesting to apply different impulse responses to different effects channels and switch among them, aurally "jumping" from place to place. (Effects configurations will be discussed in an upcoming section.)

Delayed Signals: A Matter of Interpolation
The delay-based effects that we've covered work by means of a buffer or a delay line. The buffer stores a certain number of incoming samples, tapping the line at various points. This is functionally similar to the wavetables described in Chapter 5, from which samples are read according to a sampling increment that causes every *n* values to be read from the table to obtain different pitches (wavetables will be discussed further in Chapter 10).

Because the delay line holds a discrete number of time points and sample values, and not a continuous signal (which would have an infinite number of points and values, as described in Chapter 5), inevitably there will be a need for sample values that lie "between the cracks." Depending on the resonant frequency or delay time chosen for a filter, or the nature of a modulation such as a vibrato, sample values will need to be used that fall between the time points represented by the discrete values held in the buffer. For these cases, the sampling increment needs to be a floating point value rather than an integer. *Interpolation* allows the decimal part of the sampling increment to be accounted for and values to be output that fall between the values stored in the delay line.

Suppose, for example, that given a certain frequency setting, the delay line needed to produce the value of the signal it "holds" at index value 100.25. For this phase position, the output sample may be the sum of:

$$(0.75 \times [index\ 100]) + (0.25 \times [index\ 101])$$

This can be verified by a simple, base case example. Suppose the value at [*index* 100] is 100, and the value at [*index* 101] is 200. If the value needed fell at index 100.25, it is easy to see this interpolated value should be 125. This is shown to be true if we plug these sample values into the equation above:

$$(0.75 \times 100) + (0.25 \times 200) = 75 + 50 = 125$$

This method of interpolation, called *linear interpolation*, effectively derives a straight line between successive sample values and produces the value of the line at a position between each sampling increment. However, as was described in Chapter 2, straight lines tend to produce sharp edges in the wave, which create energy at higher frequencies. For a digital system, this can produce aliasing, especially when the signal already has high energy in the higher areas of the spectrum. As a solution, linear interpolation systems often include a *decimating lowpass filter*, which smooths the output signal to eliminate aliasing. This filtering produces an inherent coloration in linear interpolation, which can sometimes have a muffling effect on the sound.

Other forms of interpolation attempt to interpolate a smooth curve between points. *Higher-order interpolation* calculates values based on a number of samples above and below the desired index point. Some software programs allow the user to select the interpolation method; besides linear interpolation, other methods include all-pass interpolation, warped all-pass interpolation, and cubic interpolation (Figure 8-12). The tradeoffs are between coloration and computational efficiency. Linear interpolation is the least expensive computationally to perform, while higher-order interpolation methods may more resemble the warmer sound of analog processors. The subject of interpolation will return in Chapter 10.

Spectral Effects

Spectral effects do not work with buffers and delays, but instead work directly on the signal's spectral content. While some of the simpler spectral effects have their origin in analog systems, the more advanced types are products of digital technology.

Ring/Amplitude Modulation

Ring modulation is the result of multiplying of two signals, as discussed in Chapter 6. (This does not produce a ringing, as the name might imply; the term derives from the analog design of these filters, which consisted of a set of diodes in a ring formation.) Multiplying signals results in spectral *sidebands* at the sum and difference frequencies of the two signals. For example, if a frequency of 440 Hz is multiplied by a frequency of 100 Hz at the same amplitude, the result will be sideband frequencies of 340 and 540 Hz, each at half the original amplitude. Ring modulation may be considered a sonic demonstration of the trigonometric identity:

$$cosAcosB = 0.5[cos(A + B) + cos(A - B)] \qquad (8\text{-}7)$$

For digital ring modulation, the sum and difference frequencies are the spectral convolution that results from the time-domain multiplication of two signals, as was discussed in Chapter 6.

A ring modulator takes at least one input audio signal. Some can take a second input signal as the multiplier, others produce the multiplier internally as a fixed waveform. With a complex audio input, the output is similarly complex and often inharmonic: every harmonic of the input is duplicated above and below the multiplier, producing a "science fiction" type of mechanical sound. When two signals are input,

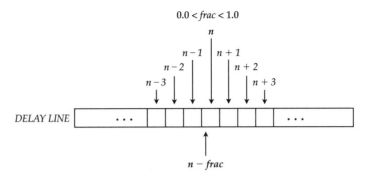

$$0.0 < frac < 1.0$$

Linear interpolation

Interpolate along a straight line between index points

$$y\,[n.frac] = ((1 - frac) \times x\,[n]) + (frac \times x\,[n + 1])$$

All-pass interpolation

Include the last output value

$$y\,[n.frac] = ((1 - frac) \times x\,[n]) + x\,[n + 1]) - ((1 - frac) \times y[n])$$

Warped all-pass interpolation

$$y\,[n.frac] = \left(\frac{1 - frac}{1 + frac} \times x\,[n]\right) + x\,[n + 1] - \left(\frac{1 - frac}{1 + frac} \times y\,[n]\right)$$

Four-point cubic interpolation

Include the values a number of indices before and after the current index

$$
\begin{aligned}
y\,[n.frac] = &\left(\frac{-frac \times (frac - 1) \times (frac - 2)}{6} \times x\,[n - 1]\right)\\
&+ \left(\frac{(frac + 1) \times (frac - 1) \times (frac - 2)}{2} \times x\,[n]\right)\\
&- \left(\frac{(frac + 1) \times frac \times (frac - 2)}{2} \times x\,[n + 1]\right)\\
&+ \left(\frac{(frac + 1) \times frac \times (frac - 1)}{2} \times x\,[n + 2]\right)
\end{aligned}
$$

Figure 8-12 Interpolating the value at a fractional index, n.frac

the result is even more complex, as every harmonic of each signal forms sum and difference frequencies with the harmonics of the other.

Amplitude modulation is the process of periodically changing the amplitude of a signal. As an example, a sine wave may be used as a control signal that modulates the amplitude of another sine wave. When the modulating oscillator operates at low (sub-audio) rates, the result is an oscillation in loudness (tremolo). For example, if the modulator is set to a frequency of 6 Hz, the result is a tremolo that changes in amplitude six times per second. When the frequency of the modulating oscillator is raised to an audible frequency (over 20 Hz or so), there is a qualitative change to the sound. As the tremolo becomes quicker, it becomes a pair of pitches at sum and difference frequencies of the initial audio frequency. The audible result is very similar to that of ring modulation, in that spectral sidebands appear; the difference is that with amplitude modulation the original audio frequency remains audible.

Amplitude modulation is essentially the same process as ring modulation, with the distinction that an offset is added to the modulator. This may be described by a variation on Equation 8-7 with a DC offset added to one factor:

$$(1 + cosA)cosB = cosB + 0.5[cos(A + B) + cos(A - B)] \qquad (8\text{-}8)$$

This is the same process that is employed in AM radio broadcasting. To broadcast AM signals, a high-frequency carrier wave has its amplitude modulated by a wave representing the broadcast material, as shown in Figure 8-13. The carrier, being a high-frequency wave, is able to travel long distances when it is emitted as an electromagnetic wave from a station's antenna. Its frequency corresponds to the station number on the AM dial. A receiving antenna may then be tuned so that it resonates at the carrier frequency, and the electromagnetic signal induces current in the antenna.

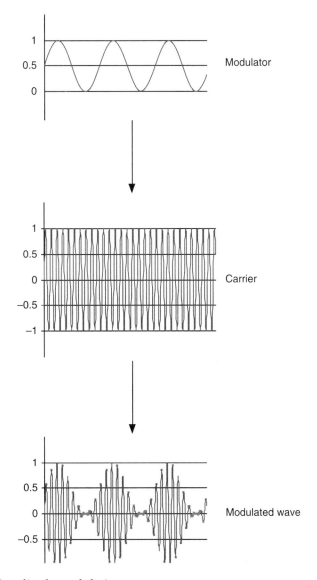

Figure 8-13 Amplitude modulation

The receiver then demodulates the received signal, a process that removes the carrier frequency and leaves only the broadcast material frequencies, which are then passed on to the amplifier.

Amplitude modulation as a form of music synthesis was explored in the radio broadcast facilities that housed the first electronic music studios, beginning in the early 1950s. In contrast to broadcasting applications, in musical applications the carrier frequency is generally in the audible frequency range, which is many octaves lower than radio broadcast carrier frequencies. There is also no demodulation, so that the modulated carrier wave is used as a musical component. Amplitude modulation and ring modulation were central, both technically and conceptually, to many works by composer Karlheinz Stockhausen, such as *Telemusik* (1966) and *Hymnen* (1967).

Channel Vocoder

The *vocoder* (*voice coder*) was introduced in 1940 as a research project carried out by Homer Dudley (1896–1987) of Bell Labs. In 1939, Dudley had introduced the *voder*, a complex speech-synthesis machine, something like a cross between a typewriter and an organ. The vocoder went a step further, as it incorporated analysis and resynthesis. A signal taken from a microphone was sent through a series of bandpass filters. The output levels of each filter were used as volume controls to a corresponding set of output filters, a configuration called an **envelope follower**. Noise and "buzzy" waveforms (such as a sawtooth wave, as shown in Figure 2-10) were sent as input signals to the output filters, with the result that these noise/buzz signals would "talk" (Figure 8-14). If desired, the signal could be manipulated in a number of ways:

- by changing the frequency of the resynthesis waveform
- by harmonizing the output by duplicating resynthesis waveforms that were tuned to different pitches
- by creating timbral variation through **cross synthesis**, whereby the outputs of the envelope followers could control synthesis filters that did not correspond to the same frequency band as the analysis filters (Figure 8-15). In this arrangement, one frequency range's volume changes controlled the filter of another frequency range

While the results were compelling, the hardware required proved too expensive to be put to practical use in telephony. A more economical facsimile was created in the Sonovox, a commercial product that consisted of two disks that were held to the throat. An audio signal was sent through them as the performer would mouth words. The result was that the audio signal was filtered by the vocal tract, and a talking effect was produced. This was used through the 1940s and 1950s in radio commercials (two prominent examples were the talking foghorn in ads for Lifebuoy soap; the talking train in Bromo Seltzer ads), films (the talking train in Walt Disney Pictures' *Dumbo*), and recordings (notably series featuring the young character Sparky, produced by Alan Livingston for Capitol Records in the 1940s and the 1950s, such as "Sparky and the Talking Train" and "Sparky's Magic Piano"). Later devices were derived from the Sonovox, notably the Talk Box used by artists such as Peter Frampton for talking guitar effects.

The vocoder was reintroduced as a musical tool in the 1970s. It reached large audiences through the singing synthesizer effects created by composer/synthesis Wendy Carlos for the film *A Clockwork Orange* (1971). It was also used by artists such as the German band Kraftwerk for futuristic techno effects. Many DAW programs feature vocoder plug-ins, as do some hardware synthesizers, some of which feature built-in microphones for vocal processing.

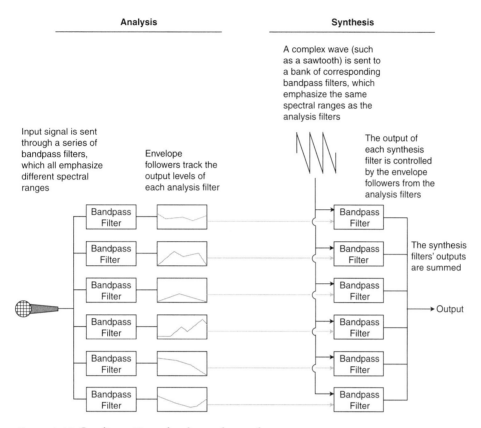

Figure 8-14 Configuration of a channel vocoder

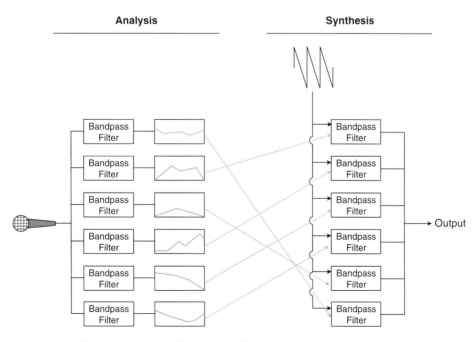

Figure 8-15 Cross synthesis with a channel vocoder

Phase Vocoder

The *phase vocoder* was first described in the 1960s, and began to be implemented in computer music systems in the 1980s. An early piece that featured it was Jonathan Harvey's *Mortuous Plango, Vivos Voco* (1980), which blurred distinctions between recordings of a boy singer and the timbre of a cathedral bell.

The functionality of the phase vocoder is commonly described with two conceptually different but mathematically equivalent interpretations (Dolson, 1986):

1. as a processor that sends a signal through a bank of bandpass filters,
2. as a series of Short Time Fourier Transforms.

In the first interpretation, the signal is considered to be sent through a bank of bandpass filters. Any signal can be created from projections of a rotating phasor within a unit circle (see Figures A1-3, A1-4, and 5-24). The phase vocoder reverses this process, taking an input signal and interpreting its samples the results of a rotating phasor function. It derives the phasor's magnitude and radian velocity from trigonometric principles described in Appendix 1. The phase vocoder is named for the process of estimating the signal's frequency by observing the difference in magnitude between each angular rotation of the phasor. Frequency deviations in the signal within each filter's passband can be tracked, making phase vocoders well suited for following the variations found in many musical signals.

Because the phase vocoder is a software-based instrument, the number of bandpass filters may be determined by the user, and represents a compromise. Ideally, the passband of each filter contains only one partial of the signal. If the passband is wide enough to contain multiple partials, the analysis may be distorted due to interference or cancellation of multiple partials between the passband. Increasing the number of filters, therefore, can create a more effective analysis of the signal. But this is more expensive computationally. Furthermore, as was pointed out in Chapter 5, the narrower a filter's bandwidth, the longer its impulse response, which in a phase vocoder may mean that the filters respond too slowly to reflect changes within the signal. The number of filters used depends on the musical signal and the effect desired by the composer. It is a matter of taste, often arrived at through experimentation.

The second interpretation considers the phase vocoder to be a series of Short Time Fourier Transforms. In this case, the number of spectral components depends on the number of samples applied to the transform, as described in Chapter 6. It is more efficient to use sample blocks that are a power of two in size, so that the FFT may be used for analysis, particularly when real-time analysis and resynthesis are needed.

Whichever interpretation is preferred, the bottom line is that once the signal is converted to the spectral domain, any number of manipulations can be done on the spectral data before it is converted back to a time-domain signal. The most common applications of the phase vocoder are pitch shifting and time stretching, although many other spectral modifications are possible.

With simple wavetable synthesis, changing a signal's pitch also changes its duration, and vice versa. This is achieved by changing the sampling increment, and is the digital equivalent of changing the playback speed of a vinyl record or analog tape. Phase vocoding allows effects such as pitch shifting without changing duration, and time stretching without changing pitch (although extreme changes in either will produce noticeable coloration). Extending the duration is a matter of either creating interpolated phase angles (filter bank interpretation) or performing inverse FFTs less often than analysis FFTs are performed (FFT interpretation). Pitch change is accomplished by altering the radian frequency of the signal—that is, by manipulating the phase angle between successive samples. This is the basis of pitch correction plug-ins (an enhancement that some artists arguably place too much reliance on).

Phase vocoding is another area of active development. Besides pitch shifting and time stretching, phase vocoding plug-ins offer effects such as morphing between instrumental timbres, averaging spectral energy in certain frequency bins over time, limiting, filtering, swapping energy between spectral regions, or providing random spectral modulations.

Dynamic Effects

Another category of effect alters a signal's dynamic range (the difference between the highest and lowest amplitude levels). These alterations go beyond simple volume modifications, and can have wide-ranging effects on the character and timbre of the sound.

Compressor/Limiter

A *compressor/limiter* reduces input levels when they exceed a certain threshold. Thus, the dynamic range of the signal is reduced, or *compressed*. Case (2007) describes compressors as automated volume faders, then goes on to stress that this deceptively simple explanation just scratches the surface. The differences among compressors include how quickly the "faders" move, and the shape of their trajectory. The effect may be described by a *transfer function* (Figure 8-16). When input level are lower than a user-specified threshold, the output level matches the input level. Above the threshold, the output level is mapped to a value below the input level. The compressor's output is described by a ratio of input change over resulting output change: the number of decibels the input must increase to result in an output change of 1 decibel. When the ratio is above a value of 10:1, the more extreme effect is called *limiting*.

The output of a compressor/limiter is typically the result of a calculation done on the RMS value of a window (block of a designated size) of samples (see Chapter 2 for an explanation of RMS). In addition to setting the threshold level and the slope of the

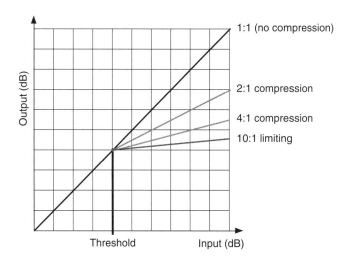

Figure 8-16 Compressor/limiter transfer function

transfer function above the threshold, users may typically adjust the attack and release times—that is, the length of time after the input level rises above the threshold that it takes until the compression is activated, and how long after the input falls below the threshold it takes for the compression to stop. A long attack time can blur an instrument's transient. For example, many percussive transients sound loud initially, but then quickly fade as the compression takes effect. A long release time can extend an instrument's release if the instrument's natural amplitude level falls below the compression threshold faster than it takes the release time to activate. Compression/limiting is useful for evening out an inconsistent signal (such as a player moving about and not maintaining a consistent distance from a microphone).

Another type of automated volume control with a compressor is called a *sidechain*. Sidechaining applies compression to one track, but activates the compression based on the level of another track. This is sometimes done for voice-overs. The vocal track controls a compressor that is applied to a music track, so that when an announcer begins speaking, the volume level on the music track drops automatically, and rises again when the announcement stops.

Special effects can be achieved by setting high attack and release times, creating unnatural-sounding transients or decays as the shape of the wave is changed. This means that compressors do not only keep volume levels within limits; they also can change the shape of the wave, significantly changing the timbre. If the amplitude goes well above the threshold, the wave may be flattened, adding harmonic distortion to the sound.

Compressors are an advanced effect that requires training and experience to learn to use well. They are essential in recorded music for focusing the sound. However, I recommend to beginning students that they avoid them altogether, particularly in projects that involve using prerecorded audio clips. Granted, avoiding them is not always possible, as softsynths often come with built-in compressors that are difficult to disable (softsynths will be covered in Chapter 10). But this is another topic that raises the subject of ear training. Compression is not some kind of magic button. Naïve users may overload the sound of their mix, thinking that compressor will prevent clipping (distortion due to exceeding the available volume range) and therefore make the sound tolerable. But lowering the volume does not necessarily solve the problem. While the compressor may control the volume levels and keep them from clipping, the sound can still suffer from a loss of clarity—a colleague and I call it the "basketball bouncing in a gym" effect, to describe the oversaturated lack of distinction. Also, different compressors respond differently, and their settings are not standardized; they often use an arbitrary scale, so that a setting of, say, 5 for a parameter may mean one thing for one brand of compressor, and something entirely different for another brand. Therefore, beginning students are often better served by first learning to mix without relying on compression, and then learning to use it for nuance as an advanced topic. At that point, compression can be introduced as an enhancement rather than as a crutch.

Compression can add vitality to a track that is lacking it. A drum may gain punch, a guitar may get a dose of nasty grittiness, vocal tracks may gain intelligibility if low levels are brought up, or a bass guitar can seem to wrap the listener in a sensual embrace due to artful adjustments of attack and decay times that change its timbre. Compression can also keep instruments from stepping on each other in a mix. If a bass and a bass drum are both keeping the beat, the combination of these two low instruments may result in a muddy sound. Adjusting the attack time on the bass can maintain its transient, while a quick decay can ensure that its sustain doesn't muddy the bass drum. By tweaking compression on the bass and the bass drum, the engineer can choose to let

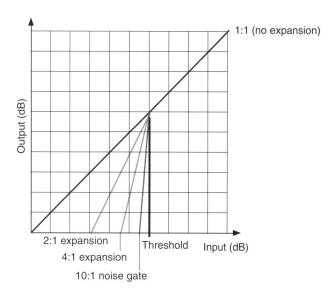

Figure 8-17 Expander/noise gate transfer function

one of them initiate the beat by emphasizing its transient and the other instrument provide the sustain. But this is likely to be a fine balance, achieved through trial and error. Using compression well means that the engineer has to rely primarily on her experience and her ears, and not just use compression as a brute-force approach to keeping volume levels down.

Expander/Noise Gate

An *expander/noise gate* performs the opposite function of a compressor/limiter. Rather than reducing a signal's dynamic range, an expander makes it larger. An input signal is windowed, with processing based on the RMS of the amplitudes in each window. As the transfer function shows (Figure 8-17), an expander reduces those levels that are below the threshold even further. The quiet sections of the signal become even quieter, so the dynamic range becomes greater. The *expansion ratio* describes the number of dB that the output will drop for every drop of 1 dB in the input. Levels that fall below the transfer function are eliminated entirely. An extreme level of expansion, greater than 10:1, is called a noise gate. As with a compressor/limiter, users may typically choose the threshold level, the expansion ratio, and the attack and release times. A common use of expansion is to remove low-level noise from a signal.

Companding

Compression and expansion may be used in combination for noise reduction or transmission over a channel with limited dynamic range, a process called *companding*. On transmission, a compressor allows the signal level to be raised, thus increasing the signal-to-noise ratio. When the signal is received, an expander restores the original dynamic range, reducing any noise acquired during transmission.

Normalization/Maximization

Normalization/maximization adjusts all sample values proportionally, typically to increase the overall volume. It's a bit like the old saying: "A rising tide raises all boats."

If we could control a harbor's water supply, we could make the boats go up or down at will. If all the boats are under a bridge, we need to take care and raise the boats only until the tallest mast brushes the underside of it. If we really must raise them further, we have to start by shortening the tallest masts.

NORMALIZATION

Normalizing is like raising all boats until the tallest mast hits the bridge. That is, a normalizing algorithm scans an audio file and finds the highest sample level. It calculates the percentage that sample needs to be raised to hit 0 dB Full Scale (0 dBFS, 100 percent of the maximum possible level). It then adjusts every sample by that same percentage. Many normalizers allow users to choose what the maximum level should be, 0 dBFS or some percentage thereof.

When mixes are assembled into an album, normalizing can be very helpful. Often, different tracks have been recorded and mixed at different times and places. Each sounds fine in isolation, but when they're put together there are often overarching differences among tracks, such as overall EQ and volume levels. Normalizing can create a volume context for the album, with carefully adjusted volume balances among the tracks. This is an important part of the mastering process, which will be discussed further at the end of this chapter.

But normalizing can only work if there is sufficient headroom. If the highest samples are already at or near the peak position, then nothing more can be done to normalize the audio file. An occasional peak from a plucked string or snare drum can disable normalizing.

MAXIMIZATION

Maximizing is an attempt to inject tracks with digital steroids, increasing the overall RMS level of a file without clipping it. The audio is first compressed (lowering those tallest masts). With the added headroom, the track can be normalized (allowing all masts to be raised). Some maximizers use look-ahead techniques to anticipate peaks and lessen them before the samples are actually read.

While maximizing can be useful, like compression it lends itself to being misused. Psychoacoustically, when the same material is played at different volume levels, the louder one often sounds more "present" (at least in the short term). This has led to a phenomenon called the "Loudness Wars" in the audio production industry, where the goal has become to make albums sound as loud as possible, even if dynamic range is lost in the process. Despite first impressions, audio that has consistently high RMS becomes fatiguing to hear. Furthermore, it lacks distinction: with everything equally loud, nothing can stand out. Music is much more effective when it contains contrasts instead of blaring constantly. (For a compelling demonstration of this phenomenon, readers are urged to view Mayfield [2009] on youtube.com.)

Some advertising for maximizers gives the impression that they perform some sort of trickery that makes audio "radio ready" (read: louder than everyone else). Like all tools, these can be useful when used correctly, but they should not be regarded as a panacea. There's a risk of creating a distorted and fatiguing sound, not to mention the added quantization error that results from all the multiplication operations involved in rescaling the audio samples. Like reducing the sample size (discussed earlier), maximization is something that should ideally be done only once, as a very last step in the production, and not something that gets done repeatedly.

Mixing and Signal Flow

The central component of an audio system is the mixer, a type of device that was introduced in Chapter 4. This is where the various audio signals are combined and processed. A mixer acts as a traffic controller for signals entering and leaving it. Signals are often split and sent to different processing operations, to be recombined later. Sometimes signals are sent out of the mixer and then sent back in again. Figure 8-18 illustrates the physical layout of a "generic" mixer. Figure 8-19 shows a block diagram of the mixer. It is fashioned after the layout of block diagrams in commercial mixer documentation manuals: the signal flow goes from left to right, with the various output routes arranged vertically.

A mixer may be an analog or digital piece of hardware, or a software program. An analog mixer routes streams of voltage, or current. A digital mixer has ADCs at the input and DACs at the output, and it routes streams of binary numbers. A software

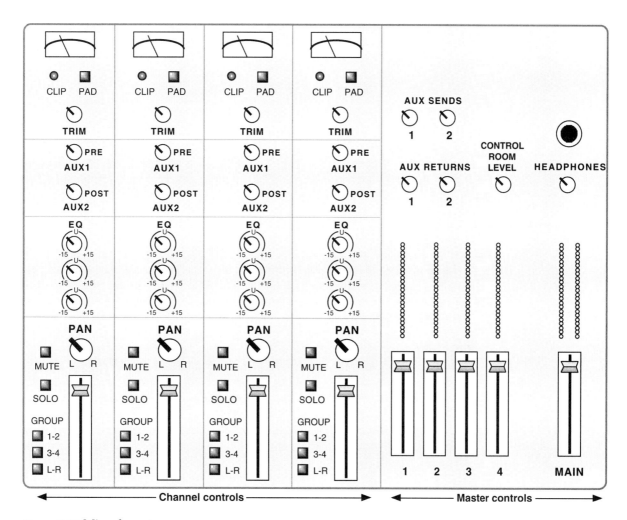

Figure 8-18 Mixer layout

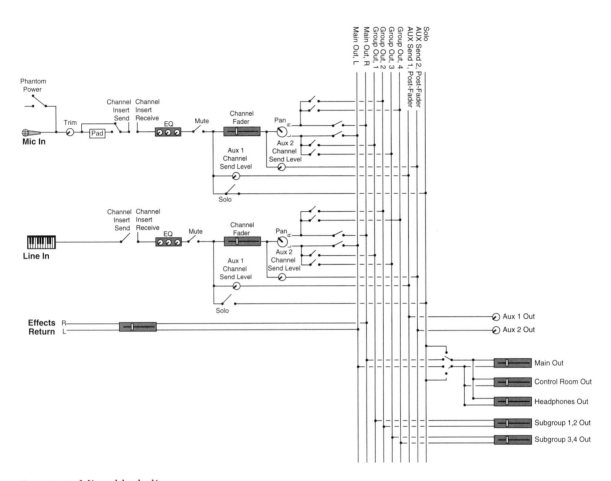

Figure 8-19 Mixer block diagram

mixer is a simulation of a hardware mixer that runs as a computer program. Its elements may be addressed either through mouse clicks or via a ***control surface***, which is a set of buttons, knobs, and sliders that can send information to corresponding elements in the software mixer. All types are similar conceptually.

Channels

Each input signal is sent to a mixer ***channel***. Often, an input channel corresponds to a single instrument, but this is not always the case. Some instruments, such as drum sets, may have multiple microphones assigned to them, each of which goes to a separate mixer channel. A large ensemble, such as a choir, may be picked up by several microphones that are suspended over different sections of musicians. Each section may then be sent to a different mixer channel, where the balance among the sections may be controlled.

Most of the controls on a mixer are ***channel controls***. Channel controls are arranged in vertical ***strips***. Recognizing the repetitiveness of the strips simplifies the array of knobs, sliders, and buttons on the surface of a mixer (just as recognizing the repetitiveness of white and black key patterns simplifies the layout of a piano keyboard).

Mixers can take two types of input: *line level* and *mic level* (see Chapter 4). Some mixers have inputs assigned specifically for line or mic-level sources. Others can take either input type and automatically make the appropriate adjustments for signal level. Still others have two jacks at each input, one for each level, such that using one jack overrides the other. Figure 8-19 shows signal paths for one line-level input and one mic-level input.

Mic level inputs typically have a *pot* (short for *potentiometer*) to adjust the input level, labeled "trim" or "gain." Mic inputs also typically have a *pad* switch that reduces extra "hot" (loud) signals. A *clip light* is a warning signal, usually in red, that turns on when the signal rises to a level that is likely to result in distortion.

Level Meters

One of the fundamental tasks of a mixing board operator is to be aware of the various input levels, as well as the overall output level. Traditionally, input levels are reflected on VU (*volume unit*) meters, which are needles that lean all the way to the left at an input level of zero, and lean to the right as volume levels go up. VU meters are typically at the very top of each channel strip, as shown in Figure 8-18. The level indications are somewhat different on analog and digital meters, which is sometimes a hurdle for engineers who transition from analog to digital mixers. Digital meters can clip when even a single sample hits peak (others have thresholds, such as five consecutive samples at maximum), even though this may not produce any audible distortion. Analog VU meters respond more slowly, closer to the response rate of the human ear. Digital meters may be informative, but their clip lights may not necessarily reflect what we hear. Still, digital clipping should be regarded as a sign of danger, as opposed to clipping on an analog mixer, where moderate amounts of it may be acceptable. The rule of thumb is that digital levels are far less forgiving of peaks than analog levels are, so it's best to avoid clipping of any kind in digital tracks.

When monitoring, it is important to make sure that the speakers, whether they are headphones or monitor speakers, are set to *unity*, which means that they do not amplify or attenuate the signal they are receiving. When a signal exits a processor at the same level at which it entered, the processor is said to be operating at unity gain. (*Gain* refers to the ratio of a signal's output power to its power on input.) A common mistake made by beginning students is to mix while wearing headphones that have their volume at a low level. They turn up the volume of their mix, somehow not noticing all of the red clip lights that illuminate. The first step in creating effective mixes to make sure the levels of the monitor speakers or headphones do not give a deceptive rendition of the actual mix levels.

Phantom Power

As discussed in Chapter 7, some microphones require a voltage input to operate. This voltage, or phantom power, is often supplied by the microphone preamplifier in the mixer and sent via the microphone input cable. The audio travels down the cable to the mixer as AC, while the phantom power travels up the cable like a DC undertow to the microphone that it powers. Phantom power may be applied globally, for the entire mixer, or assigned to only one channel.

As a troubleshooting tip, if there is no apparent signal from a microphone, the phantom power may need to be switched on. As a further caution, some devices, such as vintage ribbon microphones, can be damaged or destroyed if the phantom power is on when they are plugged in. Because all three pins of the cable will never make contact

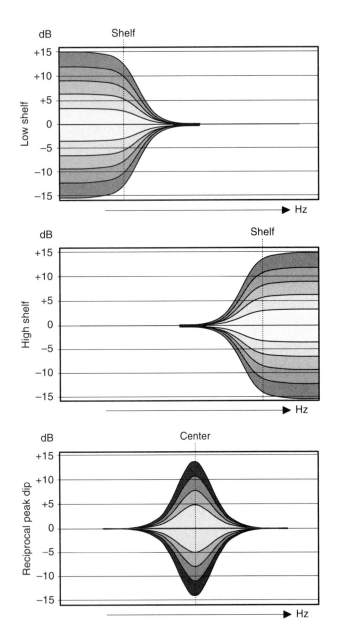

Figure 8-20 Highpass and lowpass shelf filters and reciprocal peak dip bandpass filter

at exactly the same moment, the first one that does can receive a voltage spike that can damage fragile circuitry. Therefore, phantom power should be off when the microphone is plugged in, and switched on only after the plug is securely in place. While there is some evidence that this danger may be overstated, those who prefer to err on the side of caution point out that no microphone has ever been damaged by being plugged in when the phantom power was switched off.

Channel Insert

Many mixers have a channel-level Send/ Return route to direct an input signal out for immediate processing, such as compression or expansion. Typically, this is done with a single jack that handles both the input and output signals. A special Y-shaped cable is often used for *channel inserts*. The base of the Y is inserted into the Insert jack and is capable both of sending and receiving the audio signal. The two ends of the Y go into input and output jacks of an external processing device.

Equalization

Equalization (EQ) is a set of specialized lowpass, highpass, and bandpass filters. A mixer typically features lowpass and highpass *shelf filters* and one or more midrange bandpass *reciprocal peak dip filter(s)* (Figure 8-20). When an EQ knob is at the 12:00 position, no filtering is being applied. This position is often marked "U" to indicate unity. Turning the knob to the left or right attenuates or amplifies, respectively, certain frequency ranges. The "generic mixer" shown in Figure 8-18 offers a gain of plus or minus 15 dB with each EQ range.

A shelf filter provides flat amplification or attenuation above or below a given shelf frequency. Many mixers have fixed shelf frequencies for HI EQ and LO EQ knobs. A low shelf filter affects all frequencies below the shelf, and is meant to treat bass drums or bass parts. A high shelf filter affects all frequencies above the shelf frequency, and can add extra presence to instruments such as cymbals or wood blocks. Both these high and low ranges are likely places for background noise to appear, and attenuating the shelf filters can sometimes lower the noise level.

MID EQ ranges attenuate or amplify frequencies on either side of a center frequency. A reciprocal peak dip filter is a special type of hybrid filter whose bandwidth varies with gain level. Thus, this filter type is a hybrid of both fixed Q and variable Q filters (Q, the ratio of center frequency over bandwidth, was described in Chapter 5). *Semiparametric filters* allow the center frequency to be adjusted. High-end mixers may feature *fully parametric EQ*, which allows both center frequency and Q to be adjusted.

Equalization can provide useful assistance when needed, but it is meant to be used in small doses. If all of the EQ knobs are being used in extreme positions, it is comparable to adding large amounts of salt or pepper to food in order to make it palatable. It is most likely that there is a problem elsewhere in the signal chain, such as the positioning of a microphone or player.

Channel Fader

A *channel fader* is the volume control for a channel. Adjusting the fader position for each channel sets the balance among the instruments.

Mixer Buses

Signals exit the mixer through *buses*. There are a number of different bus types. The most straightforward are the main stereo output buses at the final stage of a signal's path. But it is common to send a signal out of the mixer temporarily for additional processing, after which it is sent back into the mixer to be recombined with the rest of the signals.

The first bus along the signal path is a type called an *auxiliary send*. Auxiliary send ("aux") buses are used to tap the channel. *Aux buses* are typically used for effects processing and monitor mixes. Depending on the mixer, aux sends may also be labeled "Monitor" or "Effects."

Monitor mixes are useful in live situations where performers need monitor speakers onstage to hear the other players. Some performers may need different mixes (a drummer, for example, may need to hear the bass but not need a strong lead guitar or vocal in the monitor mix). Aux buses allow custom monitor mixes to be created. Mixers have a certain number of aux buses, each of which may correspond to a different monitor mix. The example mixer in Figures 8-18 and 8-19 features two aux buses. Each auxiliary signal tap has a volume control knob on its channel strip. This allows a channel's signal to be added to a given aux bus via the appropriate send knob on the channel strip. This allows a channel's signal to be sent to as many aux buses as needed and at the signal level needed.

Aux sends are also used to send a signal out of the mixer temporarily for effects processing in an external device. After a signal is sent out and processed, it may be returned to the mixer in one of two ways. Some mixers have a special Effects Return jack. Alternatively, a processed signal may be sent into another channel's input, allowing control of both the "dry" (unprocessed) and "wet" (processed) signal on separate mixer channels. Many DAWs create auxiliary tracks, which exist to process material from audio tracks.

An aux send may be either *prefader* or *postfader*, meaning that the signal is tapped either before or after the channel fader sets its output volume. In Figures 8-18 and 8-19, auxiliary send 1 is prefader and auxiliary send 2 is postfader. A monitor send is likely to be prefader, because the monitor mix is set by the volume levels represented by the aux knobs and does not need the extra volume information from a channel fader. An effects send may be either prefader, postfader, or it may be switchable. A prefader send is the most flexible, as it allows the dry signal to be brought to low volume levels via the channel fader, while the tap sent to the effects devices is at full level.

Mute/Solo Switches

The *mute switch* allows a channel to be silenced without moving its fader position. This allows the role of a channel in a mix to be quickly tested. The *solo switch* does the opposite, immediately silencing all channels that do not have the solo switch depressed.

Pan

The *pan pot* determines the proportion of the signal that goes to the left (odd) and right (even) output channels. A channel's output may be sent to a number of stereo outputs. When a channel's output is being sent to a subgroup pair, the pan control determines the proportion of the signal level that goes to the odd and even channels of a subgroup (subgroups will be covered in the next section). When the channel's output is being sent to the main output, the pan control determines the left-right stereo position. The section on stereophony will discuss panning in more detail.

Output Buses

The set of buttons to the left of each of the channel faders in Figure 8-18 is used to direct each channel to any number of available *output buses*. The Main Out (or L-R Out) is what is typically connected to a mixdown machine for the final mix, such as a tape deck, CD recorder, or PA system. Channels may also be sent to *subgroups*, which are also arranged as stereo pairs. Any number of channels may be combined onto one subgroup and controlled by one fader. Thus, if a recording combines a percussionist and a choir, each on multiple mixer channels, the percussion channels may be combined on one subgroup and controlled by that subgroup's fader, and the choir channels may be similarly subgrouped and controlled by another fader.

Mixers are often classified by the number of channel inputs, the number of subgroups (or group buses), and the number of main outputs (for example, 24 × 8 × 2).

Patchbay

A *patchbay* is a routing point between a studio's various devices and its mixer (Figure 8-21). Having to unplug and plug devices to send signals among them can be inconvenient and confusing. It is more intuitive to plug cables into a consolidated patch bay, where each device or mixer channel has the appropriate number of input jacks, or destinations, along the bottom row, and output jacks, or sources, along the top row. (If horror movie terminology helps, think of the bottom row jacks as signal suckers, and the top row jacks as signal spitters.) Patchbay connections are typically made with TRS cables (cable types are described in Chapter 4).

A patchbay can make custom configurations easy to assemble during a session. For example, if an instrument has a particularly large dynamic range, it may be advantageous to record its signal through a compressor and EQ unit. Depending on the context, which unit comes first may vary. With a patchbay, the instrument's output can be sent to the input of the compressor, and the compressor's output into the EQ unit, and the EQ output into the mixer input. If it's then determined that it would be better to send the

Figure 8-21 Samson S-patch plus 48-point balanced patchbay
Source: © 2015 Samson Technologies

microphone signal to the EQ before the compressor, it is a simple matter to make this change by rearranging cables at the patchbay.

In its default state, all of a patchbay's inputs are sent to its corresponding outputs. When a cable is plugged into an input, the default connection is broken, and the signal is sent over the cable. When a cable is plugged into an output, the result depends on whether the jack's configuration is *normalled* or *half-normalled*. When the jack is normalled, plugging into the input overrides any other signal connection to the device. When the jack is half-normalled, the connection between input and output is maintained, so that the input signal to the patchbay adds the cable's material to the signal path.

For example, a default routing might be to send the output of a CD player goes into channel 6 of the mixer. If a cable is inserted into the CD player's output jack in the patchbay, the connection to mixer channel 6 is broken. The signal is sent over the cable instead, to wherever the user decides to plug it. But if the connection is half-normalled, then when a cable is inserted into the output jack, the signal still goes to mixer channel 6, but it can also be sent someplace else, such as to another mixer channel, because the connection has not been broken, only tapped.

With some patch bays, inserting the cable part way creates a half-normalled connection, and inserting the cable all the way creates a fully normalled connection. In this case, the only potential caution is that half-normalled signals are not balanced, because the tip portion of the cable is not making contact. When the cord is fully inserted, all three points are making contact, and a balanced signal is possible.

Stereophony

Many DAW systems allow material to be output to a variety of multi-channel formats, and it is becoming increasingly common for electroacoustic concerts to feature experimental multi-channel configurations. This section will provide an overview of some of the more common multi-channel formats.

Localization vs. Spaciousness

As discussed in Chapter 7, our sense of musical space is the result of having two ears. Just as two eyes give us a visual perception of depth, two ears give us a sense of aural space. *Stereophony* refers to the use of more than one channel of audio to increase the tangibility of recorded music. The advantages of using multiple channels were described in the 1930s, when the first experiments took place. Early recordings and radio broadcasts were monophonic, and the effect was described as though listeners were hearing the sound through a window that was the size of the speaker, cut into the wall of a performance space. When two-channel recordings and broadcasts were introduced, the impression was not the addition of a second window; rather, it was as though there was a single large window spanning the width between the two loudspeakers. While two-channel stereophony is the norm, the term *stereophonic* can refer to any number of channels.

The addition of multiple channels enhances the listening experience through both localization and spaciousness (see Chapter 7). Localization refers to an ability to hear performers' apparent location on an aural stage. In a multi-channel system, localization effects are simulated through differences in loudness between multiple channels. To a blindfolded listener, a sound emanating from one speaker sounds as though it is located at that speaker's location. A sound produced at equal volume from two speakers is heard as a *phantom image* placed in space between them. Changing the volume balance between two speakers causes the phantom image to "drift" toward the louder speaker. Thus, the perceived sound stage, which spans the area between the speakers, can have distinct apparent locations for different instruments, achieved through phantom imaging.

Localization has been found to be accurate and consistent when speakers are spaced no more than 60° from each other. However, while localization can create highly effective listening experiences, it requires that listeners be situated in a "sweet spot" located midway between the speakers. This is not always practical, particularly in domestic settings where placement of furniture or the shape of a room may overrule optimum speaker placement. However, the second sensation, spaciousness, is less dependent on the listener's position. Although its meaning is somewhat vague, it refers to an apparently enlarged listening area, and a greater sense of the sound of the venue through diffuse reverberation.

Simulated Localization in Audio Systems

Volume controls on audio equipment adjust the amplitude level of the signal. The perceived loudness, however, is based on the power of the signal at the listener's position. The distinction is important when the goal is to create the impression that a sound moves from one speaker to another. This effect is achieved by a volume crossfade between stereo channels, and typically the desired impression is that the object maintains a constant distance from the listener, as shown in Figure 8-22.

For the perceived distance to remain constant, the total power emitted by the two speakers must remain constant during the crossfade. The total power of the sound field is the sum of the speaker's amplitude levels squared (recall Equation 2-17). As shown in the top portion of Figure 8-22, this is achieved when amplitude changes correspond to a quarter period of a sinusoidal pattern, rather than a linear crossfade pattern. The sinusoidal amplitude pattern ensures that the total power remains at the full desired level (100 percent of the level, or a constant value of 1), due to the trigonometric identity:

$$sin^2\theta + cos^2\theta = 1 \quad \text{(8-9, also shown in Equation A1-1)}$$

On the other hand, a linear crossfade creates a dip in the overall power level at the midpoint of the fade. When each channel's amplitude level is at one-half maximum, the total power emitted is:

$$(1/2)^2 + (1/2)^2 = 1/2$$

This decreased power level has implications for the perceived distance of the object, which is dependent on the intensity at the listener's position. Recalling the inverse square law, the change in intensity, I, is proportional to 1 over the change in distance, d, squared:

$$\Delta I \propto \frac{1}{\Delta d^2} \tag{8-10}$$

A change in intensity of one-half implies that:

$$\frac{1}{2} \propto \frac{1}{d^2} \text{ or } d^2 \propto 2$$

Thus, the perceived distance at the midpoint of a linear pan is $\sqrt{2}$ (or 1.414 . . .) times the perceived distance at the beginning and end points of the crossfade. The

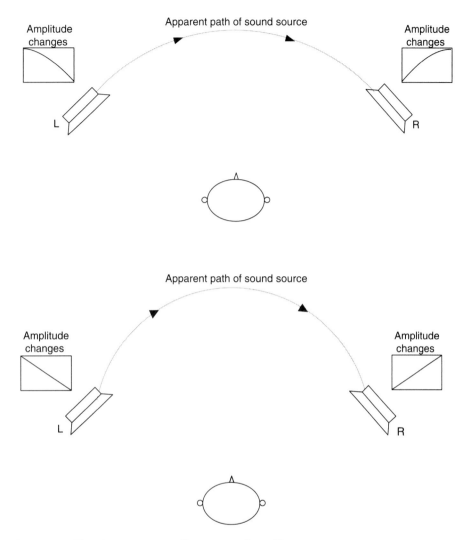

Figure 8-22 Constant power vs. linear panning effects

apparent path of a linear fade is shown in the bottom portion of Figure 8-22. This is known as the "hole in the middle" effect.

Mixer pan pots are designed to create "constant power pans," in which there is a constant power level between the two stereo channels. The amplitude levels assigned to each channel, based on the position of the pan pot, correspond to sine and cosine measurements of the pan pot's position, as shown in Figure 8-23.

Quadraphony

The early experiments in stereophony in the 1930s concluded that three channels—left, center, and right—provided optimum localization and spaciousness. But the outbreak of World War II caused industrial priorities to shift away from research into audio entertainment. When high-fidelity systems were reintroduced in the 1950s, two-channel stereophony proved to be the most practical to implement in consumer systems, which were introduced on the market in the 1960s.

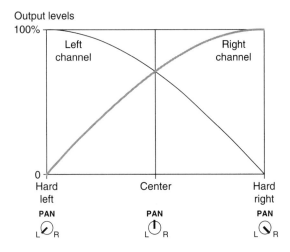

Figure 8-23 Output levels of left and right stereo channels based on pan pot position

In 1970, audio manufacturers introduced *quadraphonic* sound systems, which consisted of four channels: left and right front, plus left and right rear. This configuration put speakers 90° from each other, a good degree wider than the 60° limit required for effective localization. Thus, the advantages of quadraphony were due more to enhanced immersion and spaciousness than to localization. Some artists, notably Wendy Carlos, advocated placing speakers in an arc—at 9:00, 11:00, 1:00, and 3:00—a configuration that offered enhanced localization due to the 60° placement (Armbruster, 1984).

Ultimately, quadraphony was not a commercial success, and marketing efforts were abandoned by 1977. Its failure was a disappointment to many, and was the result of a number of factors. A primary reason was that the impetus to market these systems was more economic than aesthetic: by the early 1970s, the market for two-channel systems was largely saturated, so it was in manufacturers' self-interest to convince consumers that four channels would be better than two. However, the problem of how to encode four channels onto vinyl discs was approached differently by different companies. Four incompatible standards were introduced, and none succeeded in capturing the market. If there's one thing the public hates, it's a format war: faced with uncertainty as to which system would prove to be the most reliable investment, coupled with the logistical need of finding space for extra speakers in the household, buyers wound up avoiding the format altogether.

Commerce aside, in terms of audio production, quadraphony offered a number of valuable lessons in how *not* to use multiple channels. One mistake on some recordings was placing the listener in the middle of a virtual orchestra. The sensation of different instruments reaching the listener from different directions caused many to describe the experience as one of "a moose surrounded by wolves." (Subsequent research has shown that listeners prefer to be positioned at the "best seat in the auditorium" rather than "in the middle of the band.") The psychoacoustics of localization were often not considered. As covered in Chapter 3, humans do not localize well to the side. Tests have shown that a noise signal gradually panned through the four channels does not appear to travel in a continuous circle. As it approaches the side, it becomes unstable, also seeming to appear slightly to the rear and the front, before suddenly "jumping" to the rear channel.

Despite the commercial failure of quadraphonic recordings, the four-channel format remains an output option in many DAW systems. When used properly, it can offer enhancements over two-channel listening, particularly in concert settings where the placement of speakers and audience members can be controlled.

5.1 Surround Sound

In the 1990s, the introduction of digital audio and video systems brought about renewed interest in how to enhance the viewer experience through multiple sound channels. While various configurations were proposed, *5.1 surround sound* became the standard for cinemas and home movie players. These systems consist of three front speakers—left, center, and right—and two surround speakers—left-surround and right-surround. In cinemas, the two surround channels are typically delivered through arrays of speakers hung along the side walls. A boilerplate channel assignment is to place a movie's dialog on the center channel, the music on the left and right front channels, and Foley and ambient sounds on the front left and right plus the surround channels.

The value ".1" refers to a special subwoofer that delivers frequencies below 125 Hz or so. (The value of 0.1 is not accurate, and is really just a figure of speech to imply that this is not a full bandwidth channel.) The subwoofer channel is the sum of the low frequency content of all five main channels. Because these low frequencies are not highly directional due to their long wavelengths, and because the capacity to produce them would require added capability in the main channels, a single subwoofer speaker, typically placed on the floor, delivers the thuds and rumbles, enhancing the sounds of low basses, rockets taking off, earthquakes, stampedes, and the like.

Cinema stereo is an active area of development. In 2010, a seven-channel format came into being, which consisted of breaking each of the surround channels into two zones. Current work involves the use of ceiling speakers and increased numbers of channels. While some channels form the basic "sound bed," others are meant to contain elements that are independent of the basic channel format. Audio can be directed to these channels by metadata, which places sound effects in specific locations, according to the number of speakers and their layout within a particular venue (Dolby Laboratories, 2014).

While there have been attempts to market 5.1 channel recordings of music, the format has not been an overall success. However, it remains an option for concert settings, and the need to mix for cinema has made this a frequent output option in DAW programs.

Eight Channels and More

Multi-channel stereophony is an area of interest within the electroacoustic music community, and more and more facilities are distinguishing themselves by creating flexible multi-channel listening spaces. Mixing music for eight or more channels is common for electroacoustic events in the *acousmatic* tradition, where emphasis is often placed on the art of *diffusion*, which is the technique of distributing sound through loudspeakers that are strategically placed throughout the venue. Often, multi-channel events credit performers responsible for diffusing the audio, who may or may not be the composers of the piece being diffused.

One common arrangement of octaphonic systems is a circle surrounding the listeners. The 45° separation of the speakers means that localization effects are possible, although the weaker sense of localization to the sides and rear (discussed in Chapter 3) brings into question how much precision in localization can be perceived. Another common arrangement is to place the audience within a cube, with four upper speakers and four lower speakers. This approach makes use of spaciousness more than localization. The choice is as much due to artist preference as it is to psychoacoustics. The speaker configuration is a composer's choice, along with the choice of instruments and style of the music.

Jonty Harrison (b. 1952) from University of Birmingham recommends an alternate eight-channel configuration, shown in Figure 8-24. The Main and Wide speaker sets provide an extended arc for the primary sound imaging, while more distant sounds can be realized through the Distant and Rear sets. This is the basis of the Birmingham Electroacoustic Sound Theatre (BEAST), which has been expanded with additional arrays of eight speakers for even greater focusing of sound imagery. The sound theater functions

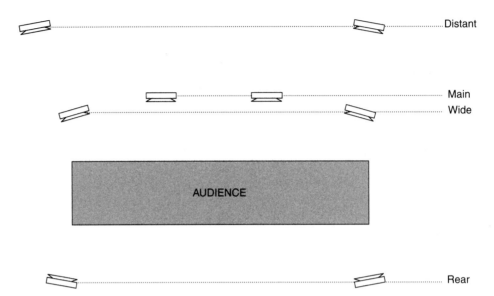

Figure 8-24 Eight-channel basis for the Birmingham Elecroacoustic Sound Theatre (BEAST) sound system

as an instrument itself, although Harrison acknowledges that it is site-specific. Pieces composed for a nonstandardized loudspeaker configuration are challenging to realize in other locations. This represents an aesthetic tradeoff: some things in life are site-specific, and some are transportable. Just as "destination weddings" are a choice that some couples make, while others choose locations that are convenient for family and friends, there are different ways of approaching music distribution. There is value in creating events that gather people in a certain location for a particular, unique listening experience, and there is value in creating music that is readily distributable. Choosing the performance and distribution format is just one of many choices that composers face when realizing a piece.

Ambisonics

Ambisonics is a surround recording technique closely associated with the Soundfield microphone (shown in Figure 7-28). Conceptually, it has parallels to MS recording, in that it simulates signals recorded with one omnidirectional and three figure-8 microphones, with stereo imaging that depends on how the signals are decoded on playback. Ambisonic production is a two-step process, by which signals are encoded when they are recorded (or synthesized). On playback, they are decoded in a manner determined by the speaker configuration. The encoding and decoding process means that the recording is configurable, in that it may be adapted for different speaker systems, depending on how it is decoded.

First-Order Ambisonics, originally described by Gerzon (1973), considers sounds to be occurring within a unit sphere, at positions that are a combination of the horizontal angle, A, and a vertical angle, B. Its distance along each of three axes can be described by these equations:

$$x = cosAcosB \quad \text{(front-back)}$$
$$y = sinAcosB \quad \text{(left-right)} \quad (8\text{-}11)$$
$$z = sinB \quad \text{(vertical)}$$

The recorded signal is encoded onto four channels, which correspond to four microphones:

$$X = input\ signal \times x \qquad \text{forward pointing figure 8}$$
$$Y = input\ signal \times y \qquad \text{left-right pointing figure 8}$$
$$Z = input\ signal \times z \qquad \text{up-down pointing figure 8}$$
$$W = input\ signal \times 0.707 \qquad \text{omnidirectional (common signal)}$$

(8-12)

On playback, each output channel is sent a weighted sum of all four of these signals. The combination varies with playback configuration, although the playback speakers are assumed to be equally spaced. For a four-channel horizontal-only playback system, the decoding equations use only the front-back (x) and left-right (y) values, and disregard the vertical value (z):

$$left\ front = W + 0.707(X + Y)$$
$$right\ front = W + 0.707(X - Y)$$
$$left\ rear = W + 0.707(-X + Y)$$
$$right\ rear = W + 0.707(-X - Y)$$

(8-13)

For an eight-channel *periphonic* (horizontal plus vertical) cube, the decoding combinations use all three axes:

$$left\ front\ upper = W + 0.707(X + Y + Z)$$
$$right\ front\ upper = W + 0.707(X - Y + Z)$$
$$left\ rear\ upper = W + 0.707(-X + Y + Z)$$
$$right\ rear\ upper = W + 0.707(-X - Y - Z)$$
$$left\ front\ lower = W + 0.707(X + Y - Z)$$
$$right\ front\ lower = W + 0.707(X - Y - Z)$$
$$left\ rear\ lower = W + 0.707(-X + Y - Z)$$
$$right\ front\ lower = W + 0.707(-X - Y - Z)$$

(8-14)

Higher-Order Ambisonics (HOA), introduced by David Malham in the late 1990s, offers improved localization and a larger listening "sweet spot." The higher orders are achieved through a greater number of encoded recording signals than the four listed above, and greater numbers of playback channels. Custom microphone arrays need to be created to record the signals, as there is no ready-made solution such as the Soundfield microphone, which provides first-order encoded recordings. But the decoding synthesis is as efficient with higher orders as it is for first-order. Ambisonic techniques have yielded good results in transmitting characteristics of the performance space for networked music performances (described in Chapter 6)—where performers in distant locations connected by high-speed Internet connections perform in tandem—as well in some gaming environments. While not a commercial format, HOA is an area of active research, with a number of recordings available online.

Mastering

Mastering is the final step in the process of producing an album of music. Once a set of tracks has been mixed, the step of mastering makes the collection of individual tracks into a consolidated album. Mastering is a final focusing to create a unified "album sound." The process is analogous to a series of paintings such as Oscar-Claude Monet's *Stacks of Wheat*. These twenty-five canvases were all painted outdoors, at the same location, from 1890 to 1891. Each was begun outdoors, on site. Monet then finished them in his studio so that he could create a harmonious look among all of the canvases.

An album of music is like this series of paintings. The individual tracks may have been recorded by different people, at different times and places, over a span of months or years. Thus, each track might have a different sound and feel to it. Mastering creates a sound quality that is consistent from track to track. This involves the use of EQ and compression to create the signature spectrum of the album. A variety of specialized software may be used to give an album its sonic flavor. Some editing programs border on the synaesthetic, allowing an audio file's spectrogram to be manipulated in a visual environment, wherein portions of the spectrum may be selected and amplified, attenuated, extracted, cut, or copied, in a manner similar to what is commonly done in visual editing programs (Figure 8-25).

Often, "stems" are brought to a mastering studio. These are submixes of each track; for example: vocals only, drums only, or guitars. The decision of which stems to use is usually unique to different albums and producers.

The mastering process also involves determining the order of tracks on the album and the amount of time that should elapse between tracks. Normalization may be employed to create a consistent volume level among the various tracks. The final result is a cohesive sound that makes all the tracks sound as if they belong together in the same "sound world."

Tracking, the stage where musician's performances are recorded, typically takes place in a different facility than does mastering, which is postproduction. A tracking studio offers enough space for the musicians and instruments, often in separate, isolated rooms, and enough channels to record them all. A mastering studio is smaller, usually a single room, and features a comprehensive set of EQ and dynamic tools, plus high-quality speakers, high-quality D/A and A/D converters, and clean listening room acoustics.

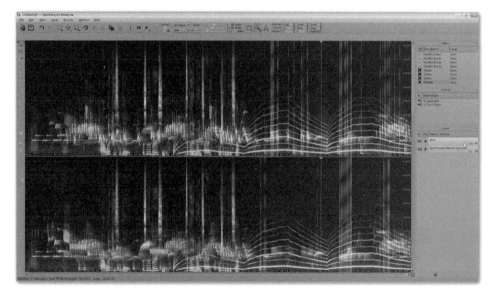

Figure 8-25 SpectraLayers software
Source: SpectraLayers software, copyright Sony Creative Software

Suggested Exercises

- Make a recording of something that shows a healthy signal level with a digital recorder. Next, lower the recorder's input level and make the same recording again. In a digital audio editor, adjust the amplitude of the second recording so that it matches the level of the first. What would account for any differences in sound quality?

- When recording or amplifying audio, there are a number of points at which the audio level may be adjusted. Each can potentially introduce distortion into the audio signal. Therefore, these points have to be kept in balance with each other when approaching the final output level. These points may include the output level of the device where the audio originates, the input and output levels of microphone preamps, a trim level on a mixer channel, the volume fader level on the same mixer channel, the master output level of the mixer, and the input level to an audio to digital converter.

  What points of gain adjustment does your equipment have, and how do they sound different when they introduce distortion? Turn down your monitors to avoid damaging them, and run through some *gain staging* tests. If you lower a mixer channel fader to zero and turn the trim up to a high level, then gradually raise the fader level, how is the signal distorted? If the trim is turned down and the fader is brought to a high level to compensate, what form of noise is introduced? Digital distortion is a different type of distortion altogether. While analog distortion "squashes" the wave, as discussed in Chapter 4, a digital signal that exceeds available limits undergoes a "hard" cutoff of the peak and trough of the wave. This causes a curved wave to approach the shape of a square wave, adding odd harmonics that introduce a metallic edge that is a different sound from analog distortion.

- Download a number of impulse responses and set up convolution reverbs on a number of auxiliary tracks. Send a recording to them, switch among them, and observe how the character of the sound differs when it is "placed" in different ambient environments.

- Work with a reverse reverberation effect (sometimes called "preverb"). Make a recording of a sound. Then reverse the audio file. Play the audio file in reverse through a long reverberation and save the result as an audio file. Then reverse this audio file. The original will be restored, but it will emerge out of a long, reverberant crescendo.

- Create a radio commercial advertising an upcoming musical event. This should feature narration and at least two pieces of music playing in the background. Listen critically so that the placement of the narration occurs at quieter moments of the music, so that the two complement each other rather than distract from each other. Create a smooth transition to the second piece somehow. Adjust volume levels so that at times the music is featured, and at other times the music fades to allow the voice to sound above it. Beware of automated volume control effects such as auto-ducking, which automatically drops a music track's volume level when a vocal track is sounding. It might work, it might not. Be sure your ears get the final determination. Using this properly involves carefully timing the narration elements to match appropriate points in the music. Be sensitive to a sense of cohesion and aural continuity. One potential pitfall is to record a vocal track in an environment that has some small amount of background noise. When the vocal part starts and stops, the appearance of the background noise sounds discontinuous and distracting. One solution to this is to record a few seconds of "silence," that is, only the background noise and no narration. This clip of background noise can be played repeatedly when the narration is not present. This renders the background noise to an environmental factor that the ear disregards since it is a constant, faint presence.

- Create a basic motif of drums, bass, chords, and some type of melody or vocal. Do at least three remixes of the tracks. What can you change in terms of balance and effects to make each sound different?
- "More cowbell": create a regular beat pattern with a cowbell or some other percussive instrument. How can you modify its sound over time to make it interesting, rather than irritating? Things to change may include EQ, compression, modulation, amplifier modeling, reverberation, echo, and any other effects that are available in your DAW environment.
- Experiment with a compressor to see how it can affect the character of a sound. Record a series of bass drum hits and observe them in a DAW waveform editor. Come up with three ways to modify the sound with the settings of a compressor. (Notice that the untreated bass drum sound is much more extended than is usually heard in recordings, where a quick decay creates a crisper sound.) Look at the compressed versions in a waveform editor and compare the difference in envelope and the sound of the different versions. Record a bass line and do the same thing, coming up with at least three different compression settings that change the quality of the sound to make it suitable for different types of music, for example, a slow ballad, an upbeat electronic dance tune, or a country hoedown.

Key Terms

5.1 surround sound	envelope follower
acousmatic	equalization (EQ)
all-pass filter	expander/noise gate
Ambisonics	expansion ratio
amplitude modulation	feedback delay
auxiliary (aux) bus	flanger
auxiliary send	fully parametric EQ
bus	gain
channel	gain staging
channel control	half-normalled
channel fader	Higher-Order Ambisonics (HOA)
channel insert	higher-order interpolation
chorus	interpolation
clip light	limiting
companding	line level
compressor/limiter	linear interpolation
control surface	mic level
convolution reverb	multitap delay
cross synthesis	mute switch
decimating lowpass filter	negative sum
diffusion	normalization/maximization
digital reverberation	normalled

output bus
pad
pan pot (potentiometer)
parallel filter
patchbay
periphonic
phantom image
phase shifter
phase vocoder
plate reverb
positive sum
postfader
pot or potentiometer
prefader
quadraphony
reciprocal peak dip filter
reverb or echo chamber

reverberator (or reverb unit)
semiparametric filter
series (or cascade) filter
shelf filter
sideband
sidechain
simple delay
solo switch
spectral effect
spring reverb
stereophony
strip
subgroup
transfer function
unity
vocoder
voder

Chapter 9

Communication Among Devices

Contemporary music production, performance, and audio art relies on inter-device communication. Just about every acoustic instrument has an electrified version, and their sounds may be modified by a variety of pedals or boxes of buttons. These instruments typically work in conjunction with at least one computer to recall settings and perform some form of processing. Many bands have complicated setups, with instruments connected and communicating via a variety of computers. The modern roadie is less the amp-schlepper of yore and more of a fleet-footed IT specialist, constantly troubleshooting networking issues among computers, control surfaces, and instruments, and finding ways to incorporate new devices into a performer's rig.

There are a number of means by which interconnected devices may exchange information. This chapter will focus mainly on the most common communication protocol in electronic music, *Musical Instrument Digital Interface (MIDI)*. But it will also touch on other protocols that have grown out of the MIDI standard, or are commonly used in conjunction with it.

MIDI: The Big Picture

MIDI is a protocol for hardware and for digital communication that allows devices to send and/or respond to instructions. MIDI information is to computers what sheet music is to humans: a series of instructions that, when properly carried out on an instrument, produce a piece of music.

MIDI was created in 1983, and it revolutionized the synthesizer industry by providing a common standard adopted by all manufacturers, which was overseen by the MIDI Manufacturers' Association (www.midi.org). For many musicians, this was their gateway into musical computing. MIDI was simple—sometimes too simple—but this drawback was also to become its greatest advantage. Hardware has evolved since 1983, and not always in ways that were anticipated. While many of the needs addressed by the MIDI specification are all but obsolete, MIDI is so easy and cheap to implement that it is used by many types of mechanical devices, both musical and nonmusical. Many of its instructions have been adapted for a variety of purposes due to their simplicity. If automation is required, MIDI is a likely candidate.

At its inception, a MIDI message to play a particular note was transmitted from a *master device* to a *slave device*. When a player depressed a particular key on a synthesizer keyboard, a message was sent to a slave device to play the same note. When the player lifted her finger from the key on the master, a message to stop playing the note was sent to the slave.

With master-slave configurations, there was often no need for a musician to use multiple keyboards. Manufacturers soon began to create *tone modules*, which were rack-mountable components that produced the sounds of synthesizers, but without the keyboard. Musicians often preferred to use a *MIDI controller keyboard*, which had no sound-generating abilities but simply sent MIDI messages to tone modules. Buyers would choose tone modules based on the types of sounds they produced, and choose a controller keyboard based on how it felt to play—the weight and size of the keys, for example.

MIDI was created at the same time that the personal computer came into being, and MIDI software was quickly created for this emerging market. Common types of MIDI programs included:

- *Sequencers*: these allowed a musical performance to be recorded and edited.
- *Notators*: these rendered MIDI as standard notation, allowing easy transposition and part extraction from a score.
- *Computer-Aided Instruction (CAI)*: these gave students training in musicianship fundamentals.
- *Accompaniment*: these provided accompaniment as a practice aid to soloists.
- *Editor/Librarian*: these provided a graphical interface for organizing, storing, and editing synthesizer patches.

The functionality of these programs will be covered more fully in Chapter 10.

A *MIDI file* is a recording of performance instructions, a computerized version of a player-piano roll. Many MIDI programs could save and import MIDI files. This allowed multi-application procedures such as recording a performance into a sequencer, exporting it as a MIDI file, and then importing this file into a notator so that it could be printed as sheet music.

Because MIDI files consist of instructions only, with the audio created by the receiving device, MIDI files are quite small compared to audio files. Personal computers now commonly have sets of musical instrument sounds as part of their multimedia library. Some multimedia players, such as Apple's QuickTime or Microsoft's Windows Media Player, can open MIDI files and play them, employing built-in libraries of instruments to render the audio. MIDI files are easy to find online, although they often sound rather robotic. (This fact actually raises interesting questions about the role of interpretation and inference in music performance. A MIDI file contains information contained on a piece of printed music. When just that information is realized, the result is stiff and canned. This gives us an idea of the degree to which a sensitive and trained performer extrapolates on what is printed to create a living piece of music.)

Connecting MIDI Synthesizers

The original MIDI devices were connected by MIDI cables, which transmitted messages through 5-pin DIN connectors, as shown in Figure 9-1. Transmission was serial, one bit at a time, at a rate of 31,250 bits per second (31.25 kilobaud), and in one direction only. Instruments had a series of MIDI jacks labeled IN, OUT, and THRU (Figure 9-2). A cable would be plugged from the OUT jack of a master device to the IN jack of a slave device (Figure 9-3). If other devices were also involved, the THRU jack could be used to receive and immediately send any incoming messages, either in a daisy-chain configuration (Figure 9-4a), or via a MIDI THRU box (Figure 9-4b).

Figure 9-1 Five-pin DIN connector

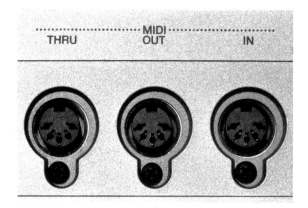

Figure 9-2 The three types of MIDI jacks
Source: Pepgooner/Shutterstock.com

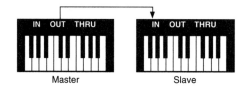

Figure 9-3 Simple master-slave configuration

A system that included a computer required a ***MIDI interface*** (Figure 9-5). MIDI interfaces came in various sizes, from simple models that enabled a single in-out pair of cables to be connected, to larger types that allowed multiple pairs of MIDI cables connected to a variety of instruments. MIDI interfaces originally connected to a computer serial port. When USB came into being in the early twenty-first century, MIDI interfaces became USB devices. Since 2005 or so, many instruments are made with USB jacks so that they may be connected to a computer directly, without the need of a MIDI interface. Audio interfaces often include MIDI cable jacks as well as audio cable plugs.

Much MIDI information is channel-based, based on the idea that each synthesizer in a studio could be uniquely identified by a channel, numbered 1–16. MIDI ***channel-voice messages*** contain a channel identifier, which would allow all devices in a studio to carry out instructions that come over their particular channel, and disregard instructions sent over other channels. Multi-jack MIDI interfaces could expand on the 16 channels by allowing each in-out pair to transmit 16 channels, making the number of available channels the number of MIDI jacks times 16.

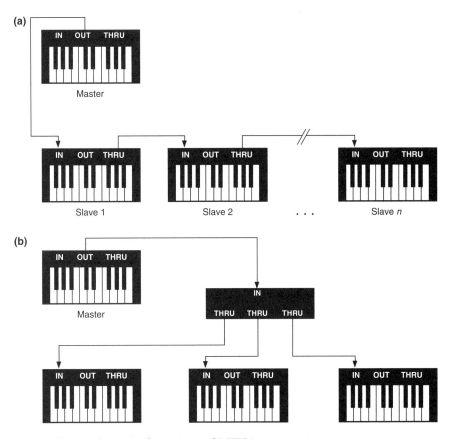

Figure 9-4 Daisy-chain configuration of MIDI instruments

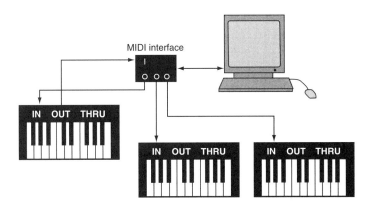

Figure 9-5 Simple configuration of computer and MIDI instruments

MIDI Messages

The MIDI specification outlined a number of message categories. The messages most commonly encountered by musicians (as opposed to programmers) were a set of seven channel-voice messages. They transmit instructions that are analogous to information that would be found in traditional music notation, and are still the message types most likely to be encountered in typical music production contexts.

Status Bytes and Data Bytes

The nature of bits, nibbles, and bytes is discussed in Appendix 4. Channel-voice messages are transmitted with two types of eight-bit bytes: *status bytes* and *data bytes*. A status byte determines the type of message and the channel number (the "what?" and the "where?").

The most significant bit (MSB) of a status byte is 1:

1nnnnnnn

(The letter "n" is used to denote a binary bit having a value of one or zero.)

The status byte is divided into nibbles (Figure 9-6). Following the defining 1 of the most significant bit, the remaining 3 bits of the most significant nibble define the message type. With 3 bits allocated to define the message type, there is a maximum of eight possible categories of messages (although only seven are assigned to channel voice messages). The 4 bits of the least significant nibble define the channel number of the message; the 16 available channels are numbered 0 through 15.

A data byte gives a value (*how much?*) The MSB of a data byte is 0:

0nnnnnnn

With 7 bits following the MSB, a data byte's range of expressible values is 2^7, 0–127.

A complete channel-voice message consists of one status byte followed by either one or two data bytes, depending on the message type.

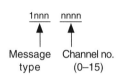

Figure 9-6 Structure of a channel-voice message status byte

Channel-Voice Message Types

There are seven channel-voice message types, outlined below. In the "Hex" (hexadecimal) column, n represents a digit from 0–F. In the "Binary" column, n represents a digit of 0 or 1.

NOTE OFF
(2 data bytes)

Hex	*Binary*	
8n	1000nnnn	*<status>*
	0nnnnnnn	*<note number>*
	0nnnnnnn	*<velocity>*

Note number:	Each chromatic pitch is assigned a note number. Middle C is note number 60; middle C# is note 61, middle D is note 62, B below middle C is note 59, and so on.
Velocity:	Reflects how quickly a note is released. A higher number denotes a quicker release, corresponding to a note fading quickly. A lower number denotes a slower release, corresponding to a note fading slowly.

NOTE ON
(2 data bytes)

Hex	*Binary*	
9n	1001nnnn	*<status>*
	0nnnnnnn	*<note number>*
	0nnnnnnn	*<velocity>*

Note number:	The note numbers are the same pitch assignments as those used with Note Off messages.

Velocity: Reflects how quickly a note is depressed. A higher number results in a louder tone. A Note On velocity value of 0 is another way of specifying a Note Off.

POLYPHONIC KEY PRESSURE (POLY AFTERTOUCH)
(2 data bytes)

Hex   *Binary*

An   1010nnnn   *<status>*
         0nnnnnnn   *<note number>*
         0nnnnnnn   *<pressure>*

Note number: The note numbers are the same pitch assignment as those used with Note Off and Note On messages.

Pressure: Reflects physical pressure applied to the keys while they are depressed. Pressure messages represent an attempt to expand the expressive capability of MIDI instruments in ways that are not possible on acoustic keyboard instruments. Pressure applied to the keys is mapped to some modulation parameter (specified by the user for the particular instrument). Thus, each key can generate its own degree of modulation. This was a feature found mainly in higher-end instruments, as separate sensors had to be installed for each key, which was more expensive than a single sensor for all keys. In reality, however, it was impractical to use this effectively. The anatomy of the hand is such that fine pressure differences among ten fingers is difficult, if not impossible, to control.

CHANNEL KEY PRESSURE (CHANNEL AFTERTOUCH)
(1 data byte)

Hex   *Binary*

Dn   1101nnnn   *<status>*
         0nnnnnnn   *<pressure>*

This is a "poor person's" aftertouch; it is less costly to implement and thus found on more instruments than poly aftertouch. One pressure value is applied to all notes on a given channel. The value is derived from the key that has the most pressure applied to it.

PROGRAM CHANGE
(1 data byte)

Hex   *Binary*

Cn   1100nnnn   *<status>*
         0nnnnnnn   *<program number>*

This message called up a specified patch number on an instrument. With one data byte, up to 128 patch numbers could be specified.

PITCH BEND
(2 data bytes)

Hex   *Binary*

En   1110nnnn   *<status>*
         0nnnnnnn   *<value, least significant byte>*
         0nnnnnnn   *<value, most significant byte>*

Like aftertouch, pitch bend is a method of modifying the sound of a held note. The *pitch-bend wheel* on a MIDI instrument is bidirectional, meaning that its default position is at the center position of its range of motion. This quality allows the pitch to be bent up or down. When the wheel is released, it snaps back to this middle position, which corresponds to no bend in pitch. When the wheel is moved, the held pitches are bent either up or down within a range that is programmable within the instrument. The range is typically from 1 semitone to 1 octave above and below the note being bent (12 semitones).

The two data bytes are concatenated so that they represent a single value range with 14 bits of resolution (once the defining MSBs of zero are discounted). Pitch-bend messages thus have a value range from 0 to 16,383: 8192 values above and 8191 values below the held pitch. This combination of two bytes into one value makes this message type unique, as MIDI's creators felt that extra resolution was needed for this parameter. If a single data byte were assigned to the pitch bend messages, they would have a value from 0 to 127: 64 values above and 63 values below the held pitch. Depending on the range of bending selected, there was the potential for discontinuities. While 64 pitch bend increments within the range of a semitone might be acceptable, the subdivision of an octave into 64 steps would result in audible discontinuities ("zipper noise").

Musically, pitch bend and aftertouch are special classes of the more general control change (the next message type). The designers of MIDI assumed that these would be commonly used forms of modulation (just as bending notes is a common expressive technique of guitarists) and assigned them unique own message types.

CONTROL CHANGE
(2 data bytes)

Hex	Binary	
Bn	1011nnnn	<status>
	0nnnnnnn	<controller number>
	0nnnnnnn	<value>

Controllers modify some quality of a sounding note, as do aftertouch and pitch bend. Control change messages, however, are a generic category, created to allow the invention of new performer interfaces that could modulate held notes.

The *controller number* specifies a stream of information. Depending on the type of stream, controller information may be described in terms of either what type of device is originating the stream (e.g., a pedal, wheel, slider, etc.) or what type of sound parameter is being controlled (e.g., volume, tremolo, pan position, etc.). Regardless of whether the stream is commonly referred to by its origin or its destination, the first data byte specifies the control stream. The second data byte determines the value (or position) of the performance controller.

Many controller numbers remain undefined, while certain conventions have become commonplace. Controllers 0–31 are typically *continuous controllers*, generating values within the range 0–127. Some examples are shown in Table 9-1. Controllers 64–69 are typically ON/OFF controllers, such that a value of 0 corresponds to an OFF position, and a value of 127 corresponds to an ON position.

System Exclusive Messages
The MIDI specifications' System Level Message category was designed to address an entire studio of instruments, rather than just a single device. Therefore, these message

TABLE 9-1 Standard controller number assignments

	CONTROLLER TYPE	CONTROLLER NUMBER	DESCRIPTION
Continuous	Modulation wheel	1	A wheel typically lying next to the pitch bend wheel on a synthesizer. It typically controls effects such as tremolo amount. In contrast to the pitch bend wheel, the modulation wheel is unidirectional, meaning that its default position is at the bottom end of its value range, and it will not "snap" back to this position automatically when the wheel is released.
	Breath controller	2	Controls similar effects to a modulation wheel but is a device that is blown into, with values taken from breath pressure.
	Foot controller	4	A continuous foot pedal, often (but not necessarily) used to control volume.
	Master volume	7	
	Pan	10	Stereo position: (value byte of 64 = CENTER) (value byte of 0 = HARD LEFT) (value byte of 127 = HARD RIGHT)
ON/OFF	Damper pedal	64	
	Soft pedal	67	

types do not contain channel identifiers. Most of these are rarely used, but one message type of particular interest is *System Exclusive* **(SysEx)**, which allows a device to be addressed in ways that are not covered by the MIDI standard. SysEx messages may be used to address programmable elements of a particular instrument. For example, Voice Editor/Librarians relied on System Exclusive messages to modify the patch parameters of a particular instrument.

START SYSTEM EXCLUSIVE

Hex   Binary

F0   11110000

This command takes the system out of normal MIDI operating mode. It is followed by a series of identification bytes. Unique identification bytes are assigned by the MIDI Manufacturers' Association to each manufacturer. Different devices by the same company may also be identified by subsequent identification bytes. The Start SysEx message puts the instrument into a state where it was ready to receive proprietary, nonstandardized instructions. Following the series of identification bytes, any number of bytes may follow.

For example, I once created a little program that could retune a particular type of synthesizer. Accomplishing this meant digging into the manual for the SysEx information, and making a few calls to the manufacturer. The procedure was to generate a series of bytes that identified particular manufacturer, instrument series, and specific instrument model; once the device was identified, there was a series of bytes to define that a tuning dump would follow; then 128 values had to be sent that represented the tuning for each MIDI note number. I had a library of tunings, each of which was a particular sequence of 128 values. After sending the instrument the values associated with the tuning I had chosen, the final step was to take the instrument out of SysEx mode with the End SysEx message.

END SYSTEM EXCLUSIVE (EOX)

Hex   *Binary*

F7   11110111

Following whatever sequence of bytes are required to carry out whatever proprietary action is desired on a particular instrument, sending it this message returns the system to normal MIDI operating mode.

MIDI Utility Programs

In many instances, particularly with newer instruments, it may be possible to plug a device into a computer's USB jack and have it be immediately operational. But in configurations that involve a computer communicating with multiple hardware units, particularly pre-USB instruments that require a MIDI interface, it may be necessary to use a MIDI studio configuration utility. These store a diagram of a MIDI studio, with the type of interface, the number and type of instruments, and the channels on which each instrument is set to respond (Figure 9-7). It is possible to rename instruments within the configuration, so that a user may personalize the name of an instrument if so desired. With such a utility acting as a message router, instruments in the user's studio appear in a sequencer or other software program when the user launches it. Users may then direct MIDI messages to conveniently named instruments in their studios, rather than having to address messages to particular MIDI channels, and having to remember which instruments correspond to what channels.

When a newly purchased instrument is connected to a computer, it can be a bit confusing to sort out what types of messages it is sending, particularly when it is not

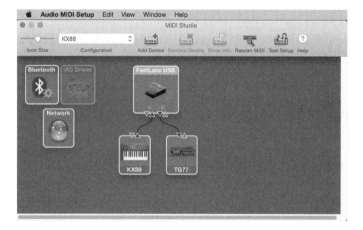

Figure 9-7 MIDI studio configuration utility. This setup uses pre-USB instruments, so a MIDI interface is needed. Here, a Fastlane USB interface supports two sets of IN-OUT MIDI cables. A KX88 keyboard controller sends MIDI information into the computer. The computer sends information to a TG77 synthesizer module. *Source: Audio MIDI Setup screenshot reprinted with permission from Apple Inc.*

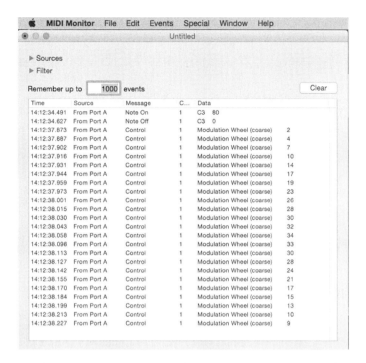

Figure 9-8 A utility to report incoming and outgoing MIDI messages. This can be helpful in diagnosing MIDI problems, or "taking the pulse" of a MIDI instrument
Source: MIDI Monitor screenshot reprinted with permission from snoize.com

something straightforward like a keyboard, but a control interface consisting of a multitude of buttons or sliders. Of course, there is always the option of studying the manual. But it can often be more efficient to start by using a utility that reports incoming and outgoing MIDI messages (Figure 9-8). Once an instrument is plugged in and is recognized by the computer, all a user needs to do is press its buttons or move its sliders and see what types of messages are being sent, in effect, taking the instrument's pulse. Once it's clear what the instrument does when fresh out of its box, then it can be more helpful to read the manual to learn how to make changes, if necessary. Depending on the context, it may be easiest to program the device to send the desired message type. Or sometimes it's easier to make adjustments in the software that receives messages from the device so that the messages have the desired effect on the sound.

Additions to the MIDI Protocol

As MIDI became ubiquitous, a number of add-ons came into being, sometimes to improve compatibility among devices, sometimes to refine what could be done with certain message types.

Standard MIDI Files (SMFs)

As more and more MIDI software was released, it became clear that there was a need for an all-purpose file type that allowed information to be exchanged among different manufacturers' programs. In 1988, the ***Standard MIDI file (SMF)*** was added to the

MIDI specification. These are to sequencers what plain text files are to word processors: a generic file format that may be opened in a variety of applications (typically sequencers and notation programs). They have the extension ".mid."

There are three types of Standard MIDI file:

- *Type 0:* All information is contained in one sequencer track. When Type 0 files are imported into a sequencer, some programs prompt the user to decide whether the file should be "exploded" into 16 tracks, with each track containing information from the corresponding channel number.
- *Type 1:* Track information is maintained. Note that sequencer tracks and MIDI channels are two different things. A single sequencer track may contain information on more than one channel (although this is probably not advisable); likewise, multiple tracks may contain information on the same channel.
- *Type 2:* Track information is maintained, with each track having its own tempo.

Because the MIDI standard includes information only about event types, but not about time, Standard MIDI Files may be considered a collection of MIDI events, each of which is timestamped. Standard MIDI files interleave MIDI events with time values, with each MIDI event preceded by a ***delta time value*** that indicates the number of elapsed clock ticks since the last MIDI event.

Standard MIDI files also allow ***meta-events*** to be stored, which may provide added information about the file. Examples of meta-events include tempo changes, track names, key signatures, lyrics, and instrument names. Meta-event types are registered with the MIDI Manufacturer's Association, and each has a unique number that allows it to be specified within a Standard MIDI File. A meta-event follows a delta time value and precedes a MIDI event. A unique byte of 11111111 indicates that a meta-event is to follow. Following this byte is the identification number of the meta-event, which is followed by a byte that indicates the number of data bytes that are necessary to describe the event. Then the actual bytes describing the event follow. The meta-event is considered complete when the specified number of bytes has been read.

Standard MIDI Files also allow SysEx data to be stored. Like meta events, SysEx events are placed between a delta time event and a MIDI channel voice event.

General MIDI

General MIDI—a "standard within a standard"—was adopted in 1991 to allow Standard MIDI files to be played easily on different instruments. Prior to General MIDI, an instrument would have to be prepared before it could play a MIDI file as it was intended to sound. The file had to be checked for Program Change patch numbers; the instrument types used in the file had to be noted and the patches on the receiving instrument had to be assigned to appropriate patch numbers to that the appropriate instrument types would be played.

General MIDI outlines a standardized set of patch assignments so that instrument types correspond to patch numbers. For example, General MIDI instruments have a piano patch assigned to patch 0, an organ assigned to patch 19, a trumpet assigned to patch 57, and so on. Naturally, the quality of patches differs from instrument to instrument. But standardized patch numbers at least ensure that MIDI files are "plug and play." Table 9-2 shows the set of instrument types that are mapped to patch ranges, and Table 9-3 shows the list of standardized patch assignments for all 128 patches.

General MIDI also ensures that drum parts are easily transferable. Drum patches differ from instrumental patches in that drum sounds are not pitched. Each note number produces the sound of a different type of percussion instrument. In General MIDI, note numbers are standardized for drum patches, as shown in Table 9-4, and channel 10 is reserved for drum tracks only.

MIDI file players, such as QuickTime and Windows Media Player, are typically General MIDI, which means that files downloaded from the Internet, or embedded on Web pages, can be played easily. The General MIDI standard democratized MIDI, so that it became a standard multimedia element. For example, computer games are generally focused more on graphics than sound, and game producers would rather use the available memory on a disc for high-resolution graphics than for high-fidelity music. General MIDI allows game soundtracks to employ MIDI files, which makes them compatible with any General MIDI sound card.

Karaoke Files

The *karaoke file* type was specified in 1998 to allow creation of sing-along arrangements for use in karaoke bars. A karaoke file is a Standard MIDI file with lyrics as meta-information and typically has the extension ".kar." A karaoke machine is able to play back MIDI tracks and project lyrics.

TABLE 9-2 General MIDI instrument families

PATCH NUMBERS	INSTRUMENT FAMILY
1–8	Piano
9–16	Chromatic Percussion
17–24	Organ
25–32	Guitar
33–40	Bass
41–48	Strings
49–56	Ensemble
57–64	Brass
65–72	Reed
73–80	Pipe
81–88	Synth Lead
89–96	Synth Pad
97–104	Synth Effects
105–112	Ethnic
113–120	Percussive
121–128	Sound Effects

TABLE 9-3 General MIDI patch assignments

1	Acoustic Grand Piano	12	Vibraphone	23	Harmonica
2	Bright Acoustic Piano	13	Marimba	24	Tango Accordion
3	Electric Grand Piano	14	Xylophone	25	Acoustic Guitar (nylon)
4	Honky-tonk Piano	15	Tubular Bells	26	Acoustic Guitar (steel)
5	Electric Piano 1	16	Dulcimer	27	Electric Guitar (jazz)
6	Electric Piano 2	17	Drawbar Organ	28	Electric Guitar (clean)
7	Harpsichord	18	Percussive Organ	29	Electric Guitar (muted)
8	Clavi	19	Rock Organ	30	Overdriven Guitar
9	Celesta	20	Church Organ	31	Distortion Guitar
10	Glockenspiel	21	Reed Organ	32	Guitar harmonics
11	Music Box	22	Accordion	33	Acoustic Bass

(Continued)

TABLE 9-3 (*Continued*)

34	Electric Bass (finger)	66	Alto Sax	98	FX 2 (soundtrack)
35	Electric Bass (pick)	67	Tenor Sax	99	FX 3 (crystal)
36	Fretless Bass	68	Baritone Sax	100	FX 4 (atmosphere)
37	Slap Bass 1	69	Oboe	101	FX 5 (brightness)
38	Slap Bass 2	70	English Horn	102	FX 6 (goblins)
39	Synth Bass 1	71	Bassoon	103	FX 7 (echoes)
40	Synth Bass 2	72	Clarinet	104	FX 8 (sci-fi)
41	Violin	73	Piccolo	105	Sitar
42	Viola	74	Flute	106	Banjo
43	Cello	75	Recorder	107	Shamisen
44	Contrabass	76	Pan Flute	108	Koto
45	Tremolo Strings	77	Blown Bottle	109	Kalimba
46	Pizzicato Strings	78	Shakuhachi	110	Bagpipe
47	Orchestral Harp	79	Whistle	111	Fiddle
48	Timpani	80	Ocarina	112	Shanai
49	String Ensemble 1	81	Lead 1 (square)	113	Tinkle Bell
50	String Ensemble 2	82	Lead 2 (sawtooth)	114	Agogo
51	SynthStrings 1	83	Lead 3 (calliope)	115	Steel Drums
52	SynthStrings 2	84	Lead 4 (chiff)	116	Woodblock
53	Choir Aahs	85	Lead 5 (charang)	117	Taiko Drum
54	Voice Oohs	86	Lead 6 (voice)	118	Melodic Tom
55	Synth Voice	87	Lead 7 (fifths)	119	Synth Drum
56	Orchestra Hit	88	Lead 8 (bass + lead)	120	Reverse Cymbal
57	Trumpet	89	Pad 1 (new age)	121	Guitar Fret Noise
58	Trombone	90	Pad 2 (warm)	122	Breath Noise
59	Tuba	91	Pad 3 (polysynth)	123	Seashore
60	Muted Trumpet	92	Pad 4 (choir)	124	Bird Tweet
61	French Horn	93	Pad 5 (bowed)	125	Telephone Ring
62	Brass Section	94	Pad 6 (metallic)	126	Helicopter
63	SynthBrass 1	95	Pad 7 (halo)	127	Applause
64	SynthBrass 2	96	Pad 8 (sweep)	128	Gunshot
65	Soprano Sax	97	FX 1 (rain)		

TABLE 9-4 General MIDI percussion key mappings

NOTE NO.	INSTRUMENT	NOTE NO.	INSTRUMENT
35	Acoustic Bass Drum	59	Ride Cymbal 2
36	Bass Drum 1	60	Hi Bongo
37	Side Stick	61	Low Bongo
38	Acoustic Snare	62	Mute Hi Conga
39	Hand Clap	63	Open Hi Conga
40	Electric Snare	64	Low Conga
41	Low Floor Tom	65	High Timbale
42	Closed Hi-Hat	66	Low Timbale
43	High Floor Tom	67	High Agogo
44	Pedal Hi-Hat	68	Low Agogo
45	Low Tom	69	Cabasa
46	Open Hi-Hat	70	Maracas
47	Low-Mid Tom	71	Short Whistle
48	Hi-Mid Tom	72	Long Whistle
49	Crash Cymbal 1	73	Short Guiro
50	High Tom	74	Long Guiro
51	Ride Cymbal 1	75	Claves
52	Chinese Cymbal	76	Hi Wood Block
53	Ride Bell	77	Low Wood Block
54	Tambourine	78	Mute Cuica
55	Splash Cymbal	79	Open Cuica
56	Cowbell	80	Mute Triangle
57	Crash Cymbal 2	81	Open Triangle
58	Vibraslap		

GS MIDI and XG MIDI

GS MIDI, an expansion of General MIDI, was created by the Roland Corporation in 1991 for its Sound Canvas® tone module. GS MIDI features multiple drum kit patches and standardizes more controllers than those listed in Table 9-1 to include effects such as reverberation and brightness.

XG MIDI was created by the Yamaha Corporation in 1994 for its MU80 tone module. This protocol also adds standardized controllers that address additional expressiveness (chorus, attack time, release time, etc.). In addition, XG MIDI includes the definition of special SysEx messages to allow processing of an input signal, such as a karaoke vocalist.

Some Web sites that offer downloadable MIDI files specify that the files are GS MIDI or XG MIDI, meaning that their files take advantage of the special features on these types of devices.

MIDI Show Control (MSC)

MIDI Show Control (MSC) is a standardized set of SysEx messages that control non-musical theatrical devices such as lighting, scenery, pyrotechnics, or sound effects. MSC allows an entire production to be controlled by a sequencer, or by a control surface. Some theatrical devices allow MIDI messages to be combined with Digital Multiplex (DMX) messages, which is a protocol that controls lighting devices. With automated controls on these devices, a complicated cue that involves changes in lights, sound, and pyrotechnics can be generated automatically by a single push of a button.

Just What Do You Mean by That?

As hardware advanced, MIDI's capabilities became dated. Some developers floated the idea of updating it, but always concluded that it was impractical to update or replace the MIDI specification. An entire marketplace of instruments had come into existence based on MIDI as it was created in 1983, and people wanted to keep these instruments as they were. But adaptations of some kind were inevitable. MIDI messages may have been created for certain purposes, but there was no reason not to repurpose them and use them in ways other than what was originally intended. A MIDI message became abstracted, a little piece of digital syntax that could mean a variety of things, based on the devices involved.

One early adaptation was the number of available patches. In 1983, synthesizers could store a dozen preset patches or so. MIDI Program Change message, which allowed 128 patches, seemed a vast number of presets. But within a few years it became common for instruments to have hundreds of patches available, leaving the problem of how to call them up, now that the once-limitless capabilities of the Program Change message had become insufficient. The solution that manufacturers devised, beginning with the Roland Sound Canvas® in 1991, was to arrange patches in *banks*, each of which contained 128 patches. Controller 0 was adopted as a bank selector, with the value byte specifying the bank number. Thus, a bank select message (controller 0) followed by a program change message allowed selection of [128 × 128] total patches. For example, patch 12 in bank 80 on channel 1 would be chosen with the following sequence of bytes:

Hex	*Binary*	
B0	10110000	*<status—Control Change, channel 1>*
00	00000000	*<controller number 0—bank select>*
01	01010000	*<value—bank number 80>*
C0	11000000	*<status—Program Change, channel 1>*
0C	00001100	*<program number—12>*

Another example of a MIDI message being repurposed from its original intent was implemented in Yamaha's 02R mixer. Many mixers have a talkback microphone, which is meant to enable communication between an engineer in a control room and a musician in a tracking room. The 02R's talkback was toggled on and off when the mixer received a NOTE ON message of Middle C. This meant that talkback could be switched on and off via a MIDI keyboard connected to the mixer, or via any programmable device, such as a foot controller or other control surface that could be configured to send this message out when the switch was depressed.

Given the rudimentary structure of MIDI messages, just about any electronic device can be equipped to generate them. It brings to mind the wisdom of Canadian handy-man comedian Red Green, whose tagline is that duct tape is the cure for everything. MIDI may be crude, but it can hold everything together, making it the duct tape of multimedia production.

One example of MIDI holding everything together is a theatrical production. Consider a dramatic scene in which a character smashes a bottle on a table. The bottle has been pre-broken by the props master so it can be reassembled and broken again, night after night. The problem is that, because nothing actually shatters, this specially prepared safety-certified prop makes little more than a dull thud when it hits the wood. With this unconvincing sound, the action looks contrived. A sound design solution is to connect a relay unit, which translates electrical pulses to MIDI messages, to a transducer surface on the table. The relay is programmed to send a NOTE ON message to a sampler, which plays a shattering glass sound effect through a hidden speaker. (Samplers are instruments that store audio files that are triggered by MIDI Note On messages. They will be discussed further in Chapter 10.) This more realistic sound effect, directly triggered by the action, makes the scene more dramatic and exciting.

MIDI Control Change messages are a common way of repurposing MIDI. These can be thought of as anonymous, constantly changing streams of information. There are a great number of control surface devices on the market. These are boxes arrayed with interface elements such as buttons, sliders, and joysticks. These interfaces are programmable and can be made to send out Control Change messages for different controller numbers and MIDI channels. With 16 MIDI channels having 128 available controllers each, there are 2048 such streams available. These streams may be generated by a slider or a pedal on a musical device, or may be generated by something else entirely.

Exactly what Control Change streams control is arbitrary. My brother, who is a puppeteer, once had to work with a mechanical puppet for a television commercial that was being made by a toy company. The movements of the puppet's limbs were all controlled by MIDI tracks, with each limb and each direction defined by a different controller number. The puppet's choreography was stored in a sequencer, as though it were a piece of music.

Many animated films rely on an expanded form of this concept. Actors perform in body suits, which are arrayed with sensors that track the actor's movements and convert them to MIDI control information. This controller data gets sent into a computer animation program, where it gets assigned to corresponding limbs of an animated character. The animated characters move and behave in tandem with the human actor, giving the animation a degree of nuance that would be difficult to obtain through drawing or programming.

Another common use for MIDI controllers is real-time video processing, where Control Change messages are mapped to video parameters (luminance, chrominance, clip selection, playback speed, layer mixing, alpha channels, effects, etc.), allowing video artists to create improvisations intuitively by riding the knobs and faders of their favorite control interface. The interface sends MIDI information into a VJ program that is handling video playback. A video clip, for example, may have its frame numbers mapped to a MIDI fader. Familiar DJ scratching effects may then be applied to the video clip by quick fader moves.

Laptop video software and MIDI controllers have simplified VJs' lives enormously. Your father's VJ needed a truck or van to transport multiple desktop computers, audio, and videotape decks, CD and DVD players, and audio and video mixers. Now they can travel to gigs by subway, carrying just a backpack with a laptop that runs their software of choice, their favorite control surface, and possibly a separate hard drive that holds all of their video and audio clips.

Open Sound Control (OSC)

Open Sound Control (OSC) was invented in 1997 at UC Berkeley's Center for New Media and Technology (CNMAT; http://opensoundcontrol.org) as a protocol to control networked sound modules and multimedia devices. In a simple configuration, one piece of software can control another on the same computer. In more a complex setup, OSC is transmitted between devices via Ethernet cables, which connect computers to the Internet. A device can control any other device connected to the Internet to create a performance that transcends geography (networked music was described in Chapters 6 and 8). In a more localized setup, computers may either be physically connected, or they may be part of a wireless network that allows them to send information among themselves.

OSC is like a "supersized" version of MIDI, with a more open-ended vocabulary and more precise time responses. MIDI is constrained by its eight-bit message format, which limits the range of values and types of messages that can be sent. Its numbering of channels, patches, and controllers is arbitrary, and can easily become confusing. OSC's message structure supports more detailed messages that consist of text and numbers (also called *name-value pairs*). This means any software or hardware synthesizer that can respond to OSC can have any combination of parameters, and any other supporting device can control those parameters by simply declaring a name-value pair, which sets that parameter to the new value in the receiving device.

Moreover, MIDI's slow transmission rate (31.25 kilobytes per second) can bog things down if there are dense streams, such as multiple continuous controllers. In contrast, OSC transmits over Ethernet some 300 times faster, typically in the range of 10-plus megabits per second, using the Internet Network Time Protocol, which synchronizes machines at the subnanosecond level. Plus, rather than send messages serially (one at a time), as happens with MIDI, OSC allows groups, or *packets*, of messages to be programmed to execute at specifically defined times. It's like a fireworks show: shoot out a packet of messages, and all the devices simultaneously flare up into action.

For communication between devices over the Internet, OSC uses an addressing scheme called an *address tree* or *hierarchical namespace*, which allows messages that resemble Internet addresses. Devices can be arranged into groups and subgroups. Figure 9-9 is a simple example, showing a set of oscillators that are arbitrarily named "bass," "tenor," "alto," and "soprano" (of course, they could be called anything). Each oscillator has controllable parameters for frequency, amplitude, and pan position. The address tree-based OSC message to set the tenor oscillator's frequency to 220 looks like this:

```
/oscillators/tenor/freq 220
```

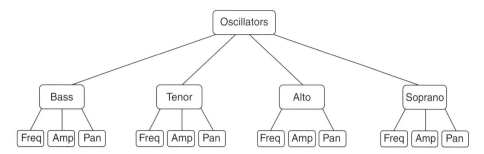

Figure 9-9 Tree structure of OSC messages

In computer networks, devices called *clients* send messages to receiving devices, which are called *servers* or *hosts*. It's like when you go to a restaurant: you're the client of that establishment. You make requests, and a server or host produces something (usually a meal) in response.

For a client to control a server, it first has to know the server's *Internet Protocol (IP) address*, which identifies a machine on the Internet. IP addresses take the form of four numbers separated by periods, sometimes called a "dotted quad" formation, which looks something like 127.0.0.1. (This particular IP address is a special one, as it is used to refer to the machine that is both sending and receiving a message, and is used when programs on the same machine are communicating via OSC. The IP address *localhost* may sometimes be used instead of the dotted quad address.)

Data to be transmitted is broken into small chunks and sent in packets. Each packet consists of the data "payload" and control information, which consists of delivery information such as source and destination addresses and information about which portion of the data the packet's payload came from, so that the data can be reassembled at the destination. Once the IP address is established, the client application then "packetizes" the OSC messages and sends them over a network port. This is typically a *UDP port (User Datagram Protocol)*, which is compatible with the time-sensitive, packetized nature of OSC messages. The arrival of a given message and the order of messages arriving are not guaranteed (earning it the nickname "Unreliable Datagram Protocol"). More reliable protocols, such as TCP/IP, require a series of queries and confirmations (*handshakes*) that ensure the integrity of the transmission. These checks, however, are time-consuming. In performance contexts, the higher priority is timeliness, even at the expense of risking an occasional missed piece of data. UDP is "connectionless," which means that no time or bandwidth is occupied with establishing connections between devices and verifying that the information was received. Messages can be sent without having to check first whether the destination device is "listening" for the information. This is the preferred protocol for time-sensitive applications, and it is compatible with packet broadcasts.

OSC is the basis of remote-control add-ons to a number of products. The Behringer X32 digital mixer, for example, includes an iPhone or iPad app that allows the mixer to be operated remotely via OSC commands. This allows a soundboard operator to be able to leave the mixer station and go into the auditorium, where she can hear the results of mixing changes executed on a mobile device. This allows sound levels to be easily set and saved. The OSC commands of products like this are largely invisible to the user.

Other apps allow users to create their own interfaces and OSC commands. The apps TouchOSC (hexler.net) and Lemur (liine.net) allow users to create custom interfaces consisting of buttons, sliders, knobs, and other interface elements, and to customize the OSC messages that these send out to receiving devices. During performance, artists have the option of moving from page to page on a mobile device, with each page containing a different interface layout. (A few specific examples will be discussed in Chapter 11.)

Remapping Values

When values are originating from one place and then being sent to another to be translated into musical material, there are times when the values need to be remapped from one range to another. Sometimes, this is a simple process. For example, to remap the value 4 within a range of 1 to 10 to a proportional value between 1 and 100, the conversion can be done by a simple multiplication by 10, resulting in a value of 40. When things aren't so obvious as that, there is a general-purpose formula that may be employed. To map a value x, which falls within the range between values a and b, to a value y, which falls between values c and d, the conversion may be performed as follows:

$$y = \left(\frac{(d - c)}{(b - a)} \times (x - a) \right) + c \qquad (9\text{-}1)$$

DIY Device Development

There is considerable overlap between digital audio, music technologies, and open-source electronics, which is sometimes called the "Makers Movement." This is an open-source community in which people use products such as the Raspberry Pi (https://www.raspberrypi.org), which is an inexpensive general-purpose computer that can run multiple programs, or Arduino™ microcontroller motherboards (www.arduino.cc) to create new products and collaborate with each other (Figure 9-10). Arduino™ DIY kits consist of a microcontroller board with both digital and analog inputs and outputs,

Figure 9-10 Arduino™ UNO board

plus a USB connector. Additional components may include jumper cables, LED displays, lights, buttons, temperature sensors, tilt sensors, and motors. A programming language allows behaviors to be programmed for these inputs and outputs and loaded into the hardware. The open-source nature of the hardware, software, and documentation allows people to share work and build on each other's projects. The 2012 TED talk "How Arduino™ Is Open-Sourcing Imagination" (Banzi, 2012) describes a variety of projects created with these systems, many of them by young students. They are limited only by the imagination, and range from the whimsical to the scientific to the humanitarian. Some of the highlights include:

- A sign-language glove that recognizes gestures and translates them into text that is displayed onto a screen.
- An earthquake detector that automatically publishes earthquake data onto Twitter.
- A pet feeder, developed by someone with two cats, one of which required special food for health reasons; sensors on the animals' collars caused a retrofitted CD player to slide from one side to another, exposing the appropriate bowl of food for the cat that approached it.
- A remote-controlled helicopter, originally developed as a toy, later used to distribute supplies to isolated areas of Africa.
- A device that automatically mutes a television when news coverage turns to celebrities that the user finds "overexposed."

Many of these are started as prototypes in basements or classrooms and then developed into full products by startup funds raised online through systems such as kickstarter.com.

Many Arduino™ musical applications can be found online. A cursory search on youtube.com reveals tutorials on how to create things such as xylophones by attaching sensors to pieces of Plexiglas; the sensors send MIDI Note On messages to a computer or tone module when the Plexiglas is struck by a mallet. Arduino™ controllers come in many forms. For example, the Lilypad is a type of disc that is meant to be sewn into theatrical costumes, sometimes with special conducting thread. This allows the costume, or different parts of the costume, to light up during dance numbers in synchronization with music or other effects that may be occurring.

In 2012 I had an opportunity to participate in a performance commemorating the seventy-fifth anniversary of the Golden Gate Bridge (Exploratorium, 2012; Ballora, 2014). The performance featured a 23-foot flexible model of the bridge created at San Francisco's Exploratorium Science Museum. It was constructed as a series of square metal segments that were joined to form a flexible "roadway" that could be shaken and twisted, with data on the motion sensed by accelerometers. The model also included a series of other interface elements placed on the towers, which included a series of flex resistors, piezo transducers, and force-sensing resistors. The model sent data via an Arduino™ Mega board, which transmitted 18 MIDI event types, some of them MIDI note numbers, and others control change streams. The buttons sent MIDI note on messages, which triggered sound effects stored in a computer. The control change values from the shaking and twisting were sent to a second computer, where the coordinate values were remapped to frequency values and wrapped in OSC messages, which were sent to a synthesis program that was playing an amorphous sound wash. The frequency values from the model's motion modulated the pitch of the sound wash, so that the model's motions were translated into a continuously shifting melody.

Suggested Exercises

- Download some standard MIDI files from the Internet. Be sure they can be opened in a MIDI file player of some kind. How does the same file differ when played with different MIDI players?
- Use a MIDI utility that monitors incoming MIDI messages to trace what is being sent to the computer from a MIDI controller of some kind. What types of messages does it send by default? How easy is it to change them to another message type?
- Using a MIDI sequencer, enter one line of a two-part invention. Save this as a standard MIDI file. Open the SMF in a notation program and complete the invention with the second line.
- Open a standard MIDI file downloaded from the Internet in a DAW. How can you "improve" it with MIDI editing functions? Examples might be to alter the velocities on a drum track so that some hits are louder than others, making subtle changes to the piece's volume, extending or shortening some durations, or playing some notes a hair early or late.
- Try creating an arrangement that combines more than one MIDI file. How can the transition between them sound seamless and inevitable? How can MIDI material be used as composers use basic ideas—fragmentation, transposition, inversion, harmonization, etc.?
- A Suggested Exercise in Chapter 5 was to create a composition from white noise and filters. Connect a MIDI controller to a DAW and do something similar, but let the changes in filtering be controlled live from your manipulations of the physical interface—sliders, knobs, and so forth.

Key Terms

address tree or hierarchical namespace
bank
channel-voice message
client
continuous controller
controller number
data byte
delta time value
General MIDI
GS MIDI
handshake
Internet Protocol (IP) address
karaoke file
localhost
master device
meta-event
MIDI controller keyboard

MIDI file
MIDI interface
MIDI Show Control (MSC)
Musical Instrument Digital Interface (MIDI)
name-value pair
Open Sound Control (OSC)
packet
pitch-bend wheel
server or host
slave device
Standard MIDI file (SMF)
status byte
System Exclusive (SysEx)
tone module
UDP port (User Datagram Protocol)
XG MIDI

Chapter 10

Digital Instruments

Digital technology has changed the definition of what an "instrument" is. Computer programs have evolved from their early form as advanced scientific calculators to becoming analogs of just about any tool imaginable, including instruments for making music. In Chapter 3, there was some reference to theories that music is an essential communication tool, and part of what makes the human species what it is. Along these same lines, Scaletti (2015) observes that language gives humans the ability to create stories about things that do not exist. She extends this to observe that software performs the same function: it is a language of symbols that effects physical change, enabling hardware to run in new ways. It makes it possible for a single machine to behave like many machines, and has led to new tools being created at unprecedented rates.

Many digital musical instruments may be thought of as component systems. The actual objects handled by musicians may not produce any sound, but could be interface components consisting of physical keys, knobs, switches, and other controls. The signals from these components may be sent to a number of devices, some of which produce sound, others of which modify the sound. The new normal is a hardware-software hybrid with levels of customizability that did not exist for earlier generations of musicians. The next section will cover hardware instruments, which are emulations of traditional acoustic instruments—typically keyboard instruments. Then the focus will shift to software instruments, which refers to digital sound-making, which may be activated by a variety of interface types.

Hardware Instruments

Samplers

Samplers are instruments that contain audio files that are triggered by MIDI note messages. Samplers are successors to an earlier, tape-based instrument called the Mellotron. Created in the 1960s, this instrument contained dozens of strips of audiotape. Depressing different keys activated different strips of tape by pressing them against a playback head. Two famous recorded examples were the flute sounds in the introductions of the Beatles' "Strawberry Fields Forever" and Led Zeppelin's "Stairway to Heaven." Although its sounds could be evocative, the Mellotron was an unwieldy instrument, both in size and in maintenance requirements. Musicians craved what it could do, but their technical crews wished there were an easier way.

In the 1980s, digital samplers became the alternative. They contained digital recordings, stored on disc or computer hard drive. In terms of computer data, a sampled audio file is very similar to a wavetable (described in Chapter 6). But samplers' contents typically originate from digital recordings made with a microphone, while the samples that comprise a wavetable tend to be calculated by a synthesis algorithm.

There is a slight difference in implication when the term "sample" is used in the context of these instruments. Whereas in a digital audio context, the term refers to an instantaneous amplitude measurement, in the context of these instruments, the term refers an audio file, to the collection of samples that comprise the recording.

Once a recording is made, the sample can be assigned to a group of MIDI note numbers. One note serves as the "fundamental," which plays the sample back unaltered. If the sample is assigned to a group of note numbers, those above the fundamental play the sample faster (and at a higher pitch), and those below the fundamental play the sample slower (at a lower pitch). Most samples are only effective over the span of a few notes before they sound "chipmunky" above the base pitch or like an extended rumble below it.

While users can certainly record their own samples (and readers are encouraged to do this in the Suggested Exercises at the end of this chapter), most musicians' first use of a sampler is likely to be with a bank of commercially prepared samples. Considerable effort goes into preparing these, as creating a convincing rendition of an instrument involves making more than just a single recording. An instrument is usually *multi-sampled*, which means that it consists of a collection of samples that span the instrument's range, with each assigned to a range within about a major third. In many cases, there may be more than one sample assigned to each note number, with different samples triggered by different key velocity values. A piano, for example, changes tone depending on the key velocity. Assigning a number of samples, all recorded at different dynamics, to the same note and setting each to be activated by different velocity ranges allows a more expressive and natural sound.

A number of steps go into preparing audio files to be used in samplers. The sound needs to be edited to ensure that it begins and ends smoothly when a key is depressed and released. Typically, a sample also has *loop points* within its steady-state region. Once the initial transient has played, the steady-state portion can repeat indefinitely until a Note Off message is received. Finding loop points is a matter of identifying two of the waveform's zero crossings between which the wave activity is fairly consistent. This allows the sample to loop continuously without glitches, and to decay convincingly when the key is released.

Special effects may be created with multilayered sample banks, in which combinations of different instruments or sounds are assigned to the same note number so that an ensemble sound is produced. With an audio editor, different recordings may be combined into the same sample, either layered, or arranged one after another in sequence. Most commercial instruments allow this type of editing to be performed via front panel controls or by software that is included with the instrument.

While most commercial sample banks may consist of instrumental samples, there is really no limit to the type of sound a sampler can produce. If something can be recorded, it can be put into a sample and activated by MIDI. Samplers are the most flexible tool for the creation of *musique concrète*, music composition from recorded sounds, which was defined by Pierre Schaeffer (1910–1995) of the Radiodiffusion Française in Paris in 1948 and introduced the era of music created from electronics.

In the twenty-first century, samplers may exist as stand-alone hardware instruments or as software packages. They have become invaluable not only to musicians but also to sound-effects artists in theater and cinema. Cinema Foley artists, for example, who create sound effects for films, typically work with sequencers and samples of footsteps, doors opening and closing, passing cars, and so forth. As will be described in Chapter 11, films are typically digitized for postproduction, so that they may be played from within a computer in a DAW environment, where the appropriate music and sound effects can be programmed to play at the precise frame number needed.

Synthesizers

Sound synthesis has undergone a number of evolutionary steps and mutations through its history. Notable early work began in 1950 at the *elektronische Musik* facility at the Nordwestdeutscher Rundfunk (NWDR) radio facility in Cologne, Germany. Early innovators included composer Karlheinz Stockhausen (1928–2007). These experiments, carried out with oscillators, filters, tape players, and specially designed keyboards, were meant as an alternative to the *musique concrète* approach practiced at Schaeffer's facility. (The divide between the two approaches began to lessen by the middle of the decade with pieces such as Stockhausen's *Gesang der Jünglinge* in 1956.) The term *synthesizer* first appeared in America in 1952 with the creation of the RCA Mark I Sound Synthesizer. In 1959, the next version of this instrument, the Mark II, became the centerpiece of the Columbia-Princeton Electronic Music Center. This was a hybrid analog and computer system. The sound was generated by analog circuits consisting of some 1,700 vacuum tubes in nine racks. The sound was controlled by binary numbers—holes were punched into rolls of paper from a typewriter-like keyboard; as the paper was unrolled across sensing brushes, the series of holes were read in horizontal rows as ones and zeroes. These binary values were applied to frequency, octave transposition, timbre, envelope, and volume. Time was represented by the spacing between the binary values, so that numbers close together produced changes more quickly than did numbers that were spread farther apart. This formidable instrument was the basis of many groundbreaking pieces; some of the most notable were by composers Milton Babbitt (1916–2011), Mario Davidovsky (b. 1934), and Charles Wuorinen (b. 1938).

Commercial synthesizers were introduced in the 1960s, and were an outgrowth of *modular component systems*, which were DIY electronics developed by inventors such as Harald Bode (1909–1987) at NWDR in Cologne, and Bob Moog (1934–2005) and Don Buchla (b. 1937) in the United States. These modular systems consisted of oscillators, filters, noise generators, and amplifiers that could be assembled on open circuit boards that allowed flexible configurations. The *voltage-controlled modular synthesizer* was introduced by Moog in 1967, at about the same time that Buchla (who did not care for the term "synthesizer") introduced the Modular Electronic Music System. These came into the public eye via recordings such as Morton Subotnick's (1933-) *Silver Apples of the Moon* (1967) and Wendy Carlos's (1939-) *Switched on Bach* (1968). These instruments produced sound by an approach called *subtractive synthesis*, wherein complex waveforms, such as those shown in Figure 2-10, were controlled by filters and amplifiers (synthesis techniques will be discussed in more detail in the next section).

Modular component systems were conceptually similar to the MUSIC N acoustic compiler software programs that Max Mathews was developing at about the same time at Bell Labs (see Chapter 5). However, acoustic compilers offered potentially unlimited complexity. Because they were based in code, and not in hardware, MUSIC N could be configured to virtually any level of complexity, without the physical limitations of hardware. *Additive synthesis*, the creation of complex waveforms through combinations of sine wave oscillators, had been theorized and attempted with analog systems. But it did not become feasible until the creation of acoustic compilers, which allowed dozens of oscillators to be created.

The seemingly limitless potential of computer music attracted a number of researchers to this sonic frontier. James Tenney (1934–2006) was composer in residence at Bell Labs from 1961 to 1964, and carried out the earliest computer music research, exploring ways to program musical intelligence into software. He was followed by Jean-Claude Risset (b. 1938), who carried out some of the first systematic studies of timbre, which were made possible with the capabilities of additive synthesis and early digital recording (Risset, 1965; Risset and Mathews, 1969). Another notable pioneer was John Chowning (b. 1934) at Stanford University, who studied stereo localization and vibrato. His vibrato experiments led him to unwittingly discover *frequency modulation (FM) synthesis*, whereby complex timbres could be created with great efficiency through very high vibrato rates (Chowning, 1974). (Late in his life, Mathews was known to quip that the best thing about his early writing on computer music [Mathews, 1963] was that Chowning and Risset read it.) Composer/historian Kyle Gann (b. 1955) observes that one thing that attracted these composers was the capability to specify characteristics that could unfold slowly, in a controlled manner (Gann, 1997). Vibrato, filter frequency, pitch, or anything else could be made to change by any amount over any length of time. This level of precision was not available through any kind of analog or acoustic instrument, and represented a new level of musical control that only a computer could offer.

As compelling as they were, computer music systems were high-end technology, and only available to those with access to large university or corporate mainframe systems. Learning to use them was not for the faint of heart, although Chowning points out in lectures that it is much easier to write a simple computer program than it is to write a simple piece of musical counterpoint. Commercial analog synthesizers were far more accessible to the general public. An active market formed for them following the early recordings by Carlos and Subotnick, and the 1970s featured a great number of competing companies and products. The synthesizer sound infused popular music, thanks to the efforts of artists such as Keith Emerson and Stevie Wonder (among many others).

While analog synthesizers could produce new worlds of sound, they were unpredictable. They would gradually drift in tuning, and having to pause and readjust them periodically was a fact of life. Their unpredictability also made it difficult to replicate results from one session to another. Even if the cables were set up in the same fashion, the actual sonic results could vary from session to session. To many, this was part of the appeal of using these instruments. They were described as having their own personality, which needed to be tamed. A common hack to the popular Moog Ladder Filter, for example, was to turn off its input and turn its feedback setting up. Since there was always some amount of noise present in the circuit, it would recirculate within the filter, which effectively turned it into a sinusoidal oscillator (Puckette, 2015).

In the 1980s, digital synthesizers became commercially available at consumer price levels. The Yamaha DX7, introduced in 1983, made FM synthesis and MIDI available to proletarian musicians, and its sales levels were unprecedented. In 1984, low-cost samplers became available. For the remainder of the 1980s, any self-respecting keyboardist's studio would be expected to have both synthesizers and samplers, as well as a personal computer that integrated everything.

In the 1990s, manufacturers began to market hybrid instruments that combined synthesis algorithms with sampled recordings of actual instruments. A patch might combine the attack from a digital recording and a synthesized steady-state portion. This hybrid sound could then be molded with synthesis editing functions such as filters, effects, or other wavetables. By the end of the 1990s, instruments typically had far fewer programmable synthesis functions, as manufacturers found that few users took the time to explore them in any great depth, and instead used either presets or samples.

Users who did have an interest in delving into sound synthesis started gravitating towards computer solutions in the 1990s. As computer processing speeds increased dramatically, synthesis software based on MUSIC N programs became available for personal computers. The term "synthesizer keyboard" became more informal. Depending on who was using the term, it might refer to any type of hardware instrument that had MIDI capability, whether it was an electronic piano, organ, or a keyboard workstation, which is a "one-person band" machine that includes a keyboard and built-in sequencer. DAW programs began offering alternatives to tape-based recording systems, usually in tandem with extensive libraries of software synthesizers (*softsynths*) that could be played by MIDI messages. These messages might come from a standard MIDI file, or they might originate from a MIDI keyboard or control surface.

Alternate MIDI Controllers

MIDI technology has also brought about the creation of new types of instrumental interfaces. Some are based on motion within a light field, allowing movements and gestures to be translated into MIDI information. Some are new types of boxes that may be squeezed, shaken, or otherwise manipulated. Others are based on bioelectric signals, taking signals from muscle or eye movement or brainwave signals. Three such alternate controllers are shown in Figures 10-1, 10-2, and 10-3.

Figure 10-1 The Skoog sends MIDI control change signals when it is tapped, squeezed, pressed, or shaken
Source: Courtesy of skoogmusic.com

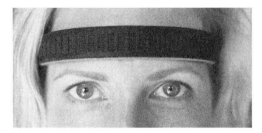

Figure 10-2 The BioVolt captures the skin surface voltage on the head, including signals from facial muscles (EMG), eyes (EOG), and some signals from the brain (EEG)
Source: Courtesy of infusionsystems.com

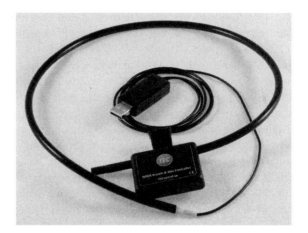

Figure 10-3 The USB MIDI Breath and Bite Controller generates MIDI controller information from breath and bite pressure
Source: Courtesy of TEControl AB; http://www.tecontrol.se

The development of new controller types redefines the act of music making and brings about new types of performances. It creates new forms of musical instruction, allowing children to make music without the standard learning curve of learning to manipulate a physical instrument. (This is in no way meant to suggest that traditional instruments are obsolete. However, children are taking up musical instruments in fewer numbers than in prior generations, as the admissions numbers of any university music program can attest. Giving children ready access to making music may give them the motivation to take the next step of learning to master an instrument.) Perhaps most significant, these new interface types can enable music making for people with restricted movement due to disabilities. This can be life-transforming for people in motorized chairs, who have limited mobility or speech ability, as it makes it possible for them to compose music or to participate in performances that have historically been unavailable to them (Graham-Knight and Tzanetakis, 2015).

Software Instruments

As described in the chapter's introduction, software allows new types of tools to be created. This section will explore instruments that exist as software programs, rather than as physical pieces of dedicated hardware.

MIDI-Based Software

The first type of software instruments to be examined will be those that are based in MIDI messages, although it will soon become clear that many software instruments incorporate MIDI and other functionalities, blurring distinctions among them.

SEQUENCING SOFTWARE

A *sequencer* stores a musical performance, which may be recalled, played back, or edited. Sequencers have existed in various forms for hundreds of years. Among the first were music boxes, which consisted of a revolving wooden drum with raised pins that plucked musical tines as they rolled past. Later, the player piano operated by means of a paper roll with holes punched in it, which activated the notes of a musical work. In electronic music, hardware sequencers have existed since the 1960s, when they were created for the Buchla Modular Electric Music System. These allowed sequences of numbers to be assigned to musical parameters such as pitches, filter cutoff frequencies, volumes, or other qualities. Sequences were a distinctive feature of Subotnick's early recordings, and sequencer modules soon became available for the Moog modular synthesizer.

MIDI software sequencers came into being in the 1980s, and became the most comprehensive type of software for handling MIDI information. In a nutshell, sequencers combine MIDI transmission with a clock and attach **timestamps** to each MIDI event to specify when it happens. Figure 10-4 shows features common to many sequencing programs.

There are typically a number of ways to record material in a sequencer. The most straightforward approach may be to use the sequencer like a tape recorder: create a new track, click on the record button, and play the material on an instrument. **Punch recording** allows a segment of a recording to be replaced: if, out of a twenty-measure recording, measures 12 through 15 contain mistakes, measure 12 beat 1 may be designated a **punch-in point**, and measure 16 beat 1 may be designated a **punch-out point**.

Tracks view
tape recorder–like interface for playback and record control

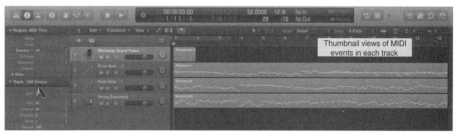

Piano roll view
MIDI events are represented graphically.
Note events are represented as horizontal lines; vertical position corresponds to pitch, length to duration.

List view
MIDI events are represented as text.

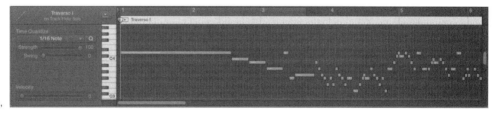

Sample screens from the program Apple Logic Pro X.

Figure 10-4 Sequencing program
Source: Screenshots reprinted with permission from Apple Inc.

Activating the record function results in simple playback until measure 12 is reached, at which point the sequencer records material for the next three measures before returning to playback mode.

Loop/overdub mode allows a complicated part to be recorded in successive passes by specifying a series of measures that are to play repeatedly. If, for example, the first eight measures are selected, then as soon as eight measures have been recorded, the time position jumps back to the beginning of measure 1, and anything played will be added to what was recorded previously. This can be an effective way to create an intricate percussion part, gradually layering one instrument at a time.

The tempo of a MIDI sequence is arbitrary. A fast passage may be recorded with the sequencer metronome set to a slow tempo. The tempo may then be sped up when the completed track is played back. Once recorded, material may be *quantized* on playback, meaning that the timing of notes and other events is adjusted to occur at the nearest user-specified subdivisions of a measure: typically at 16th notes, 32nd notes, or 8th notes.

Step entry allows MIDI notes to be entered one at a time, without the clock ticking. A user selects a note duration value, then plays a MIDI note on a controller, and this note gets recorded with the selected note value. Another note duration may be selected, another note entered, and so on. In this way, parts may be entered at the musician's own pace.

The contents of a sequencer track may be viewed in a number of formats. Many sequencers feature a notation screen. MIDI note messages can be represented as notes on a staff. A wrong note may be edited by moving it up or down to another staff position. New material may also be entered by clicking on note values from a menu and then clicking on the staff.

A less intuitive but more complete view is the *event list*. An event list is sometimes the easiest way to determine the order of events in a sequence and may be the place to correct problems that would not appear on a notation screen or piano roll view, such as instrument changes not occurring at the right time due to misplaced Program Change messages, or a tremolo continuing too long because the modulation wheel (Controller number 1) is not set back to zero.

A *piano-roll view* displays MIDI note events as colored bars that lie along a horizontal timeline. The length of each bar indicates the note's duration, its vertical position indicates pitch, and often its color indicates velocity. A note bar may be moved up or down to change its pitch, across to play at another point in time, or stretched or shortened horizontally to change its duration. Controller information from devices such as a volume pedal, pitch-bend wheel, or modulation wheel may also be "drawn" in. Once material is entered, it may be cut, copied, and pasted in a manner akin to editing done on a word processor. A series of measures may be recorded, then copied and pasted elsewhere, eliminating the necessity of recording the same material more than once.

NOTATION SOFTWARE

Notators translate MIDI information into common-practice notation so that professional-quality musical scores may be printed (Figure 10-5). Notators have many things in common with sequencers. Both can import and export Standard MIDI files, record MIDI from an instrument, and play files back with variable tempo and instrument assignments. The difference between the two is that sequencers are meant primarily to store performance information, while notators focus on the graphic dimension of creating standard notation.

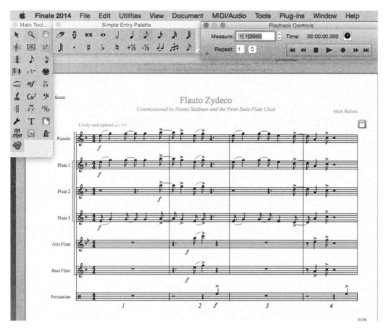

Figure 10-5 Notation program
Source: Screenshot reprinted with permission from MakeMusic.com.

Once an ensemble score is complete, the parts for each instrument may be extracted. This is probably the greatest advantage to creating computer-printed music. Entering the score can be time consuming, and in many cases may take about the same amount of time as it would to write the score by hand. But once the score is complete, the next step of writing parts by hand carries the inherent possibility of human error creating discrepancies between the score and parts. Sorting out these unexpected surprises can waste valuable rehearsal time. The ability of computer-notated scores to generate parts automatically gives composers peace of mind that the score and parts will match.

Many notators also have the capability of creating graphic files from a selected portion of the screen. An excerpt may be created in a notator, saved as a graphic file, and then brought into another program such as a word processor, drawing program, or presentation program to be used as an example figure with text or other graphics incorporated.

EDITOR/LIBRARIAN SOFTWARE

Creating patches on the original voltage-controlled modular synthesizers was an intricate affair. Complex sounds could require a veritable spaghetti of patch cables. Compact synthesizers, such as the Minimoog, began to appear in 1969. These were smaller and lighter, had buttons instead of patchcords to connect modules, and they could store patches internally. Although they did not have the range of capabilities offered by larger modular systems, many musicians preferred them due to their suitcase dimensions, plus the ease with which they could store and recall patches for performances.

When digital synthesizers were introduced in the 1980s, their patches were far more complex than those of modular synthesizers. It often took more than 100 values to specify the various aspects of a given patch. Paradoxically, it seemed that the greater the

Figure 10-6 Editor/librarian program for the Minimoog Voyager synthesizer
Source: Image used courtesy of Moog Music Inc.

number of available parameters, the smaller the display screen manufacturers provided on the instruments. With only one value visible at a time, it was difficult to keep a sense of perspective on the overall patch: some described it as "looking at the world through a keyhole." *Editor/librarian software* allowed complex synthesizer patches to be created more intuitively with the aid of a graphical user interface (Figure 10-6). As described in Chapter 9, by the early 1990s it was common for synthesizers to store sounds in banks of 128 patches. Editor/librarians allowed groups of banks to be stored in a computer and quickly transferred to the instrument.

Digital Audio-Based Instruments

DIGITAL AUDIO WORKSTATION SOFTWARE

Digital Audio Workstations (DAWs) have become the heart of a music production studio. Much of what was once done with tape decks, mixers, and outboard equipment is now done in integrated music production software packages. Some DAWs are low priced, or even come bundled with a computer at no extra cost. Many musicians use these low-cost programs to start projects, getting the basic elements in place before taking them into professional studios to complete. At the higher-priced end, DAWs such as those found in professional recording studios can cost hundreds of dollars. Many are expanded versions of the MIDI sequencers that date back to the early 1980s.

Computer-based recording systems were introduced in the late 1980s. They were expensive and required extra hardware to do the conversions between digital and analog, as well as to perform DSP operations. The mid-1990s bought a dramatic increase in standard processing power and speed on personal computers, and sequencers began incorporating audio tracks along with MIDI tracks. By 2007 or so, many sequencing programs were blurring the distinction between audio and MIDI-based tracks, often making it easy for users to copy data from one track type to the other. On the main session screen, audio-based tracks appear as waveforms, while MIDI tracks appear as miniature versions of the piano roll view. If a user drags material from a MIDI track to a track that has been defined to play an audio track, the computer takes into account the type of MIDI instrument associated with the region (based on the Program Change message it contains and its library of General MIDI patches), and generates samples that correspond to the note events. Depending on the length of the region, this conversion can take place within seconds. Some workstations also automatically adjust the tempo of an audio segment to match the sequence tempo, although the sound quality becomes noticeably colored if a file is stretched or compressed too much. Many DAWs are loop-based environments, which are created to be suitable for DJ work in which excerpts, or *loops*, from diverse sources are mixed and matched to create a collage of new and recycled material.

Many DAWs have an extensive mixer screen. Mixes may be automated, either by recording movements of a knob or fader made while the tracks are playing, or by drawing envelopes over an image of the waveform. Mixing a complex piece in an analog system used to be a choreographed sequence of moves that had to be rehearsed and performed. In a digital system, automation makes the mix sound exactly the same each time the tracks are played, and fine adjustments can easily be made.

In a DAW, an audio clip may be used over and over. Although it may appear as though the audio material is duplicated, it would be impractical to do this, given the size of audio files. A project's audio files are stored in a collection of media files associated with it. A segment of audio that is used more than once is not copied each time it is reused; rather, the program references the same file whenever it needs to use it. Thus, audio data is kept separate from editing operations. A DAW project folder typically contains the session file, and a series of folders containing the audio files, information about fades, and other information used by the session file. A common mistake made by beginning students is to believe that the session file stands alone and can work without the accompanying audio files. Good housekeeping habits are important to learn early, especially if a project is created on different computers over multiple work sessions. When the project is stored between work sessions, it is imperative that all of its components be stored together.

As discussed in Chapter 6, plug-ins are a major feature of DAW environments. These are modular processing units that can be inserted into the audio signal chain, software versions of the outboard effects that are part of the analog studio environment. Some of these were discussed in Chapter 8. Many plug-ins and softsynths are part of libraries that are available as additional purchases. Interestingly, while digital processing allows for many types of operations that are not possible in the analog domain, digital effects can also sound artificial, and effects designers often take steps to create a sound that approaches that of analog systems. There are, for example, analog tape plug-ins that add transient response and added harmonics in emulation of the saturation found on analog tape; some even add other analog "flaws" such as electrical hum and hiss.

Just as audio may be digitized and stored on hard disk, so may video and animation. DAW programs usually allow audio and visual elements to be combined, so that multimedia projects may be realized on one computer workstation. Such a production system once might have consisted of a videotape player, an audiotape recorder, synthesizers, and a computer. A good deal of time had to be spent ensuring that all these components were properly synched. Combining multimedia elements is greatly simplified now that a single computer can store all of the media and work with it in an integrated production environment (scoring for video will be discussed further in Chapter 11).

SOFTSYNTHS AND SAMPLE LIBRARIES

In the twenty-first century, as computers commonly function as instruments in and of themselves, many synthesizers and samplers exist in software form. Softsynths can be assigned to MIDI-based tracks, and MIDI information recorded there can control the instrument. Some softsynths are samplers, and may access extensive sample libraries stored on a hard drive. Others carry out different forms of synthesis, sometimes emulating vintage analog models. Besides being responsive to note messages, many of these instruments also feature extensive editable parameters that can be mapped to MIDI controllers. This represents another historical reverse: analog modular synthesizers had a knob for every element of the sound. Digital synthesizers were button-based, with a series of button pushes needed to switch a single slider's control to a particular sound parameter. While the sound was cleaner on digital instruments, the multi-function buttons gave the musician less performance control over the character of the sound. With softsynths, this control is returned. Synthesizer parameters may be associated with incoming MIDI messages from a keyboard controller, slider box, or some other physical user interface, giving musicians as much expressive control as they care to assign to an interface.

Many softsynths are not DAW plug-ins, but fully featured, stand-alone software programs. The direct descendant of MUSIC N is Csound (https://csound.github.io), which is free and open source, and can run on any computer platform. Given its long history and numerous developers, it has a rich library of synthesis and signal processing modules.

Synthesis programs take many forms. Some are extended additions to DAW software, some are apps for portable devices. Some are graphic emulators of classic analog synthesizers, others are programming languages. But it's important to note that all of them have their basis in the same fundamental principles. Synthesis techniques do not become obsolete when a particular instrument is no longer manufactured. The building blocks of synthesis have been in place for decades, and will be the subject of the next section.

Sound Synthesis

Many musicians who favor working with synthesizers rely on the computer as their instrument. Contemporary computers are much faster than those on which the first software synthesis programs ran, fast enough to realize audio in *real time*. This means, for example, that instead of using a commercial synthesizer, a musician may create her own synthesis patches and trigger the audio instantaneously via MIDI input from a control interface. Audio input may also be processed immediately. A signal taken from an instrument via a microphone may be sent to the computer, processed by filters and/or effects, and output with no appreciable time lag, allowing such processing to be used in concert situations.

Wavetables

As described in Chapter 5, one of the first concepts developed by Max Mathews was the wavetable, a tool by which a waveform could be described by a formula and pre-rendered so that it could serve as an efficient template of an instrument or timbre. For example, a wavetable might specify which harmonics should be present in the wave, and at what relative amplitudes to each other. A collection of wavetables might be defined for a particular piece, serving as its "instrumental ensemble."

The wavetable is incremented in circular fashion, like the hands of a clock face. If a clock is checked every five hours, starting at 12:00, it will show the times 12:00, 5:00, 10:00, 3:00, 8:00, 1:00, and so on. The same type of progression occurs when a wavetable is traversed. It outputs samples at the sampling rate, but, depending on what the desired pitch is, some samples in the wavetable are likely to be skipped. Which samples are sent to the DAC depends on the desired pitch. As shown below, the factors that determine how the wavetable's values are read include the sampling increment, initial phase, and method of interpolation.

If each sample in a wavetable is read, the resulting frequency, f, is:

$$f = \frac{sampling\ frequency}{wavetable\ size} \tag{10-1}$$

For example, a 512-point table read at the CD audio rate produces a frequency of:

$$f = \frac{44100}{512} = 86.132\ \text{Hz} \tag{10-2}$$

To generate a frequency an octave higher, every second sample is skipped, that is, a sampling increment of 2 is used, so the table is traversed twice as fast.

As the sampling increment changes, the resulting frequency is:

$$f = \frac{sampling\ increment \times sampling\ rate}{wavetable\ size} \tag{10-3}$$

To obtain the sampling increment for a particular frequency, Equation 10-3 may be rewritten as:

$$SI = wavetable\ size \times \frac{desired\ frequency}{sampling\ rate} \tag{10-4}$$

For example, a 512-point table with a sampling increment of 4 produces a frequency of 344.53 Hz:

$$SI = 512 \times \frac{344.53}{44100} = 4$$

Many wavetables can be iterated with a phase offset, which adds a constant value to each sampling increment position. For example, with a sampling increment of 4 and a phase offset of 3, the values will be taken from the table at points (0 + 3), (4 + 3), (8 + 3), (12 + 3), and so on. Recall from Chapter 1 that phase refers to a wave's position. Applied to a wavetable, the term refers to a position (index) within the wave.

In these examples, integer sampling increments produced non-integer frequencies. As was the case with delay lines, described in Chapter 8, not all desired frequencies will necessarily be produced with integer sampling increments. In fact, integer sampling increments are probably the exception, rather than the norm. For example, to produce a frequency of 440 Hz from a 512-point table at the CD audio rate, the sampling increment is:

$$SI = 512 \times \frac{440}{44100} = 5.1083$$

This sampling increment implies that the first value is to be read from the table's phase position zero, the next value from phase position 5.1083, the next from phase position 10.2166, and so on. That is, values need to be retrieved that fall between values stored in the table. This is done through interpolation, which factors in the decimal part of the sampling increment and derives intermediate values. As shown in Figure 8-12, if linear interpolation is used, for a phase position of 10.2166, the output sample would be:

$$(0.7834 \times [index\ 10]) + (0.2166 \times [index\ 11])$$

Unit Generators and Signal Flow Charts

Analog synthesis consisted of building blocks that were termed *modules*, which could be patched together to create complex instruments. Software synthesis systems also consist of modular building blocks called *unit generators*. A unit generator is an algorithm that creates or modifies an audio signal. Like wavetables, they are templates. The nature of the signal they output depends on certain parameters that are input to them. The output of one unit generator may be sent to the input of another unit generator. Unit generator configurations are illustrated in flowcharts that show connections of unit generators and mathematical operations that are performed on their outputs. Three simple examples are shown in Figure 10-7.

Unlike the orientation of electrical diagrams (such as the mixer block diagram of Figure 8-19), signal flow in unit generator flowcharts is usually oriented vertically, with signal flow going from the top down. The sound-producing unit generators shown in Figure 10-7 are oscillators, which produce periodic waves. Most software synthesizers allow musicians to employ oscillators that create the classic wave shapes shown in Figure 2-10 or to create their own wavetables.

Figure 10-7a is a simple sine wave oscillator. This oscillator has three inputs (also called *arguments*): (1) a frequency (440 Hz); (2) a phase offset (zero); (3) and amplitude. In this example, the amplitude is controlled by another unit generator, an *envelope generator*. As described in Chapters 3 and 6, envelope generators control output level. Like oscillators, they output a series of values over time, but they do not cycle repeatedly. The envelope generator in the figure is a classic four-segment type, with arguments for attack time, decay time, sustain level, and release time (how long it takes a note to fade to silence after it is released). These envelope types are called *ADSR envelopes*. While envelope generators are often applied to volume, they can control any parameter; pitch or filter cutoff frequency are two sound features commonly controlled by envelope generators.

Figure 10-7b illustrates amplitude modulation, which was described in Chapter 8. A second sine wave oscillator is added to the output of an envelope generator, and their sum controls the amplitude input of the audio oscillator. In principle, there is no difference between the two audio oscillators, although to speed computations many programs offer the capability for modulating oscillators to produce samples at a slower rate than the audio rate of 44.1 kHz. This slower rate is often called the *control rate* to distinguish it from the audio rate. The control oscillator has a frequency of 5 Hz, well below the threshold of human hearing. Thus, in this patch it functions as a *low-frequency oscillator (LFO)*; that is, its signal is not meant to be heard, but rather to modulate another oscillator's output. If the frequency of the modulator were brought to an audio frequency (above 20 Hz), the spectral sidebands described in Chapter 8 would become audible.

Figure 10-7c illustrates ring modulation, also described in Chapter 8. The outputs of two audio oscillators are multiplied to create the sum and difference sideband frequencies.

Another common unit generator is a *noise generator*. These output random sequences of values to create noise signals, such as the one shown in Figure 2-1. A

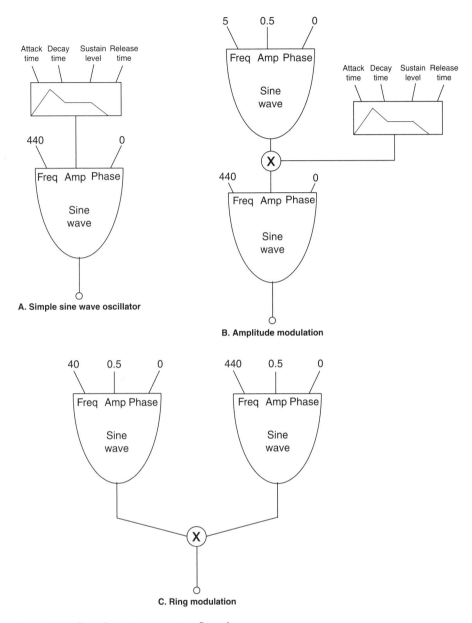

Figure 10-7 Simple unit generator flowcharts

simulation of a flute, for example, might combine outputs of a noise generator with a triangle wave. The noise generator might have a shorter envelope time and a lower overall volume than the triangle wave so that it is only heard during the initial onset of a note, just as the sound of breath is audible during the onset of a note from a flute. Percussion instruments typically contain a high degree of noise, so a noise generator sent through various filters may be useful for the creation of percussive sounds.

As described in Chapter 2, the term "noise" refers to an aperiodic wave. A more nuanced definition defines noise as some degree of randomness. Different types of noise are created from different degrees of randomness, and many synthesis programs offer a choice of different noise generators. The noise plot shown in Figure 2-1 is generated from total randomness, a complete absence of any correlation (predictability) between one value and the next. Noise of this type generates a spectrum that averages equal energy at all frequencies, and is called white noise. Its name is a reference to white light, which contains equal energy at all light frequencies. It has a shrill hissiness to it, similar to the noise of a shower or static between radio stations.

Pink noise (or *1/f noise*), in contrast, contains equal energy over every octave. Its spectrum is a curve, with energy levels that are the inverse of the frequency value, which gives it greater intensity at the low end. Its name also references visible light, which has lower frequencies at the red end of the spectrum. As described in Gardner (1978), a series of numbers with a $1/f$ distribution can be generated by using a series of dice. To start, all the dice are rolled, and the sum of their values is recorded. Then each die is assigned to correspond to a binary digit in a number that is continually incremented by one. Each time a bit changes from 1 to 0 or from 0 to 1, a new value on its associated die is generated. At each increment, the appropriate dice are rolled, and the sum of all the dice is taken. Thus, some numbers change more rapidly than others: The die associated with the 1 bit changes with every increment; the die associated with the 2 bit changes every two increments; the die associated with the 4 bit changes every four iterations; and so on. Numbers produced in this fashion "have a memory," as the numbers representing the larger bits change less frequently.

Given its lower spectrum, pink noise is less shrill than white noise; it is sometimes compared to the sound of ocean waves. Its equal distribution of energy per octave makes it suitable for many testing purposes. When audio systems are tested in movie theaters, for example, pink noise is played over the loudspeakers, and a microphone is placed at various spots in the auditorium. The spectrum picked up by the microphone is observed, and if it does not match the known pink noise signal, adjustments are made to the loudspeakers' output spectra. This ensures that the entire spectrum of audio frequencies sounds as it should.

Brown noise is named after botanist Robert Brown (1773–1858), whose observations of the erratic motion of pollen grains in a glass of water later became the basis of Einstein's proof of molecular diffusion. Gardner (1978) also describes a method for creating a "Brown" distribution of numbers by starting from an initial value, and continually adding a random number in the range of ± 1 to the total with each iteration. Brown noise also favors the low end, with even less energy at the high end. It has a spectrum of $1/f^2$, and is often referred to as a *drunken walk* or *random walk* statistical distribution: an inebriate's impaired sense of equilibrium causes him to walk in a different direction with each step; the distance travelled after n steps is proportional to $\sqrt{n}$.

The spectra for white, pink, and Brown noise are shown in Figure 10-8.

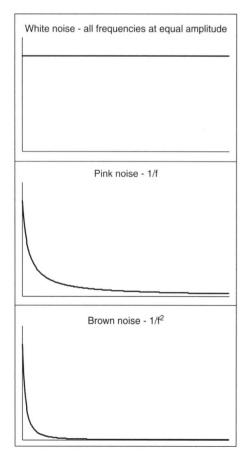

Figure 10-8 Spectra of white, pink, and Brown noise

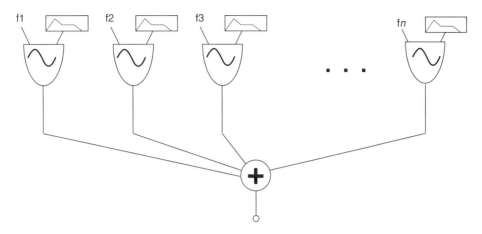

Figure 10-9 Additive synthesis flowchart

Additive Synthesis

As mentioned earlier in this chapter, some of the first studies of timbre were performed with additive synthesis (sometimes called Fourier synthesis). A series of sine oscillators is used to create each partial of a complex tone. With each oscillator controlled by a different frequency envelope and amplitude envelope, in theory any complex sound can be synthesized, given enough oscillators (Figure 10-9). The trumpet tones in Figure 6-11 were resynthesized using additive synthesis. Similar work was carried out by Jean-Claude Risset in the analysis and resynthesis of bell tones (Risset, 1969). Additive synthesis offers musicians the maximum level of flexibility, but is also data-intensive. Dozens of oscillators are needed to synthesize an instrument of any complexity. Because the spectra of acoustic instruments vary depending on their amplitude and pitch being played, a given instrument is likely to require an extensive library of oscillators and envelopes to be synthesized convincingly.

Subtractive Synthesis

Additive synthesis might be compared to needlepoint, where many strands are assembled to create a greater whole. Subtractive synthesis could similarly be compared to sculpting, where a rough mass of material has elements removed until a refined shape is left. In subtractive synthesis, noise signals and complex waveforms—such as the classic sound synthesis waveforms shown in Figure 2-10—are put through filters to shape a spectrum in broad strokes. While complex additive synthesis is only feasible with computer music systems, analog modular synthesizers—which synthesized waveforms through the manipulation of electronic voltage levels—were based on subtractive synthesis. Typical modules included the *voltage-controlled oscillator (VCO)*, the *voltage-controlled filter (VCF)*, and the *voltage-controlled amplifier (VCA)*. Musicians could purchase these small modules separately and put them together to create larger synthesis systems. In addition to filtering, different forms of modulation were also employed in classic subtractive synthesis to create variation in the sound. Some of the more common forms are described next.

LOW-FREQUENCY OSCILLATOR (LFO)

Figure 10-10 is a flowchart illustration of the subtractive patch that was used to create Figure 5-15. A sawtooth wave with a frequency of 220 Hz is input to a lowpass filter. The

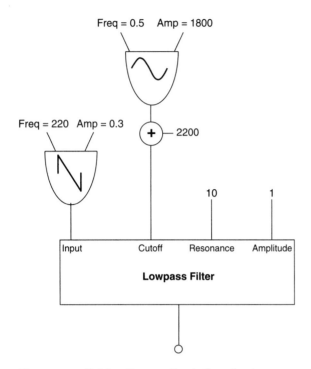

Freq = 0.5   Amp = 1800

Freq = 220   Amp = 0.3

+ — 2200

10   1

| Input | Cutoff | Resonance | Amplitude |

Lowpass Filter

Figure 10-10 Subtractive synthesis flowchart

resonance value controls the volume of the spectral peak that is characteristic of feedback filters. The filter's cutoff frequency is modulated by an LFO sine oscillator with a frequency of 0.5 Hz. The LFO has an amplitude of 1800, meaning that its values oscillate in the range of ±1800. The LFO's offset value means that 2200 is added to all values generated by the oscillator. With the amplitude and offset combined, the oscillator outputs values that oscillate between 400 and 4000 (the sum and difference between the amplitude value and the offset).

A kind of "decelerated" noise generator can be used as an LFO. Rather than generating random values at an audio rate, the values are generated much more slowly, and used as a control source. This kind of LFO noise generator is sometimes called a *sample and hold generator*. Random values are generated at some regular time increment. Each is applied to some parameter, such as pitch, and held until another random value is output.

DETUNE

Detuning is an effect that puts a number of similar oscillators out of tune with each other by small fractions of a wavelength. As discussed in Chapter 3, small tuning differences produce a beating at a rate that is the difference between two frequencies. When the difference is very slight, on the order of tenths or one-hundredths of a second, this produces a very slow modulation that is less like a tremolo and more like a gradual ebb and flow. By combining several versions of a simple wave, such as a sawtooth or triangle, and detuning each of them just slightly from each other by differing amounts, the various beating patterns become superimposed and indistinct. The net result is an indefinite shifting quality that is a classic signature of analog synthesis.

PULSE WIDTH MODULATION (PWM)

Another common form of modulation is *pulse width modulation (PWM)*. A square wave, as shown in Figure 2-10, is a special case of a wave type called a *pulse wave*, which alternates between two levels, high and low. A pulse wave is described by its *duty cycle*, which describes the percentage of each cycle that is at the high level. This means a square wave is a type of pulse wave having a duty cycle of 50 percent, or 1/2. Pulse width modulation varies the duty cycle of a pulse wave, as shown in the top part of Figure 10-11.

Because the period of the wave's cycle does not change, this modulation does not change the wave's pitch, but the change in duty cycle alters its timbre. The spectrum of a pulse wave may be described by the *sinc function*, which is shown in the bottom left of Figure 10-11. The spectrum follows the contour of the pulse wave, with the denominator of the duty cycle determining which harmonics occur at the zero crossing points, and have zero amplitude. For example, with a duty cycle of 1/2, every second harmonic has an amplitude of zero (which is another way of saying that only odd harmonics are present in the wave, which is the description shown in Figure 2-10). The

Pulse width modulated waveform

Pulse width modulated spectrum

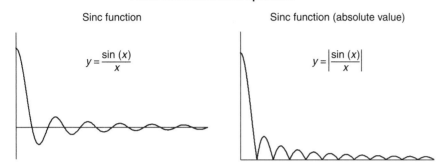

Figure 10-11 Pulse width modulation

amplitude of those odd harmonics is at the level of the sinc curve at the points half-way between the zero crossings (which happens to be one over the harmonic number, as described in Figure 2-10). But if the wave has a duty cycle of 25 percent, or 1/4, every fourth harmonic has an amplitude of zero. The amplitude of the three harmonics between each of these is the height of the sinc curve at the three points evenly spaced between the zero crossings. With a duty cycle of 12.5 percent, or 1/8, every eighth harmonic is missing from the spectrum. Thus, every eighth harmonic has an amplitude of zero, corresponding to the zero crossings of the sinc plot. The amplitude of the seven harmonics between each of these is the height of the sinc curve at the seven points evenly spaced between the zero crossings.

Thus, as the pulse width is modulated, its spectrum changes according to this pattern. The effect is similar to slight chorusing or detuning. As shown in the plot, this would mean that some amplitudes are negative, that is, polarity inverted. As discussed in Chapters 2 and 3, this would sound the same to our ears as a positive amplitude. So it is more accurate to consider the amplitudes as following the contour of the *absolute value* of the sinc plot, as shown in the bottom right of Figure 10-11. (Recall that the absolute value refers to the distance a number is from zero, which is the same for both positive and negative numbers. For example, both 3 and –3 are the same distance from zero on a number line, so the absolute value for both is 3. The absolute value converts negative numbers to positive numbers by disregarding the sign.)

OSCILLATOR SYNC
Another shifting qualitative effect may be obtained through *oscillator sync*, where a sync oscillator (or master oscillator) controls a secondary oscillator (or slave oscillator). Each time the sync oscillator begins a new cycle, it causes the secondary oscillator to break its cycle and start another cycle immediately, as shown in Figure 10-12. This

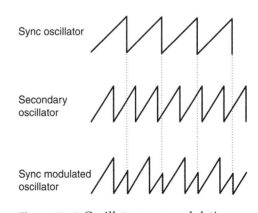

Figure 10-12 Oscillator sync modulation

is often done with sawtooth waves, although some synthesis programs allow any type of wave to be hard-synchronized to the cycles of another. Typically, the slave oscillator is at a higher frequency than the master oscillator. The pitch of the synced modulated waveform is that of the master waveform, because its cycles begin at the same time as those of the master. But using an LFO to vary the pitch of the slave has the aural effect of varying the timbre of the sync modulated waveform.

VOWEL SYNTHESIS

Some of the earliest work in subtractive synthesis were simulations of human speech with the voder and vocoder, which were described in Chapter 8. The vocal apparatus is akin to a quarter-wave resonator tube (described in Chapter 1), with the throat acting as the closed end and the mouth acting as the open end. The larynx produces a rich harmonic wave, and the shape of the vocal cavity introduces formants in the spectrum (as described in Chapter 2). The frequency centers and relative amplitudes of the formants are what create vowel sounds. (This can be demonstrated by tapping your pharynx, just under the Adam's apple, and silently mouthing the vowels. The tapping is equivalent to an impulse signal, and the shape of your mouth filters this impulse to create a "vowel-tap" sound.)

By sending a rich wave, such as a sawtooth, through a set of 3–5 bandpass filters that are set to the same center frequencies and amplitudes as vocal formants, vowel-like qualities can be produced. Table 10-1 shows charts of average formants corresponding to vowels produced by male, female, and child voices.

Frequency/Phase Modulation

As was described earlier, digital instruments revolutionized the commercial synthesizer industry in the early 1980s with the expanded sound palette of frequency modulation synthesis, which was first described by Chowning (1977). This technique applies high-frequency vibrato to an oscillator, as shown in Figure 10-13. It is similar to amplitude modulation (described in Chapter 8) in that it is adapted from radio broadcast techniques of modulating a carrier wave. At low modulation frequencies, the effect is a vibrato. But at high modulation frequencies (above 20 Hz or so), frequency modulation produces a change in timbre that is far richer than the sideband pair produced by amplitude modulation. The timbre will be described below, following a clarification of terminology.

Although the properties of frequency-modulated waves had been known for decades to broadcasters and electrical engineers, the precision of digital technology made it realizable as a synthesis approach. FM synthesis revolutionized the music industry and quickly became a household word among synthesists. In practice, the term was actually a misnomer. Although the audible results are equivalent, the actual implementation in synthesizers was *phase modulation*. Because some synthesis programs use the latter term, the distinction is shown and discussed in Figure 10-14.

The spectrum of a phase-modulated wave is like an expanded version of the spectrum that results from amplitude modulation. As discussed in Chapter 8, amplitude modulation produces the carrier frequency plus sideband spectral components at the sum and difference of the carrier frequency (f_c) and the modulator frequency (f_m). In phase modulation, the result is *many* such sideband pairs that lie at the carrier frequency plus and minus *integer multiples* of modulator frequency, as shown in Figure 10-15. Although the number of sideband pairs is theoretically infinite, Chowning and Bristow (1987) describe that in practice the number of sideband pairs with significant energy is the ***index of modulation*** (amplitude of the modulator) plus two.

TABLE 10-1 Averages of fundamental and formant frequencies and formant amplitudes of vowels

Phonetic Symbol	Typical Word	Average Fundamental	dB	Formant 1	dB	Formant 2	dB	Formant 3	dB
ADULT MALE									
i	beet	136	0	270	−4	2290	−24	3010	−2
ɪ	sit	135	0	390	−3	1990	−23	2550	−27
ɛ	bet	130	0	530	−2	1840	−17	2480	−24
æ	cat	127	0	660	−1	1720	−12	2410	−22
ɒ	hot	124	0	730	−1	1090	−5	2440	−28
ɔ	bought	129	0	570	0	840	−7	2410	−34
ʊ	foot	137	0	440	−1	1020	−12	2240	−34
u:	food	141	0	300	−3	870	−19	2240	−43
ʌ	up	130	0	640	−1	1190	−10	2390	−27
ɜ:	bird	133	0	490	−5	1350	−15	1690	−20
ADULT FEMALE									
i	beet	235	0	310	−4	2790	−24	3310	−2
ɪ	sit	232	0	430	−3	2480	−23	3070	−27
ɛ	bet	223	0	610	−2	2330	−17	2990	−24
æ	cat	210	0	860	−1	2050	−12	2850	−22
ɒ	hot	212	0	850	−1	1220	−5	2810	−28
ɔ	bought	216	0	590	0	920	−7	2710	−34
ʊ	foot	232	0	470	−1	1160	−12	2680	−34
u:	food	231	0	370	−3	950	−19	2670	−43
ʌ	up	221	0	760	−1	1400	−10	2780	−27
ɜ:	bird	218	0	500	−5	1640	−15	1960	−20
CHILD									
i	beet	272	0	370	−4	3200	−24	3730	−2
ɪ	sit	269	0	530	−3	2730	−23	3600	−27
ɛ	bet	260	0	690	−2	2610	−17	3570	−24
æ	cat	251	0	1010	−1	2320	−12	3320	−22
ɒ	hot	256	0	1030	−1	1370	−5	3170	−28
ɔ	bought	263	0	680	0	1060	−7	3180	−34
ʊ	foot	276	0	560	−1	1410	−12	3310	−34
u:	food	274	0	430	−3	1170	−19	3260	−43
ʌ	up	261	0	850	−1	1590	−10	3360	−27
ɜ:	bird	261	0	560	−5	1820	−15	2160	−20

After Petersen and Barney (1952)

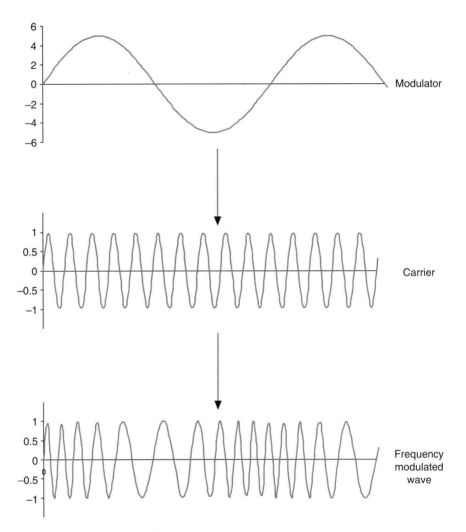

Figure 10-13 Frequency modulation

The relative amplitude of each sideband pair may be found by pairing the modulation index with a graph of **Bessel functions** of the first kind. Bessel functions are plotted in terms of an **order**. These functions are used to describe a variety of behaviors, including the vibrational modes of circular membranes such as drum heads, electromagnetic waves in tubes, and acoustical radiation. Figure 10-16 shows plots of Bessel functions ordered 0 through 9. In FM signal processing, the orders of Bessel functions correspond to the sideband pair: the zero-order function corresponds to the unmodulated carrier; the first order corresponds to the first sideband pair at $f_c \pm f_m$; the second order corresponds to the second sideband pair at $f_c \pm 2f_m$; and so on. The horizontal axis of each graph corresponds to the index of modulation. The amplitude of each sideband pair may be determined by a three-step process:

1. To get the amplitude of sideband pair n, select the graph of the Bessel function order n.
2. Read across the horizontal index to the modulation index value.
3. The value of the curve at that point is the amplitude of the sideband pair.

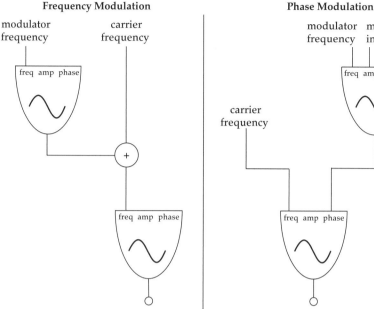

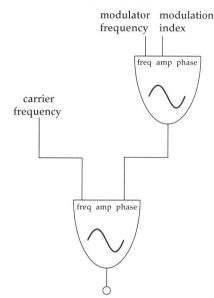

Frequency Modulation   Phase Modulation

modulator frequency   carrier frequency

modulator frequency   modulation index

carrier frequency

The sample increment is modulated.

The sample increment is constant; each output index value gets an additional offset value from the modulating oscillator. The results are similar, with distinctions between the two algorithms discussed below.

Phase modulation is an indirect way of modulating the frequency of an oscillator. Recall that phase refers to the position of a wave at a given time. Imagine the crest point of the oscillator wave is pulled to the left or pushed to the right a bit. When the crest is pulled to the left, the effect is that cycles occur more often, with a resulting higher frequency. Similarly, when crests are pushed to the right, cycles appear less frequently, with a resulting lower frequency.

When a wavetable is incremented, the phase refers to the position of the incrementer. Frequency is derived from the rate at which the table is incremented. Therefore, the audible frequency is the result of the incrementer's speed. When the speed of the incrementer is modulated, the audible frequency is also modulated. Frequency is analogous to acceleration, which is the derivative (rate of change) of velocity. (Since the incrementer moves through the table in one direction only, speed is synonymous with velocity in this example.) Therefore, frequency is the derivative of phase.

This means that the same audible results may be obtained from both configurations, as long as the derivative of a sine wave (a cosine wave) is used as the modulator in the frequency modulation algorithm.

Phase modulation is what has been implemented in most commercial synthesizers. It is a more economical configuration. Phase modulation also makes it more practical to implement cascades of phase modulators (modulators modulating other modulators, the last of which modulates the carrier). In phase modulation, any DC offset in the chain of modulators only results in a constant phase shift, which is inaudible. In a frequency modulation cascade, any DC offset in the modulators would result in a constant change in frequency, which would be audible.

Figure 10-14 Frequency modulation and phase modulation synthesis

Because only the first-order Bessel function curve is not zero at horizontal position zero, a modulation index of zero produces only the carrier frequency. As the modulation index increases, the power of the carrier frequency is distributed to the sidebands that emerge; thus, the bandwidth increases while the total power produced by the

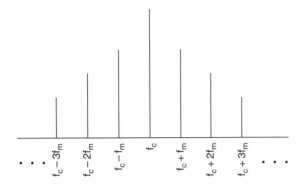

Figure 10-15 Spectrum of a phase modulated wave

complex wave remains consistent. Because all the Bessel functions oscillate at different rates, a small change in the modulation index can produce complex spectral variations as different sideband pairs are amplified or attenuated.

The resulting spectra can be predicted from the ratio of the modulator to the carrier. When the frequencies of both are equal (a ratio of 1:1), all harmonics are produced, producing sawtooth-like waveforms. When the modulator frequency is twice the carrier frequency (a ratio of 2:1), every second harmonic is produced, thus removing all even harmonics and producing a square-like waveform. In general, if the modulator frequency is an integer multiple of N times the carrier frequency, the spectrum is harmonic, somewhat like the pulse width modulated waves described above, with every Nth harmonic removed. If the modulator:carrier ratio is not an integer relation, the spectrum is inharmonic, as the sideband pairs do not occur at harmonics of the carrier frequency. Thus, the complex inharmonic spectrum of a bell or percussion instrument can be produced with a small number of oscillators. With an amplitude envelope applied to the modulator, dynamic spectral changes can be produced. It was this computational efficiency that made this synthesis method so successful: a great variety of sounds could be produced with just a few oscillators.

Depending on the fundamental frequency of the carrier and the level of the modulation index, there are scenarios in which lower sidebands could extend below 0 Hz. In this case, the negative frequencies correspond to the aliased frequencies represented in the polar graph in Figure 5-7. Negative components are "wrapped around" 0 Hz to a frequency below the Nyquist frequency and their polarity is inverted. This can have the effect of altering the uniform spacing of sidebands and producing inharmonic timbres. Should the "wrapped" sidebands coincide with any positive sidebands, the polarity inversion can cause cancellation or attenuation of the positive sideband.

More variation can be introduced by using more than a simple oscillator pair. One possibility is to combine multiple oscillator pairs, so that their spectra are added. Or a single modulator may modulate a group of carriers, all of which are set to different frequencies. If one of the carriers has a fixed frequency, it can create formants in the spectrum (formants are discussed in Chapter 2, and also above, in the context of vocal synthesis). Other multi-oscillator configurations contain cascaded modulators that produce even more complex spectral patterns, whereby a modulator-modulator pair may produce a spectrum containing multiple sidebands, which produce groups of sideband pairs when this wave is applied to the carrier (sidebands of sidebands).

Nonlinear Waveshaping

Phase modulation is the most common example of a class of synthesis algorithms called *nonlinear waveshaping*. If waveshaping is considered a "black box" that makes changes of some kind to an input wave, the term "nonlinear" means that more comes out than was put in. While a linear system can alter frequencies and phases of input waves, a nonlinear system generates entirely new spectral components. Other examples were given in Chapter 5, where the effects of distortion were discussed. Nonlinear waveshaping is also termed *modulation synthesis* or *distortion synthesis* in some literature.

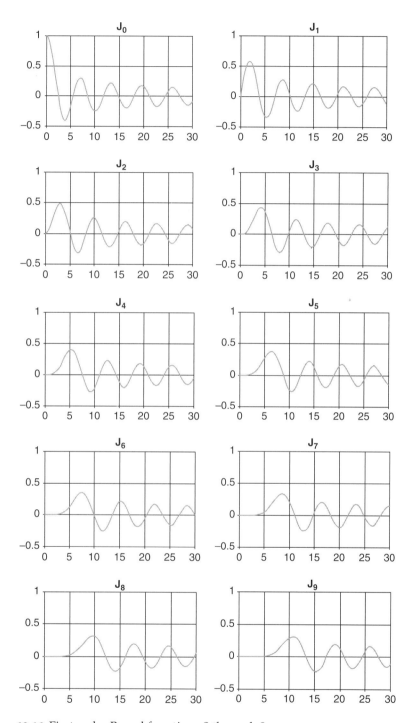

Figure 10-16 First-order Bessel functions 0 through 9

Waveshaping often involves the use of a transfer function, which rescales samples in an input waveform to change its shape. A common type of transfer function waveshaping makes use of *Chebyshev polynomials of the first kind*, which have the effect of adding harmonics to a waveform as its amplitude increases. This is similar to the distortion introduced by some tube amplifiers, and adds a similar warmth to the sound. The fact that it is amplitude-dependent gives it a natural-sounding quality; the distortion is not a constant effect, but varies with the nature of the signal.

Physical Modeling

By the 1990s, commercial synthesizers seemed ready for a new direction. In the 1960s and 1970s, analog synthesizers had an attractive warmth to their sound, but they were unstable, and it was difficult to simulate acoustic instruments with them. In the 1980s, FM synthesizers offered new ranges of timbres, but after the initial excitement over them wore off, people began to find their sound cold and clinical. While samplers produced effective reproductions of acoustic instruments, they were limited in that their sounds were snapshots that were triggered, rather than being actually played with expressive variation.

Manufacturers began to show interest in a new approach called *physical modeling* (also called *waveguide synthesis*). The model is based on physical measurements of an instrument, acoustical data on the spectra produced by the instrument under varying conditions, the mechanics of how the instrument is played, and an understanding of how the instrument's playing techniques correspond to changes in the sound it produces.

As a starting point, string vibration can be described mathematically with the *wave equation*, which factors in characteristics such as string length, tension, density, and level of displacement. The wave equation can be extended to wind instruments, as the wave equation can also describe vibrating columns of air, with the transverse motions of the string substituted with longitudinal compressions and rarefactions of air.

Other physical modeling parameters include the initial source of excitation—*lips* for a brass instrument such as a trombone or tuba; a *jet* for an instrument such as a flute; *reed* for a clarinet, oboe, or bassoon; *bowing* or *plucking* for string instruments—plus features such as the instrument body's shape and length, changes in embouchure, changes in breath pressure, changes in bite pressure, and changes in bow pressure or direction.

Physical modeling creates a much more dynamic sound than the static snapshot of an audio sample. As discussed earlier, researchers such as Risset, Moorer, and Grey analyzed how the spectral content changed in trumpets as the volume changed (Moorer and Grey, 1977 and 1978; Risset, 1965; Risset and Mathews, 1969). It can be difficult to model this change effectively with additive or FM synthesis, as it is difficult to assign appropriate sound parameters to a characteristic such as change in breath pressure. Sampled sounds offer some improvement, but still are lacking in *control intimacy*, which is an instrument's responsiveness to small, complex gestures from the musician. The change in sound is usually due to a combination of factors. For example, vibrato usually involves some combination of changes in pitch, volume, and timbre. It varies from instrument to instrument, as well as according to musical context. It is difficult, if not impossible, to get this level of control with standard interface elements such as a slider, modulation wheel, or pitch-bend wheel.

Physical modeling synthesizers were introduced in the 1990s, but were not commercially successful. They proved difficult to play, which kept them from gaining a foothold in the market, and were discontinued. Still, research in this form of synthesis continued at institutions such as the Center for Computer Research in Music and Acoustics (CCRMA) at Stanford University, and it remains an active area of investigation. Besides synthesizing facsimiles of existing instruments, physical models make the creation of imaginary instruments possible—composer Trevor Wishart (b. 1946) has remarked that this approach gave him the possibility of playing "a two-mile long trumpet, powered by a jet engine." A number of physical modeling-based plug-ins are available, and are akin to convolution reverbs (described in Chapter 8) in their capability of producing realistic results based on physical measurements. Besides DAW plug-ins, there are also dedicated software packages for physical modeling.

A commonly cited drawback to physical models is that they can be difficult to explore while they're under construction. They can be complex, and a complete model needs to be created before the sound can be heard. Emerging software is allowing physical models to be constructed incrementally, giving the designer more flexibility to test and modify the design as it is being built.

A conceptually simple form of physical modeling is the *Karplus-Strong string model*. This consists of a buffer that gets filled with a noise signal, and is recirculated through a lowpass filter. Because any type of signal that repeats, even noise, sounds pitched, the noise burst sounds pitched yet somewhat pointed, like a guitar string at the moment it is plucked. Users select a delay time at which to tap the buffer, so that the perceived pitch is the inverse of the delay time (for example, to generate a frequency of 440 Hz, a delay time of 1/440 can be selected). As the signal is recirculated through the lowpass filter, with each pass some of the high frequencies are removed, so that the sound becomes gradually less pointed and more like a sine wave. The result is remarkably similar to the sound of a plucked string. Each initiation of the model generates a new buffer. Even if the pitch and essential timbre remain the same, the quality of the attack is slightly different with each note, just as a plucked guitar string never sounds exactly the same way twice.

The Karplus-Strong model may be expanded by sending the signal through other filters to model resonances of an instrument body and create more complex waveforms. For example, a frequency-dependent delay, implemented through a series of all-pass filters, might simulate string stiffness or variations due to bowing motion. The wave equation may also be applied to two-dimensional systems, so that drum membranes may also be modeled.

A related type of physical modeling is *modal sound synthesis* (also called *damped sinusoidal synthesis*). It models mass-spring vibrating systems, based on the mass, damping, and restoring spring force. Equations describing this kind of decaying sinusoid are standard IIR filters such as those described in Chapters 5 and 6. These may be used to describe modes of vibrating bodies such as ceramic bowls, metal bars, bells, or anything else. Some software allows users to define an arbitrary number of ringing filters, each at its particular ringing frequency, volume, and decay time. By sending either an impulse signal or a high-bandwidth continuous signal (such as noise) through these, a remarkable range of timbres can be created.

Another variation on the modeling idea is *analog modeling synthesizers*, which are digital models of the circuitry found in vintage instruments from the 1960s and 1970s. Like the analog tape plug-ins that reintroduce the "imperfections" of tape machines into digital audio production, these instruments and/or plug-ins are meant to couple the warmth of analog instruments with the stability of digital instruments.

Granular Synthesis

Like FM synthesis and physical modeling, *granular synthesis* is only realizable with computer music systems. Granular synthesis is the equivalent of what pointillism is to painting, a technique practiced by artists such as Georges Seurat in works like *Sunday Afternoon on the Island of La Grande Jatte* (1884–1886), which is composed of thousands of small dots. The idea of sound grains was described by composer/theoretician Iannis Xenakis (1922–2001) in 1963 (reprinted in Xenakis, 2001). It was based on his 1960 work *Analogique B*, which consisted of sine tones recorded onto tape, which was cut into small pieces and reassembled according to various probability theories. But it fell to later, computer-based composers such as Curtis Roads (b. 1951) and Barry Truax (b. 1947) to develop these ideas into working musical systems.

In granular synthesis, a composer outlines in broad strokes the nature of *sound clouds* created from extremely short grains of sound (durations are typically on the order of milliseconds). Parameters typically include the number of grains played per second, their average duration, the waveshapes of the grains, and envelope shapes of the grains. *Tendency masks* outline the upper and lower limits within which values may be chosen at random. Rich overall textures may be created through the sum of such microscopic sound particles. One side effect is that amplitude modulation results from the quick succession of grains, producing added spectral richness from the resulting sidebands. In the earliest granular works, composers synthesized sound grains. Today, the term is often associated with audio sample work, whereby grains are created by playing extremely short excerpts of audio files.

Algorithmic and Interactive Composition

Algorithmic composition refers to a composer setting up processes and rules for music generation, and leaving it to computers to carry out the lower-level work of generating the actual music events. It was first explored by Lejaren Hiller (1924–1994) with programs he wrote for the Illiac computer at the University of Illinois at Urbana-Champaign, where he also founded the first American computer music research center. His *Illiac Suite for String Quartet* (1957) was divided into four movements, each of which represented a particular musical experiment. The first was based on simple counterpoint, with notes generated at random that were retained if they met the rules of classical counterpoint, or discarded and replaced by a new note if they did not. The second began with random notes, with rules gradually being applied throughout the movement that imposed order, resulting in correct counterpoint by the movement's end. The third movement explored varying rhythms and string playing techniques, with pitches first being the same for each instrument while rhythms and techniques were highlighted. The pitches were first chosen at random, then from simple compositional rules, then according to twelve-tone serial rules. The fourth movement was based on probability functions.

As computer music was developed at Bell Labs in the 1960s, composers such as James Tenney (1934–2006), Emmanuel Ghent (1925–2003), and Laurie Spiegel (b. 1945) developed algorithmic composition systems. Spiegel later created Music Mouse in 1986, which was a commercial MIDI-based algorithmic composition program. The descendants of this work are programs such as Max/MSP (www.cycling74.com) and SuperCollider (www.supercollider.sourceforge.net). These are general-purpose musical programming environments. Among many other things, users can set up synthesis algorithms from scratch and create musical processes that outline ways for the computer to generate musical material. Many users of these programs participate in *live coding sessions* (Collins, McLean, and Rohrhuber, 2014). These are computer jam sessions that feature composers onstage, typing code. Their computer screens are projected so that audience members can see the code that is generating the audio (and often video).

A related area is that of *interactive composition*, which is the process in which a performer shares control of the music's creation with a computer. These performances are often improvised, and involve a computer system that "listens to" and analyzes salient musical features such as individual phrases, tempo, density, loudness, register, and harmonic progression. The computer then responds, "composing" music based on what the performer has played. Leading composers in this area include Tod Machover (b. 1953), from the Massachusetts Institute of Technology Media Lab, and Robert Rowe (b. 1954), from New York University.

Suggested Exercises

- Find a film clip online. Download it and open it in a DAW program. Remove its soundtrack or lower the volume, so that the film is effectively silent. Recreate a soundtrack to the film, using the DAW to enter music and some "hit points." You'll find that a hit point sounds somewhat unconvincing and awkward until the precise moment is found. At that moment, the film will seem to come alive, and the sound and action will blend seamlessly. It is usually best to understate the sound. When it matches the action exactly, it doesn't need to be loud to be present. A common mistake of beginning students is to turn up the volume for the hit point sound effects, as though the high volume level can somehow compensate for the fact that it doesn't precisely match the action. Try to go for effects that are understated and effective.
- Create a sound collage using only clips that last two seconds or less. Use editing and effects to make all clips sound as though they are part of the same "sound world."
- Make a set of recordings from common household objects—water running, doors closing, running a comb along an edge for a "zipper" sound, light switches, tapping pot lids, etc. Assign these recordings to different keys of a sampling instrument. Use this as a drum machine, and play some drum-like patterns. Expect that each recording will need to be edited. At the very least, you will want to trim silence off of the beginning and end of the recording. You will probably also do multiple "takes" of each object. For example, if you are holding a pencil at the sharp end and dropping it downwards onto a counter so that it bounces a few times on its eraser, you may want to try this a few times in succession so that you can record the "perfect bounce." Later, you can extract this from your recording. You may find a number of useful bounces that you want to use. The next step will be to assign each recording to a different set of MIDI notes in the sampler. Through trial and error, determine how many keys a recording may be transposed up or down and still sound effective. Depending on the sounds, it may be desirable to overlap different sounds and key ranges, so that depressing a single MIDI key plays more than one sample simultaneously. Some samplers allow different samples to be assigned to different velocity ranges. Returning to the eraser bounce example above, if there are a number of useful bounces that you record, you may want to assign them to different key ranges. Alternatively, you may wish to assign more than one bounce to a single key, but with different recordings triggered with different velocity values. Still another possibility is to get a multi-layered polyrhythmic effect by

assigning several bounces to the same set of keys, so that a number of recordings are heard simultaneously.

- Make some recordings of longer, sustained sounds. Examples might be sung vowels, bowed strings, rubbing the top of a wine glass. Store these in a sampler and edit their loop points so that they can sustain indefinitely and continuously. Play a piece made up of these longer sounds, just as you played a rhythmic piece made up of short, percussive samples above.
- Create a cluster of sine waves, and put a different, slow amplitude changes on each so that the result is a quasi-harmonic timbre with overtones emerging, disappearing, and reappearing again, all at different rates. Also try working with a rich harmonic oscillator, such as a sawtooth. Put multiple sawtooths into multiple filters, all with slow, sweeping cutoff frequencies at different rates. Distribute the sawtooths to different spots in the panning field to create a shifting curtain of sound.
- Using only electronic sounds, nothing recorded, create clips no longer than 5 seconds that express the following words:
  o Speckly
  o Sparkly
  o Rocky
  o Cloudy
  o Philosophical
  o Barren
  o Splendiferous
  o Noncommittal
  o Spicy
  o Zesty
  o Effervescent
  o Ticklish
  o Flirtatious
  o Melancholy
  o Reminiscent

Feel free to come up with other descriptive words that create sound design challenges.

- Create a short piece using softsynths. Turn off all post-synthesis processing—reverb, modulation, compression, delay, EQ, etc. What does the raw softsynth sound like on its own? Recreate these effects using buses and effects tracks.

Key Terms

additive synthesis
ADSR envelope
algorithmic composition
analog modeling synthesizers
argument
Bessel function
Brown noise
control intimacy
control rate
detuning

drunken walk or random walk
duty cycle
editor/librarian software
elektronische Musik
envelope generator
event list
frequency modulation (FM) synthesis
granular synthesis
index of modulation
interactive composition

Karplus-Strong string model
live coding session
loop
loop point
loop/overdub mode
low-frequency oscillator (LFO)
modal sound synthesis or damped
    sinusoidal synthesis
modular component system
module
musique concrète
noise generator
nonlinear waveshaping (modulation
    synthesis or distortion synthesis)
notator
order
oscillator sync
phase modulation
physical modeling or waveguide
    synthesis
piano-roll view
pink or 1/f noise
pulse wave

pulse width modulation (PWM)
punch recording
punch-in point
punch-out point
quantize
sample and hold generator
sampler
sequencer
sinc function
softsynth
sound cloud
step entry
subtractive synthesis
synthesizer
tendency mask
timestamp
unit generator
voltage-controlled amplifier (VCA)
voltage-controlled filter (VCF)
voltage-controlled modular
    synthesizer
voltage-controlled oscillator (VCO)
wave equation

Chapter 11

Tales from the Trenches: Survival Tips in Specific Contexts

Much of the material in this book has been theoretical. The goal has been to cover the basic groundwork of computer music and audio technology principles. This final chapter will be more miscellaneous and hands-on, covering some practical issues that come up in certain working contexts. While a chapter such as this cannot be exhaustive, hopefully it will be a useful collection of tips and tricks that do not normally fall within the scope of a reference textbook.

Live Sound Mixing

Conceptually, live mixing is simple: a number of microphone sources are connected to a mixer, and a soundboard operator adjusts the relative volume levels for the mix that is sent to a PA system. It sounds easy enough, and not that different from adjusting volume levels on a home audio system. But the reality is that different performance venues and ensembles present different challenges, making mixing more multifaceted than it appears at first.

There are limits to how loud volume levels may be set before a microphone feeds back, picking up its signal from the PA and recirculating it. It is rarely possible simply to set a level and leave it. Performers tend to move about, varying the distance between themselves and the microphone(s). Signals typically need constant monitoring, so that they remain audible when the level lowers, but stay low enough to avoid feedback. Broadway sound mixers who adjust the levels of actors' microphones are known to learn hundreds of small movements, sometimes emphasizing just part of a word and de-emphasizing another part, quickly turning the fader down for a sibilant and back up again for the vowel.

In musical venues, the concert sound is typically a combination of sound from the PA combined with sound that originates from the stage. Rock bands playing in bars are notoriously challenging to mix, as there are a number of variables that are outside the control of the sound mixer. Drum kits are usually loud enough on their own to over-power the other instruments even when the drums have no amplification. Electric guitars usually have onstage amplifiers that provide ample volume levels. Vocals and acoustic guitars are typically what need amplification, but there is inevitably some bleed from the onstage guitars and drums that blends with the microphone signal. Often, there is no such thing as a good mix in this environment. Rather, the goal of the sound mixer is to make the sound as tolerable as possible, given the inevitable shortcomings.

Many directional speakers, such as guitar amplifiers, produce a focused, laser-like cone of sound. The result in a theater is that people seated in the front rows who are outside this dispersion cone hear very little of the guitar, while those seated in the back, where the cone is wider, may find the guitar to be far too loud. Often the solution is to turn the guitar amplifier so that it faces either upwards or toward the back wall, away from the audience. A microphone may then be placed near the amplifier so that its sound may be sent to the PA system, which presumably has a more even distribution over the seating area.

Another challenging issue is onstage monitoring. Because the PA system is often in front of or above the performers, they are unable to hear what is being sent to the audience. They require additional loudspeakers that are directed at them so that they can hear themselves and each other. Sometimes these are in the form of a "wedge," a loudspeaker that rests on the floor, pointing upwards at the player. To prevent monitors bleeding into microphones, many bands now use *in-ear monitor (IEM)* systems, which consist of an earpiece worn by each player, along with a small mixing console so that each player can customize her mix.

An important lesson to be learned by both musicians and audio technicians is that not everyone has to hear everything in the monitors. Often, less is more. Musicians who are new to these systems will often turn everything up, listening to all instruments at full volume, and then wonder why they can't hear a particular instrument. The solution is often to turn down all instruments but their own, often eliminating some of them altogether, and then to raise their mixer's master volume.

Setting Up a Recording Studio

Working in a recording studio is in some ways like working in a kitchen. There are a variety of tasks that rely on tacit knowledge. Two people may follow the same recipe steps, but a more experienced baker's cake may turn out far superior to a cake made by a novice: just how one beats an egg, sifts flour, or adds a pinch of salt is not typically described anywhere, and these are skills gained by hands-on experience. The same can be said about many tasks involved in working in a music studio. There are many books that are dedicated to the subject. What follows here are simply some tips that will hopefully help ease the transition from novice to veteran.

A music production studio can be put together at just about any size and budget, depending on the user's needs, preferences, and pocketbook. In the simplest scenario, a laptop computer and a pair of headphones can serve as the entirety of a musician's workspace. For mixing and playback, this may be all that is necessary in terms of hardware. To facilitate creating new material, some sort of MIDI keyboard is likely to be the first thing added to the computer and headphones. These few components can fit into a small carrying bag, and can be suitable for a musician on the go.

For a permanent or semipermanent workspace, additional steps may be taken to optimize the working environment.

Room Coloration
Ideally, the room will not have parallel walls and will be free of lingering, unwanted reflections. In reality, most buildings are made with rooms that have parallel walls, and so steps may need to be taken to minimize room resonances. This may involve some trial and error. Chapter 8 contained distinctions between absorbing sound and diffusing

reflections. You can get a quick sense of a room's qualities by snapping your fingers or clapping your hands and listening for reflections or echoes. Ideally, a room should sound pretty "dead." Furniture, absorbers, or diffusers can all help to minimize room resonances. Some should be attached to the wall. Others can be movable panels, which resemble office space partition walls on wheels, to make the space adaptable to different performer configurations.

Electrical Noise

After you've spent some time with the room factors, the next step should be the electrical system. Chapter 4 discussed ground loops. Besides minimizing this unwanted hum, another consideration is to ensure that the power supply is consistent and free from noise originating from other devices in the building. In addition to generating audible interference, system noise can distort or mask low-level high frequencies that provide the resolution for clean transients and full timbral reproduction.

The likelihood of ground loops is reduced if everything leads to a single outlet, rather than having devices plugged into a series of outlets distributed around the studio. Extension cords and power bars can ensure that all power originates from the same place. If possible, this outlet should be connected to a breaker box circuit that does not power other devices that may experience power surges (washer/dryers, refrigerators, space heaters, and the like). Ideally, this circuit should operate at 20 amperes or more to ensure sufficient power for all devices.

A number of additional steps may be taken to ensure that current flows smoothly throughout the studio. A *power conditioner* can be used for additional stability and insulation from outside interference. The power conditioner should be plugged into the wall outlet, and be the end point for all extension cords and power bars leading to studio devices. A *power regulator* ensures that voltage is delivered consistently, and is not subject to sudden spikes due to outside interference (such as lightning or solar storms). The most expensive and physically heaviest treatment is a balanced power conditioner. In addition to regulating voltage, balanced conditioners inhibit noise by sending a balanced signal, such that the current-carrying wires are no longer hot and neutral (as discussed in Chapter 4), but rather carry two versions of the current at opposite polarity, as is the case with balanced audio cables (also discussed in Chapter 4).

Another possible source of electrical interference is the audio cables themselves, particularly if they are running alongside power cords. Try to separate audio and power cables whenever possible. If they must occupy the same real estate, they should cross at right angles to each other. Another way to ensure clean signal flow is to minimize excess cable. The most inexpensive approach (dollar-wise) is to make your own cable. Connectors and spools of cable can be purchased at much lower prices than pre-made cables, and cable can be cut to lengths that match the actual run lengths needed in a particular studio. A more inexpensive approach, time-wise, is to use a cable ordering site like monoprice.com, which allows customers to specify cable types, connector types, and lengths.

Sometimes devices use a "wall-wart," which transforms AC to DC and sets the current at the precise voltage needed by the device. Besides taking up extra outlet space, wall-warts are only meant to be used with their particular device. If the device is removed and stored somewhere else, it's advisable to label the plug that goes with it. Wall warts often do not have a metal shield to isolate them and prevent them from causing interference, so they should be kept as far as possible from any signal-carrying cables.

While many studios are centered on mixing boards, it is becoming more common for mixing to be done in software, in which case all sources are directed to the studio's audio interface. Depending on how many inputs are needed, it may be helpful to use an audio snake, which is a bundle of cables wrapped together, with a set of connectors at either end (looking something like squid tentacles). It's a good idea to label each end of the cable so that it's easy to know which device leads to which inputs. Many snakes come with prelabeled connectors for this reason. At this writing, an alternative to audio snakes is emerging, which is to send audio over a computer network cable. This approach will be discussed further in this chapter's section on networking.

Many outboard components can be mounted into 19″ racks, which keeps things tidy and ergonomic. Many rack-mountable units generate heat, so it's advisable to leave space above the heat vent, rather than placing devices right on top of each other. Using nylon washers on the rack screws can lessen the possibility of ground loops originating from the rack assembly.

Other housekeeping tasks include using dust covers and keeping dust cloths and air sprayers on hand. Polishing cable connectors regularly removes oxidation that can build up and interfere with the electrical flow. An unused mascara brush can be used for cleaning female connectors: spray the brush, gently clean the connector, then wipe the brush with a paper towel; repeat the process until the paper towel is clean after wiping the brush. Switching off a piece of gear and turning all its knobs back and forth a few times can keep corrosion from building up, especially in knobs that aren't used very often.

Common-Sense Procedures

A recording studio is a singular kind of environment, and it may take some adaptation to learn to work effectively in it. One person's common sense is another person's learning curve. While some of the following tips may sound silly or obvious, they are all based on actual experiences with beginning students.

- Don't underestimate the value of organization. Store all cables together, grouped by cable type and length. Keep supplies like pens, tape, and blank CDs within easy reach.
- Learn to look before you step. Recording spaces are in a constant state of flux, with different instrument setups coming in and out on a daily basis. At any given moment there may be cables, microphone stands, or instrument stands in a place where there was empty space the day before. In daily life at home, we usually have a fairly fixed configuration of furniture and objects, and we habitually set out for a destination in the house while looking in another direction. In the studio, get in the habit of looking before you move to avoid slapstick-style mishaps.
- During sessions, arrange your audio cables in designated paths along the floor to avoid having to step through a random tangle of cables to move something. If there is extra cable, be sure to coil it so that it does not splay out and create a trip hazard.
- It's a good idea to establish a workflow wherein things are cabled in a certain order. This makes it easier to remember the order in which cables were laid so that they can be dismantled in reverse order at the end of a session without tangling.
- Sometimes both close mics and overhead mics are used simultaneously to record a variety of simultaneous perspectives. Set up the close mics first, then the overhead mics. If the overhead mics are set up first, it's easy to forget to leave room for the close mics, which means you need to take extra time to dismantle and move the overheads.

- Microphones are fragile, so handle them accordingly. Put a microphone stand in place, attach the microphone, and then connect the cable as a last step. Secure the cable to the stand with a cable wrap or a piece of string.
- Never tap a microphone to check for signal. This can damage the diaphragm. Scratch it instead.
- If you want to move a stand slightly, be sure you do this by picking up the stand and placing it in a new location. Do not tug on the cable on the floor to nudge the stand toward you.
- When you are finished with a microphone, start by removing the cable from it. Then remove the microphone from the stand and place it safely in its case. Then put away the cable and the microphone stand.
- When working on a project that has many tracks, give them short names to avoid running out of DAW screen real estate ("EG" takes up less space than "killer lead guitar," for example). It can also simplify things to use a system of colors or capitalization, capitalizing auxiliary tracks and using lower case for audio tracks, or using different colors for different instrument groups.

Cable Wrapping

When cable is stored, there is a standard technique for wrapping it that keeps the cables in good shape and makes them easy to unwrap later. This is *not* done by holding your arm in an L shape and wrapping the cable around your elbow and the crook of your thumb. Proper technique involves changing directions for odd and even loops. It isn't difficult to do, but it is cumbersome to describe in words. The best way to learn this is from someone with experience who can show you in person, or to watch an online video. Enter "how to wrap an audio cable" into an Internet search engine and a number of videos will appear.

Once you have wrapped a cable once or twice, the cable will "remember" how it was wrapped, and you can rewrap it by working with its tendencies. If the cable is wrapped properly, it can be quickly cast out when it is used again; if it is not wrapped properly, casting it out will create "pretzels" along the cable.

Order of Operation

Monitor speakers and phantom power should be the last things turned on and the first things turned off. When beginning a session, leave these switched off while setting up the gear. The gear should be turned on first, then the speakers. When changing anything, turn down the speakers to avoid damaging them if something is suddenly unplugged or plugged in. When powering down, switch off the speakers first, then switch off the gear. The procedure is akin to getting dressed and undressed, with the gear being like the undergarments, and the speakers being like the outer garments. When getting dressed in the morning, the undergarments go on first, then the outer garments. When getting undressed in the evening, the outer garments come off first, followed by the undergarments.

Scoring for Video

The nuts and bolts of scoring music and sound effects to video are far simpler in the twenty-first century than they were in the twentieth, when the process was much more dependent on synchronizing multiple devices. The most common synchronization

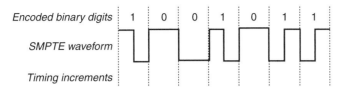

Figure 11-1 Biphase modulation of SMPTE Timecode signal

method was via **SMPTE Time Code** (SMPTE stands for Society of Motion Picture and Television Engineers). This form of time code represents an absolute time clock that gives a precise encoding to each film or video *frame*. Each frame is a single image on film or tape, and SMPTE encodes each in the format `01:02:03:04` (one hour, two minutes, three seconds, four frames). The most common frame rate was 30 frames per second, although different playback devices used variants on this rate (the most common of these will be listed later in this chapter).

A device called a *SMPTE signal generator* would be used to record (or "stripe") time code onto the highest-numbered track of a multitrack tape. The timecode was in the form of an audio signal that was a pulse width modulated square wave. In an encoding method known as **biphase modulation**, a half-cycle that was entirely in the up or down position through the span of a timing increment represented a binary digit of 0, while a transition in this same period—either from up to down or from down to up—represented a binary digit of 1 (see Figure 11-1; note the similarity with the NRZI encoding used on CDs, shown in Figure 6-13b). Each `hour:minute:second:frame` coordinate was encoded as an 80-bit timecode word: 20 groups of 4 bits identified the hour, minute, second, frame, along with extra bits for optional binary information and sync data, which identified the ends of frames. Because the values were encoded as shifts in the pulse, rather than in the polarity of the pulse, and because the sync data identified frame endings, information could be read whether the tape was moving forward or backward, in play, fast-forward, or rewind mode.

The SMPTE signal was not something anyone wanted to hear in the finished recording, so some care needed to be taken to record it at an optimum level. At too low a level, other machines might not be able to read it well. At too high a level, there was the possibility that the signal could "leak" onto the adjacent track on the tape; often, this adjacent track was left blank to ensure that the SMPTE signal did not blend with any of the recorded audio, which meant that the number of available audio tracks on the tape was reduced by two, one for the SMPTE track, another for the blank "guard" track.

In a MIDI studio, a SMPTE-to-MIDI converter would generate SMPTE time code to be recorded. Once this step was accomplished, the SMPTE audio track would be sent from the tape player to the converter, which would convert the absolute-timed SMPTE to **MIDI Time Code (MTC)**, which was a version of the SMPTE values that was represented in MIDI bytes, which could be transmitted over MIDI cables. The MTC would then drive the studio's sequencers and drum machines. Thus, the tape deck acted as the master device, and all other devices were set to slave mode, advancing to the time code read from the tape.

If the tape were cued to start at some point other than the very beginning, the converter would read the time and start the sequences and drum patterns at the appropriate place. For example, if it were necessary to record a synthesizer part that lasted two and a half minutes, from `1:05:00:00` to `1:07:30:00`, the slave could be set to observe a SMPTE offset of five minutes so that it wouldn't be necessary to record five minutes of silence in the DAW before the synthesizer part began.

If more audio tracks were needed than could be recorded onto a single tape, multiple tape decks could be locked together. The SMPTE signal could be copied to other tapes, and each deck could be connected to the synchronizer via an external control connector, which was available on professional-grade tape decks. The synchronizer would receive the time code signals from each deck, and adjust the motor speed of the slave deck so that it remained synchronized with the master deck. If the master was put into fast-forward or rewind mode, the synchronizer would put the slave deck into the same mode, and adjust the slave unit as necessary when playback resumed to ensure that both were in the same place.

SMPTE Time Code allowed albums to be produced in separate studios. Some bands who became very successful found it difficult to assemble all members in a studio at the same time due to various commitments. Although it was not considered an ideal method of collaboration, each member could be sent a time-coded version of the works in progress. They could record their parts on their own, and the various tapes could then be synced onto the final master. If there were any differences in time code between versions, an offset could be programmed into the synchronizer that accounted for differences between a master's and a slave's time codes, and make the necessary adjustments.

An SMPTE track could also be recorded onto an audio channel of a videotape. When music and sound effects were added, a video playback deck would act as the master device that controlled all sequencers and audiotape decks. If the sound effects editor were recording Foley (specific cues such as footsteps, doors closing, objects dropping, etc.), samples could be played by a slaved sequencer at a specific frame. Composers who wanted to have a specific beat of music match a specific screen event would need to perform some arithmetic and bookkeeping, converting the music tempo from beats-per-minute to beats-per-frame for each music sequence and each tempo change.

Film composers today are far less preoccupied with syncing devices. It is far more common to work with digitized video or film that is added to a DAW project and played synchronously with it. The most common film format is QuickTime, which automatically embeds material with SMPTE timings. When a movie is imported into a DAW project, both the DAW and the movie are frame-locked. Users can use playback controls in either the DAW or in the movie window and the effect is the same: the two play in tandem. Furthermore, the DAW clock can display timing either in SMPTE format, bar/beat format, or both, which eliminates the need for arithmetic conversions from tempo references to absolute time references. Any existing audio in the video file, such as dialog, may be imported into the DAW as an audio track so that it can be mixed along with the sound effects and music. The tempo and absolute times are autonomous, yet interlocked. The music tempo may be changed without affecting the absolute time display.

Although the memory and processing speed available on today's computers has made synchronizing multiple devices largely a thing of the past, there are still times when syncing multiple devices is necessary, such as when multiple computers are used to play animations when large game projects are being assembled, or when a film project is only available on a videotape. While most DAW programs run more smoothly when they are acting as the clock master, it is possible to change the clock source so that the DAW is slaved to another master device. Most DAWs can work at all standard frame rates. The most common are:

- 24 frames per second (fps) for film
- 25 fps for PAL-encoded video (Phase Alternation by Line, used in European countries)
- 30 fps for NTSC-encoded video (National Television System Committee, used in the United States and Asia)
- 29.97 fps drop frame (This rate was adopted when color television was introduced; black and white broadcasts were at 30 fps, with 60 Hz household AC used as a timing reference. To keep color broadcasts compatible with black and white television sets, a black and white frame was sent first, slowed down ever so slightly so that color information could be sent next, before the next frame. The difference amounts to 18 frames every ten minutes, or about 3.6 seconds per hour. In this format, video is played at 30 frames per second, but a single frame is surreptitiously dropped every so often to keep the average rate of 29.97 fps.)

The default timing correspondence is for measure 1, beat 1 to correspond to SMPTE time 1:00:00:00. It is common practice for video content to begin at this position of one hour to allow for smooth pre-rolling of content. When playing the video from the start, normally one starts playback a few seconds early, particularly when multiple devices are synced together, to allow everything a few seconds to begin synchronization and for the motors to settle into a stable speed. If the content were to begin at time zero, 00:00:00:00, the pre-roll would bring the tape position to a time prior to "midnight," perhaps at 23:59:45:00. The reset of all numbers to zero can cause syncing problems with some tape machines, hence the practice of using a start time at one hour. The DAW clock may be set with a SMPTE offset if necessary.

Important locations may be noted by *scene markers,* which give an absolute time reference to onscreen events and content changes, such as scene cuts. This ensures that they will always play at the same absolute time even if the tempo of the music is changed later. Events such as sound effects may be placed into the DAW's event list (such as the one shown in Figure 10-4), which can be set to display time in SMPTE format. The timestamps of each event may then be changed to match the onscreen action precisely. Saving events as scene markers also enables easy navigation throughout the film by advancing to positions in a scene markers' list, rather than using play, fast-forward, or rewind.

With the ability to import movies into DAW projects, scoring is greatly simplified. There is rarely any need to spend the time that was once necessary to sync machines. There is also less need for meticulously prepared cue sheets for music and sound effects, given how flexibly audio events can be created and edited within the DAW. If live musicians are recording the score under the direction of a conductor, it is easy to program the tempo and tempo changes into the DAW, and to have them reflected in a click track that the musicians and/or conductor may listen to over headphones. When the audio work is completed, the soundtrack may be mixed in the DAW and exported to the movie file as its soundtrack.

Networking Devices

It is becoming more and more common to create small computer networks to perform a variety of tasks. The process often involves some trial and error, and it's usually wise to dedicate at least one work session to ironing out connection issues and ensuring that everything is communicating as desired. This may involve spending some time checking the product reference manuals to ensure that sending and receiving addresses between devices are compatible. There are various components to networking addresses. Some of the most common ones are described next.

Network Address Components

ROUTER

A device that connects a network to the Internet is a *gateway*. Many Internet connections, however, are handled by a specialized type of gateway called a *router*, which does a bit more than a general gateway. While a gateway is passive in the way it sends and receives packets, routers analyze what is being sent or received and find the most efficient path from sender to receiver. A broadband router creates wired connections among computers and some types of telephone lines. A wireless router connects to a modem and generates a wireless signal, allowing any computer within its range to connect to the Internet.

IP (INTERNET PROTOCOL) ADDRESS

Every device on a network is identified by a unique *IP address*. These addresses are 32-bit values, which are typically written in "dot decimal" (or "dotted quad") notation. This consists of four subdivisions of 8 bits (octets) derived from the 32-bit number, which are written as decimal numbers. An example is shown in Table 11-1.

Some of the octets of an IP address identify the network (like the area-code portion of a telephone number), and the remaining octets identify specific devices (like the seven-digit telephone number). Two addresses are reserved for special use, which means that the number of available devices is determined by the number of identifying bits minus two. Three classes of IP address use three different octet allocations, based on how many octets identify the network, how many octets identify individual devices, and how the first four bits of the first octet are allocated:

- Class A addresses, meant for very large networks, use the first octet to identify the network and the remaining three octets to identify each device; 24 identifying bits mean that the number of available devices is 2^{24}–2, or 16,777,214. If the first bit is a zero, the address is identified as Class A, which means these networks fall into the address range 1–126.x.y.z.
- Class B addresses allocate the first two octets for the network ID and the third and fourth octets for the device IDs, which means that the number of available devices is 2^{16}–2, or 65,534. If the first bit is one and the second bit is zero, the address is identified as Class B, which means these networks fall into the address range 128–191.x.y.z.

TABLE 11-1 IP address structuring

a 32-bit binary identification number

01100100100101101100100011111010

is divided into four 8-bit octets

01100100.10010110.11001000.11111010

commonly written with each octet as a
decimal number in the range of 0–255

100.150.200.250

- Class C addresses allocate the first three octets for the network ID, and one octet to identify each device, which means the number of available devices is 2^8-2, or 254. If the first two bits are both one and the third bit is zero, the address is identified as Class C, which means that these addresses fall into the range `192–223.x.y.z`.

Because most networks need more addresses than are allowed in a Class C bit allocation, but far fewer addresses than are allowed in a Class B bit allocation, a technique called *subnetting* allows network administrators to allocate the 32 bits of IP addresses more flexibly to suit the needs of a particular network. This technique is the subject of the next section.

SUBNET MASK

The *subnet mask* is a 32-bit binary number that defines how many IP addresses may be allocated within its network. Besides allowing greater flexibility in IP address allocation, it also allows a network to be subdivided into *broadcast domains*. Broadcast domains allow traffic to be filtered to the appropriate devices, making transmission more efficient.

The leftmost values of the subnet mask are 1; these identify the network. Rightmost values are 0, and identify individual devices on the network. Thus, each octet that is part of the network identification consists of eight binary digits of 1, or a decimal value of 255. (A string of eight ones, a value of 255, is not a valid first octet value for any IP address, since, as described above, the definitions of Class A, B, and C networks all have at least one zero among the first four bits. This makes the subnet mask distinct from IP addresses.)

For example, the following subnet mask

```
11111111  11111111  11111111  10000000
   255        255        255       128
```

indicates that the first 25 bits are used to identify the network, and the remaining 7 bits identify devices on that network.

PORTS

Hardware ports are plugs for physical devices on a computer. The most common type is probably the USB port. (Hardware ports are sometimes called *jacks* to distinguish them from virtual ports, which identify types of requests that servers may provide.) The *virtual port* is a 16-bit number that is appended to server messages to identify the type of process being requested. Some common port numbers are shown in Table 11-2.

Examples of Network Connections

The basics of OSC transmission were covered in Chapter 9. This section will outline some of the steps involved in setting up a few specific software connections. Hopefully these examples will help to illustrate what kinds of measures need to be taken in other specific contexts.

MIXER CONSOLE APP

The Behringer X32 Digital Mixing Console has an associated app, X32 Mix, which allows the board's mix levels and routings to be controlled from an iPad. This enables the board operator to make adjustments to the mix from a position away from the board. For example, sound files may be played while the operator walks through the auditorium, hearing the mix from the audience's perspective, and making adjustments

TABLE 11-2 Commonly used network port numbers

PORT	REQUEST TYPE
20	FTP—Data
21	FTP—Control
22	SSH Remote Login Protocol
23	Telnet
25	Simple Mail Transfer Protocol (SMTP)
53	Domain Name System (DNS)
79	Finger
80	HTTP
110	POP3
115	Simple File Transfer Protocol (SFTP)
143	Interim Mail Access Protocol (IMAP)
156	SQL Server
443	HTTPS
445	Microsoft-DS
458	Apple QuickTime

accordingly without having to run back and forth between the console to make adjustments and the auditorium to hear the results.

The app works by sending OSC messages between the iPad and the mixer. The nature of these messages is largely invisible to the user, who simply sees a graphic animation of the mixing board on the tablet screen. Moving a fader on the tablet screen causes the corresponding fader to move on the mixing console. The console needs to have an IP address identified with it (normally 192.168.0.x) as well as a subnet mask (normally 255.255.255.0). When the tablet app is first launched, a prompt appears that asks to have the IP address of the tablet and the console entered, as well as their respective subnet masks. Once the two are connected, they work seamlessly for the most part, making it easy to forget that these connection steps were ever necessary.

MAX/MSP AND SUPERCOLLIDER
Both of the Max/MSP and SuperCollider music programming environments were described in Chapter 10. In Max/MSP, the programming is visually based: users select *objects* (akin to MUSIC N unit generators, also described in Chapter 10) and create communication among objects by connecting patch cords between *outlets* of some objects and *inlets* of others. SuperCollider is a programming language: users type descriptions of *Ugens* (unit generators) or *SynthDefs* (synthesizer definitions) as functions. These functions can take arguments that describe aspects of a particular unit generator or synthesizer. SuperCollider runs as two components: a *server* holds predefined SynthDefs, and generates audio when it receives commands from the *language*. Users

interact primarily with the language, creating SynthDefs and instantiating them to create audio. OSC messages may be sent that communicate either with the language or with the server directly.

While it is possible to create *graphical user interfaces* (*GUIs*) in SuperCollider, there are times when it may be easier to use Max/MSP to create a GUI that sends information to SuperCollider via OSC messages. Two basic examples of how to do this are shown in Figure 11-2.

Figure 11-2a demonstrates Max/MSP sending messages to the SuperCollider server. In SuperCollider, a Synthdef called "testOSC" is loaded to the server. When it is instantiated, it outputs to either the left channel (0) or the right channel (1) at random, generating a sine wave at a random frequency between 500 and 1200 Hz, with a short, smooth envelope that lasts 0.35 seconds.

(a) SuperCollider

```
(
SynthDef("testOSC", {
    Out.ar(
        IRand(0, 1),
        SinOsc.ar(Rand(500, 1200), 0, EnvGen.kr(Env.sine(0.15, 0.2), doneAction: 2))
    )
}).load(s);
)
```

Max/MSP

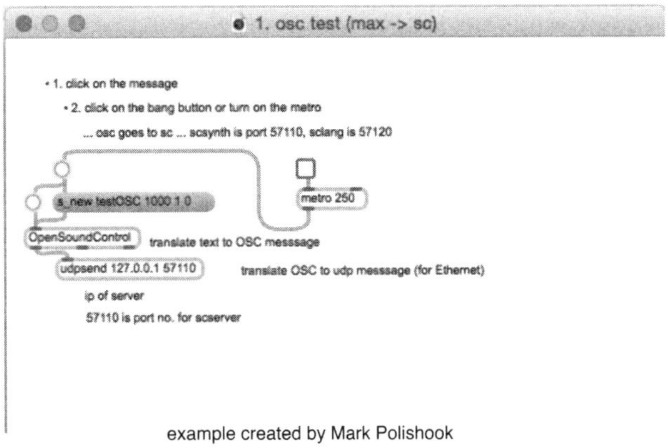

example created by Mark Polishook

(b) SuperCollider

```
n=NetAddr.new("127.0.0.1", 1500);
a = {1.0.rand}!3;
n.sendBundle(0, ['/dingbat'] ++ a);
n.sendMsg('/hi',37);
```

Max/MSP

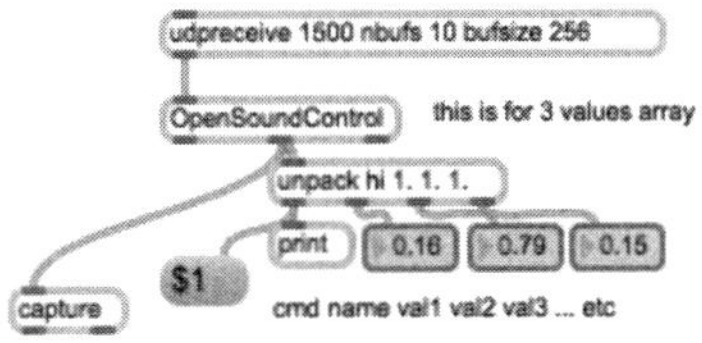

Figure 11-2 OSC Communication between SuperCollider and Max/MSP
Screenshot reprinted with permission from Cycling74.com

In Max/MSP, switching a **checkbox** to the ON state sends impulses once every 250 milliseconds. The impulse first causes a text message to be sent to an **OpenSoundControl** object, then causes the **OpenSoundControl** object to output the text message in OSC format to a **udpsend** object, which sends the OSC message to a specified IP address and port number. The IP address 127.0.0.0 (sometimes referred to as *localhost*, as described in Chapter 9) refers to the same machine that is sending the message, meaning that the message is transmitted internally from one software program to another that is running on the same machine. The default value of the SuperCollider server port is 57110. Thus, activating the **metro** object with the **checkbox** causes SuperCollider to produce a short beeping sound, at a random frequency and stereo channel, every quarter of a second.

Figure 11-2b demonstrates sending values from SuperCollider to Max/MSP. In SuperCollider, each line is executed individually. The first line assigns to a variable called "n" an instance of a Netaddr Ugen, which defines a network address by its IP address (here, this is again the localhost) and port number (1500 in this example). The second line assigns to a variable called "a" an array of three random numbers between zero and 1.0. The third line bundles the text string "dingbat" and the array of numbers stored in variable "a" and sends this bundle at a timestamp of zero (i.e., immediately) to the address defined in variable "n."

In Max/MSP, a **udpreceive** object is set to receive messages over the same port number (1500). This raw data is sent to an **OpenSoundControl** object to be unpacked into its four components. The text string **"dingbat"** is printed in a message box (marked with **$1** to indicate a changeable argument), and is printed in Max/MSP's **Max** window, which posts information for purposes of notification and debugging. The three values in the array "a" appear in three number boxes. A **capture** object stores everything output by the **OpenSoundControl** object so that the material can be used later, if desired.

In SuperCollider, executing the fourth line sends a message with no timestamp. The text string "hi" appears in the message box and the Max window, and the single integer value 37 appears in the leftmost number box, while the rightmost two number boxes remain as they were.

If Max/MSP and SuperCollider are running on two separate computers, they may be connected into a mini-network via an Ethernet cable. Each computer needs to have a unique IP address, such as 10.x.y.z, which is an unused Class A subnet, meant for private networks like this example. Once each computer has been set to its respective IP address, then the IP address in SuperCollider's NetAddr Ugen needs to match the IP address of the computer running Max/MSP, and the **udpsend** object in Max/MSP needs to be set to send to the IP address of the computer running SuperCollider.

The Golden Gate Bridge performance described in Chapter 9 was a bit more complicated than these two examples, but here is a description in a nutshell. The data from the model bridge's accelerometers was sent as MIDI Control Change messages to a computer running both Max/MSP and SuperCollider. In Max/MSP, copies of the Control Change values were sent into a number of converters that performed the conversion shown in Equation 9-1, remapping the values to various ranges that were applicable to two SynthDefs that were running in SuperCollider. Two **OpenSoundControl** objects sent messages to the localhost, which directed them to the SuperCollider language port (57120). Changes in the position of the bridge model generated a series of name-value pairs that were sent as OSC messages to the SuperCollider language. In the SuperCollider language, the OSCdef unit generator defines incoming message names. If the incoming message has a name that matches that defined in an OSCdef, then a function is executed. For this performance, the OSCdefs were programmed to start, stop, or update the two Synths as messages came in. In this way, the motion of the bridge model was sent to SuperCollider, which played a low droning sound that was modulated in various ways according to changes in the model's position. Technically speaking, it was not necessary to use Max/MSP for this; MIDI could have been sent directly to SuperCollider, its values converted, and sent to the SynthDefs. However, given the complexity of the synthesis patch, it seemed prudent to divide the synthesis from the graphics and conversions, so we used both programs.

LEMUR AND SUPERCOLLIDER

As described in Chapter 9, the Lemur app allows a custom playing interface to be created on a portable tablet device such as an iPhone or iPad. The interface can consist of knobs, buttons, sliders, switches, and a number of other elements. In many ways, Lemur's history encapsulates trends in technology. Originally introduced in 2005, Lemur was a hardware touchscreen that could be connected to a computer via an Ethernet cable. Its versatility was unprecedented, and it was enthusiastically received by those who could afford its $2,500 list price. When smartphones and tablets came into being, a Lemur app was soon created that sold for $60. It duplicated the functionality of the touchscreen and sent OSC and MIDI commands wirelessly. The hardware Lemur was discontinued by 2011, but the app enjoys a strong user base.

To establish wireless communication between the portable device and a target computer, Bluetooth must be turned off on both. (Bluetooth is a wireless technology that allows computers to communicate with peripherals without cables. While it is useful for everyday devices such as mice or printers, it can cause interference in this context.) A *wireless ad hoc network* (*WANET*; or *IBSS*, for *Independent Basic Service Set*) needs to be created on the computer. These are dynamic, self-configuring networks that can be created and joined on the fly, without any kind of router or administrative setup. Setting up the WANET gives the computer a self-generated IP address, which should be noted (Figure 11-3). After taking these initial steps, the tablet's Wi-Fi settings should show the name of the wireless network created on the computer, which should be selected.

Interfaces are created on the computer in an associated software program called Lemur Editor, shown in Figure 11-4. These interfaces then may be transferred to the tablet, which runs the Lemur app. On the tablet, the **Settings** window of the Lemur app reflects a self-generated IP address for the tablet (Figure 11-5), which is labelled **Lemur IP**, consisting of the IP address followed by the app's port number, which defaults to 8000, in the form xxx.xxx.xxx.xxx:8000. Another field, labelled **Host**, needs to have the IP

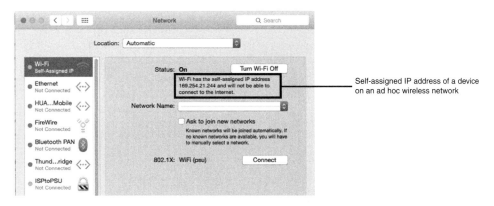

Figure 11-3 A device on an ad hoc wireless network creates an IP address for itself
Screenshot reprinted with permission from Apple Inc

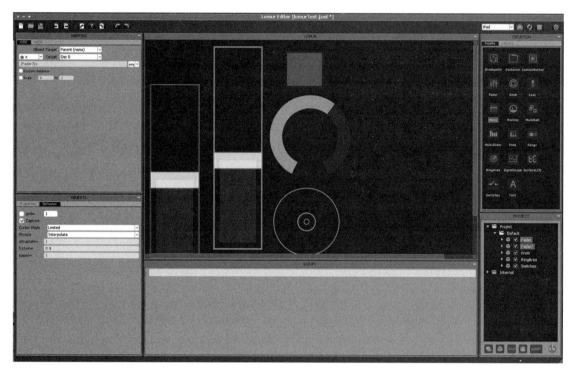

Figure 11-4 Lemur Editor software, where custom interfaces are created and sent to a tablet device
Screenshot reprinted with permission from liine.net

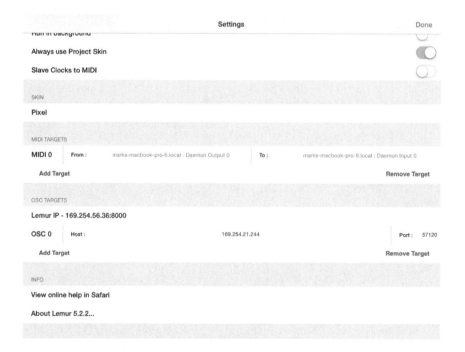

Figure 11-5 Settings window of the Lemur app
Screenshot reprinted with permission from liine.net

address of the computer entered, along with a port number (57120 for the SuperCollider language port).

In the computer's Lemur Editor application, the **Settings** menu has three tabs. The **Editor** tab may be ignored at this stage. The **Lemur** tab (Figure 11-6) shows the IP address of the computer in the **Local IP** field, and the IP address of the tablet (without the port number) in the **Lemur** field. The **OSC** tab (Figure 11-7) shows the IP address of the tablet in one of the available **IP address** fields, with the port number 57120 in the **Port** field.

When objects are created, they may be assigned names that will be transmitted as part of the name-value pair when the object is manipulated. These assignments are done in the **MAPPING** window on the left portion of the Interface Editor. In Figure 11-4, the highlighted fader's position is shown to transmit with the name **/Fader2/x**, which will be followed by a number reflecting the slider's position. The default is a value between 0 and 1, but this may be scaled in the Lemur Editor to transmit values within any desired range.

In SuperCollider, a NetAddr unit generator may be defined that contains the IP address of the tablet and the port number 8000 (Figure 11-8). Then a series of OSCdef unit generators may be created that contain a key name ("fadertest," "test," and "buttontest" in the figure) that identifies each OSCdef in Super-Collider's memory, a function to be carried out when this OSCdef is activated (in the figure, the simple example function prints each value received), the name of an object in the Lemur interface (**/Fader/x**, **/Fader2/x**, **/Switches/x**), and the source address that was defined in the NetAddr object, the variable *n*. When these objects are manipulated in Lemur, SuperCollider prints the values received, as shown in Figure 11-9.

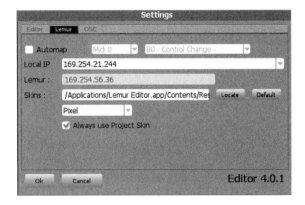

Figure 11-6 Lemur Editor Settings window, Lemur tab
Screenshot reprinted with permission from liine.net

Figure 11-7 Lemur Editor Settings window, OSC tab
Screenshot reprinted with permission from liine.net

A more musical implementation can be seen in Figure 11-10. In SuperCollider, a SynthDef is defined that plays a sine tone. It has four *changeable arguments*, which are properties of the Synth that may be changed while it is sounding: an off switch (gate), frequency, pan position, and volume. In the Lemur Editor, an interface is created that consists of:

- an On/Off switch, which sends a value of 1 if it is activated, and 0 if it is deactivated;
- a slider that sends values with the label **Frequency**, and is scaled to operate in the range of 110 to 880;

```
n=NetAddr("169.254.56.36", 8000);
OSCdef.new(\fadertest, { arg msg, time, addr, recvPort; msg[1].postln; }, '/Fader/x', n);
OSCdef.new(\test, { arg msg, time, addr, recvPort; msg[1].postln; }, '/Fader2/x', n);
OSCdef.new(\buttontest, { arg msg, time, addr, recvPort; msg[1].postln; }, '/Switches/x', n);
```

Figure 11-8 OSCdefs in SuperCollider

```
[ [ /Switches/x, 1 ] ]
[ [ /Switches/x, 0 ] ]
[ [ /Fader/x, 0.65901637077332 ] ]
[ [ /Fader/x, 0.65987700223923 ] ]
[ [ /Fader/x, 0.66047948598862 ] ]
[ [ /Fader/x, 0.6609011888504 ] ]
[ [ /Fader/x, 0.66119641065598 ] ]
[ [ /Fader/x, 0.66140305995941 ] ]
[ [ /Fader/x, 0.66154772043228 ] ]
[ [ /Fader/x, 0.66164898872375 ] ]
[ [ /Fader/x, 0.66171985864639 ] ]
[ [ /Fader/x, 0.66176944971085 ] ]
[ [ /Fader/x, 0.66180419921875 ] ]
[ [ /Fader/x, 0.66182851791382 ] ]
[ [ /Fader/x, 0.66184550523758 ] ]
[ [ /Fader/x, 0.66185742616653 ] ]
[ [ /Fader/x, 0.6618657708168 ] ]
[ [ /Fader/x, 0.66187161207199 ] ]
[ [ /Fader/x, 0.66187566518784 ] ]
[ [ /Fader/x, 0.66187852621078 ] ]
[ [ /Fader/x, 0.66188055276871 ] ]
[ [ /Fader/x, 0.66188192367554 ] ]
[ [ /Fader/x, 0.661885201931 ] ]
[ [ /Fader2/x, 0.40420001745224 ] ]
[ [ /Fader2/x, 0.40294000506401 ] ]
[ [ /Fader2/x, 0.40205800533295 ] ]
[ [ /Fader2/x, 0.40144062042236 ] ]
[ [ /Fader2/x, 0.4010084271431 ] ]
[ [ /Fader2/x, 0.39770591259003 ] ]
[ [ /Fader2/x, 0.39479413628578 ] ]
[ [ /Fader2/x, 0.39215588569641 ] ]
```

Figure 11-9 When the code in Figure 11-8 is run and the Lemur interface elements are manipulated, the values received are printed

- a knob that sends values labeled **Pan2**, which is scaled to send values between –1 (extreme left) and 1 (extreme right);
- a slider that sends values with the label **volume**, which is scaled to operate in the range of 0 to 1.

In SuperCollider, a SynthDef may be instantiated by the command

```
Synth("name")
```

By assigning the Synth to a variable, such as x, the Synth's properties may be changed by using the set message, followed by the name of one of the changeable arguments and a value, as in:

```
x.set('freq', 440)
```

In the example, there are four OSCdefs that receive messages from the four items in the Lemur interface. The first instantiates the Synth if a value of 1 is received from the button, and deactivates it if a value of 0 is received by setting the Synth's gate value to zero. The second, third, and fourth OSCdefs update the frequency, pan, and volume respectively with values received from the interface elements that are addressed to them.

MIDI OVER LAN

The theoretical maximum cable length over which MIDI can be sent is 30 feet, although in reality cables often should be shorter to transmit reliably. Longer cable runs may be created by replacing a MIDI connector with an XLR connector. Although the MIDI DIN connector has five pins, only three of them are used. These may be connected to the three pins of an XLR cable and the signal can travel much farther, more reliably.

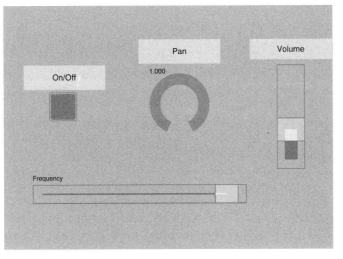

```
(
SynthDef("sinetest", { arg gate=1, freq=220, pan=0, vol=0.3;
      o=SinOsc.ar(freq, 0, vol);
      p=Pan2.ar(o, pan);
      e=Env.asr(0.1, 1, 1);
      Out.ar(0, EnvGen.ar(e, gate: gate, doneAction: 2)*p)
}).add;
)

n=NetAddr("169.254.164.90", 8000);

(
~synthactivate= OSCdef.new(\onoff,
      { arg msg, time, addr, recvPort; [msg, time, addr, recvPort].postln; v=msg[1].asInteger;
      if ( (v ==1), { x=Synth("sinetest"); }, { x.set(\gate, v) });
      }, '/Switches/x', n);

~synthfreq = OSCdef.new(\freqfader, { arg msg, time, addr, recvPort; [msg, time, addr, recvPort].postln; v=msg[1]; x.set(\freq, v); }, '/Frequency/x', n);

~synthpan = OSCdef.new(\panner, { arg msg, time, addr, recvPort; [msg, time, addr, recvPort].postln; v=msg[1].asFloat; x.set(\pan, v); }, '/Pan2/x', n);

~synthvol = OSCdef.new(\volset, { arg msg, time, addr, recvPort; [msg, time, addr, recvPort].postln; v=msg[1].asFloat; x.set(\vol, v); }, '/Volume/x', n);
)
```

Figure 11-10 Lemur interface that controls a SuperCollider Synth with changeable arguments
Screenshot reprinted with permission from liine.net

However, many are turning to the possibilities of *local area networks* (*LANs*) to get around MIDI's limitations. Programs such as ipMIDI (http://www.nerds.de) packetize MIDI information and send it over UDP connections. The connections may be wired or wireless, although wireless connections have higher latency. For wired connections, an unmanaged *Ethernet switch* may be used, which contains a number of Cat5 Ethernet cable jacks. The switch acts as a hub, creating a closed network with no connection to the Internet. A series of computers may be connected to its jacks, each set to a specific IP address, typically in the 10.x.x.x domain, described above. This connection makes every computer accessible by every computer.

If each computer on this LAN has the ipMIDI driver installed, ipMIDI appears to the computer just like a synthesizer or any other MIDI instrument. It is selectable within any MIDI program, such as a DAW, or within a MIDI configuration utility, such as the one shown in Figure 9-7. This allows MIDI messages to be sent to this "instrument" and out to the network.

Besides eliminating the length limitation of MIDI cables, MIDI over a LAN is also faster. As discussed in Chapter 9, transmission via a MIDI interface is 31.25 kilobaud, a rate that can become insufficient when multiple lines of Continuous Control Change messages are being generated. But the 7-bit message structure of MIDI is trivial for network transmission, which is on the order of a gigabit per second.

AUDIO OVER LAN

Network technology is also poised to create a paradigm shift in audio transmission. Just as MIDI data can be packetized and sent over network cables, the same can be done with audio signals. At this writing, this is an emerging area, with "prosumer"-level devices just becoming available. The devices use different protocols, and it is unclear which will eventually become the standard.

In traditional concert setups, microphones are plugged into a *microphone splitter*, which sends the audio signals to multiple locations: a recording desk, a front-of-house console where the PA mix is created, and a monitoring desk, where the audio is sent back to the onstage musicians. Splitters are large, expensive, and they color the sound.

As an alternative, microphones may be plugged into a *stage box*, which digitizes and packetizes the audio and then sends it to an Ethernet switch. This allows anyone connected to the switch's network to access a copy of the audio signal via one of its jacks. These are redundant copies of the microphone signals, which open up a number of possibilities. Besides the various stations receiving identical, uncolored copies of the audio, multiple computers may be recording, which means that there is a backup in case one of them should fail.

In a recording studio, sending audio over a network simplifies a number of things. Cat5 cable can transmit 256 monophonic audio channels (at least in theory—the limit is being tested as new hardware is introduced). This means that a series of audio cables may be replaced by a single, smaller Cat5 cable, with much less risk of interference, ground loops, and other noise that can creep into audio cables. Buildings with computer networks installed in them can share audio between rooms via the networking infrastructure, rather than having to connect audio cables.

Key Terms

....

biphase modulation	power conditioner
Ethernet switch	power regulator
film/video frame	router
gateway	scene markers
graphical user interface (GUI)	SMPTE Time Code
in-ear monitor (IEM)	stage box
Independent Basic Service Set (IBSS)	subnet mask
IP (Internet Protocol) address	subnetting
local area network (LAN)	virtual port
microphone splitter	wireless ad hoc network (WANET)
MIDI Time Code (MTC)	

Appendix 1

Geometric View of a Sine Wave

Phasors, Radians, and the Unit Circle

A sine wave can be described completely by three properties:

1. *Frequency* or how often the cycle repeats itself
2. *Amplitude* or how far from equilibrium the wave moves at its extreme points
3. *Initial phase* or the starting position in the cycle

If we know these three things about a sine wave, we can determine its position at any time: past, present, or future.

Remarkably, these three properties, which are fundamental to so many types of motion found in nature, can be illustrated as a function of a rotating radius within a circle, as shown in Figure A1-1. Each position of the radius may be described in terms of the *radius length*, or *magnitude*, and the angle of the radius. To keep things simple, the radius is given a length of 1, and thus this type of illustration is called a *unit circle*.

While in everyday life angles are commonly measured in degrees, the division of a circle into 360 degrees is an arbitrary subdivision (based on the ancient Babylonians' estimation of the number of days in a year). When continuous functions are being studied, it is more common to express angles in *radians*, a measurement unit that is more intrinsic to a circle's structure. A radian is the angle that produces an arc along the circumference that has the same length as the circle's radius. If just over three radians are traversed, half the circle is covered (Figure A1-2). The precise number of radians in half

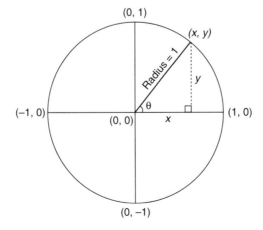

Figure A1-1 Unit circle

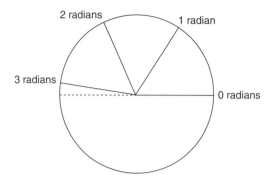

Figure A1-2 Half a circle spans an angle of just over three radians

of a circle is a non-repeating, infinite irrational number, 3.14159 . . ., commonly abbreviated with the Greek letter π (pi).

The 3:00 position is commonly considered the starting point, 0 radians. A half circle is traversed when the radius is rotated π radians, and a complete circle is traversed when the radius is rotated 2π radians. To convert from degrees to radians, we multiply the degree measurement by $\pi/180$. To convert from radians to degrees, we multiply the radian measurement by $180/\pi$.

The unit circle is plotted on a Cartesian plane, with its center at the origin, (0, 0). If the length of the radius is one unit, then 0 radians appears at point (1, 0), $\pi/2$ radians at point (0, 1), π radians at point (–1, 0), and $3\pi/2$ radians at point (0, –1).

Any angle can be described by a pair of points (x, y) lying along the circumference (Figure A1-1). When a vertical line is dropped from (x, y) to the radius along the zero radian line, a right triangle is constructed. The triangle serves to show a number of trigonometric relationships:

- *Sine* (opposite over hypotenuse): Because the rotated radius, the *hypotenuse*, has a length of 1, the sine value of angle θ is the ratio of the opposite side's length over the length of the hypotenuse, $y/1$, or, more simply, y.
- *Cosine* (adjacent over hypotenuse): The cosine value of angle θ is the adjacent length over the hypotenuse, $x/1$, or, more simply, x.
- *Tangent* (opposite over adjacent): The tangent of angle θ is the ratio between the two sides, y/x. Angle θ is also called the arctangent of the ratio y/x.

Because the hypotenuse has a length of 1, this demonstrates a connection between the Pythagorean theorem and a common trigonometric identity:

PYTHAGOREAN THEOREM: **TRIGONOMETRIC IDENTITY:**

$$x^2 + y^2 = 1 \qquad\qquad \cos^2\theta + \sin^2\theta = 1 \qquad\qquad (A1\text{-}1)$$

When the hypotenuse has a length other than 1, its length at any angle is $\sqrt{x^2+y^2}$

If the radius, or *phasor*, is made to rotate counterclockwise, and the height of its edge is measured and plotted at regular intervals (which correspond to regular angular rotations of the phasor), the result is a sine wave, as shown in Figure A1-3. Thus, a sine wave is called a *projection* from the vertical axis (called the *imaginary axis* in signal processing). If a projection is taken from the horizontal axis (called the *real axis* in signal processing), the result is a cosine wave, as shown in Figure A1-4. With this graphic

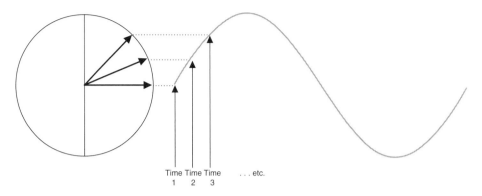

Figure A1-3 A sine wave plot produced by projections from a phasor

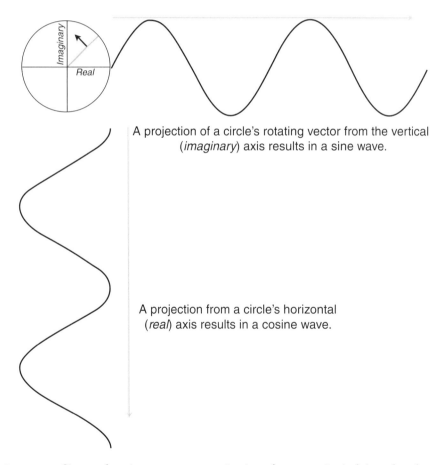

A projection of a circle's rotating vector from the vertical (*imaginary*) axis results in a sine wave.

A projection from a circle's horizontal (*real*) axis results in a cosine wave.

Figure A1-4 Sine and cosine waves are projections from a unit circle's real and imaginary axes

interpretation, it can be seen that the only difference between a sine wave and a cosine wave is the initial phase value, the starting angle of the phasor from which the projection is taken. Thus, we often refer to waves of this shape as sinusoidal waves. The frequency corresponds to the speed at which the phasor is rotated, and the amplitude corresponds to the length of the phasor. A number of important digital signal processing operations that are shown in this book rely on converting signals to this visual interpretation, whereby the signal can be described by a function of a particular magnitude and incrementing phasor angle (also called the *radian frequency*).

Sinusoidal Equation

The radian frequency of a phasor is often notated ω, which is defined as:

$$\omega = 2\pi f$$

This can be interpreted as:

2π is one cycle

f is the number of cycles per second

Thus, the height of a sine wave, y, with a maximum amplitude of A, at any time t can be described as:

$$y = A\sin(\omega t + \phi) \qquad\qquad \text{(A1-2)}$$

We can understand this to mean that the height of the phasor is determined by the sine of the angle shown by a phasor that has been spinning at rotation frequency for some amount of time. If it began rotating from a position other than zero, then the phase offset, φ, needs to be taken into account. This equation incorporates the three pieces of information about a sinusoidal wave that tell us everything about it: amplitude, frequency, and initial phase.

Key Terms

amplitude

cosine

frequency

hypotenuse

imaginary axis

initial phase

magnitude

phasor

projection

radian

radian frequency

radius length

real axis

sine

tangent

unit circle

Appendix 2

Plotting Sine Charts in a Spreadsheet

While specific features of spreadsheet programs vary, they all have features in common. Using basic formulas and plotting functions, it can be instructive to learn to generate graphs of sinusoidal functions. The steps are outlined here.

Creating a Basic Sine Wave Plot

Step One: Create a Series of 360 Values (from 0 to 359)

A spreadsheet is a grid of cells. Columns are labelled by letters, and rows by numbers. Cell A1 is the top left cell.

> Go to cell A1 and enter the value "0" and hit ENTER.
> This brings the cursor to cell A2. Go to the formula bar and enter the character

=

and click in cell A1. The cell number appears. Now enter

+1

The complete formula should appear as

=A1+1

A value of "1" should appear in the cell. With cell A2 selected, navigate to cell A360 and SHIFT-CLICK to select all cells from A2 to A360. Use the **Fill → Down** function to paste the formula from cell A2 into all cells. (In addition to doing this via a menu option, some spreadsheets allow it to be done by clicking on a marker that appears in the lower-right corner of the cell and dragging downwards.) Pasting the formula in this way causes each cell to "look" up to the cell above it and add 1 to whatever it finds there. A series of values from 0 to 359 now appears in column A.

Note: This is a *relative* formula, because no specific cells are entered, just a command to refer to the cell immediately above it and to do something (in this case, simply add 1) with whatever value may appear there.

This sequence of 360 values represents 360°, one complete period of a sine wave (Figure A2-1).

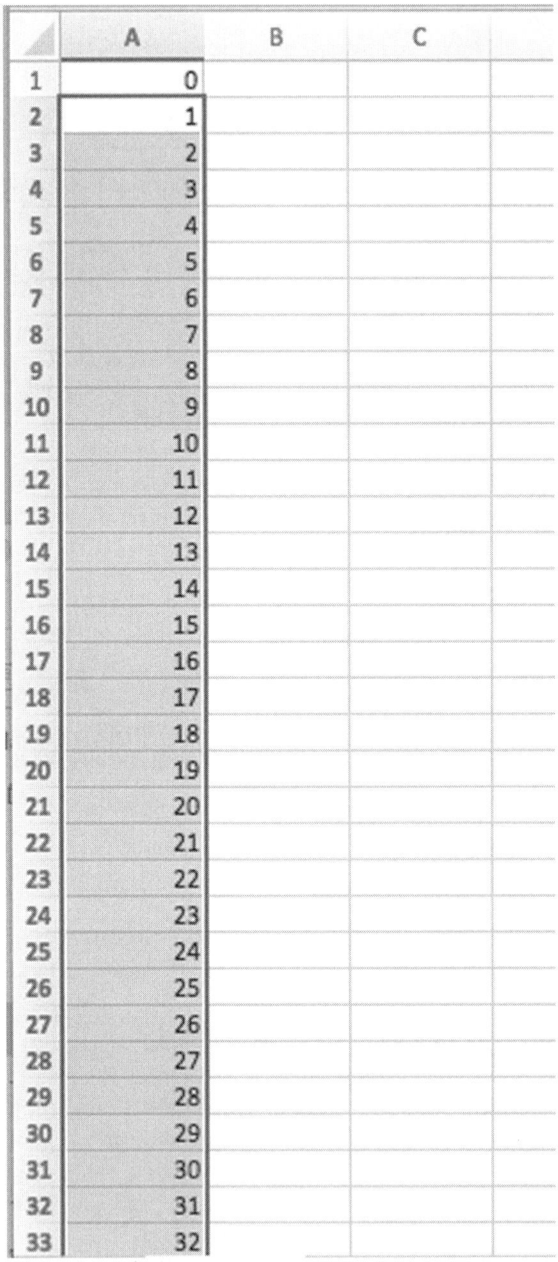

	A	B	C
1	0		
2	1		
3	2		
4	3		
5	4		
6	5		
7	6		
8	7		
9	8		
10	9		
11	10		
12	11		
13	12		
14	13		
15	14		
16	15		
17	16		
18	17		
19	18		
20	19		
21	20		
22	21		
23	22		
24	23		
25	24		
26	25		
27	26		
28	27		
29	28		
30	29		
31	30		
32	31		
33	32		

Figure A2-1

Step Two: Convert the Degrees to Radians

The next step is to convert the degree values in column A to radian values in column B. Move the cursor to cell B1. In either the cell itself or the formula bar, type

```
=
```

then click in cell A1, which appears in the formula bar. Then enter

```
*PI()/180
```

The entire formula should appear as

```
=A1*PI()/180
```

Note that this is another relative formula. It instructs the program to "look" one cell to the immediate left and to multiply whatever value is there by $\pi/180$. Use the **Fill → Down** function again to copy this formula down through cells B360 (Figure A2-2).

B1		X	✓	$f\!x$	=A1*PI()/180	

	A	B	C	D
1	0	0		
2	1	0.01745329		
3	2	0.03490659		
4	3	0.05235988		
5	4	0.06981317		
6	5	0.08726646		
7	6	0.10471976		
8	7	0.12217305		
9	8	0.13962634		
10	9	0.15707963		
11	10	0.17453293		
12	11	0.19198622		
13	12	0.20943951		
14	13	0.2268928		
15	14	0.2443461		
16	15	0.26179939		
17	16	0.27925268		
18	17	0.29670597		
19	18	0.31415927		
20	19	0.33161256		
21	20	0.34906585		
22	21	0.36651914		
23	22	0.38397244		
24	23	0.40142573		
25	24	0.41887902		
26	25	0.43633231		
27	26	0.45378561		
28	27	0.4712389		
29	28	0.48869219		
30	29	0.50614548		
31	30	0.52359878		
32	31	0.54105207		
33	32	0.55850536		

Figure A2-2

Step Three: Create a Sine Wave

Position the cursor in cell C1. In either the cell or the formula bar, enter

```
=sin(
```

Then click in cell B1 so that this cell appears in the formula bar, then enter

)

The complete formula should appear as

=SIN(B1)

After entering this formula in cell C1, return the cursor to cell C1. Once again, use the **Fill → Down** function to paste this formula into all cells from C1 to C360.

This is another relative formula that translates as, "Look immediately to your left, take the sine of whatever value you find there (Figure A2-3)".

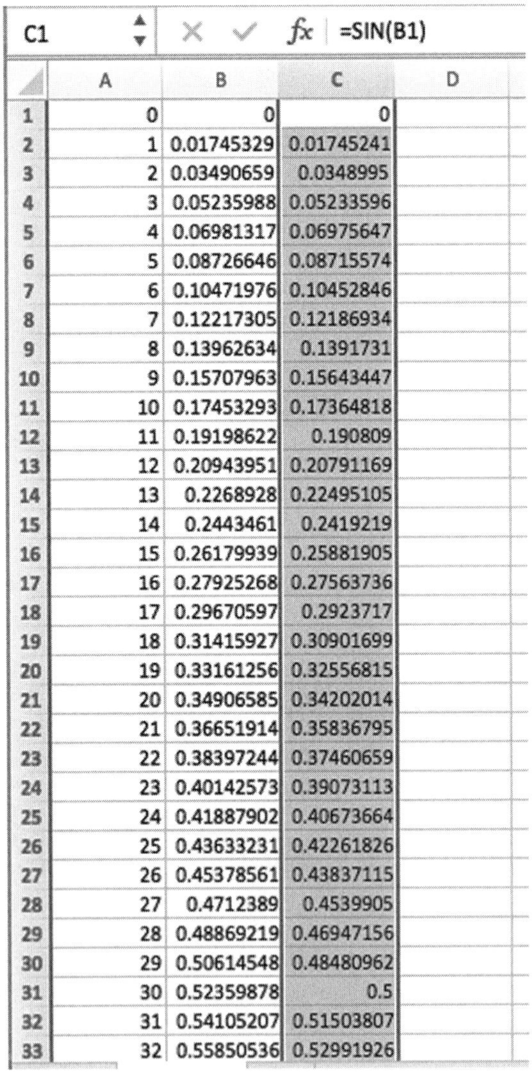

C1			fx	=SIN(B1)	
	A	B	C	D	
1	0	0	0		
2	1	0.01745329	0.01745241		
3	2	0.03490659	0.0348995		
4	3	0.05235988	0.05233596		
5	4	0.06981317	0.06975647		
6	5	0.08726646	0.08715574		
7	6	0.10471976	0.10452846		
8	7	0.12217305	0.12186934		
9	8	0.13962634	0.1391731		
10	9	0.15707963	0.15643447		
11	10	0.17453293	0.17364818		
12	11	0.19198622	0.190809		
13	12	0.20943951	0.20791169		
14	13	0.2268928	0.22495105		
15	14	0.2443461	0.2419219		
16	15	0.26179939	0.25881905		
17	16	0.27925268	0.27563736		
18	17	0.29670597	0.2923717		
19	18	0.31415927	0.30901699		
20	19	0.33161256	0.32556815		
21	20	0.34906585	0.34202014		
22	21	0.36651914	0.35836795		
23	22	0.38397244	0.37460659		
24	23	0.40142573	0.39073113		
25	24	0.41887902	0.40673664		
26	25	0.43633231	0.42261826		
27	26	0.45378561	0.43837115		
28	27	0.4712389	0.4539905		
29	28	0.48869219	0.46947156		
30	29	0.50614548	0.48480962		
31	30	0.52359878	0.5		
32	31	0.54105207	0.51503807		
33	32	0.55850536	0.52991926		

Figure A2-3

Step Four: Plot the Sine Values

Select the values from cell C1 to C360. With this cell range selected, use the spreadsheet chart function to create a Line Chart. A plot of the sine wave appears (Figure A2-4).

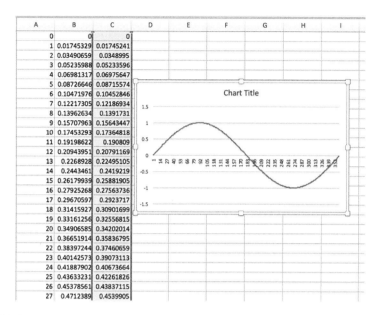

Figure A2-4

Building on the Foundation

. . . .

Change Amplitude, Frequency, and Initial Phase

By generalizing the sine formula, it is easy to change the values for the three characteristics of a sine wave (amplitude, frequency, initial phase) to see how they affect the plot.

The equation of a sine wave is given in Equation A1-2. It can be translated into a spreadsheet formula by making a few additions to the basic sine formula entered in the last section (Figure A2-5).

Go to cell C1. Change the formula from

`=SIN(B1)`

to

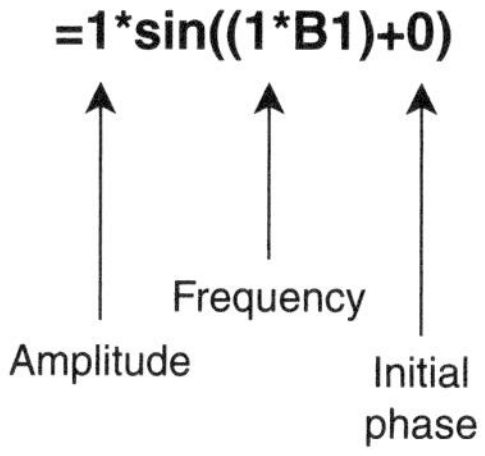

$$=1*sin((1*B1)+0)$$

Amplitude   Frequency   Initial phase

Figure A2-5

Use the **Fill** → **Down** function as before to copy this new formula over the range of cells from C1 to C360.

These new values, the two 1s and a 0, are the default values for a textbook sine wave—one cycle, an amplitude of 1, and an initial phase of 0. Adding them to the formula will not change the appearance of the plot.

But return to cell C1, change the multiplier of the value in cell B1 from 1 to 2, then
Fill → Down, and see how the plot updates. There are now two cycles instead of one.
Experiment with plotting different amplitudes, frequencies, and initial phases.

Use Absolute Cell References
Delete the chart created above.

Insert three blank rows above the cells. The wave's values now begin in row 4.

In cells B1 through B3, enter the labels "amplitude," "frequency," and "phase," respectively. (These three text cells are just labels for convenience, they have no function in the actual plot.)

Enter a value of 1 in cell C1, a value of 1 in cell C2, and a value of 0 in cell C3.

Go to cell C4, and change the formula to look like this:

```
=$C$1*SIN((1*B1)+$C$3)
```

The dollar sign creates an *absolute* reference. In contrast to the relative references used previously, this one specifies a fixed cell. It translates as, "No matter where you are, look at cell C1 and use the value there." This value is the amplitude value of the wave.

Fill → Down so that the formula appears from cells C4 to C364.

Create another chart. It should look like a standard sine wave. But now, by simply changing the value in cell C1, the chart's amplitude will update accordingly.

Do the same thing for the frequency and phase components of the formula. Changing any of the of the sine wave's characteristics now takes just a few keystrokes (Figure A2-6).

[Note: to change the value for initial phase in C3, it will be necessary to use a formula that puts the offset in terms of π, for example, **=pi()/4**.]

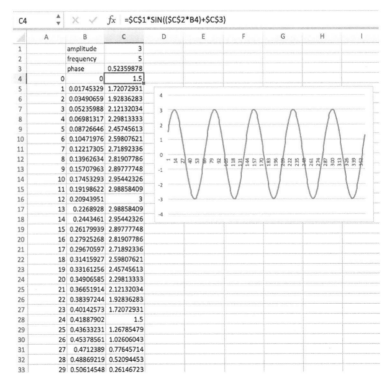

Figure A2-6

Use an Absolute Column Reference and a Relative Row Reference

To easily copy a set of sine wave values to create additional waves, combinations of absolute and relative cell references may be used.

Go to column C4. Change the formula to

```
=C$1*SIN((C$2*$B4)+C$3)
```

The **$B4** represents an absolute column reference (the dollar sign preceding the B) but a relative row reference (no dollar sign preceding the 4). For the cells containing amplitude, frequency, and phase values, the column is relative (no dollar sign preceding it), but the cell number is absolute (always the top cell for amplitude, row 2 for frequency, and row 3 for phase). Cells C1 through C364 may now be copied to column D. If new values are entered in cells D1 through D3, they will be reflected in the sine wave values contained in cells D4 through D364. But since the reference to the cell holding the radian values now has an absolute column reference, that Column B will continue to act as the column containing the radian angle.

Plot More Than One Sine Wave

Delete the chart created above. Keep the values in columns C and D as they are.

Select both columns of sine values: cells 4 to 363 in columns C and D. Plot a line chart as before. Since two columns of values are selected, two sine waves will be plotted (Figure A2-7).

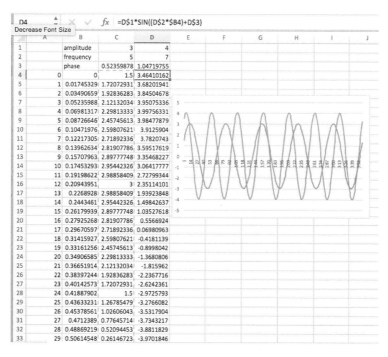

Figure A2-7

Change the values in the top three cells in rows C and D, and the waves update automatically.

Repeat this procedure to create charts that contain more than two sine waves.

Add the Separate Sine Waves to Create a Composite Sine Wave

After adding some number of sine waves, create an additional column. Suppose that three sine waves were created in columns C, D, and E. Go to cell F4. Enter

=SUM(

then drag across, from cell C4 to E4. The cell range will appear in cell F4. The cursor should still be in the formula bar. Then enter

)

The complete formula will look something like

=SUM(C4:E4)

Fill → Down to copy this sum formula from cell F4 to F364.

Select all the component sine wave plots and the composite sine wave plot—that is, the cells 4-364 in column C through cells 4-364 in column F.

Create a chart from all of these columns. All selected waves, the component sine waves and the composite wave, will be plotted (Figure A2-8).

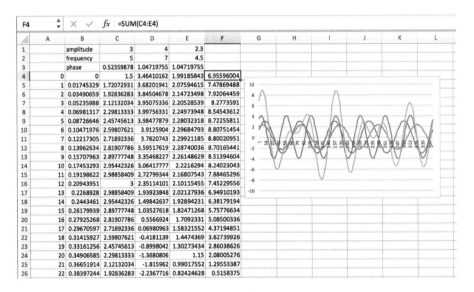

Figure A2-8

This shows how waves of different amplitudes, frequencies, and phases combine, as in the case of complex waves appearing in nature or from musical instruments.

By changing the amplitude, frequency, and/or phase values above the columns for each of the component sine waves, the plot will update, reflecting the changes in the component and composite waves.

Appendix 3

Overview of Logarithms

Exponents, Viewed from Another Angle

Any number can be expressed in exponential terms, for example:

$$10^2 = 100 \qquad \text{or} \qquad 10^3 = 1000$$

Using exponents to express a value in this way is akin to asking the question, "This number, raised to that power, results in what value?"

The subject of logarithms takes another view of the same question, focusing instead on the exponent. Starting with the value on the right side of the equals sign in the exponential equations above, the question asked is: "This value is the result of what power applied to that number (base)?"

The two examples may be rewritten as:

$$\log_{10} 100 = 2 \qquad \text{and} \qquad \log_{10} 1000 = 3$$

(Read: "log to base 10 of 100 equals 2" and "log to base 10 of 1000 equals 3.")

Now consider the range of numbers *between* 100 and 1000, for example 400 and 625. These examples may be written as

$$10^{2.60205999} = 400 \qquad \text{or} \qquad \log_{10} 400 = 2.60205999$$

$$10^{2.79588002} = 625 \qquad \text{or} \qquad \log_{10} 625 = 2.79588002$$

These examples show that if the focus is on logarithms, the value range from 100 to 1000 may be expressed with values that are between 2.0 and 3.0, thus compacting the terms that express a large range of numbers. Compacting numeric ranges this way is particularly valuable when the range is large, as is the case with audible sound power levels, described in Chapter 2.

Before the invention of calculators, logarithms were extremely useful to mathematicians because principles of logarithms simplified a variety of operations. Today's scientific calculators can readily provide values for logarithms, but mathematicians and scientists used to rely on thick books of tables for logarithms ("what power of 10 results in this number?") and *antilogarithms* ("10 to this power results in what number?"). It was helpful to use these to simplify the operations of multiplication, division, and exponential values.

Property 1

$$\log_a (M \times N) = \log_a M + \log_a N$$

(i.e., the answers to multiplication problems can be found by using addition)

Examples:

a. $\log_{10}(1000 \times 10) = \log_{10}1000 + \log_{10}10$
$$= 3 + 1$$
$$= 4$$

antilog: $10^4 = 10,000$

b. $\log_{10}(400 \times 625) = \log_{10}400 + \log_{10}625$
$$= 2.60205999 + 2.79588002$$
$$= 5.39794001$$

antilog: $10^{5.39794001} = 250,000$

Property 2

$$\log_a \frac{M}{N} = \log_a M - \log_a N$$

(i.e., the answers to division problems can be found by using subtraction)

Examples:

a. $\log_{10} \dfrac{1000}{10} = \log_{10}1000 - \log_{10}10$
$$= 3 - 1$$
$$= 2$$

antilog: $10^2 = 100$

b. $\log_{10} \dfrac{400}{625} = \log_{10}400 - \log_{10}625$
$$= 2.60205999 - 2.79588002$$
$$= -0.19382$$

antilog: $10^{-0.19382} = 0.64$

Property 3

$$\log_a M^n = n \log_a M$$

(i.e., the answers to exponential problems can found by using multiplication)

Examples:

a. $\log_{10}100^3 = 3 \times \log_{10}100$
$$= 3 \times 2$$
$$= 6$$

antilog: $10^6 = 1,000,000$

b. $\log_{10}625^4 = 4 \times \log_{10}625$
$$= 4 \times 2.7958002$$
$$= 11.1835201$$

antilog: $10^{11.1835201} = 152,588,000,000$

Appendix 4

Representing Numbers

Given the graphics-oriented nature of computing and the ability of computers to display a variety of multimedia types, it is easy to forget that they are essentially very speedy calculators. Everything they do involves information in the form of numbers, including the manipulation of musical information. To understand how computers do their work, it's necessary to have some understanding of how numbers are represented in computer systems.

Numbers Are Power

Numbers are represented as successive powers of a *base,* or *radix.* The powers increment upwards to the left, starting with zero to the far right. The number 1234 for any base *b* represents:

one times *b* to the third power
+
two times *b* to the second power
+
three times *b* to the first power
+
four times *b* to the zeroth power

(Note: Any number in any base to the power of zero is 1.)

Any value may be expressed with any radix. A base of 10, termed the *decimal system*, is most commonly used (perhaps because we have ten fingers and toes, it makes sense to us to think of numbers in terms of tens). Thus, the columns in base 10, moving from right to left, are termed the ones column, the tens column, the hundreds column, the thousands column, and so on. A digit placed in each column is a multiplier for each successive power. Therefore, the value 1324 represents:

one times 10 to the third power
+
three times 10 to the second power
+
two times 10 to the first power
+
four times 10 to the zeroth power

Of What Value Power?

For any base b, there exist b distinct numerical symbols. For example, in base 10, there are 10 distinct symbols: 0 through 9. In any base b, if there are n digits, the range of values that may be represented is b^n. For example, with two digits in base 10, $b = 10$ and $n = 2$. With two digits, the range of values that may be represented is 10^2 (100) values: 0 through 99.

Very large and very small numbers are usually described with prefixes recognized by the International System of Units (SI), as shown in Figure A4-1.

Numbers in Computers

Computers do not store values in decimal form. They store values with circuits that have two possible states: ON and OFF. Computers are therefore able to represent numbers in a system consisting of two symbols. Base 2, the *binary system*, meets this requirement.

The Binary Number System

The binary number system consists of only two digits: 0 and 1. That distinction aside, the system of representing numbers is exactly the same as in the decimal system. The binary number columns are shown in Table A4-1. Table A4-2 compares a sequence of numbers in the decimal and binary systems.

Some Essential Terminology

- A single digit of a binary number stored in a computer is called a *bit* (an abbreviation of binary digit) (Figure A4-2).

Power of ten	Number	Symbol
10^{-12}	0.000000000001	ρ (pico)
10^{-9}	0.000000001	η (nano)
10^{-6}	0.000001	μ (micro)
10^{-3}	0.001	m (milli)
10^{-2}	0.01	(centi)
10^{-1}	0.1	(deci)
10^{0}	1	
10^{1}	10	(deca)
10^{2}	100	(hecto)
10^{3}	1,000	k (kilo)
10^{6}	1,000,000	M (mega)
10^{9}	1,000,000,000	G (giga)
10^{12}	1,000,000,000,000	T (tera)
10^{15}	1,000,000,000,000,000	P (peta)

Figure A4-1 Powers of 10
Source: Adapted from "LHC: The Guide" (p. 1.) ©CERN.
https://cds.cern.ch/record/1165534/files/CERN-Brochure-2009-003-Eng.pdf

TABLE A4-1 Binary number columns

...	2^4	2^3	2^2	2^1	2^0
	Sixteens column	Eights column	Fours column	Twos column	Ones column

TABLE A4-2 A sequence of numbers in decimal and binary systems

DECIMAL	BINARY
0	0
1	1
2	10
3	11
4	100
5	101
6	110
7	111
8	1000

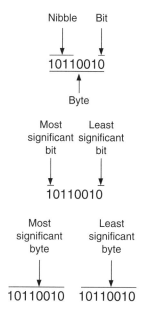

Figure A4-2 Bits, nibbles, and bytes

- A group of 8 bits is called a *byte*. Computers typically are able to store values within the range of some multiple of 8 bits—16 bits, 24 bits, 32 bits, etc.
- A group of 4 bits, half of a byte, is called a *nibble*.
- The rightmost bit, which represents the lowest power, is called the *least significant bit* (or LSB).
- The leftmost bit, which represents the highest power, is called the *most significant bit* (or MSB).
- Larger numbers need to be represented with two or more bytes (16 or more bits).
- The byte that represents the lower powers of the number is called the *least significant byte*.
- The byte that represents the higher powers of the number is called the *most significant byte*.

A digital system is often referred to as an *n-bit system*, meaning it has *n* digits available to represent numbers. The range of values can be determined the same way as was described above. In a binary system, $b = 2$, so an *n*-bit system is a statement that describes the resolution of the system. An 8-bit system can represent 2^8 (256) values. A 16-bit system can represent 2^{16} (65,536) values.

The Hexadecimal Number System
Because the number of digits in binary numbers can quickly add up, base 16, the *hexadecimal system*, is often used as a convenience. Because the arabic number system does not have digits to represent values greater than 9, alphabetic characters are used, as shown in Table A4-3.

The convenience of hexadecimal notation is that a 4-bit nibble can be expressed as one hexadecimal bit, since a binary nibble can express 16 values: the range of one hexadecimal digit. Frequently, an 8-bit byte will be expressed as two hex bits, as shown in Table A4-4. Hexadecimal notation can be helpful because it takes less space on a page to write a number. It can also be easier to read than an extended sequence of ones and zeroes.

TABLE A4-3 Decimal, hexadecimal, and binary numbers

DECIMAL	HEXADECIMAL	BINARY
0	0	0
1	1	1
2	2	10
3	3	11
4	4	100
5	5	101
6	6	110
7	7	111
8	8	1000
9	9	1001
10	A	1010
11	B	1011
12	C	1100
13	D	1101
14	E	1110
15	F	1111
16	10	10000
17	11	10001

TABLE A4-4 8-bit bytes can be expressed with two hexadecimal bits

Binary	1010	0110
Hexadecimal	A	6
Decimal	10	6

To convert two hex bits to decimal, multiply the most significant nibble by 16, then add the least significant nibble. For the 8-bit number shown in Table A4-4, the process is:

$$(10 \times 16) + 6 = 166$$

Integers and Floating Points

Numbers within the set of positive whole numbers (1, 2, 3, . . .), negative whole numbers (−1, −2, −3, . . .), and zero (0) are called *integers*. To represent negative numbers in computers, the values of bits are switched—0s to 1s and 1s to 0s—and a value of 1 is added to the result:

$$6_{10} = 0110_2$$

$$-6_{10} = 1001_2 + 1 = 1010_2$$

This form of representation is called *two's complement*. For a two's complement system of n bits, the upper half of the range (MSB = 1) represents negative numbers, while the lower half of the range (MSB = 0) represents positive numbers. Thus, with 4 bits, the values −8 to +7 may be represented.

The advantage of two's complement representation is that it allows subtraction to be performed as addition. To subtract B from A, A is added to the two's complement representation of B. If the result requires a 1 to be carried over to the leftmost bit, the sum is a positive number. If there is no carry bit, the answer is negative and is represented in two's complement form, as shown in Table A4-5.

Numbers that include a decimal point (for example, 3.14159) are called *floating-point numbers*. Floating-point representation in computers usually involves a base (sometimes called a *mantissa*) and an exponent. Typically, 3 bytes represent the mantissa and 1 byte represents the exponent. Floating-point numbers can be difficult to define with absolute precision, and in computers they are stored as approximations. The fraction 1/3, for example, cannot be represented with complete accuracy in decimal form (0.33333 . . .; an infinite series of the digit 3 is required). To represent such numbers in a computer, rounding has to occur after some maximum number of available bits has been used up. For example, the number 1/3 may need to be represented with only 3 three decimal places, as 0.333. This can lead to a certain degree of error in arithmetic operations. As a simple example:

$$1/3 \times 1/3 = 1/9 = 0.11111 \ldots$$

but

$$0.333 \times 0.333 = 0.110889$$

This degree of error may be insignificant or it may be crucial, depending on the circumstances. A series of operations involving floating-point numbers has the potential to accumulate error with each operation. This issue is discussed in Chapter 8 in the context of audio processing operations.

TABLE A4-5 Subtraction using two's complement numbers

$7_{10} - 6_{10}$	$6_{10} - 7_{10}$
0111 + 1010	0110 + 1001
10001	1111
The leftmost carry bit indicates a positive result.	Since there is no carry bit, the result is the two's complement representation of a negative number: 0001_2, or -1_{10}.

Key Terms

base or radix
binary system
bit
byte
decimal system
floating-point numbers
hexadecimal system
integers

least significant bit (LSB)
least significant byte
mantissa
most significant bit (MSB)
most significant byte
n-bit system
nibble
two's complement

Glossary

1/f or **pink noise**
Type of noise that contains equal energy over every octave. Its spectrum is a curve, with energy levels that are the inverse of the frequency value, and which has greater intensity at the low end. Its name also references visible light, which has lower frequencies at the red end of the spectrum.

5.1 surround sound
The multichannel standard for cinemas and home movie players. These systems consist of three front speakers—left, center, and right—and two surround speakers: left-surround and right-surround. The ".1" refers to a special subwoofer that delivers frequencies below 125 Hz or so.

absorption coefficient
Value describing the degree to which a particular material absorbs a particular frequency. A low absorption coefficient indicates that the majority of sound energy striking a surface is reflected away from it. An open window does not reflect any incident sound, so it is considered to be 100 percent absorptive.

acousmatic
"Loudspeaker music"—a tradition of concert events in which music is distributed through loudspeakers that are strategically placed throughout the venue.

acoustic compiler
A type of software built to create musical sounds.

acoustics
General term referring to sound, hearing, and the science of sound

acoustic signature
The factors making up the character of a sound—the instrument, the venue, the microphone, the audio production, etc.

active loudspeaker
A speaker that has a built-in amplifier.

additive synthesis
The creation of complex waveforms through combinations of sine wave oscillators.

address or **index**
The position of a sample within an audio signal; expressed as an ordinal number (the first sample, second sample, third sample, etc.).

address tree or **hierarchical namespace**
A method of referring to a computer file that describes its location within a series of folders, or directories, with each folder level separated by a slash, as in: folder/subfolder/filename.

ADSR envelope
A classic four-segment envelope, with parameters for attack time, decay time, sustain level, and release time.

AES/EBU transmission format
Professional-grade digital transmission format for two-channel audio, typically delivered over three-pin balanced connectors; low in jitter and capable of being transmitted up to 100 meters.

air particle velocity
The speed at which individual molecules move back and forth during a sound event. Air particle velocity increases when there is an increase in pressure level and/or frequency, since increased air pressure levels at the same frequency implies that individual molecules move farther back and forth each cycle than they do when pressure levels are lower.

air pressure
The density level of air molecules. For sound events, pressure levels alternate between compressed and rarefied states.

air suspension speaker
A speaker made of an airtight enclosure.

algorithmic composition
An approach to composition involving the definition of processes and rules for music generation, with computers doing the lower-level work of generating the actual music events.

alias
A misrepresented frequency in a digital recording due to a sampling rate that is too low.

all-pass filter

A type of filter that passes the average amplitudes of all frequencies equally during its steady state, but can color sound due to a complex phase response. It can also create a metallic ringing when the input is a sharp transient; this ringing frequency is unrelated to the input spectrum, as it is dependent on the filter's delay time.

alternating current (AC)

Current that constantly changes direction; electrons moving back and forth along a conductor.

ambisonics

A surround recording technique that relies on an encoded recording, which can be decoded on playback to play through an arbitrary number of speaker configurations.

ampere

Unit measurement for current level; describes the number of electrons that pass over a point over a given period of time. Named after the French physicist and mathematician André-Marie Ampère (1775–1836).

amplitude

The degree to which a vibrating object deviates from equilibrium, i.e., how high and low the wave's oscillations are.

amplitude envelope

The shape of a sound's amplitude changes over time.

amplitude modulation

The process of periodically changing the amplitude of a signal. When the modulation operates at low (subaudio) rates, the result is an oscillation in loudness (a tremolo). When the modulation frequency is brought to higher values (over 20 Hz), there is a qualitative change in the effect. In addition to the frequency of the audio-producing oscillator, extra frequencies are added to the sound at sum and difference frequencies with the modulator's frequency.

analog

An imitation; in electronics and telecommunications, the creation of AC voltage variations that mirror variations in acoustic pressure levels.

analog audio

Audio created by imitating of a continuous wave, such as on vinyl disc, tape, or voltage-controlled synthesizers.

analog modeling synthesizers

Digital synthesizers that model the circuitry found in vintage voltage-controlled instruments.

analog-to-digital converter (ADC)

Component that converts a continuous signal to a series of discrete samples.

analytic listening

Learning to "hear out" the individual harmonics of a sound like a plucked string, which is composed of multiple frequencies.

antinode

Point of maximum deviation in a standing wave.

aperiodic wave

Refers to a phenomenon (such as a wave) that has no repeating pattern.

argument

Inputs to a computer function.

asymmetrical distortion

Different misrepresentations of the high and low portions of an audio wave; tends to produce additional high harmonics.

atmospheric pressure

Change in molecular density of the atmosphere, used to describe weather changes. Although sound events are also due to changes in air pressure, weather events are of lower frequency and greater magnitude than sound events.

attack or **transient**

The initial onset of a note played by an instrument; tends to have noise and high frequency content; this segment of a note's evolution characterizes the sound of a particular instrument.

audibility threshold

The intensity level at which a sound becomes audible. If a sound is played at a volume level that is too low to be heard, and the volume is gradually increased, the level at which the sound becomes audible is the audibility threshold.

auditory scene analysis

The study of the organizational principles exercised in hearing, how the auditory system parses the complex wave that stimulates the eardrum into distinct events in the environment.

auditory stream

The identification of discrete entities in the listening environment. An example is the sound of footsteps, which consists of a series of discrete sound events, but is automatically grouped by the auditory system into a single identity.

auxiliary (aux) bus

An internal mixer path that directs an audio signal to a processing component of some kind before the signal is output.

auxiliary send
A type of signal path found on an audio mixer that sends a copy of an audio signal elsewhere to be processed in some way.

axial mode
Standing waves within a room along its axes that run left-right, up-down, and front-back.

backplate
Stationary capacitor plate in a condenser microphone.

backward masking
A louder sound masking a softer sound that precedes it.

balanced cables
Cables that deliver duplicate versions of the signal over two wires, at opposite polarities. Noise induced along the line is eliminated when both polarities are made the same again.

balancing transformer
Device on the receiving end of a balanced cable that reverses the polarity of one of the wires' signals.

bandpass filter
Filter that allows, attenuates, or eliminates frequencies outside a defined band.

band-reject filter
Filter that attenuates or eliminates frequencies within a defined band.

bandwidth
Frequency content of a complex tone or noise.

bandwidth (BW) of a filter
The difference between spectral components on either side of the bandpass or band-reject filter's center frequency that the filter affects in power by 3 dB.

bank
In a synthesizer, a group of 128 patches, or timbres.

Bark scale
Divides human hearing into twenty-four critical bandwidths, in a spectrum that goes up to 15.5 kHz.

basis set
A set of linked (dependent) basis vectors in a system, such as the x, y, and z coordinates of a Cartesian system. Any point in the system may be described as a linear combination of these basis vectors; conversely, these basis vectors are able to describe any point in the system.

bass-reflex speaker
A loudspeaker with a vented box design; a porthole in the speaker cabinet allows it to act as a tuned resonator and to effectively reproduce low frequencies.

battery
A vessel containing a chemical solution that tends to break down into positively and negatively charged ions. Current can flow along a wire that connects the positive to the negative region. Devices placed along the flow of current may be powered by it.

beating (first-order)
A modulation in amplitude when two tones are played simultaneously that are close in frequency to each other.

bel (B)
A logarithmic, comparative measurement of sound power levels, named after Alexander Graham Bell.

Bessel function
A set of solutions to a differential equation. Various forms of these functions are used in a variety of applications, including signal processing and FM synthesis.

bidirectional microphone
A microphone directional pattern that is sensitive to wavefronts arriving from the front and rear, but not from the sides.

biphase modulation
A form of encoding binary digits with a pulse wave, wherein a half-cycle that is entirely in the up or down position represents a binary digit of 0, while a transition in this same period—either from up to down or from down to up—represents a binary digit of 1.

bit depth (or sample size, word size, or quantization level)
The number of bits used to represent sample values. The more bits that are used, the more accurate the sample measurements are.

Blumlein configuration or **XY microphone configuration**
Two directional microphones with identical directional sensitivities placed at the same spot, one directly on top of the other, at an angle. A common configuration consists of two bidirectional microphones oriented 90° with respect to each other.

Braunmühl-Weber dual-diaphragm variable pattern microphone
A condenser microphone design in which two diaphragms are placed on opposite sides of a

single backplate. By various combinations of the cardioid patterns from each diaphragm, virtually all first-order patterns directional can be produced.

Brown noise

A type of noise with high-intensity low-frequency components, having a spectrum described as $1/f^2$, and a pattern sometimes described as a drunken walk or random walk.

buffer

A temporary set of memory to hold audio samples for processing of some kind.

bus

Signal paths in an audio mixer. The output buses send the signal to loudspeakers so that they can be heard. Internal buses direct the signal to processing devices.

capacitance

Measurement of an object's ability to hold extra electrons.

capacitor

A device that holds two oppositely charged elements, used to control current flow.

cardioid

Microphone directional pattern resembling a heart shape; sensitive to wavefronts arriving from the front, less so to side-arriving wavefronts, and little-to-no sensitivity to wavefronts arriving from the rear.

carrier

A high-frequency signal that delivers program material signals in classic radio broadcasting.

cascade (or **series**) **filter**

A filter configuration in which an input signal is sent through a succession of filters.

cat's whisker diode

A type of vacuum tube used in early radio receivers.

center frequency (CF)

Frequency component at the center of a bandpass filter's passband, or at the center of the frequencies attenuated by a band-reject filter.

channel

A signal path within an audio mixer; each input source is a channel, which may be adjusted and directed in ways that differ from the other audio channels.

channel control

Controls on an audio mixer that pertain to a single channel, rather than to the overall sound mix that is made up of a number of channels.

channel fader

Volume control for an audio channel in an audio mixer.

channel insert

A special type of send-and-return route in an audio mixer that is meant to provide immediate processing, such as compression or expansion, before the audio signal passes farther into the signal chain where it may be processed further and mixed with other audio signals.

channel-voice message

MIDI messages that are to take place on a particular channel.

characteristic frequency

The frequencies that can function as standing waves in a vibrating object; these are frequencies at which the object "likes" to vibrate. Also called "resonant frequencies."

Chladni patterns

Illustrations of vibrations on a vibrating plate, created by spreading fine sand on the plate. When the plate is brought to vibration, the sand collects at nodal points, forming different patterns for different frequencies.

chord

A set of pitches played simultaneously.

chorus

Audio effect that combines input with an oscillating delay; composed of a feedforward comb filter with a delay time on the order of 20–30 ms; the effect sounds something like human singers, who can never sound at exactly the same time and thus have a "group" sound.

chroma

A defined pitch class, such as steps of a scale (do, re, mi, . . . etc.)

client

In a computer network, a device that sends a message to a receiving device (which is termed the host or server).

clip light

A warning light on an audio mixer that indicates that the audio signal has exceeded system limits and is likely to clip or distort.

closed circuit

A system in which electrons may flow from a negatively charged element to a positively charged element.

cluster system
Stack of loudspeakers that are calculated to produce different frequencies in different directional patterns. These systems are the most versatile and the most expensive, but are the most effective for moving the larger volumes of air needed to fill a large theater, arena, or stadium.

codecs
Encoder/decoder, used in encoding multimedia files for various distribution formats, such as compressed versions for the Internet.

coefficient
Values by which variables are multiplied in an equation. In digital filter operation, past samples are multiplied by a set of values that determine the frequency response; these values are the filter's coefficients.

coincident microphone recording or **intensity recording**
A microphone configuration consisting of two directional microphones at the same location with them oriented in different directions from each other. Because there is no time difference between the signals arriving at the two microphones, the resulting stereo imaging is due to pressure differences between them. The two main coincident configurations are XY and MS.

comb filtering
An uneven frequency response due to regular frequency cancellations that can result when a signal is combined with a delayed version of itself.

common pin
Component of a wall outlet that leads electrons to ground.

companding
Component that combines compression and expansion for noise reduction or transmison over a channel with limited dynamic range. On transmission, a compressor allows the level of the signal to be brought up, thus increasing the signal-to-noise ratio. When the signal is received, an expander restores the original dynamic range, minus the noise.

compressed state
Air molecules at higher pressure levels (greater density) than in the normal, undisturbed state.

compressor/limiter
An automated volume controller that reduces input levels when they exceed a certain threshold. The speed at which they operate is adjustable, so that they can control the envelope of a sound, which can significantly affect its timbre.

condenser
Microphone transducer that operates by means of a capacitor system.

conductor
A medium that allows electrical current to pass through it.

consonance
A sound quality that is pleasing or agreeable when pitches played in combination.

constant Q filters
Bandpass filters that maintain a constant ratio of center frequency over bandwidth when the center frequency is adjusted.

constructive interference
Result of two waves of similar polarity encountering each other; they combine briefly, creating a moment of greater amplitude than either possesses individually.

continuous controller
MIDI channel voice message type that consists of a stream of information, usually from a movable interface element, such as a modulation wheel or a volume pedal.

control intimacy
An instrument's responsiveness to small, complex gestures from the musician.

control rate
A slower sample rate used for creating modulating signal generators in digital synthesizers.

control surface
A interface device consisting of buttons, knobs, or sliders that may be programmed to operate an audio device of some kind.

controller number
An identifier for a continuous control stream of MIDI messages. By convention, some streams may be described in terms of what type of device is originating the stream (e.g., a foot pedal is commonly assigned to controller number 4, modulation wheel to controller number 1) or what type of sound parameter is being controlled (e.g., volume is commonly assigned to controller number 7, pan position to controller 10).

convolution
A vector operation that involves sliding one vector over another, multiplying overlapping members,

and taking the sum of all multiplications. The vectors are then slid by another increment, and the process repeats. When two time-domain signals are multiplied, their spectra are convolved. When two time-domain signals are convolved, their spectra are multiplied.

convolution reverb
A type of reverberation plug-in that uses an impulse response recorded at an actual site to function as the filter's impulse response, thus "placing" the audio in the space where the impulse response was recorded.

Core Audio Format (CAF)
Audio file type that can serve as a wrapper for many other file types, is unrestricted as to its file size, can record more efficiently, and can hold additional data about the file.

cosine curve
Describes displacement pattern due to simple harmonic motion; a sinusoidal shape that begins at a value of 1.

critical band (basilar membrane)
A region of hair cells along the basilar membrane that fire when stimulated by a particular frequency.

critical band (frequency proximity)
A range of frequency proximity; two tones that fall within each other's critical band sound like a single pitch, with varying degrees of modulation or "roughness" occurring as the pitches are moved farther apart.

critically sampled
An audio signal that is sampled with a Nyquist frequency that matches the signal's frequency exactly. Critical sampling runs the risk of capturing only the zero crossings instead of the peaks and troughs.

cross synthesis
Applying characteristics of one sound to another; often done by filters, whereby a set of filters analyzes a sound, and then applies this analysis to another sound. The result is a kind of cross-breeding between the two sounds.

crossover network
System of filters within a loudspeaker that breaks the audio spectrum into subregions, each of which is reproduced with its own cone-coil system.

crystal set
Early type of radio receiver that operated by means of a quartz crystal.

cube root intensity law
When instruments play the same pitch, the perceived loudness is proportional to the cube root of the number of instruments playing. For example, eight instruments are required to create an effect of loudness doubling (since $2^3 = 8$).

current
The movement of electrons from one place to another.

cutoff frequency
Frequency component that indicates a level of significant attenuation in a lowpass or a highpass filter.

cycles per second or **hertz (Hz)**
Unit of measurement describing how often a wave repeats itself

damped sinusoidal synthesis or **modal sound synthesis**
Synthesis based on a model of a mass-spring vibrating system, based on the mass, damping, and restoring spring force.

data byte
A byte in a MIDI channel-voice message that gives a value to be applied to the message (e.g., note number in a note on message).

DC content or **DC offset**
A constant value added to all points in an AC signal.

decibel (dB)
A variation on the bel that yields more useful values for sound power levels.

decimating lowpass filter
A type of lowpass filter used to smooth a signal that has been processed, removing aliasing but potentially adding a muffling effect on the sound.

delta-sigma encoding (or **sigma-delta encoding)**
An alternative to PCM encoding; used on the Super Audio Compact Disc (SACD) format.

delta time value
A time increment in a Standard MIDI File that describes the amount of time to transpire between two MIDI events.

destructive interference
Result of two waves of opposite polarity encountering each other; they combine briefly, creating a moment of lesser amplitude than either possesses individually.

detuning

Synthesis technique whereby oscillators are put out of tune with each other by a small fraction of a wavelength, adding modulation and richness to the sound.

diaphragm of a microphone

A thin membrane that vibrates in response to air pressure changes.

difference or **Tartini tones**

When two pitches are played loudly together, a third tone at the difference between the two can sometimes be heard (e.g., a combination of frequencies at 2200 and 2300 Hz can sometimes produce an audible pitch at 100 Hz).

diffraction

A wavefront bending around an obstacle. This occurs when the wavelength is larger than the dimensions of the obstacle.

diffuse reverberation

Second- and higher-order reflections that occur as sound wavefronts bounce off the surfaces of a space, producing a diffuse wash of sound that is sometimes called the "room sound."

diffusion

The art of distributing music through a series of loudspeakers strategically placed throughout a venue, which makes the sound appear to move in ways that enhance the music.

Digital Audio Workstation (DAW)

A software-based music production studio, emulating the functions of an analog tape deck and effects processors.

Digital presence workstation

A control panel used in setting up networked music connections.

digital reverberation

Reverberation accomplished by digital components that process a digitized audio signal.

digital-to-analog converter (DAC)

A component that translates sample values into voltage levels, which may then be used to drive an amplifier to generate audio.

digital signal processing (DSP)

Manipulation of digital material, such as filtering or spectral analysis.

diode

Type of vacuum tube, used to control current.

Direct Box (DI)

A device that receives audio input signal, lowers the signal's impedance, and outputs it over a balanced line.

direct current (DC)

Flow of electrons from one place to another in a manner akin to water flowing along a pipe; the type of current produced when battery terminals are connected in a closed circuit.

direct sound

Sound wavefronts that travel directly from the source to the listener. These wavefronts provide the cues for localization of the sound source.

discharge

The flow of electrons from one object to another, which equalizes the number of electrons in each, thus eliminating an electrical charge.

Discrete Fourier Transform (DFT)

An adaptation of the Fourier transform for finding spectra of discrete digital signals.

dissonance

A sound quality that is clashing or disagreeable when pitches played in combination.

distance factor or **reach**

A comparison of the relative distance a microphone may be placed from a sound source, compared to an omnidirectional microphone, to produce the same direct-to-reverberant response.

distortion

The way in which a component's output signal does not match the input signal, such as an audio wave being reshaped in some way.

distortion synthesis (modulation synthesis or **nonlinear waveshaping)**

A form of processing in which new spectral components are added to an input signal.

distributed cognition

A mutual sharing of ideas within a community, creating cumulative experiences that result in culture.

distributed creativity or **networked music**

Concerts that feature performers located in different places, performing together with the aid of high-speed, high-bandwidth Internet connections.

dither

Low-level noise added to the audio signal before it is sampled, or to a digital signal before its sample size is reduced. Allows low-level audio signals to be reproduced in digital systems, and allows information contained in large sample sizes to be retained when the sample sizes are reduced.

Doppler shift
The change in pitch perceived when a moving object passes by a listener. The motion toward and away from the listener causes the sound wavefronts to be compressed and expanded, producing a drop in pitch when the object passes.

drunken walk or **random walk**
Pattern of noise that follows a pattern similar to that of an inebriate's impaired sense of equilibrium, which causes him to walk in a different direction with each step; the distance traveled after n steps is proportional to $\sqrt{n}$.

duty cycle
The percentage of a pulse wave's cycle during which it is in its high position.

dynamic range
The difference between the highest and lowest amplitudes in a signal.

dynamic transducer
Microphone transducer consisting of coils attached to the diaphragm that move back and forth within a magnetic with the diaphragm's motion, producing electrical current in response to the motion.

early reflection
First-order sound wavefront reflections that reach the listener after reflecting once from the floor, ceiling, walls, or furniture. It gives cues for a space's size, and can provide additional clarity if the delay times cause the early reflections to arrive within 35 ms of the direct wavefronts.

echo or **reverb chamber**
The earliest form of artificial reverberation; audio played into a highly reflective room is picked up with at least one microphone; the signal from this room is then mixed with the original signal.

editor/librarian software
Software for creating synthesizer patches and organizing them in banks.

electromagnet
A magnet created by an electrical current directed through a coiled wire.

electromotive force (EMF)
The force that induces electrons to flow from a negatively charged object to a positively charged object.

electron
Negatively charged particles that orbit an atom's nucleus.

elektronische Musik
Early form of electroacoustic composition based entirely on electronically generated sounds in the creation of serial music.

emergent property
Something that comes into being as a result of a number of factors, a whole that is greater than the sum of its parts.

encoding
Translation of data from one form to another; with audio samples, encoding is necessary to convert them to a form that may be stored reliably on storage media.

entropy encoding
An approach to file compression whereby, rather than storing every sample of a cyclic waveform, a cycle can be identified, and the number of cycles can be encoded.

envelope follower
A control signal that originates in a bandpass filter that tracks levels within a particular band of an input signal, and applies these level changes to a different signal that is being output.

envelope generator
Synthesizer component that controls an output level over time.

equalization (EQ)
A set of specialized lowpass, highpass, and bandpass filters found on an audio mixer or an audio amplifier that allows the spectrum of a signal to be adjusted.

Ethernet switch
A hardware module containing a number of Cat5 Ethernet cable jacks.

event list
A text-based view of MIDI events in a DAW program.

expander/noise gate
A component that expands a signal's dynamic range, making soft sections quieter and loud sections even louder.

expansion ratio
A ratio in an expander that describes the number of dB that the output drops for every 1 dB drop in input.

Fast Fourier Transform (FFT)
A more efficient version of the Discrete Fourier Transform, fast enough to allow real-time analysis; requires a window size that is a power of 2.

feedback delay
A delay component that combines the delayed output with the input signal, producing a decaying series of echoes.

feedback filter (or resonant or recursive filter)
A filter that recirculates its output back into its input, blending past output with present input values.

feedforward filter
A filter that processes incoming samples and outputs them without directing any of the output back into the input.

film/video frame
A single image on a film or videotape.

filter difference equation
An equation describing how a digital filter treats both present and past input, and past output samples.

finite impulse response (FIR) filter
Another term for a feedforward filter. Since there is no recirculation of the output back to the input, an impulse signal will produce a finite number of samples before the output returns to zero.

first-order cardioid microphone
A set of microphone directional response patterns that are variations on the heart-shaped cardioid pattern, and can be described by a polar equation containing a cosine term to the first power.

flanger
A feedback comb filter that has a short, oscillating delay time—typically in the range of 1 to 10 ms. The delay time oscillations result in a dynamic comb filter with sliding teeth to create a pronounced "whooshing" sound.

flutter echo
A "reverberation tail" that results from an impulsive sound wavefront bouncing back and forth between two surfaces.

force
A push or pull on an object, causing it to move.

formant
Consistent spectral peaks, regardless of the pitch or fundamental frequency being sounded. An instrument's body colors the sound with formants, and one instrument body may introduce different formants than another, accounting for the instruments' difference in sound quality

forward masking
A louder sound raising the audibility threshold of another sound that is played within 100–200 ms later.

forward-oriented omni microphone or subcardoid microphone
First-order cardioid directional pattern that resembles an omnidirectional pattern with reduced sensitivity to energy arriving from the rear.

Fourier analysis or transform
The decomposition of a complex wave into its harmonic components, or spectrum. Each harmonic has a particular relative amplitude and phase with respect to the other harmonics. The analysis gives information about the relative amplitudes and phases of a complex periodic wave.

frame
A group of samples representing each moment of a digital recording. Each sampling increment contains a new frame of samples, with one sample per channel of audio. A monophonic file has one sample per frame, a two-channel stereo file has two samples per frame, a quadraphonic file has four samples per frame, and so on.

frequency
How often a wave repeats itself, measured in cycles per second, or hertz (Hz).

frequency domain masking
Masking phenomena involving sounds that are played simultaneously.

frequency modulation (FM) synthesis
The creation of complex timbres through high vibrato rates.

frequency response
Describes the spectral content of an audio device. A filter's frequency response describes how it amplifies or attenuates different spectral regions.

friction machine
Early electronic device used to charge objects by turning a crank to spin them against each other.

Fukada Tree configuration
A microphone configuration to record surround sound consisting of seven microphones for left, center, right, left and right rear, and left and right wide.

fully parametric EQ
EQ that allows both center frequency and quality (Q) to be adjusted.

fundamental frequency
The lowest standing wave a vibrating object can support. For a musical vibration, the fundamental frequency corresponds to the perceived pitch the object produces.

fundamental tracking
If combinations of harmonically related tones are played in succession, a lower tone can often be perceived that would be the common fundamental to each of these tone groups if it were, in fact, present.

gain
The ratio of a signal's output power to its power on input.

gain staging
Working with various volume levels along a signal path to prevent noise and distortion.

gateway
A device that connects a network to the outside Internet.

General MIDI
A standardized set of patch assignments so that instrument types correspond to patch numbers within a synthesizer, as well as assignments of drum sounds within a drum patch, which is assigned to MIDI channel 10.

Gestalt principles
A set of rules that account for perceptual completion and pattern formation, whereby the visual and auditory systems infer patterns and wholes based on incomplete information.

glitching error
An error that can result during the digital-to-analog conversion process due to some bits being translated before others; under some circumstances this can lead to voltage spikes in the output that are not present in the audio signal.

gradient or **pressure gradient**
Microphone constructed with a diaphragm that responds to pressure changes arriving from both the front and the rear, with the signal produced according to the difference in pressure wavefronts arriving from either side of the diaphragm.

granular synthesis
The creation of sound clouds from many extremely short grains of sound.

graphical user interface (GUI)
A visual computer control interface that resembles a hardware interface with images of siders, knobs, buttons, etc.

ground loop
Electrons circulating in a kind of whirlpool between devices; produces an audible hum in audio equipment.

grounding
A connection to the earth in an electrical system that allows stray electrons to drain away.

GS MIDI
An expansion of General MIDI, created by the Roland company in 1991; features multiple drum kit banks and standardized controller numbers to include effects such as reverberation and brightness.

half-normalled
Patchbay configuration that maintains flow from input to output along a connection, so that the input signal to the patchbay adds the cable's signal to the signal path, rather than overriding it.

half-wave resonator
A tube that is either open on both ends or closed on both ends. Its length is one-half the lowest wavelength (fundamental frequency) it may support. A half-wave resonator can also support all harmonics of the fundamental.

Hamming window
Window type commonly used in Short Time Fourier Transform analyses.

handshake
A series of queries and confirmations that ensure the integrity of file transmissions over the Internet, used by some transfer protocols, such as TCP/IP.

hanning window
Window type commonly used in Short Time Fourier Transform analyses.

harmonic series

The set of frequencies that are integer multiples of the fundamental.

hertz (Hz) or **cycles per second**

Unit of measurement describing how often a wave repeats itself.

hierarchical namespace or **address tree**

A method of referring to a computer file that describes its location within a series of folders, or directories, with each folder level separated by a slash, as in: folder/subfolder/filename.

Higher-Order Ambisonics

An improvement on First-Order Ambisonics, offering improved localization and a larger listening "sweet spot." The higher orders are achieved through a greater number of encoded recording signals than in First-Order Ambisonics, and greater numbers of playback channels.

higher-order interpolation

Interpolation of values based on the values of a number of samples above and below the index point being interpolated.

highpass filter

A filter that removes low-frequency components (it "lets the highs pass").

Hooke's law

The relationship between force (F), tension (K), and displacement (y):

$$F = -Ky$$

Used to describe vibrating bodies such as mass-spring systems.

host or **server**

Devices on a network that provide information or services on demand; requests are received from client devices.

hot pin

Component of a wall outlet that supplies electrical current.

hot wire

One of two wires in an electrical cable, makes contact with the outlet's hot pin.

hypercardioid pattern

First-order cardioid directional response having a tight forward-magnitude response.

Ideale Nierenanordnung **(INA 5; "ideal cardioid") microphone configuration**

Also called INA 5, a microphone configuration to record surround sound consisting of five cardioid microphones, each of which records one of the five surround channels.

impedance (Z)

Frequency-dependent resistance in alternating current.

impulse response (filter)

The set of coefficients in a filter difference equation. An impulse signal input to the filter will produce an output that matches these coefficients.

impulse response (reverberation)

Echo and reverberation patterns in a room that result from a brief, impulsive sound; used to characterize a room's acoustics.

impulse train

Wave created from a series of regular impulses; its spectrum consists of all harmonics of the fundamental, all at equal amplitude.

in-ear monitor (IEM)

Earpieces worn onstage by musicians that allow them to hear a mix of all the instruments being played.

Independent Basic Service Set (IBSS)

A dynamic, self-configuring network that can be created and joined on the fly, without any kind of router or administrative setup.

index or **address**

The position of a sample within an audio signal; expressed as an ordinal number (the first sample, second sample, third sample, etc.).

index of modulation

Output level of the modulating oscillator in FM synthesis.

inductance

The result of electrical current mingling with magnetism; the property by which a change in current emits magnetism, which affects current in nearby conductors.

induction

The creation of magnetism when there is a change in electrical current, or the creation of electrical current when a conductor is made to move within a magnetic field.

induction coil

A device created to demonstrate the properties of electromagnetic induction. A power source regularly switched on and off generates alternating current in a nearby conductor.

infinite impulse response (IIR) filter

Another term for a feedback filter. Since the output is recirculated back to the input, there is the theoretial potential that an impulse signal can produce an output sequence that never returns to zero.

inner product
A vector operation in which corresponding points between vectors are multiplied.

insulator
Material that does not allow electrical current to flow through it.

integrated circuit
Systems of transistors wired together onto a single silicon wafer, allowing complex electrical devices to be created in small sizes.

integrated unit
Loudspeaker in which both the woofer and tweeter, and possibly a midrange speaker, are contained within the same enclosure along with the crossover network.

integrator
A component that keeps a running total of the values input to it.

intensity (I)
Power with respect to distance; the power level at a listener's position, measured in watts per square meter.

intensity recording or **coincident microphone recording**
A microphone configuration consisting of two directional microphones at the same location oriented in different directions. Because there is no time difference between the signals arriving at the two microphones, the resulting stereo imaging is due to pressure differences between them. The two main coincident configurations are XY and MS.

interactive composition
A piece in which a performer shares control of the music's creation with a computer.

interaural cross correlation (IACC)
The degree of similarity between the wavefronts reaching each of a listener's two ears.

interaural level delay (ILD)
A function of the angle at which a sound wavefront reaches a listener, ILD describes the difference in the spectra of pressure patterns reaching the near and far ear. This is the primary localization cue for frequencies above 1500 Hz or so.

interaural time delay (ITD)
A function of the angle at which a sound wavefront reaches a listener, ITD describes the difference in time between the wavefront's arrival at the near and the far ear. This is the primary localization cue for frequencies below 1500 Hz or so.

interleaving
Changing the order of samples before storing the signal; a form of encoding that ensures that if a portion of the medium is damaged, the affected samples will not be contiguous on playback, and the damage may be repairable with a correction algorithm of some kind.

Internet Protocol (IP) address
A 32-bit number that identifies a device on the Internet.

interpolation
A method for creating values that fall between the index points of a delay line buffer.

intonation
Refers to pitches that are related by each other by simple integer ratios.

inverse Fourier transform
The reverse of a Fourier analysis. Spectral components are combined to create a complex wave.

inverse square law
A change in intensity by a factor of one over a change in distance squared; applies to many forms of energy, including sound intensity levels.

inverted sine wave
A sinusoidal wave that starts at zero and begins with the negative portion of its cycle.

ion
A charged atom; a negative ion has more electrons that protons; a positive ion has more protons than electrons.

IP (Internet Protocol) address
A number that identifies a device on a computer network.

jitter
Timing irregularities in a digital transmission.

just intonation
A tuning system that relies on simple integer ratios to derive each interval of a musical scale.

karaoke file
A type of MIDI file that includes a display of lyrics for sing-along use in karaoke parlors.

Karplus-Strong string model
An algorithm involving a buffer of noise that recirculates through a lowpass filter, creating extremely realistic plucked string sounds.

kinetic energy
The energy of a body in motion. Dependent on its mass (m) and its velocity (v):
$$KE = \tfrac{1}{2} mv^2$$

Note that the energy increases as a factor of velocity squared. This is why so many football injuries occur during kickoffs: players of large mass who have run the length of the field acquire high velocities, and thus collide with much greater force than they would if they had only run a short distance first.

Lambert's cosine law
A principle stating that the intensity of the reflections is proportional to the cosine of the angle of incidence with a line perpendicular to the surface.

lands
Areas between the holes (pits) in the surface of an optical disc. Binary information is encoded in the form of pits and lands.

Leyden jar
Invented in 1746, a jar lined with foil that could hold a charge. An early form of capacitor that eventually led to the development of the battery.

Lightpipe transmission format
Multi-channel high-resolution audio transmission protocol, typically delivered over fiber optic cables.

limiting
High level of compression, where large changes in input volume result in comparatively small changes in output volume.

line level
Mixer input at the level output by keyboards and most processing devices, delivered over unbalanced cable.

linear mass density
Mass per unit length, usually applied to long and narrow objects, such as rods and strings. Expressed as kilograms per meter.

linear interpolation
Interpolation method based on creating an imaginary straight line between values held in a delay buffer, and outputting a point that lies on that line, between values held in two successive buffer indices.

linear progression
A sequence of values obtained by continually adding a constant value, such as: 2, 4, 6, 8, 10 . . .

live coding session
A kind of jam session based on improvised coding, in which computer screens are projected so that audience members can see the code as it is typed by the composers that generates the audio (and often video) as it is being created.

local area network (LAN)
A network that consists only of machines in physical proximity to each other and that is not connected to the Internet.

localhost
Another term used for the special IP address 127.0.0.0, which refers to the machine sending the message, meaning that the message is being transferred from one program to another within the same machine.

localization
Quality of a recording's stage picture; the degree to which the apparent positions of different players can be heard.

localization blur
The margin of error found in studies of sound localization, the degree of certainty to which listeners can identify the apparent locations of sound sources.

lodestone
Term given to the magnet by ancient Greek writers.

logarithm
The power to which a number may be raised.

loop
A brief segment of musical material used by a DJ as part of a sound collage pattern.

loop point
Designated points within a sampled audio recording; when the sample is played in response to a MIDI note on message, the sample loops between these points until a note off message is received.

loop/overdub mode
A sequencer recording mode in which a passage repeats, recording whatever is played; this allows a complex passage to be created gradually as the user records new material with each pass.

lossless encoding
A form of file compression that does not remove any material from the original file.

lossy
A form of file compression that removes material deemed expendable from a file to reduce the file size.

loudness
Perception of sound volume; related to intensity levels, but also affected by a variety of other qualities, such as frequency, envelope, and bandwidth.

low-frequency oscillator (LFO)
An oscillator producing a subaudio frequency (below about 20 Hz); its signal is not meant to be heard, but rather to modulate another oscillator in some way.

lowpass filter
A filter that removes high-frequency components (it "lets the lows pass").

magnetic induction
The generation of electrical current by moving a conductor within a magnetic field.

magnetism
A property by which some objects are attracted to or repelled from each other, and by which a force field causes particles to align themselves around two poles.

main mic
Principal microphones of a concert recording configuration; these are meant to provide the overall aural picture, the "master shot" of the performance.

masking
A phenomenon by which certain sounds may cause other sounds to disappear perceptually.

master device
A device that sends instructions to other devices ("slaves"), which carry out the instructions.

mechanical coupling
When contact is made between two objects, motion from one object may be passed to the other.

meta-event
Information about the information contained in a file; in a Standard MIDI file, this refers to information about the MIDI events it contains, such as tempo, track names, key changes, lyrics, and instrument names; this information is not required for the file to be played, but it can be handy when it is displayed in certain programs.

mic level
Mixer input at a level output by microphones, which are low impedance and delivered over balanced cable.

microphone splitter
An analog junction box where microphones can be plugged, and their signals distributed to various receiving devices.

microprocessor
Groups of microscopic transistors wired together on a single chip or wafer, forming a complete computation engine.

microtonality
Pertaining to pitches that fall "between the cracks" of equal tempered pitches, such as those found on a concert piano.

MIDI (Musical Instrument Digital Interface)
A protocol for hardware and for digital communication that allows devices to send and/or respond to instructions.

MIDI controller keyboard
A keyboard that sends MIDI information but does not produce any audio.

MIDI file
A file that contains MIDI information, which may be played in a number of media programs, such as Windows Media Player and QuickTime.

MIDI interface
A translating device that converted MIDI bytes into a form that could be read by a computer, and converted information generated by MIDI software into MIDI bytes that could be transmitted to MIDI instruments.

MIDI Show Control (MSC)
A standardized set of MIDI SysEx messages that control nonmusical theatrical devices such as lighting, scenery, pyrotechnics, or sound effects.

MIDI Time Code (MTC)
A version of SMPTE timecode values that represented them in MIDI bytes, which could be transmitted over MIDI cables and a MIDI interface.

missing fundamental
A phenomenon observed when two tones are played together that could be harmonically related; listeners often report hearing a third tone that would be the fundamental for both of them. For example, if tones at 440 and 660 Hz are played together, listeners often report hearing a tone of 220 Hz that is not actually being played.

mixer
Central unit of a music production studio, where signals from various devices are combined, balanced, and processed.

modal enhancement
Amplification of certain frequencies within a room due to standing waves at those frequencies.

mode of vibration
Pattern by which an object, such as a system of masses and springs, may vibrate: all masses may move in the same direction, or some may move in opposing directions.

modal sound synthesis or **damped sinusoidal synthesis**
Synthesis based on a model of a mass-spring vibrating system, based on the mass, damping, and restoring of spring force.

modular component system
DIY audio components assembled on a "breadboard" (blank circuit board); eventually evolved into the modular synthesizer.

modulation synthesis (distortion synthesis or nonlinear waveshaping)
A form of processing in which new spectral components are added to an input signal.

module
Building block of analog synthesizers; modular synthesizer systems were created by attaching any number of modules into a complex system of oscillators, filters, amplifiers, envelope generators, etc.

monitor speaker
Loudspeakers meant for critical listening facilities, designed to deliver all frequencies as equally as possible with little or no coloration.

Moore's Law
A 1965 observation by Gordon Moore, the cofounder of Intel, predicting that the number of transistors per square inch on integrated circuits was likely to double each year.

MS microphone configuration
A recording configuration consisting of one cardioid microphone and one bidirectional microphone; creates a recording in which the stereo image can be adjusted in postproduction.

multimeter
A basic electronics testing tool that measures current, voltage, or resistance.

multiplexer
Component of the digital recording process that transforms parallel sample streams from each audio channel into a single stream for storage.

Samples from the different channels are alternated in the stream.

multitap delay
Combination of a succession of simple delays; users may typically adjust the delay time and gain of each delay.

musique concrète
Music form introduced in the late 1940s based on creating pieces from recorded sounds.

mute switch
A button on a mixer to silence a channel without moving its fader position.

mutual induction
A phenomenon that occurs when voltage changes in one wire coil induce voltage in another due to the electromagnetic field that the primary voltage changes produce.

name-value pair
A messaging format in which a parameter name is followed by a value that is to be applied to that parameter, such as "frequency 440" to tell a device to play a pitch of middle A.

near-coincident microphone configuration
Also called quasi-coincident configurations, the term refers to pairs of directional microphones that are close but not coincident; meant to record some of the localizability of coincident configurations and some of the sense of spaciousness of time-of-arrival configurations.

negative charge
A condition due to an excess of electrons held in an object.

negative sum
Type of comb filter that subtracts a delayed sample from the current input sample.

networked music or **distributed creativity**
Concerts that feature performers located in different places, performing together with the aid of high-speed, high-bandwidth Internet connections.

neutral wire
One of two wires in an electrical cable, which makes contact with the outlet's common pin.

newton
Measurement unit of force. One newton causes a 1 kg object to accelerate by 1 meter per second every second (1 m/s^2).

nodes
Points of no displacement in a standing wave.

noise floor
A constant level of noise present in any audio signal.

noise generator
A kind of oscillator (in a modular synthesizer) or unit generator (in a software synthesis program) that generates a random signal of some kind.

noise shaping
A process that highpass filters quantization error so that the distortion is pushed to frequencies above the audible range.

nondestructive editing
Editing of digital material that can be undone without any damage to the original version.

nonlinear waveshaping (modulation synthesis or distortion synthesis)
A form of processing in which new spectral components are added to an input signal.

Non-Return to Zero (NRZ) encoding
A form of encoding used to represent digital information by which ones and zeroes are represented by high and low voltage levels.

Non-Return to Zero Inverted (NRZI) encoding
A form of encoding used to represent digital information by which ones and zeroes are represented by transitions between high and low voltage levels.

nonstationary signal
A signal that has an irregular pattern.

normalization/maximization
A processing operation that raises the volume level of an audio file. First, extreme peaks are lowered. Then all sample values are raised proportionally.

normalize
The process of transposing values so that they fall within a desired range.

normalled
Patchbay setting that causes an input signal to override any other signal connection to a device.

notator
A software program that produces music notated in the common practice staff system.

Nyquist frequency
Half the sampling rate; also the highest frequency that can exist in a digital recording.

Nyquist theorem or **sampling theorem**
"To represent digitally a signal containing frequency components up to X Hz, it is necessary to use a sampling rate of at least $2X$ Hz."

oblique mode
Standing waves within a room along its axes that run diagonally between opposite corners, such as from ceiling front right to floor back left.

OCT (Optimum Cardioid Triangle) surround configuration
A configuration meant for surround-sound concert recording consisting of a front-facing cardioid microphone combined with two hypercardioids that face 90° to the left and right, supplemented by two cardioid microphones placed some distance behind the front triangle.

octave
A duplication of pitch class that results from doubling or halving a given frequency (or multiplying a given frequency by any power of two).

octave generalization
Musical equivalence of notes separated by an octave.

ohm
Unit of measurement for electrical resistance. Named after German physicist Georg Simon Ohm (1789–1854).

Ohm's Law
Describes the relationship between voltage, current, and resistance:
$$voltage_E = current_I \times resistance_R$$

omnidirectional microphone
A microphone that responds with equal magnitude to pressure changes arriving from all angles.

open circuit
A broken connection between positive and negative battery terminals, which makes current flow impossible.

Open Sound Control (OSC)
A protocol to control networked sound modules and multimedia devices; messages are sent over a network to a particular IP address, which may refer in theory to any machine connected to the Internet.

opposing force
A pull in the opposite direction. When a pulse is sent along a string that has a fixed end, the fixed end acts as an opposing force on the pulse, causing it to reflect at the opposite polarity of its onset polarity.

optical disc
Storage format that is read by a laser beam, which reflects from pits and lands imprinted onto its

surface. This is the medium used for audio CDs, CD-ROMS, and DVDs.

order
A type of Bessel function; different orders of Bessel functions are based on variations of a basic nonlinear equation.

ORTF microphone configuration
A near-coincident stereo microphone configuration consisting of two cardioid microphones separated by 17 cm (6.7″), the approximate width of the human head, and angled 55° away from the center.

orthogonal
In coordinate systems, this term refers to axes that are perpendicular to each other. It has been generalized to describe properties that are independent of each other, or nonoverlapping.

oscillator
An electronic device that produces a repeating waveform of some kind.

oscillator sync
A type of synthesis in which a sync oscillator (or master oscillator) controls a secondary oscillator (or slave oscillator). Each time the sync oscillator begins a new cycle, it causes the secondary oscillator to break its cycle and start another cycle immediately.

oscilloscope
A testing device that displays electrical waveform signals.

out of phase
Two waveforms that have the same frequency but begin at different points in their cycles, so that they do not have simultaneous zero-crossings.

output bus
Buses on a mixer that send audio out to another device, such as a destination machine where the mix is recorded, or to monitor speakers.

oversampling
Sampling audio at a rate higher than is necessary to store all frequencies in the signal.

overtone
A frequency component of a complex wave other than the fundamental.

packet
Groups of messages sent over the Internet; large messages are often subdivided into packets, which are reassembled by the receiving device.

pad
A switch on a mixer that reduces high-level signals originating from a microphone.

pan pot (potentiometer)
A mixer knob that determines the proportion of the signal that goes to the left (odd) and right (even) output channels.

parallel filter
Filter configuration by which an input signal is split and each copy of the signal is sent through one or more filters, after which the signals are recombined.

partial
Any frequency component of a complex wave.

pascal (Pa)
Unit of measurement for air pressure, describing newtons per square meter.

passband
The spectral range that passes through a bandpass filter.

passive loudspeaker
A loudspeaker that needs to be powered by an external amplifier.

patchbay
A routing point between a studio's various devices and its mixer. Allows signal flow among devices to be changed easily.

peak pressure level or **peak amplitude level**
The highest level of deviation a vibrating object undergoes as it moves back and forth; the maximum distance from the equilibrium point.

perceptual coding
An approach to file compression that aims to remove material that would not be perceived by the auditory system.

perceptual completion
The human tendency to infer the presence of an entire object based on incomplete information (e.g., seeing a few orange and black stripes behind bushes might lead us to think there is a tiger back there; we can infer its presence without needing to see the entire tiger).

perfect fifth
A consonant interval obtained by multiplying a given frequency by a ratio of 3/2.

period
The time interval of one cycle of an object's vibration.

periodic
A wave with a repeating pattern (strictly speaking, a repeating pattern that has never changed and never will change).

periodicity theory
A theory stating that pitch perception is based on repetitive patterns within sound waves, suggested as an alternative to place theory.

periphonic
Stereophony that includes vertical imaging as well as horizontal imaging.

phantom image
A sound image that appears to fall between two loudspeakers.

phantom power
An external power source needed to charge the capacitor plates of a condenser microphone. Typically supplied by a mixer or audio interface.

phase
The position of a wave at a certain time.

phase modulation
A type of synthesis based on applying a high-frequency vibrato to an oscillator; the correct term for a process often termed frequency modulation (FM) synthesis.

phase response
A description of how different spectral components are delayed by a filter on output.

phase shifter
An effect consisting of a series (cascade) of all-pass filters with oscillating delay times. It is sometimes described as an "underwater-like" sound.

phase vocoder
A digital effect that allows signals to be shortened or lengthened without changing their pitch, or to have their pitch raised or lowered without changing the duration, as well as a number of other spectral effects.

phon
A subjective loudness measurement that uses a pure tone at 1000 Hz as a reference. At 1 kHz, the phon level matches the dB level. Sounds that are perceived as matching this loudness are considered to be at the same phon level.

phonograph
Invented by Thomas Alva Edison in 1877, this device was the birth of recorded sound.

physical modeling or **waveguide synthesis**
A computer model of the body of an instrument, with analyses of its resonances and vibrating parts.

piano-roll view
A view of MIDI events in a sequencer that displays notes as colored bars. The length of each bar indicates the note's duration, its vertical position indicates pitch, and often its color indicates velocity.

piezoelectricity
A property of quartz crystal that describes its ability to emit an electrical current when the crystal is put under physical pressure.

pink or **1/f noise**
Type of noise that contains equal energy over every octave. Its spectrum is a curve, with energy levels that are the inverse of the frequency value, and which has greater intensity at the low end. Its name also references visible light, which has lower frequencies at the red end of the spectrum.

pinnae filtering
Filtering of sound due to reflections within the pinnae before wavefronts enter the auditory canal; pinnae filtering is a primary cue in judging elevation of sound sources.

pitch-bend wheel
A bidirectional wheel found on most synthesizers, used to dynamically control the instrument's pitch.

pits
Holes between the lands (surface level segments) in the surface of an optical disc. Binary information is encoded in the form of pits and lands.

place theory
A theory stating that pitch perception is based on the motion of the cochlea (the place of maximum deviation) in response to auditory stimulus.

plane wave
A spherical wavefront that takes on a flat appearance due to its expansion as it travels from its origin.

plate reverb
Reverberation effect created in the 1950s, consisting of a transducer that converts the audio signal into mechanical vibrations that are spread over a metal plate. Transducers on the plate convert the vibrations into a signal that is mixed with the original.

playback head
On an audio tape device, this object in the tape path made contact with the tape during playback

mode, transducing the signal encoded onto the tape into alternating current, which was sent to loudspeakers for playback.

plug-in
Specialized software modules that may be used in conjunction with a larger program to provide processing operations.

polarity
A wave's orientation, up or down.

poles (of a magnet)
The ends of a magnet, which operate at opposite attraction. Termed north and south, a magnet's north pole is attracted to the south pole of another magnet, but the north pole is repelled by the north pole of another magnet.

poles or **resonances (of a filter)**
Areas of spectral amplification produced by a feedback filter.

positive charge
A condition due to an imbalance of protons and electrons. An object that has a greater number of protons has a positive charge.

positive sum
Type of comb filter that adds a delayed sample to the current input channel.

postfader
A mixer setting by which a signal is copied and sent over an auxiliary bus after the channel fader has adjusted its volume.

pot (or potentiometer)
A type of variable resistor that adjusts electromotive force.

potential energy
Property of an object that is being held in place by some force; it "wants" to move, but is restrained.

potentiometer (or pot)
A type of variable resistor that adjusts electromotive force.

power
Work done per unit of time, measured in watts.

power conditioner
A receptacle for a number of plugs that provides stability to the current received from a wall outlet and protects the plugs powered from it from outside interference. A balanced power conditioner converts AC into a balanced signal, adding further protection from induced noise mingling with the signal.

power regulator
An electrical device that ensures that voltage is delivered consistently, and is not subject to sudden spikes due to outside interference (such as lightning or solar storms).

precedence effect
The auditory system's tendency to perceive a sound source based on the first wavefront that reaches the ears.

prefader
A mixer setting by which a signal is copied and sent over an auxiliary bus before the channel fader has adjusted its volume.

pressure
The amount of force applied to an object or a given area of mass (spiked heels create more pressure than snowshoes).

pressure (microphone)
Pressure microphones contain a diaphragm that responds to sound pressure changes on only one side of the diaphragm, with no differentiation between wavefronts arriving from different directions.

pressure gradient or **gradient microphone**
Microphone constructed with a diaphragm that responds to pressure changes arriving from both the front and the rear, with the signal produced according to the difference in pressure wavefronts arriving from either side of the diaphragm.

principle of superposition
Describes the phenomenon of encounters between waves. Their fronts may meet, the wave shapes combine, and then separate again with their original characteristics intact.

proton
A positively charged particle in an atom's nucleus.

proximity effect
A "bass tip-up" effect of pressure gradient microphones caused by a corrective curve applied by an output transformer to compensate for the lower pressure gradient of longer wavelengths. It was exploited by crooners and announcers in the 1930s and 1940s, who learned to make subtle adjustments in their distance from the microphone to give their voices a husky, warm timbre.

psychoacoustics
The study of issues that connect acoustics and perception.

pulse code modulation (PCM)
Method of translating audio signals into discrete sample values, whereby a certain number of bits are used to represent instantaneous amplitude values taken at regular intervals.

pulse density modulation (PDM)
A form of digital encoding that uses very high sampling rates and a sample size of one bit, with a value of 1 indicating an increase in instantaneous amplitude level, and a value of 0 representing a decrease in instantaneous amplitude level. The density of alternating pulses reflects the shape of the audio wave. Used in the Super Audio Compact Disc (SACD) format.

pulse wave
A waveform that alternates regularly between a high and a low state.

pulse width modulation (PWM)
Synthesis technique in which a pulse wave has its duty cycle modulated, which results in a dynamically changing spectrum.

punch-in point
Designated point defined in punch-in recording at which recording commences.

punch-out point
Designated point defined in punch-in recording at which recording ends.

punch recording
A sequencer mode in which a certain segment of a piece is earmarked to be recorded over, replaced by new material. Recording is not activated until the beginning of this segment begins, and stops automatically when the end of this segment is reached.

pure tone
A sinusoidal wave, which consists of only a single frequency component.

quadraphony
Stereo systems consisting of four output channels.

quality (Q)
The ratio of center frequency over bandwidth in a bandpass or band-reject filter.

quantization level (or bit depth, word size, or sample size)
The number of bits used to represent sample values. The more bits that are used, the more accurate the sample measurements are.

quantize (MIDI sequencer)
Setting a sequence of MIDI events so that they only occur at specified subdivisions of a measure: at 16th notes, 32nd notes, 8th notes, or some other resolution.

quarter-wave resonator
A tube that is open on one end and closed on another. The tube's length is one-quarter the wavelength of the fundamental frequency. The tube can support odd harmonics of its fundamental.

quasi-coincident microphone configuration
Also called near-coincident configurations, the term refers to pairs of directional microphones that are close but not coincident; meant to record some of the localizability of coincident configurations and some of the sense of spaciousness of time-of-arrival configurations.

quasi-periodic wave
A wave that is repetitive but not truly periodic; finite in duration, with some changes in the repeating pattern over time.

random access
The ability to jump instantly to any point in an audio file without having to fast-forward or rewind, as is necessary with the linear format of audio tape.

random energy efficiency (REE) or random efficiency (RE)
A comparison of a microphone's response to sounds arriving from the front to sounds with equivalent power arriving from other directions. For example, a hypercardioid has a 0.25 REE, which means that its signal consists of one-quarter off-axis reverberations, and three-quarters on-axis direct sound.

random walk or drunken walk
Pattern of noise that follows a pattern similar to that of an inebriate's impaired sense of equilibrium, which causes him to walk in a different direction with each step; the distance travelled after n steps is proportional to $\sqrt{n}$.

rarefied state
Air pressure levels that are lower (having less molecular density) than the equilibrium (undisturbed) state.

reach or distance factor
a comparison of the relative distance a microphone may be placed from a sound source, compared to an omnidirectional microphone, to produce the same direct-to-reverberant response.

reactance
The property of impedance that causes its effects to vary with AC frequency.

receptor
Device that receives acoustic information; in a microphone this is the diaphragm, which responds to changes in air pressure in a manner similar to the eardrum.

reciprocal peak dip filter
A type of bandpass filter used in audio equalizers; the bandwidth varies with gain level.

record head
On an audio tape device, this object in the tape path made contact with the tape during record mode, saturating an AC signal that originated from the audio material onto the tape particles.

rectangular window
Window type that can be used in Short Time Fourier Transform analyses, although it is usually held up as an example of a poor window function.

reflected sound
Acoustic energy interacting with the boundaries of the performance space and the objects within it before reaching the listener.

reflection
When wavefronts encounter an obstacle of greater dimension than their wavelength, the wavefronts bounce back at an angle equal to the angle of incidence.

refraction
A change in the direction that a wave propagates due to a change in the transmission medium.

resistance
Inhibition of DC current flow. Greater resistance lowers the number of electrons that may flow, but increases their voltage, or their impetus to flow.

resonance
An object that is made to vibrate at one of its characteristic frequencies undergoes maximum displacement and is said to be "at resonance."

resonances or **poles (of a filter)**
Areas of spectral amplification produced by a feedback filter.

resonant frequency
Also called "characteristic frequencies," the set of frequencies that can produce standing waves in a vibrating object; the frequencies at which the object "likes" to vibrate.

resonator
A object or device that is particularly responsive to certain frequencies.

resonz
A type of bandpass filter found in some software synthesis programs.

restoring force
A force that acts to counteract displacement, such as a spring force, which acts to pull a stretched spring back to its equilibrium position.

Return to Zero (RZ) encoding
Early form of encoding digital information to tape in which values of 1 were represented as a high voltage level, values of 0 were represented as low voltage levels, and voltage levels returned to a midpoint of zero between each binary value.

reverb or **echo chamber**
The earliest form of artificial reverberation; audio played into a highly reflective room is picked up with at least one microphone; the signal from this room is then mixed with the original signal.

reverb unit (or **reverberator)**
Audio effect component that simulates the natural propagation of sound in an enclosed space.

reverberation radius
The distance from the performer at which the direct and reverberant sound are roughly equal in intensity.

reverberation time
The time it takes for the sound pressure level to drop 60 dB, effectively to silence.

reverberator (or **reverb unit)**
Audio effect component that simulates the natural propagation of sound in an enclosed space.

ribbon microphone
A classic dynamic pressure gradient microphone used in early broadcasting; these had a bidirectional response pattern, and consisted of a diaphragm in the form of a thin metal ribbon that was suspended vertically.

ring modulation
A classic analog synthesis effect in which two signals are multiplied. When done to sinusoidal waves, the result is sum and difference frequencies of the two. When done with complex waves, sum and differences are produced of each spectral component, leading to more complex output.

RMS (root-mean-square)

A method of deriving an average energy level of a sine wave that avoids the zero value that a simple mean would yield (since the positive and negative portions would cancel each other out). All values are squared to produce a wave with only positive values, the mean of the squared values is taken, and then the square root of the mean is taken. The RMS of a sine wave that oscillates between ± 1 is, $1/\sqrt{2}$, or 0.707.

room mode

Resonant frequencies, or standing waves, that arise within the confines of a performance space.

router

A device that receives messages from the Internet and sends them to the appropriate machine on its network, calculating the most direct path through the network to the destination machine.

sample

A discrete instantaneous amplitude measurement of a wave at a point in time.

sample and hold circuit (digital recording)

A component in the digital recording process that measures analog voltage levels and holds them long enough so that they may be read by the analog-to-digital converter.

sample and hold generator (synthesis)

A type of noise generator that generates random values at regular time intervals; each random value is held until the next value is generated.

sample frame

Each set of successive of samples that is to be played simultaneously on different channels.

sample size (or bit depth, word size, or quantization level)

The number of bits used to represent sample values. The more bits that are used, the more accurate the sample measurements are.

sampler

Instruments that contain recordings that are triggered by MIDI note messages.

sampling increment

The time interval between successive samples in a digital audio recording; the inverse of the sampling rate.

sampling rate

The rate at which samples of an audio signal are taken during digital recording; the inverse of the sampling increment.

sampling signal

A view of the digital recording process that considers each incoming sample value to be multiplied by a pulse with a value of 1, thereby scaling each pulse of the sampling signal. The sampling signal is a pulse train with the frequency of the sampling rate.

sampling theorem or **Nyquist theorem**

"To represent digitally a signal containing frequency components up to X Hz, it is necessary to use a sampling rate of at least $2X$ Hz."

sawtooth wave

Wave composed of all harmonics of the fundamental, with amplitudes that are the inverse of the harmonic number.

scene markers

An annotation to an audio event that is synced to a film or video that links that event to an absolute time, regardless of musical tempo.

second-order beats

A phenomenon that occurs for tones that are below 1500 Hz. If two tones are played that span an interval very close to an octave, for example 219 Hz and 440 Hz, a beating pattern occurs that does not have a clear acoustic explanation.

self-clocking

A method of encoding binary values that ensure that regular voltage transitions, which prevents clock drift that may occur in the case of a long stream of the same digit.

semiconductor

A material that allows current to flow through it under certain conditions; silicon is an example.

semiparametric filter

An EQ bandpass filter with which the center frequency may be adjusted, but not the quality (Q).

sequencer

A program that stores a musical performance, which may be recalled, played back, or edited.

series (or cascade) filter

A filter configuration in which an input signal is sent through a succession of filters.

server or **host**

Devices on a network that provide information or services on demand; requests are received from client devices.

shelf filter

A highpass or lowpass filter on an EQ that produces amplification or attenuation. In a lowpass filter, the frequency response is flat below the cutoff frequency, and has a sharp cutoff. In a highpass filter the frequency response has a sharp cutoff below the cutoff frequency and is flat above the cutoff frequency.

shield
A braided metal sleeve used to reduce interference in some audio cables.

Short Time Fourier Transform (STFT)
A Fourier transform performed on a segment (window) of samples excerpted from a signal. A series of STFTs are employed for real-time spectral analyses.

sideband
Certain audio processing operations produce spectral components that appear alongside the original spectral components, typically at equal distances above and below. These added spectral components on either side of the original spectral components are called sidebands.

sidechain
Automated volume control with a compressor; used to automatically lower background music when an announcer speaks, and raise the music volume when the speaking stops.

simple delay
A signal combined with a delayed version of itself.

simple harmonic motion
Sinusoidal vibratory pattern exhibited by many objects, such as pendulums, mass-spring systems, and strings.

sinc function
Curve described by the formula $\sin(x)/x$.

sine wave
Shape traced by an object vibrating in simple harmonic motion.

sinusoidal wave
A wave having the overall shape of a sine or a cosine wave, without regard to initial phase.

slave device
Device that carries out instructions received from a master device.

SMPTE Time Code
Time code developed by the Society of Motion Picture and Television Engineers that encoded an audio track with time references, which allowed multiple tape machines to lock in to each other and play in synchronization.

softsynth
A synthesizer that is a software plug-in as a component of a DAW environment, and which is "played" by MIDI messages.

solder
A type of conducting metal that may be melted and use to attach electrical components.

solid state
Current control via parts made from semiconductors; the term differentiates them from vacuum tubes, which do the same thing. Semiconductors are less expensive, smaller, and generate less heat than vacuum tubes.

solo switch
Button on a mixer that allows all channels but the soloed channel(s) to be silenced, without having to move any faders.

sone
A subjective loudness measurement. At pure tone of 1000 Hz at 40 dB is assigned a level of one sone. Each increase of one sone meant to describe a perceptual doubling of loudness.

sound cloud
A sound texture created from hundreds or thousands of extremely short sound events.

sound pressure
Air pressure changes associated with music or acoustics; at greater frequencies and less magnitude than atmospheric pressure changes.

sound waves
Sequence of compressions and rarefactions in air pressure that are perceived as sound.

Soundfield microphone
A microphone consisting of four directional microphones arranged in a tetrahedron, used in conjunction with a signal processor, which encodes the signal in a way that allows the recording to be configurable for different numbers of playback channels.

spaciousness
A quality of recorded or broadcast sound that makes it appear to spread over the listening space, with a sense of diffuse reverberation.

S/PDIF transmission format
Consumer-grade digital transmission format for two-channel audio, typically delivered over TCA cables.

spectral effect
A class of effects that change a signal's spectral content.

spectral plot
A graph showing frequencies (or wavelengths) along the horizontal axis, with intensities plotted as a function of frequency components, on the vertical axis.

spectral shadow

When a sound event occurs to one side, frequencies above 1500 Hz or so have wavelengths that are shorter than the width of the human head (7″ or 17 cm). Thus, these wavefronts reflect back away from the head. As a result there is less high-frequency content at the farther ear. This shadowing effect is the predominant localization cue for frequencies above 1500 Hz.

spectrogram plot or **sonogram**

A graph that shows both frequency and amplitude are shown as a function of time. Frequency is illustrated as a function of time, with higher frequencies appearing at higher vertical positions. Intensity levels are represented by shading or color level.

spectrum

The set of frequencies produced by a vibrating object, with their relative amplitude levels and initial phase values.

specular reflection

Acoustic reflections from smooth, regular surfaces.

speed of sound

Rate at which acoustic waves travel through a medium. In air, this is approximately 344 meters per second, with slight variations due to altitude, humidity, and temperature.

spherical stereo microphone

Ball-shaped objects that are roughly the size of the human head, containing two omnidirectional microphones placed on opposite sides to correspond to the position of the ears. Spherical microphones create interaural delay and spectral shadowing similar to that perceived by the auditory system.

spring reverb

Type of reverberation effect consisting of electrical fluctuations transduced into mechanical fluctuations, which are reflected back and forth along a spring, then transduced into electrical fluctuations and mixed with the original signal.

square wave

Wave composed of odd harmonics of the fundamental, with amplitudes that are the inverse of the harmonic number.

stage box

A digital microphone junction device that receives analog microphone signals, digitizes them, and sends the signals out as packets to an Ethernet switch.

standard cardioid microphone

A common microphone directional pattern that emphasizes pressure changes arriving from the front and de-emphasizing pressure changes arriving from the side and rear.

Standard MIDI file (SMF)

A generic MIDI file format that specifies MIDI events, delta times between events, and other meta-information. Allows songs to be played on a variety of devices.

standing wave

A series of pulses moving along a medium and reflected back and forth at a frequency such that the superposition of oncoming and reflected pulses creates a pattern in which certain points along the medium are motionless.

static electricity

Interactions between charged objects.

stationary signal

A signal that possesses a regular pattern.

status byte

Type of MIDI channel-voice message that specifies the message type and MIDI channel number.

steady-state or **sustained sound**

A waveform that undergoes regular repetitions; when musical instruments play, the onset of a pitch is typically noisy and irregular, followed by a more regular portion of the sound.

steady-state response

The response of a filter to an input signal once the filter has "become accustomed" to taking in and treating the signal.

step entry

A sequencer recording method in which MIDI notes are entered one at a time, without the clock ticking. A note duration is selected, a MIDI note is played on a controller, and this note gets recorded with the selected note value. Another note duration may be selected, another note entered, and so on. A recording may be entered at the composer's own pace, without having to play it in tempo.

stereophony

Delivery of music over multiple audio channels.

stopband

The region of spectral components that are attenuated by a filter.

streaming

The process by which a computer can receive a signal and buffer it, rendering the media when the buffer fills and then discarding the material, leaving room for the buffer to be continually refilled so that playback may proceed without interruption.

strip

On a mixer, a vertical array of controls that control an audio channel in various ways.

subband coding

A method of file compression in which short blocks of samples are applied to a bank of bandpass filters. The output of each filter is then put through a spectral analysis. Comparison of the activity in each band allows the transform to select where material may be removed or rendered in lower resolution based on predictions of whether the quantization error distortion would be masked by activity in the other bands. Tends to be strong in time localization at the expense of spectral resolution.

subcardoid pattern or **forward-oriented omni microphone**

First-order cardioid directional pattern that resembles an omnidirectional pattern with reduced sensitivity to energy arriving from the rear.

subcode

Information stored along with audio samples when they are stored to CD; subcode identifies the frame number and stereo channel of each sample, as well as marking the beginning of each frame. Allows a CD to be fast-forwarded or rewound.

subgroup

A combination of some number of audio channels on a mixer; sending these channels onto a subgroup allows their balance to remain consistent while their overall volume may be adjusted with just one fader.

subnet mask

A number that subdivides a network into broadcast domains, allowing transmission to be occur more efficiently, with a flexible configuration of bits to define either the network or particular devices on the defined network.

subnetting

A method of flexibly allocating IP addresses in a network.

subtractive synthesis

Synthesis method in which noise signals and complex waveforms are put through filters to shape a spectrum.

supercardioid pattern

First-order cardioid directional pattern having a tighter front response than standard and subcardioid patterns.

support or **accent microphone**

Microphones used in concert recordings that supplement the overview provided by the main microphones; used to focus on something that might need extra emphasis, such as a solo line or a soft instrument that may be overshadowed in the main mics.

symmetrical distortion

Equivalent alteration of a wave's high and low portions by an audio playback device; tends to flatten a wave, thus adding odd harmonics as the shape approaches a square wave.

sympathetic vibration

Motion of one vibrating body passed to another via vibrations of air molecules that are at a characteristic frequency of the objects.

synthesizer

An electronic music-making device that allows the creation of new timbres through oscillators, filters, envelope generators, audio recordings, or processing algorithms.

System Exclusive (SysEx) message

A special MIDI message type that allows a device to be addressed in ways that are not covered by the MIDI standard.

tangential mode

Standing waves within a room along its axes that run diagonally from ceiling to floor—ceiling left front-back to floor right front-back, ceiling right front-back to floor left front-back, ceiling back left-right to floor front left-right, ceiling front left-right to floor back left-right.

Tartini or **difference tones**

When two pitches are played loudly together, a third tone at the difference between the two can sometimes be heard (e.g., a combination of frequencies at 2200 and 2300 Hz can sometimes produce an audible pitch at 100 Hz).

temperament

A musical scale in which the ratios of each pitch to the fundamental are irrational numbers.

Twelve-tone equal temperament, in which the octave is subdivided into twelve perceptually equal steps, is a common example.

temporal masking
Masking phenomena involving sounds that are played one after another, rather than simultaneously.

tendency mask
An outline of boundary points, within which parameters will be chosen at random; used to outline pieces created with granular synthesis.

tension
A resistance to motion exhibited by a body that is deviated from its equilibrium position.

terminal
A conductor plate on a battery.

three-way system
A loudspeaker enclosure containing crossover networks that send various frequency ranges to tweeter, woofer, and midrange cone-coil systems.

timbre
The difference in sound quality between different instruments. Is the result of a number of factors, including spectrum and envelope shape.

timbre space
A multidimensional plot created in an attempt to classify timbres, in which timbres are placed according to overtone content, envelope, and attack time.

time-domain plot
A graph that illustrates changes that occur over time.

time localization
Accuracy of transient events when a signal is put through a Fourier analysis.

time-of-arrival recording
A recording configuration consisting of spaced microphones, typically situated in an arc around the performers. Wavefronts reach the various microphones at different times, creating an aural sense of spaciousness.

timestamp
A clock value attached to a stored musical event that indicates when it is to occur when it is played.

tinnitus
A constant perceived ringing in the ears resulting from damaged auditory nerves.

tip-ring-sleeve (TRS) connector
A 1/4″ connector used on balanced cables

tip-sleeve connector
A 1/4″ connector used on unbalanced cables to deliver line level signals.

tone height
Octave transpositions of pitch classes. Pitches retain their identify, e.g., *do* remains *do*, even when transposed up or down by some number of octaves. Tone height describes these octave transpositions.

tone module
A synthesizer device that does not include a keyboard or other type of player interface, but is meant to respond to MIDI messages.

transducer
A component that changes energy from one form into another; in a microphone, the change is from acoustic energy to electrical voltage.

transfer function
A function that describes how a processor adjusts an input signal, comparing the input to the output.

transform coding
A method of file compression in which longer blocks of successive samples are subjected to an FFT that yields a more detailed spectral view than that of subband coding. Tends to be stronger in spectral resolution and weaker in time localization.

transformer
Two coils placed in proximity for the purpose of inducing current.

transient or **attack**
The initial onset of a note played by an instrument; tends to have noise and high frequency content; this segment of a note's evolution characterizes the sound of a particular instrument.

transient response
The initial response of a filter to an input signal.

transistor
Early solid state component that revolutionized electronics by making small, inexpensive devices available, such as radios.

transverse wave
Waves that vibrate in a direction that is perpendicular to the direction of propagation.

triangle wave
Wave composed of odd harmonics, at amplitudes that are at the inverse square of the harmonic number, and are at alternating polarities.

triangular window
Window type sometimes used in Short Time Fourier Transform analyses.

triode
Type of vacuum tube, used to control current.

twelve-tone equal temperament
Scale used in Western common practice music. The octave is subdivided into twelve perceptually equal steps. This allows a piece to be re-tonicized, and the harmonies to modulate, a hallmark of Western musical composition.

tweeter
Loudspeaker component designed to deliver the higher end of the audio spectrum.

two-way system
A loudspeaker that contains both tweeter and woofer components, with a crossover network to separate the audio signal into its high- and low -frequency ranges.

UDP port (User Datagram Protocol)
User Datagram Protocol, used in Internet transmissions; does not feature the handshakes that are included in other protocols, but is more suitable for some time-sensitive messages since no time or bandwidth is used to establish and confirm connections.

unbalanced cable
Cables that deliver line-level signals over a single wire.

uncertainty principle
A theorem of quantum physics that states that the more accurately a particle's position can be observed, the less accurately its velocity can be estimated; whereas a more accurate measurement of velocity introduces more uncertainty as to a particle's precise position.

undersampling
Sampling audio at a rate below what is necessary to store all frequencies in the signal.

unity
A gain setting that does not amplify or attenuate an input signal.

vacuum tube
A glass tube that contains no air, used to control current.

variable pattern microphone
A microphone that allows the directional response to be changed between a variety of patterns.

velocity
Speed and direction of an object in motion

vibrating system
A body undergoing repetitive motion, returning to the same position at regular time intervals.

virtual port
A number that is added to a message sent over a computer network that defines the type of process being requested. Certain types of programs running on a network are associated with different port numbers.

vocoder
An analysis/resynthesis device invented in 1940, by which an input signal (typically a voice) was analyzed by a set of bandpass filters, the output of which controlled an artificial signal, with the result that the artificial signal appeared to "talk."

voder
A voice synthesizer created in 1939, the predecessor to the vocoder.

voice coil
In a loudspeaker, these are wire coils that lie within a magnetic field and are connected to the speaker cone. As alternating current is sent through the coils, it causes the coils to move in response. The voltage variations are mirrored and amplified in corresponding motions of the cone, which moves in and out in a way that mirrors the audio signal, pushing the air to create corresponding acoustic energy, thus recreating the sound.

volt
Unit of measurement for electromotive force, the degree of attraction between oppositely charged objects. Named for the Italian physicist Alessandro Volta (1745–1827).

voltage-controlled amplifier (VCA)
Amplifier component of an analog modular synthesizer.

voltage-controlled filter (VCF)
Filter component of an analog modular synthesizer.

voltage-controlled modular synthesizer
Analog synthesizer that generates or modifies sound according to voltage changes.

voltage-controlled oscillator (VCO)
Oscillator component of an analog modular synthesizer.

watt (W)
Measurement unit for power. One watt equals one newton of work performed per second.

wave equation
An equation that describes the motion of a string based on characteristics such as its length, tension, density, and displacement.

wavefront
An advancing crest or trough of a wave.

waveguide synthesis or **physical modeling**
A computer model of the body of an instrument, with analyses of its resonances and vibrating parts.

wavelength
Distance between corresponding points from cycle to cycle of a vibrating body.

waveshape
The outline traced by a vibrating body's motion.

wavetable
A waveform stored as a series of samples; the wavetable may be read through at varying rates, allowing different pitches to be produced.

Welch window
Window type sometimes used in Short Time Fourier Transform analyses.

white noise
A waveform that is completely random, with no correlation between any of the points; i.e., given a particular set of values of the waveform, it is impossible to predict what shape the wave will take in the future; its spectrum contains average equal energy at all frequencies. Its name is a reference to white light, which contains equal energy at all light frequencies.

window
An excerpted segment of an audio signal that is subjected to spectral analysis.

window function
Symmetrical signals that are multiplied by each window of samples before the window is subjected to spectral analysis.

wireless ad hoc network (WANET)
A dynamic, self-configuring network that can be created and joined on the fly, without any kind of router or administrative set up.

woofer
Loudspeaker component designed to deliver the lower end of the audio spectrum.

word size (or **bit depth, quantization level,** or **sample size**)
The number of bits used to represent sample values. The more bits that are used, the more accurate the sample measurements are.

work
The application of force to an object; the product of force and distance moved.

wow
Slight variations in the motor speed of vinyl turntables.

XG MIDI
An expansion of General MIDI, created by the Yamaha corporation to work on its devices; adds conventions to the list of standardized controllers that address additional expressiveness (chorus, attack time, release time, etc.), as well as defining special SysEx messages to allow processing of an input audio signal, such as reverb applied to a karaoke vocalist.

XLR connector
A three-pin connector, found on balanced and unbalanced cables; may make connections for line level or mic level signals.

XY microphone configuration or **Blumlein configuration**
Two directional microphones with identical directional sensitivities placed at the same spot, one directly on top of the other, at an angle. A common configuration consists of two bidirectional microphones oriented 90° with respect to each other.

zero line
Midpoint of a vibratory motion, also the point of equilibrium to which the body returns when the force causing the vibration has dissipated (the point of zero displacement from equilibrium).

Bibliography

Music, Acoustics, and Psychoacoustics

American Academy of Arts and Sciences. "Creative Arts: New Tools and Technology & the Democratization of Craft." Public Good—The Impact of Information Technology on Society. Mountain View, CA. 28 Feb.–1 Mar. 2009. Panel discussion with Charles Geschke, Dale Dougherty, Carl Rosendahl, and Jonathan Berger, moderated by Pat Hanrahan.

Backus, John. *The Acoustical Foundations of Music.* New York: Norton, 1977. Print.

Ballora, Mark. "Square One: Standing Tall." *Electronic Musician* 21.1 (2005): 76–81. Print.

Barron, Michael. "Science & Music: Raising the Roof." *Nature* 453.7197 (2008): 859–60. Web.

Beranek, L. L. *Acoustics.* Woodbury, NY: American Institute of Physics, 1996. Print.

Blauert, Jens. *Spatial Hearing: The Psychophysics of Human Sound Localization.* Rev. ed. Cambridge, MA: MIT Press, 1997. Print.

Blesser, Barry. *Spaces Speak: Are You Listening?* Cambridge, MA: MIT Press, 2006. Print.

Bregman, A. S. *Auditory Scene Analysis.* Cambridge, MA: MIT Press, 1990. Print.

Bryan, M. E., and W. Tempest. "Hearing Above 20 kHz." *British Journal of Audiology* 4.3 (1970): 67–71. Web.

Carlos, Wendy. *A Clockwork Orange.* East Side Digital, 1972. Vinyl.

———. *Switched on Bach.* East Side Digital, 1967. Vinyl.

Chowning, John. *Turenas.* Wergo, 1972. Vinyl.

Deutsch, Diana. *The Psychology of Music.* 3rd ed. Waltham, MA: Academic Press, 2012. Print.

Dunbar, Robin. *Grooming, Gossip, and the Evolution of Language.* Cambridge, MA: Harvard University Press, 1998. Print.

Fletcher, Harvey, and W. A. Munson. "Loudness, Its Definition, Measurement, and Calculation." *Journal of the Acoustic Society of America* 5.2 (1933): 82–108. Print.

Fourier, Jean Baptiste Joseph. *The Analytical Theory of Heat.* 1822. Trans. Alexander Freeman. Mineola, NY: Dover Phoenix 2003. Print.

Gann, Kyle. *American Music in the Twentieth Century.* New York: Schirmer, 1997. Print.

Handel, Stephen. *Listening: An Introduction to the Perception of Auditory Events.* Cambridge, MA: MIT Press, 1989. Print.

Harvey, Jonathan. *Mortuous Plango, Vivos Voco.* Sargasso, 1990. CD.

Helmholtz, Hermann. *On the Sensation of Tone.* 1885. Trans. Alexander J. Ellis. New York: Dover, 1954.

Hermes, D. J. "Synthesis of the Sounds Produced by Rolling Balls." Eindhoven, Netherlands: IPO Center for User-System Interaction, Eindhoven University of Technology, 2000. Technical report.

Hiller, Lejaren. *Illiac Suite for String Quartet.* Wergo, 1957. Vinyl.

Lakoff, George, and Mark Johnson. *Metaphors We Live By.* 2nd ed. Chicago: University of Chicago Press, 2003. Print.

Laurence Olivier: A Life. Dir. Bob Bee. Exec. Prod. Nick Elliot and Nick Evans. 1982. Homevision, 2000. VHS Cassette.

Lefevre, Christian. *LHC: The Guide.* Geneva: CERN Communication Group, 2009. <http://cds.cern.ch/record/1165534/files/CERN-Brochure-2009-003-Eng.pdf>.

Lerdahl, Fred. *Tonal Pitch Space.* Oxford: Oxford University Press, 2004. Print.

Levarie, Sigmund, and Ernst Levy. *Tone: A Study in Musical Acoustics.* 2nd ed. Kent, OH: Kent State University Press, 1980. Print.

Levitin, Daniel J. *This Is Your Brain on Music: The Science of a Human Obsession.* New York: Dutton Penguin, 2007. Print.

Loy, Gareth. *Musimathics: The Mathematical Foundations of Music.* Vol. 1. Cambridge, MA: MIT Press, 2006. Print.

Mathews, Max V. "The Digital Computer as a Musical Instrument." *Science* 142.3592 (1963): 553–557. Print.

Minsky, Marvin. "Music, Mind and Meaning." *Computer Music Journal* 5.3 (1981): 28–45. Print.

Mithen, Steven. *The Singing Neanderthals: The Origins of Music, Language, Mind, and Body*. London: Weidenfeld & Nicholson, 2007. Print.

Moore, Brian C. J. *An Introduction to the Psychology of Hearing*. 3rd ed. London: Harcourt Brace Jovanovich, 1989. Print.

Moorer, James A., and John Grey. "Lexicon of Analyzed Tones. Part 1: A Violin Tone." *Computer Music Journal* 1.2 (1977): 39–45. Print.

———. "Lexicon of Analyzed Tones. Part 2: Clarinet and Oboe Tones." *Computer Music Journal* 1.3 (1977): 12–29. Print.

———. "Lexicon of Analyzed Tones. Part 3: The Trumpet." *Computer Music Journal* 2.2 (1978): 23–31. Print.

Norman-Haignere, Sam, Nancy G. Kanwisher, and Josh H. McDermott. "Distinct Cortical Pathways for Music and Speech Revealed by Hypothesis-Free Voxel Decomposition." *Neuron* 88.6 (2015): 1281–296. Web.

Petersen, Gordon E., and Harold L. Barney. "Control Methods Used in a Study of the Vowels." *Journal of the Acoustical Society of America* 24.2 (1952): 175–84. Print.

Pierce, John R. *The Science of Musical Sound*. New York: Scientific American Books, 1983. Print.

Pinker, Steven. *How the Mind Works*. New York: Norton, 1997. Print.

Risset, Jean Claude. "Computer Study of Trumpet Tones." *Journal of the Acoustical Society of America* 38.5 (1965): 912. Print.

Risset, Jean Claude, and Max V. Mathews. "Analysis of Musical-Instrument Tones." *Physics Today* 22.2 (1969): 23–40. Print.

Roads, Curtis. *The Computer Music Tutorial*. Cambridge, MA: MIT Press, 1996. Print.

Robinson, D. W., and R. S. Dadson. "A Re-determination of the Equal-Loudness Relations for Pure Tones." *British Journal of Applied Physics* 7.5 (1956): 166–81. Print.

Roederer, Juan G. *The Physics and Psychophysics of Music*. 3rd ed. New York: Springer-Verlag, 1995. Print.

Rossing, Thomas D. *The Science of Sound*. 2nd ed. Reading, MA: Addison-Wesley, 1990. Print.

Rothenberg, David. *Thousand Mile Song: Whale Music in a Sea of Sound*. New York: Basic, 2008. Print.

Schoenberg, Arnold. *Style and Idea: Selected Writings of Arnold Schoenberg*. Ed. Leonard Stein. Trans. Leo Black. New York: St. Martin's, 1975.

Stockhausen, Karlheinz. *Gesang der Jünglinge*. Kürten, Germany: Stockhausen-Verlag, 1956. Print.

———. *Hymnen*. Kürten, Germany: Stockhausen-Verlag, 1967. Print.

———. *Telemusik*. Kürten, Germany: Stockhausen-Verlag, 1966. Print.

Subotnick, Morton. *Silver Apples of the Moon*. Wergo, 1967. Vinyl.

Sundberg, Johan. *The Science of Musical Sounds*. San Diego, CA: Academic Press, 1991. Print.

Tyndall, John. *Sound*. New York: Philosophical Library, 1867. Print.

Wessel, David. "Timbre Space as a Musical Control Structure." *Computer Music Journal* 3.2 (1979): 45–52. Print.

Wilkinson, Scott R. *Tuning In: Microtonality in Electronic Music*. Milwaukee, WI: Hal Leonard, 1988. Print.

Wilson, E. O. *Consilience: The Unity of Knowledge*. New York: Vintage, 1998. Print.

Xenakis, Iannis. *Analogique A and B for 9 Strings and Tape*. DRAM, 1960. Vinyl.

MIDI

Ballora, Mark. "Square One: New Tricks for an Old Dog." *Electronic Musician* 22.10 (2006): 84–86. Print.

———. "Square One: Open Sound Control." *Electronic Musician* 24.11 (2008): 64–66. Print.

Banzi, Massimo. "How Arduino Is Open-Sourcing the Imagination." June 2012. Web. 10 Aug. 2015. <www.ted.com/talks/massimo_banzi_how_arduino_is_open_sourcing_imagination>.

Center for New Music and Audio Technology (CNMAT). "Open Sound Control." University of California Berkeley. Berkeley, CA. 1997. Web. www.opensoundcontrol.org.

Chadabe, Joel. *Electronic Sound: The Past and Promise of Electronic Music*. Upper Saddle River, NJ: Prentice Hall, 1997. Print.

Cutler, Marty, Gino Robair, and Scott Wilkinson. "In Control." *Electronic Musician* 17.5 (2001): 64–109. Print.

Graham-Knight, Kimberlee, and George Tzanetakis. "Adaptive Music Technology: History and Future Perspectives." *Proceedings of the 41st International Computer Music Conference*. University of North Texas. Denton, TX. 25 Sept.–1 Oct. 2015. Presentation.

Loy, Gareth. "Musicians Make a Standard: The MIDI Phenomenon." *Computer Music Journal* 9.4 (1985): 8–26. Print.

MIDI Manufacturers' Organization. Technical documents. <http://www.midi.org>.

Moore, F. Richard. "The Dysfunctions of MIDI." *Computer Music Journal* 12.1 (1988): 19–28. Print.

Raschke, Peter. "Exploring MIDI Web Site." Northwestern University. Evanston, IL. 1997. Web. <http://nuinfo.nwu

.edu/musicschool/links/projects/midi/expmidiindex
.html>.

Rona, Jeffrey. *Synchronization from Reel to Reel*. Milwaukee,
WI: Hal Leonard, 1990. Print.

Rothstein, Joseph. *MIDI: A Comprehensive Introduction*.
2nd ed. Madison, WI: A-R Editions, 1995. Print.

Webster, Peter Richard, and David Brian Williams. *Experiencing Music Technology*. New York: Schirmer, 1999. Print.

Digital Audio

Apple Core Audio Format Specification 1.0. Technical Specifications. <https://developer.apple.com/library/mac/
documentation/MusicAudio/Reference/CAFSpec/
CAF_overview/CAF_overview.html#//apple_ref/doc/
uid/TP40001862-CH209-TPXREF101>.

Ballora, Mark. "Square One: Look Through Any
Window." *Electronic Musician* 20.8 (2004): 70–75. Print.

———. "Square One: What's in a Word?" *Electronic Musician* 21.5 (2005): 88–90. Print.

Bosi, Marina, and Richard E. Goldberg. *Introduction to Digital
Audio Coding and Standards*. Boston: Kluwer Academic
Publishers, 2003. Print.

Boyk, James, et al. "There's Life Above 20 Kilohertz! A
Survey of Musical Instrument Spectra to 104.2 kHz." Web.
<www.cco.caltech.edu/~boyk/spectra/spectra.htm>.

Brandenburg, Karlheinz. "MP3 and AAC Explained." *Proceedings of the Audio Engineering Society 17th International
Conference: High-Quality Audio Coding*. Florence, Italy.
Aug. 1999. Presentation.

Bregman, Albert S. *Auditory Scene Analysis: The Perceptual
Organization of Sound*. Cambridge, MA: MIT Press, 1990.
Print.

Cayko, Ethan. "Network Gyre—Exercising the Network's
Rhythmic Potential." *Proceedings of the 41st International
Computer Music Conference*. University of North Texas.
Denton, TX. 25 Sept.–1 Oct. 2015. Presentation.

Chamberlin, Hal. *Musical Applications of Microprocessors*.
Rochelle Park, NJ: Hayden, 1980. Print.

Cutler, Cassius C. "Transmission Systems Employing
Quantization." US Patent 2,927, 962, 1960. Print.

Deutsch, Diana, ed. *The Psychology of Music*. 3rd ed. New
York: Academic Press, 2012. Print.

Di Justo, Patrick, "Raspberry Pi or Arduino? One Simple
Rule to Choose the Right Board?" *Make: We Are All
Makers* (2015). Web. <http://makezine.com/2015/12/04/
admittedly-simplistic-guide-raspberry-pi-vs-arduino>.

European Broadcasting Union. *Tech 3364: Audio Definition
Model Metadata Specification v. 1.0*. (2014). Technical

Specification. <https://tech.ebu.ch/docs/tech/
tech3364.pdf>.

Hresko, Christian Adam. "The Internal Structure of Audio
Files: RAW, NeXT/Sun, AIFF/AIFC, RIFF WAVE." *Audio
Anecdotes*. Ed. Ken Greenebaum. Natick, MA: A. K.
Peters, 2001. Print.

Inside Macintosh: Sound. Cupertino, CA: Apple Computer
Co., 1999. Print.

Loy, Gareth. *Musimathics: The Mathematical Foundations
of Music*. Vol. 2. Cambridge, MA: MIT Press, 2007.
Print.

Mandelbrot, Benoit. "How Long Is the Coast of Britain?
Statistical Self-Similarity and Fractional Dimension."
Science 156.3775 (1967): 636–638. Print.

McClellan, James H., Ronald W. Schafer, and Mark A.
Yoder. *DSP First: A Multimedia Approach*. Upper Saddle
River, NJ: Prentice Hall, 1998. Print.

Moore, F. R. *Elements of Computer Music*. Englewood Cliffs,
NJ: PTR Prentice Hall, 1990. Print.

Nyquist, Harry. "Certain topics in telegraph transmission
theory", *Transactions of the AIEE* 47 (1928): 617–644.
Reprint as classic paper in: *Proceedings of the IEEE* 90.2
(2002): 280-305. Print.

Oohashi, Tsutomu, et al. "High-Frequency Sound Above
the Audible Range Affects Brain Electric Activity and
Sound Perception." *Proceedings of the 91st Audio Engineering Society Convention*. New York. 1991. Presentation.

Park, Tae Hong. *Introduction to Digital Signal Processing:
Computer Musically Speaking*. Singapore: World Scientific,
2010. Print.

Pohlmann, Ken C. *Principles of Digital Audio*. 3rd ed.
New York: McGraw-Hill, 1995. Print.

Puckette, Miller. *The Theory and Technique of Electronic Music*.
Singapore: World Scientific, 2007. Print.

———. 41st International Computer Music Conference.
University of North Texas. Denton, TX. 25 Sept.–1 Oct.
2015. Keynote Address.

Scavone, Gary. "MUMT 618: Computational Modeling of
Musical Acoustic Systems." Web. 5 Aug. 2015.
<www.music.mcgill.ca/~gary/618/week1/delayline
.html#SECTION00029000000000000000>.

Schroeder, Franziska. "Network[ed] Listening—Towards
a De-centering of Beings." *Contemporary Music Review*
32.2–3 (2013): 215–29. Print.

Smith, J. O. "Fundamentals of Digital Filter Theory."
Computer Music Journal 9.3 (1985): 13–23. Print.

Steiglitz, Ken. *A Digital Signal Processing Primer*. Menlo Park,
CA: Addison-Wesley, 1996. Print.

Todd, Craig C., et al. "AC-3: Flexible Perceptual Coding for Audio Transmission and Storage." *Proceedings of the 96th Audio Engineering Society Convention.* Amsterdam. 16–19 May. 1994. Presentation.

Watkinson, John. *The Art of Digital Audio.* Oxford: Focal Press, 1999. Print.

Yamamoto, Takeo. "Industry Seminar on DVD." Faculty of Music, McGill University. Montreal. 12 Apr. 1997. Presentation.

Electronics, Audio Recording, Processing and Synthesis

Amdahl, Kenn. *There Are No Electrons: Electronics for Earthlings.* Broomfield, CO: Clearwater, 1991. Print.

Armbruster, Greg, ed. *The Art of Electronic Music.* New York: GPI, 1984. Print.

Ballora, Mark. "Sonification, Science, and Popular Music: In Search of the 'Wow.'" *Organised Sound* 19.01 (2014): 30–40. Web.

———. "Square One: Some Like It Hot." *Electronic Musician* 21.6 (2005): 88–90. Print.

———. "Square One: Vive La Difference." *Electronic Musician* 22.3 (2006): 70–72. Print.

Beauchamp, James. "Will the Real FM Equation Please Stand Up?" In Letters, *Computer Music Journal* 16.4 (1992): 6–7. Print.

Begauld, Durand R. *The Sonic CD-ROM for Desktop Audio Production: Electronic Guide to Producing Computer Audio for Multimedia.* New York: Academic Press, 1996. Print.

Blackmer, David E. "The World Beyond 20 kHz." Web. 22 Dec. 2015. <http://recordinghacks.com/articles/the-world-beyond-20khz>.

Bracewell, John. *Sound Design in the Theatre.* Upper Saddle River, NJ: Prentice Hall College Division, 1993. Print.

Case, Alex. *Sound FX: Unlocking the Creative Potential of Recording Studio Effects.* London: Focal Press, 2007. Print.

Cheney, Margaret. *Tesla: Man Out of Time.* New York: Simon & Schuster, 2001. Print.

Chowning, John. "The Synthesis of Complex Audio Spectra by Means of Frequency Modulation." *Journal of the Audio Engineering Society* 21.7 (1974): 526–34. Repr. *Computer Music Journal* 1.2 (1977): 46–54.

Chowning, John, and David Bristow. *FM Theory and Applications: by Musicians for Musicians.* Tokyo: Yamaha Music Foundation, 1987. Print.

Cleveland, Barry. "Mixed Signals." *Electronic Musician* 16.11 (2000): 62–81. Print.

Collins, Nick, Alex McLean, and Julian Rohrhuber, eds. *Computer Music Journal: Special Issue on Live Coding.* 38.1 (2014). Print.

Cook, Perry R. "Sound Synthesis for Auditory Display." In *The Sonification Handbook*, ed. Thomas Hermann, Andy Hunt, and John G. Neuhoff, 197–235. Berlin: Logos, 2011. Print.

Cooper, Michael. "The Big Squeeze." *Electronic Musician* 17.2 (2001): 70–74. Print.

Costello, Sean. "The Halls of Valhalla." Web. <https://valhalladsp.wordpress.com>.

Datorro, Jon. "Effect Design Part 1: Reverberator and Other Filters." *Journal of the Audio Engineering Society* 45.9 (1997): 660–84. Print.

———. "Effect Design Part 2: Delay-Line Modulation and Chorus." *Journal of the Audio Engineering Society* 45.10 (1997): 764–88. Print.

de Campo, Alberto. *The CREATE Tutorial for SuperCollider 2.* Technical Documentation Bundled with SuperCollider Software. <www.audiosynth.com>.

Dickreiter, Michael. *Tonmeister Technology: Recording Environments, Sound Sources, and Microphone Techniques.* New York: Temmer Enterprises, 1988. Print.

Dodge, Charles, and Thomas A. Jerse. *Computer Music: Synthesis, Composition, and Performance.* New York: Schirmer, 1984. Print.

Dolby Laboratories. "White Paper: Dolby® Atmos® Next-Generation Audio for Cinema." 2014. Technical Specifications. <http://www.dolby.com/us/en/technologies/dolby-atmos/dolby-atmos-next-generation-audio-for-cinema-white-paper.pdf>.

Eargle, John. *Handbook of Recording Engineering.* New York: Van Nostrand Reinhold, 1992. Print.

———. *The Microphone Book.* Boston: Focal Press, 2001. Print.

———. *Music, Sound, Technology.* New York: Van Nostrand Reinhold, 1995. Print.

Erne, Markus, producer. *Perceptual Audio Coders: What to Listen For.* Audio Engineering Society Technical Council. 2001. CD-ROM.

Exploratorium. "Mickey Hart Performs at the Golden Gate Bridge 75th Anniversary Celebration." 27 May 2012. Web. <www.exploratorium.edu/explore/videos/mickey-hart-performs-golden-gate-bridge-75th-anniversary-celebration>.

Fukada, Akira. "A Challenge in Multi-channel Music Recording." *Proceedings of the Audio Engineering Society's 19th International Conference on Surround Sound: Techniques, Technology and Perception.* Bavaria, 21–24 June. 2001. Presentation.

Gardner, Martin. "Mathematical Games: White and Brown Music, Fractal Curves and One-over-f Fluctuations." *Scientific American* 238.4 (1978): 16–31. Print.

Gerzon, Michael. "Periphony: With-Height Sound Reproduction." *Journal of the Audio Engineering Society* 21.1 (1973): 2–10. Print.

Giles, Jeff. "Neil Young Unveils New Hi-Def Digital Music Player on 'Letterman.'" 1 Oct. 2012. Web. 22 Dec. 2015. <http://ultimateclassicrock.com/neil-young-unveils-new-hi-def-digital-music-player-on-letterman>.

Harrison, Jonty. 41st International Computer Music Conference. University of North Texas. Denton, TX. 25 Sept.–1 Oct. 2015. Keynote Address.

Hosken, Dan. *An Introduction to Music Technology.* 2nd ed. New York: Routledge, 2015. Print.

Huber, David Miles, and Robert E. Runstein. *Modern Recording Techniques.* 7th ed. Burlington, MA: Focal Press, 2010. Print.

Isaacson, Walter. *Benjamin Franklin: An American Life.* New York: Simon & Schuster, 2004. Print.

Katz, Bob. *Mastering Audio: The Art and the Science.* 3rd. ed. London: Focal Press, 2014. Print.

Keen, Andrew. "Keen on . . . Bob Weir: Why MP3 Music Is an Assault on Your Nervous System." 14 Feb. 2012. Web. 22 Dec. 2015. <http://techcrunch.com/2012/02/14/keen-on-bob-weir-mp3-music-tctv>.

Keene, Sherman. *Practical Techniques for the Recording Engineer.* Sedona, AZ: SKE, 1981. Print.

Keltz, Al. "High and Low Impedance Signals." Whirlwind Music Distributors. Web. 20 July 2015. <http://whirlwindusa.com/support/tech-articles/high-and-low-impedance-signals>.

Malham, David G. "Higher-Order Ambisonic Systems for the Spatialisation of Sound." *Proceedings of the 1999 International Computer Music Conference.* Beijing, China. 22–28 Oct. 1999. Presentation.

Malham, David G., and Anthony Myatt. "3-D Sound Spatialization Using Ambisonic Techniques." *Computer Music Journal* 19.4 (1995): 58–70. Print.

Martin, Geoffrey Glen. *A Hybrid Model for Simulating Diffused First Reflections in Two-Dimensional Acoustic Environments.* PhD dissertation, Faculty of Music, McGill University. Montreal. 2001.

Mathews, Max V. *The Technology of Computer Music.* Cambridge, MA: MIT Press, 1969. Print.

Mayfield, Matt. "Loudness War." 29 May 2009. Web. 8 Sept. 2015. <https://www.youtube.com/watch?v=TqQX3htzhSY>.

Meyer Sound Laboratories, Inc. "Restaurants, Bars & Nightclubs." Web. 21 July 2015. <http://www.meyersound.com/applications/restaurantsbarsclubs>.

Moore, F. Richard. *Elements of Computer Music.* Englewood Cliffs, NJ: PTR Prentice Hall, 1990. Print.

Pellman, Samuel. *An Introduction to the Creation of Electronic Music.* Belmont, CA: Wadsworth, 1994. Print.

Pirkle, Will. *Designing Software Synthesizer Plug-Ins in C++ with Audio Signal Processing Theory.* London: Focal Press, 2012. Print.

Porter, Scott. "Loudspeaker Tutorial." Penn State Audio Engineering Society. State College, PA. 22 Sept. 2008. Presentation.

Pras, Amandine, Rachel Zimmerman, Daniel Levitin, and Catherine Guastavino. "Subjective Evaluation of MP3 Compression for Different Musical Genres." Audio Engineering Society 127th Convention. New York. 9–12 Oct. 2009. Convention Paper.

Reid, Gordon. "Synth Secrets: Links to All Parts." Web. 12 Sept. 2015. <www.soundonsound.com/sos/allsynthsecrets.htm>.

Roads, Curtis. *Microsound.* Cambridge, MA: MIT Press, 2004. Print.

Ross, Alex. "Wizards of Sound." *New Yorker* 23 Feb. 2015. Print.

Rowe, Robert. *Interactive Music Systems.* Cambridge, MA: MIT Press, 1993. Print.

———. *Machine Musicianship.* Cambridge, MA: MIT Press, 2001. Print.

Scaletti, Carla. "Looking Back, Looking Forward: A Keynote Address for the 2015 International Computer Music Conference." *Computer Music Journal* 40.1 (2016): 10–24. Print.

Sound Performance Lab. *Yes, You Can Mic Multichannel Music.* Niederkrüchten, Germany: SPL Electronics, 1999. Print.

Thiele, Günther. "Multichannel Natural Music Recoding Based on Psychoacoustic Principles." 2001. Extended Version 3 of Audio Engineering Society Preprint 5156. <www.tonmeister.de/foren/surround/texte/multi-mr.pdf>.

Upton, Monroe. *Electronics for Everyone.* New York: Devin-Adair, 1957. Print.

Wilson, Alex, and Bruno Fazenda. "Perception and Evaluation of Audio Quality in Music Production." *Proceedings of the 16th International Conference on Digital Audio Effects (DAFx-13).* Maynooth, Ireland. 2–5 Sept. 2013. Presentation.

Xenakis, Iannis. *Formalized Music: Thought and Mathematics in Composition.* 2nd ed. Hillsdale, NY: Pendragon, 2001. Print.

Index